EDUCATION IN DEPRESSED AREAS

A. Harry Passow, editor

Teachers College Press | Teachers College
Columbia University
New York

© 1963 by Teachers College, Columbia University
Library of Congress Catalog Card Number: 63-15449
Printed in the United States of America
Sixth Printing, 1966

To Shirley

FOREWORD

Have public schools a special responsibility for educating culturally disadvantaged children in depressed urban areas? This problem is among the most crucial ones facing public education today. In July of 1962, educators from twenty-four cities were invited to Teachers College, Columbia University, to explore the layers of this enigma at a two-week Work Conference on Curriculum and Teaching in Depressed Urban Areas. Each school system was represented by a team of two key people —individuals actively engaged in planning and research in their respective school systems and charged with leadership responsibility for educational programs in disadvantaged areas. In addition, there were several persons who, rather than representing particular school systems, participated out of personal concern for the problem area.

The purposes of the conference were to examine the many dimensions of education in depressed urban areas and to develop sound guiding principles for program planners in city school systems. Participants attempted to analyze the unique characteristics and roles of the school in the urban setting and in urban development; the nature of existing and required instructional procedures; the characteristics of personnel and material resources; and other aspects of the problems faced by schools in depressed urban areas.

Thirteen specialists in various fields prepared working papers as starting points of the discussions. The invitations asked paper writers to address their manuscripts to major theoretical and empirical considerations of the broad topic and, where possible, to confront participants with implications for educational planning. Conferees received each paper in advance of the session at which the writer appeared to discuss his ideas with the group.

Each participant, either as an individual or as a member of his team, reported on local problems and efforts in educating culturally disadvantaged children. The participant-prepared materials, together with reports of additional projects and activities under way, bulwarked the specialists' working papers. At seven of the twenty sessions, the group heard these reports of local projects, shared experiences and problems, and recommended possible further actions. Mr. Paul Bisgaier, School Program Coordinator, Mobilization for Youth, Inc., served with me as co-director of the conference. Mr. David Elliott, Research Assistant at the Horace Mann-Lincoln Institute of School Experimentation, was conference recorder and summarized the high points of each session.

This book offers the thirteen working papers plus two additional papers that were shared by the group. In addition, some of the highlights of the discussions and the ideas which were germinated are included. The conference was an exploratory one in which problem definition took high priority. What emerged from the two weeks of discussion and probing were sharper insights and understandings of the dimensions of the problem of educating children and youth in depressed urban areas. The practical how-to-do-it-in-a-classroom questions still remain, but guides for suggestive solutions are a bit more visible.

The conference coordinators and participants are grateful to the Ford Foundation for its grant in support of the conference and of this publication.

A. HARRY PASSOW
Professor of Education

Teachers College, Columbia University
January, 1963

CONTRIBUTORS

David P. Ausubel is a Professor of Psychology at the University of Illinois at Urbana and a member of the staff of its Bureau of Educational Research.

Pearl Ausubel is the wife of David Ausubel and frequently assists with research and writing.

Kenneth B. Clark is a Professor of Psychology at The City College of the City University of New York. He is Director of Research for the Northside Center for Child Development in New York City.

Richard A. Cloward is a Professor of Social Work at Columbia University's New York School of Social Work and Director of Research for Mobilization for Youth, Inc.

Martin Deutsch is an Associate Professor in the Department of Psychiatry at the New York Medical College and the Director of its Institute for Developmental Studies.

John H. Fischer is the President of Teachers College, Columbia University, and Chairman of the Educational Policies Commission of the National Education Association.

Miriam L. Goldberg is an Associate Professor of Education at Teachers College, Columbia University, and a Research Associate at the Horace Mann-Lincoln Institute of School Experimentation.

Vernon F. Haubrich is an Assistant Professor of Education in the Department of Education of Hunter College in New York City.

Robert J. Havighurst is a Professor of Education and a member of the Committee on Human Development at the University of Chicago.

James A. Jones is a Research Associate with Mobilization for Youth, Inc. and the Director of Research at Harlem Youth Opportunities Unlimited in New York City.

Leonard Kornberg is an Assistant Professor of Education, Department of Education at Queens College in Flushing, New York.

Carl L. Marburger is Director of the Detroit Great Cities School Improvement Project and an Instructor at Wayne State University.

A. Harry Passow is a Professor of Education at Teachers College, Columbia University, and a Research Associate at the Horace Mann-

Lincoln Institute of School Experimentation. He is educational consultant for Mobilization for Youth, Inc.

Mel Ravitz is an Associate Professor of Sociology and Anthropology, College of Liberal Arts at Wayne State University. He is a Councilman for the City of Detroit.

Henry Saltzman is a Program Associate in the Public Affairs Program Division of The Ford Foundation.

Sloan R. Wayland is a Professor of Sociology and Education at Teachers College, Columbia University.

Alan B. Wilson is an Assistant Professor of Education, School of Education, University of California at Berkeley. He is a Research Associate at the University of California Survey Research Center.

CONTENTS

Part I Schools in Depressed Areas   I

Mel Ravitz
   The Role of the School in the Urban Setting   6

Robert J. Havighurst
   Urban Development and the Educational System   24

Sloan R. Wayland
   Old Problems, New Faces, and New Standards   46

Miriam L. Goldberg
   *Factors Affecting Educational Attainment in Depressed
   Urban Areas*   68

Part II Psychological Aspects of Education in Depressed Areas   101

David P. Ausubel and Pearl Ausubel
   Ego Development Among Segregated Negro Children   109

Kenneth B. Clark
   *Educational Stimulation of Racially Disadvantaged
   Children*   142

Martin Deutsch
   The Disadvantaged Child and the Learning Process   163

Part III Sociological Aspects of Education in Depressed Areas   181

Richard A. Cloward and James A. Jones
   Social Class: Educational Attitudes and Participation   190

Alan B. Wilson
   Social Stratification and Academic Achievement   217

Part IV Teachers for Depressed Areas   237

Vernon F. Haubrich
   Teachers for Big-City Schools   243

Leonard Kornberg
   Meaningful Teachers for Alienated Children   262

Part V   School Programs in Depressed Areas   279

          John H. Fischer
              Educational Problems of Segregation and Desegregation 290
          Carl L. Marburger
              Considerations for Educational Planning   298
          Henry Saltzman
              The Community School in the Urban Setting   322
          A. Harry Passow
              Education in Depressed Areas   332

Part VI   Bibliography   353

EDUCATION IN
DEPRESSED
AREAS

PART I

Schools in
Depressed Areas

Figures alone—massive as they are—scarcely hint at the impact of urbanization on all aspects of life in the cities. The 1960 census reports indicate that 61.3 per cent of the nation's population lives in the 189 standard metropolitan areas. From 1950 to 1960, more than 80 per cent of the total population increment took place in these areas. For education, the more dramatic fact is that almost one of every six elementary and secondary school children now attends a public school in one of the sixteen largest American cities. Statistics do not depict the physical and economic deterioration of the central city gray areas, the movement of the middle class to the suburbs, the transiency and instability of the in-migrant families, the concentration and intensification of social problems in depressed areas. City slums have existed for generations, even though their tenants have changed with each migration. Ethnic, racial, and socioeconomic groups have coalesced in areas of the city, creating de facto segregation in the schools even where laws imply non-segregation. School buildings in the depressed urban areas seem to house the greatest array of educational problems.

It is in the depressed urban areas that the web of social problems is thickest: "crime, alcoholism, drug addiction, poverty, illiteracy, disease, unemployment, and broken families are found in city slums in massively greater degree than in society as a whole."[1] Typically, the depressed area population tends to be a stratified group of predominantly unskilled or semi-skilled workers, largely in-migrant, who have moved to the city from a rural region. The ethnic and racial composition tends to be primarily from the so-called minority groups—southern Negro, Puerto Rican, Appalachian white, American Indian, Mexican, and, most recently, Cuban. However, there are other subcultures—which are not in-migrant, low-

[1] Office of Education, *The Impact of Urbanization on Education.* Washington, D.C.: U.S. Government Printing Office, 1962, p. 6.

I

socio-economic, or minority-status—whose values resemble those of the depressed-area dwellers and whose children do not achieve adequately in school.

The children in the depressed areas seem severely hampered in their schooling by a complex of conditions at home, in the neighborhood, and in the classroom. Unlike the immigrants of the past, who settled in a community for many years before moving to better neighborhoods or to the suburbs, the present in-migrants are highly mobile and transient. The parents seem unprepared for the perplexities of urban life. Their educational level is lower than that of the rest of the urban population; illiteracy hits a peak among them. There are, of course, variations among subgroups. Because the reasons for migration are usually basically economic, the established cultural and behavioral patterns are different from those of the other urban dwellers.

Although the differences among culturally disadvantaged children tend to invalidate stereotypes, certain characteristics are frequent enough to trouble the schools. Generally, these schools have higher than normal rates of scholastic failure, truancy, disciplinary problems, dropouts, pupil transiency, and teacher turnover. Poor health, inadequate motivation, malnutrition, lack of personal cleanliness, absence of basic learning skills —all are found to a greater extent among children in depressed urban areas than among students in other parts of the city or in the suburbs.

The basic problem stemming from the present in-migration, Professor Mel Ravitz suggests in the first of the following papers, is how to educate and assimilate the culturally different. Reviewing the primacy of the school in helping to acculturate nineteenth- and twentieth-century immigrants, Ravitz argues that the schools must again play a leading role. Although cultural assimilation affects housing, employment, family life, community organization, and government, as well as education, schools are a primary element in the process. Specifically, Ravitz advocates modern, adequate educational facilities; the development of schools as community meeting places for various activities; assignment of the "best" teachers to depressed areas; addition of sufficient teachers and counselors to enable individual attention to students; more men in the schools to set patterns of socially acceptable male behavior; free summer schools; teacher-training programs to adapt people to work with culturally different pupils. The channels of assimilation—education, assistance, and involvement—must all function for success. Professor Ravitz calls for better-coordinated relations between educators and government officials.

The social and educational consequences of economic segregation and urban lower-class schools are examined by Professor Robert Havighurst who views growing stratification as a threat to effective education. Pupils in a lower-class school will achieve less well, have lower educational aspirations, show less promise, and have fewer opportunities to rise socially than lower-class pupils in mixed- or middle-class schools. Havighurst proposes teamwork by educators and social scientists to improve lower-class schools and to reduce economic discrimination. His suggestions for upgrading the lower-class school include enrichment programs at the kindergarten-primary level; intellectual stimulation and access to cultural opportunities at the elementary-school level; talent discovery and development programs; and work-study programs for maladjusted youth at the junior and senior high-school levels. Havighurst would have educational planners work for all-class or mixed-class schools. Locating such schools at the borders of depressed areas might plug the outflow of the middle-class by re-creating a center city desirable as a residential area to all classes. Havighurst sees the school as taking major leadership and acting as a catalyst in relation to the other agencies involved in "social urban renewal."

For some 10 to 20 per cent of the school population aged 13 or 14 to 16, youth who have demonstrated their inability to profit from the normal academic high-school program, Havighurst would develop work-study centers and provide these pupils with an alternative way to adulthood. The emphasis in the work-study centers would be on building the habits, attitudes, and skills which would make them employable. For girls, the emphasis might be on upgrading their contributions, as adult women, to marriage and family living. One danger to avoid is that the work-study program might become too attractive and enticing for students who belong in other kinds of secondary school programs.

The central theme of Professor Sloan Wayland's paper is that the urban education problems of today are in reality new expressions of century-old problems. The crisis arises not from our past deficiencies and inadequacies but, rather, from our past successes and their yield of higher aspirations. New standards and expectations have forged discontent with existing school programs; they have stimulated a search for new courses of action adapted to the new urban dwellers. Precisely because America has succeeded in raising the standard of living for all classes, Wayland argues, the contrast between urban depressed and other classes has been sharpened. He advises a re-examination of the concepts of social class indigenous to small cities and towns. These may clarify our thinking about differentiations in the large urban areas.

Unlike Ravitz and Havighurst, Wayland suggests that the school, in its task of cultural assimilation, is circumscribed. The school is only one institution in a much larger structure, strictly limited in its work of helping assimilate in-migrants. It can link with other agencies and groups at all levels to influence decision making, but a fairly low ceiling restrains any single agency. For example, says Wayland, the schools cannot open up new job opportunities for minority groups, nor can the schools alone determine the nature or location of urban-renewal projects.

Professor Miriam Goldberg surveys forces affecting the achievement and performance of children from depressed urban areas. Citing the historical role of the cities in assimilating newcomers into the American stream, Professor Goldberg sees the problems of the urban areas changed by the nature and mobility patterns of the present in-migrants. Higher school-leaving ages, ethnic-group differences, shifts in employment opportunities for the uneducated and unskilled, and an in-migrant rather than an immigrant group are factors differentiating the present central-city core-area dweller from the preceding generations.

The composite portrait of the disadvantaged pupil which Professor Goldberg presents shows a child unready for academic learning, either intellectually or attitudinally. Schools must ask themselves, "What modifications in staffing, curriculum, organization, and resources will compensate for the early deprivations of the children from depressed urban areas?" Professor Goldberg prescribes compensatory education, especially at the pre-school and elementary levels. Drawing on existing research and experience from the social and behavioral sciences, Professor Goldberg suggests experimentation to test the hypothesis that schools can overcome widespread motivational and intellectual unreadiness for learning. Specifically, she urges re-evaluation of present programs and practices in terms of the present school populations and their environments. She cautions against doing ever more of the same and stresses the need for controlled research.

In the final report of the five-year New York City Juvenile Delinquency Evaluation Project, Professor Robert M. MacIver declares:

> The school's function is to educate, and, where the family and the community fail to provide the social adjustment and the psychological development necessary to prepare the young to receive the education the school offers, it must step in to provide it within the area of its capacity. The school is in a peculiarly strategic position to perform such a preventive and rehabilitative function.[2]

This broad role for the school was discussed at considerable length by the conferees, who raised these issues: Should the school play a welfare

[2] Robert M. MacIver, *Final Report: Juvenile Delinquency Evaluation Project.* New York: The City of New York, 1962.

role as well as an educative role in the depressed urban area? Is the educative role of such a school a welfare one as well? Does the school have an obligation to attack community problems which are not directly connected with its basic instructional functions—such as housing, employment opportunities, family life, community organization? Primarily, should the school determine or reflect society's needs and demands? Can the school develop an adequate educational program without resolving, or at least dealing with, problems of desegregation—racial and economic, de facto and de jure?

Schools in depressed areas are often perceived as "difficult" schools. To counteract their high rates of academic retardation, failure, truancy, staff turnover, pupil mobility, and disciplinary problems, educators have initiated special projects and services. These programs are seen as compensatory or remedial, requiring greater concentration of specialized personnel and cost per child. What effect do programs of compensatory and remedial education have on the school system as a whole? Can school programs, for instance, affect the exodus of the middle-class to suburban and independent schools? If, in gross numbers, there is a large reservoir of undeveloped talent in the schools of depressed urban areas, how can this potential best be realized and developed?

The unemployment rate of youth between the ages of 14 and 21 is twice that of the labor force as a whole and is even greater among youth from minority groups. Dr. James B. Conant characterizes the situation as follows: "Social dynamite is building up in our large cities in the form of unemployed out-of-school youth . . ." Should a school in an urban depressed area put greater stress on vocational education than the school in the suburb or better parts of the city? Does general education have one meaning in the slum-area school and a different meaning in American schools elsewhere? When parental support and understanding of school purposes and goals are lacking, must the school behave differently than it does in situations where there is ambition, parental support, high academic motivation? How can the school in the depressed area best open opportunities for children at the bottom? How can it attract them to the skills, knowledge, insights, attitudes, and aspirations that will help them make their own futures? We will move closer to the American ideal of *equal educational opportunity for all* through programs which face and make up for the inequalities in potential, aptitudes, and motivations. Success in school has been the key to social mobility in the United States—another way of saying a better living standard for more people than in any other country at any other time.

Mel Ravitz | The Role of the School in the Urban Setting

Much has been written about education in America, especially in the period since the Soviet satellite. Actually, of course, the problems that beset our educational system have been with us for years and were not generated by any Soviet achievement. The satellite simply dramatized a long-standing need to re-examine our educational system locally and nationally. This re-examination has been continuing now for the past several years and almost everyone considers himself an educational authority of one sort or another.

Any educational system is simply a formal arrangement of social relationships, personnel, and equipment to meet the need to transfer knowledge, skills, and values from one generation to the next. It is the chief means by which the people of any community extends its way of living into the future; breakdown or inadequacy of that educational system means breakdown or inadequacy of the community or society itself.

It should be apparent that we do not educate our children in a vacuum; we educate them in an existing and very real physical and social world that at any given moment is capable of only so much knowledge and skill, that has certain prevailing values, fears, and ignorance. We educate our children not only in and for a metropolitan community but also in and for a national and international community.

Any educational system always reflects the dominant values and attitudes of the particular community which it serves. Realistically, teachers and administrators cannot be expected to be any wiser, less prejudiced, more courageous than the general level of a community. All of us—teachers, counselors, administrators, parents, citizens—are responsible for the educational system we tolerate and support. By and large, we get just about what the majority of us want and will pay for. As our values change, so too can and should the nature, direction, and program of the educational system change. Indeed, we hold educational conferences and workshops to explore some of the significant, current characteristics of our

6

urban community that are provoking changes in our values and that ought, ultimately, to persuade us to make necessary changes in our educational system.

One such significant change—the launching of the Soviet satellite—has already been noted. That event brought home to most of us the fact that, in our competition with the Soviet Union, we could no longer take for granted our scientific and technological supremacy. However, before attempting to imitate the Soviet system, we ought to recognize that, unlike the Soviet Union, our society is a democratic one which requires more than just scientists and technicians to save it. Indeed, a more insidious danger is that we shall lose the race to the Soviet Union not because it overtakes and surpasses us in the production of technicians or missiles, but becaus we have failed to appreciate and transmit to all our children the ideal democratic values in which we *say* we believe. It is the full internationalization and living expression of these values which chiefly distinguishes our society from others. Among other things, such living expression of our values means providing equal educational opportunity to all children, regardless of race or social class.

Another significant national and international change that modern technology emphasizes is that we live today in an age where time and space have become interchangeable elements. This means that we are but hours away from anywhere in a steadily shrinking and increasingly interdependent world. This social, cultural and economic interdependence which will become increasingly impressive as our technology improves, has important implications for our educational system. An ideology of isolation or superiority that may have sufficed a century ago has now no place in the minds of any of our children.

A third new international fact of life is that all over our shrinking world non-white peoples of Asia and Africa are rising swiftly to positions of power and influence. A key feature of this rising power are the many overt acts of resentment and resistance that serve as reminders that we do not live alone in the world and that some of those whose friendship we seek and need for our survival do not view with unmixed approval everything we do. What we teach our children—all our children, how we teach them, under what circumstances, and the goals toward which we encourage them are noted elsewhere as the real evidence of our sincerity and integrity; these deeds and not our smooth words are known and their import understood by the colored peoples of the earth as they rise to positions where they can be of help or hindrance. So much for these relevant national and international changes.

In describing some of the major characteristics of the local urban community, we may begin by considering a basic physical feature. The generalized urban community is composed of three main growth areas: the old central core of the city, a large middle-aged area, and the newly developed sections and the suburbs. Within the old core area of American cities are dwellings generally built prior to the turn of the century. Many show obvious signs of decay and obsolescence and require clearance and redevelopment. Just outside this core area are the homes in middle-aged neighborhoods. These are the homes and neighborhoods in need of conservation and improvement to prevent them from becoming future slums. Finally, the third area of the city is the newly developed portion near the boundaries and in the suburbs. The new homes in these neighborhoods are in good condition at the moment, but they, too, can and will deteriorate if they are neglected.

In recent years, the urban community has grown in an almost fantastic fashion. Not only has it increased in population, but this population has redistributed itself in the region. It has spilled over the city boundaries, and there is a rapidly growing population now living in our suburbs and in sprawling fashion beyond them. In some metropolitan areas a majority of the population already lives outside the city limits in the surrounding suburbs.

A Mobile Population

Another obvious social characteristic of the urban community is the mobility of its population. The city itself is a result of population movement from the farms and countryside; that movement from rural to urban centers is still continuing. It is no secret that people from the rural sections of the South have moved and still are moving to northern industrial points, such as Cleveland, Chicago, Philadelphia, New York, and Detroit. This movement has been especially heavy during periods of war and war preparation; the early 1940's and early 1950's. Many of the people who have come have stayed to make these cities their home. Many of these people have been Negroes, who, because insecure jobs and generally lower incomes and because of formal or informal restrictions elsewhere, were forced to crowd into the oldest and most deteriorated areas of the city.

In addition to this rural to urban mobility, the urban community may be characterized by another type of movement: that from the interior—especially from middle-aged areas of the city—to its fringes or suburbs. What is essential to recognize about this movement is that it has not been simply random, individual, or isolated families who are moving out, but rather that one whole category of people is moving out while another whole category of people is gradually moving into these interior neighborhoods, especially the middle-aged conservation areas. It is to the newly developed sections of the city and to the suburbs beyond that this mass movement is directed. To be sure, some of these people moving out are seeking larger or smaller houses, as the case may be, to meet the changed needs of the changed family cycle. Other people move because they want a more-expensive or less-expensive home, depending on their different economic conditions, and depending on their need to "keep up with the Joneses." Moreover, many new families have formed and sought available housing. Any of these reasons for moving is acceptable given the mass values of our society. However, one compelling reason why many of these people are rushing from the middle-aged neighborhoods to the edge or out of the city is their fear of the people moving in. Though their fear is frequently rooted in prejudice, it is nonetheless real to them. This fear is at work in the community as we see many whites moving away because they believe terrible things will happen to them, their families, and their property if they stay. Actual evidence from many places in every city shows that, were they to stay, none of these dire things would befall them, their families or their property. Especially is this true where the incoming families have been middle-class Negroes. On the other hand, it is not possible to ignore the fact that in some other neighborhoods, where the newcomers—whether Negro or white—are of a lower social class than the present residents, various kinds of conflict and disturbance may occur which prompt some residents to leave. Such situations as knifings, extortion, and beatings do take place in some changing neighborhoods. However, these are essentially class rather than racial characteristics. While these situations do occur in some changing neighborhoods, we must not make the mistake of thinking that they are an inevitable aspect of the pattern of change in all neighborhoods. Where these situations do exist, there is sound basis for concern and even fear. Indeed, you will find the middle-class Negro families as concerned and as fearful as the middle-class whites about such intimidation and violence. Certainly, this constitutes a problem of major importance in our cities. Its solution involves and requires the active coordination of the police and all related public and voluntary agencies. Even with such total and comprehensive cooperation, the problem will not be easy to solve because the persons who engage in this violence are the products of long years of deprivation, neglect, and frustration. Even with the most careful, coordinated, and immediate efforts aimed at adapting these people to urban living, it is a difficult and long-range job.

With this as background, we are prepared at this point to focus on one of the really difficult issues of present day American society: the issue posed by the in-migration in recent years of vast numbers of rural peoples to the large urban centers, especially the northern industrial ones. Actually, the basic problem is not new; it is as old as cultural differences among and between people who meet. It is, however, a problem that comes in a new guise each time it arises. It is the problem of the "culturally different," and how to educate and assimilate them.

In-migration and Aid to Underdeveloped Countries

One way to start to consider this important problem is by pointing out a rather interesting parallel between American efforts to help different peoples all over the world and the efforts now beginning to assist those American migrants, who have in recent years been coming to such cities as Detroit, Cleveland, Chicago, New York, and Philadelphia, and who live in what have been variously called "the slums," "blighted areas," "depressed areas," "multi-problem neighborhoods."

There are several similarities worth noting. First, of course, there is the essentially rural character of both peoples; those who come to the cities are chiefly from the rural south at the present time. Second, both peoples have generally low levels of formal schooling, but they are by no means unintelligent. Third, both peoples are proud of their cultural traditions and are quick to resent any hint of condescension. Fourth, both peoples are willing to learn, but they must be taught on their own terms; they cannot be cajoled, intimidated, or embarrassed. They must be dealt with as mature adults. These people cannot be expected to realize their full potential unless they are helped at the point of interest and education they now are at. Fifth, and finally, it is very expensive in many ways to try to help either people to modify their traditional values, attitudes and behavior.

These lines of similarity between working with the so-called underdeveloped countries (really, culturally different countries), and working with rural in-migrants to American cities ought certainly to be understood and appreciated. What has been happening these past several years in many American industrial communities is this: they have been the destination for countless thousands of Negroes and whites, individuals and families, who have come mainly in search of jobs. With hope and a general willingness to work, they have come from some of the isolated portions of the back country of the South; they have come without money, and they have brought their problems with them.

Most have come to these cities to stay. The large and continuing growing number of these people have crowded into the deteriorated interior core of the city to which they have come, there to live until they make some money; after that, if they are white, they may choose either to return to the South or try to raise their living standards enough to step onto the outward-bound escalator that moves from the core towards the suburbs. If they are Negro, they will probably not seek to return to the South, but will, instead, try to raise their living standard to board the shorter escalator to move into the better neighborhoods that beckon beyond the interior core of slums. Not many of these whites and Negroes will easily move upward in the social structure; most will continue to live in the blighted core of the city, trying to raise families without much knowledge of the city and its ways, and remaining there only because it was—in economic terms—worse where they came from. These are the people too who get shifted and shunted around as the processes of expressway construction and urban renewal proceed. The inner core of the central city is being remade and those who now live there are sooner or later to be displaced. They will be forced out into the present middle-aged or conservation neighborhoods, bringing with them their cultural habits that are so threatening to the lower-middle- and middle-middle-class Negroes and whites who now reside there. Indeed, the gradual influx of these lower-class rural people of whatever race into these neighborhoods is one of the chief factors prompting the exodus of middle-class residents. Middle-class whites are moving to the fringes and out of the city; middle-class Negroes, of whom there is a growing number, strive desperately to find some opening in the surrounding wall of housing segregation through which they and their families, too, can escape again from lower-class rural influences.

This, then, is one significant part of the pattern of movement in American industrial cities. Everywhere groups of people are moving away at the approach of other groups with real or fancied differences.

As noted at the outset, the problem is an old one, but it is nonetheless critical; the specific issue is essentially: how do those who are of the middle class and who administer and control the schools, the churches, the government, the social welfare agencies, and all the other organizations of the urban community, learn to relate effectively to these people who have come and who are coming to these cities and who want to remain and be accepted? What do they do?

Obviously, one answer is to have nothing to do with them and hope they will go away; this alternative, however, is naive and ridiculous. These newcomers and some not-so-newcomers cannot be ignored. Their impact on neighborhoods, on schools, on health and welfare agencies, and on churches, is tremendous and will continue to be so. There is no real choice but to recognize the existence of these people and then to seek to integrate them into the community in such a way that they will be able to live in the urban environment with some greater degree of civic-mindedness, convenience, and satisfaction, both to themselves and to others around them.

Obviously, recognition of these lower class rural people, these presently "culturally different" people, and concern for and with them does not arise simply out of superior urban nobility. Doubtless, most present residents of these northern industrial communities would breathe a hearty sigh of relief if these people could be persuaded to return to their rural birthplaces. It is only because they cannot be persuaded to return, and because they have a full right to be here, that anyone even pretends to be willing to help them. There is a growing awareness, too, that they must be helped to assimilate because failure to do so threatens the cohesion and stability of the urban community.

When these people come to the city—and some have been here many years—they come primarily because they hope that life's circumstances will be better than they were in the agriculturally blighted areas of the South, from which most came. They moved to these cities to find jobs in order to live and make their modest contributions to society. They arrived, bringing with them the habits of the world they left: its costume, its speech, its cooking patterns, its standards, its beliefs, its attitudes, its values. Just as, a generation or more ago, America hosted large number of newcomers from western and eastern Europe, so, too, today a domestic population shift is bringing to these northern cities fresh waves of newcomers who arrive culturally encumbered with the ways of their rural birthplaces.

In those earlier days of this century, Americans marshalled their resources, established day and night schools, developed a comprehensive social work pattern suited to the problems of the European newcomers, and proceeded in a relatively short time to assimilate these people into the mainstream of American life. It was not easy, it was costly, and it was not done overnight, but ultimately there was a reasonably successful assimilation, to the greater enrichment of the American culture.

This assimilation was achieved without the insistence that every newcomer pass through the "melting pot" and emerge with standardized beliefs, customs, and behavior. It was done with a deep appreciation that social diversity—cultural pluralism—was the true basis of heterogeneous American life. The principle was accepted that assimilation in America does not require that all religious, verbal, culinary, fashion folkways of the subgroup be surrendered. The principle was accepted that people may retain many of their own cultural patterns and still be regarded as loyal, contributing members of the society. It was even implied that American society would face grave danger if this cultural pluralism disappeared and the mass culture of the emerging society smashed all diversity before it to produce a low level cultural monotony. Indeed, that is a significant threat of the present day.

Here again, in the middle of the twentieth century, American society is confronted with a challenge to the belief in cultural pluralism; present and still arriving in our great cities are these newcomers who are different, different in cultural background even though the root of their language, their religion, and their basic values is similar. Their major differences are these: they are poor, some very poor; they have never known comfort and convenience in material things; they were reared on the hard hearths of country cabins and they knew few of the graces or niceties of urban living; they have many different standards of health, of sanitation, of education; their religion is, by middle-class urban criteria, pentecostal and primitive with much appeal to emotion—a frontier religion with emphasis on elementary Christianity; they speak a language filled with the colloquialisms of their region, and they have various kinds of southern accents that set them apart. Finally, most of them have had little formal schooling; they are thus untrained for most work in the industrial community, and if they get work at all, they must accept the menial, unskilled, low-paying, transient jobs.

These, then, are some of the characteristics of both Negroes and whites, who have come to the city and will doubtless continue to come. Although, in their northern trek, these people travel by several different routes, one way or another they get to their destinations, and when they arrive they must be assimilated as immediately and as adequately as possible.

In the face of any vexing and sensitive issue, it is particularly essential that people be honest with themselves. The presence of these culturally different people in many American cities poses such an issue. Most of those people already in the city are urbanized and either already middle-class or middle-class in their orientation. Most of those who have come recently and who are still coming are neither; they are both rural and lower-class. The issue to be considered is simply: how can these two sets of culturally different people relate more effectively and harmoniously with each other?

Some Principles of Cultural Assimilation

At this point, it is appropriate to suggest a basic principle of social interaction: if, in any community, two culturally different peoples meet on a continuing basis, community integration requires one or the other of these peoples to attempt at least the partial assimilation of the other. An adequately integrated community cannot remain with two or more significantly diverse cultural groups. In the particular instance under consideration here, this principle may be translated as follows: an adequately integrated community cannot continue to exist with both large numbers of lower class, rural people and large numbers of middle class, urban people. Either one group or the other will have to try to assimilate the other, or one of them will solve the situation created by withdrawal. Some of the lower-class, rural people will withdraw back to their southern birthplaces when and if the economic conditions become so desperate that things are worse in the city than they were in the country. Some others will withdraw to other cities, especially in the West. Still others will withdraw when and if the various forms of subsistence assistance that are available are reduced, restricted, or terminated. On the other hand, some of the middle-class residents of the city will withdraw, as many have been doing, when these lower-class people begin to move into their neighborhoods. Their withdrawal will be and has been to the fringes of the city or to the suburbs.

As a corollary principle to the one just cited, it may be suggested that the group that is numerically, educationally, politically, economically superior will try to assimilate the other group. It will seek to do this eventually, after it has tried to avoid the issue altogether. It will seek to do this, because it will slowly dawn upon its members that they have most to lose by inaction and the most to gain by successful assimilation. If this larger group proceeds with care and concern in its assimilation attempt, it may well succeed. Indeed, unless it desires to withdraw, there is no reasonable alternative for the urban middle-class but to try to change some of the values, attitudes, and behavior patterns of its own members and of the existing and continually arriving members of the rural lower class. The middle-class must change its own ideas and ways to be better able to understand and accept these newcomers; the middle class, because it is the dominant category, must take the initiative in helping the newcomers shed some of their thornier and no longer functional traits. The issue is really not whether assimilation shall occur, but rather how best can it be accomplished.

The basic instruments of successful assimilation are three: education, assistance, and involvement. The greatest of these is education. None will deny that the most important tools in the assimilation of the foreign born a generation and more ago were the several educational agencies that were made available. Particularly effective were the public day and night schools. Once again the public schools must bear the brunt of the burden. Again the resources must be mustered to work with both the children and the adults who need help in becoming a bit more urban and more middle-class in their aspirations, in their values and attitudes, and in their daily behavior. Certainly no one seriously believes this tremendous transformation of hundreds of thousands of people can occur quickly or easily. It took a long time to produce the residents of depressed urban areas and it will take even longer to assimilate them to function adequately in the complex urban environment.

One specific place to begin is the school building itself which to many people represents what the community is and can become. In the depressed and corroded cores of many of our cities, there are a number of schools that are physically inadequate. Yet, even in such neighborhoods the school is the one building viewed with some community pride. Through its very physical appearance and functional design, the school building can contribute much to improved community morale and even to an enhanced self-image. In depressed areas particularly, it is important that every effort be made to provide adequate, modern, educational facilities.

These buildings should be used not just by the children of the neighborhood. The task of educating children will be significantly eased if their parents perceive the school more favorably by finding it available to them as a convenient community meeting place for various interests and activities. Schools should be kept open afternoons and evenings for as wide a range of community uses as possible. Certainly the school cannot become the community-oriented facility many want it to until and unless the people of the community begin to use it, and that cannot happen until it is made readily available. Nor is it sufficient for the building only to be available. A well-trained staff must also be present to assist those who want to use the school facility to do so quickly and conveniently.

Testing Innate Aptitude

In the depressed areas of the inner city are many children of significantly diverse backgrounds. Here are youngsters with different personality traits, different cultural experiences, different mental abilities, different levels of preparation for school work. We now recognize that it is no longer sufficient to rely on traditional IQ tests as measures of innate intelligence, learning ability, or creativity. Much evidence suggests not only that the test itself is the product of middle-class attitudes and values, but that many children who take such tests are wholly unfamiliar with both the materials of paper and pencil and the language patterns used. We are beginning to suspect that if some youngsters who do poorly on IQ tests were to function in their familiar environment, we might well see their performances improve. Finally, we are slowly coming to appreciate that the real damage of the IQ test is its subtle influence upon the mind of the teacher. Teachers, often unconsciously, expect the level of performance from the child that his IQ test indicated, a practice which, taking into account the weaknesses and inadequacies of these tests, really doesn't give some children half a chance to succeed. Paradoxically, the teacher herself may be the greatest impediment to the child's successful learning experience.

Far better than testing children's intelligence and then using the scores to anticipate their performance, the sensitive teacher will pay scant heed to such tests, if she gives them at all. Instead, she will assume the highest potential for each child and seek to individualize her attention to elicit it.

While it is, of course, a cliché to speak of greater individualized student attention, obviously this is not easy to achieve in crowded, often inadequate, urban schools. If this individualized teaching of depressed-area children is to occur, then the school board will have to make that a basic policy decision and support it in tangible ways.

One such way will be to provide sufficient teachers and counselors so that individual attention is really possible. Another way will be to provide special coaching teachers, particularly in the areas of reading, speech and abstract skills. Every effort should, of course, be made to encourage the very best teachers in the school system to volunteer for the critical assignments of the depressed areas. In this segment of the city especially, emotionally disturbed or mentally defective children should be removed from normal classrooms and provided adequate facilities elsewhere. Certainly, the task of carrying out the teaching-learning process in depressed-area schools is great enough without further complicating the matter with children who deserve to have appropriate therapeutic facilities to correct their mental or emotional ailments.

Many of these children of the depressed areas come from home situations that are deplorable, where the primary need is for the services of a nurse, a dentist, a dietician, where there is abject poverty, where there is much physical overcrowding in poor housing, where many kinds of psychological problems beset members of the family. Often, too, the families are split, with the mother assuming responsibility for both parents. Even if the family is not split, the controls that once applied in the rural setting have been broken in an urban setting that is hostile, uncaring and anonymous, and this has forced the restructuring of the family. The parental images the children now see are images of despair, of frustration, and of enforced idleness. It is absurd, too, for a middle-class teacher to set these children down each day to try to focus their attention on ancient history or on the multiplication table or on nouns or verbs, when simple good sense demands a concern with situations and circumstances under which these children live, conditions which they cannot ignore sufficiently to concentrate on what to them are really other-worldly matters.

The teacher dare not forget that the child has a life that goes on before and after school and this life may be by far the more significant one for the child. Usually it is. Somehow the teacher or perhaps the visiting teacher must penetrate the home world of the child and begin to work more extensively and more intensively with the social, economic and psychological problems of the family. Although social work ordinarily does not cut to the root of social problems, better coordinated social work activity is an important adjunct of successful teaching.

One particular approach the school should take in depressed areas is the assignment of a trained community organization person to work with the parents of school children. Anything that can be done to improve the parents' understanding of what the child is learning and why, every avenue that can help involve the parents in strengthening their own concern with education and development of the community, should redound to the advantage of the child in the classroom. Certainly, it is not far-fetched to establish the kind of adult education the parents themselves want and need. In so many instances what is most lacking in the child's approach to education is an appreciation of it as a basic instrument to survive and succeed in today's complex, specialized world. What better way to help change the child's perception of education than by working with parents in a meaningful program of adult education?

Although it may be a small point, it is also a significant one: the image of the school is an image of a world dominated by women. This is particularly true at the elementary level. Moreover, one of the unfortunate facts of life of the depressed area is the scarcity of socially acceptable male models. Many broken families, much racial discrimination, generally poor education all add up to few men who are socially successful types for the children to see and emulate. Assignment of more male teachers, counselors, and principals to the schools of the depressed areas especially would be helpful. The benefit would be a double one: the school itself would come to have some higher prestige in the eyes of depressed-area residents who view male participation as an indication of importance, and the children, both boys and girls, would have some additional desirable male models to help them to develop their personalities.

A curious social psychological obstacle confronting the children of depressed areas is the unreality of the textbook world they are expected to explore and understand. The usual textbooks are those that draw their characters, their language patterns, their attitudes, and their values from the world of the white middle class. Such a world is an unreal one for most residents of depressed areas. It is a world beyond their experience and they falter in it. Textbooks must be so rewritten that they reveal not only the vast range of racial, social-class, and occupational types that constitute our society, but they must also indicate to the depressed-area Negro child that there are successful Negro physicians, accountants, engineers, nurses, teachers, professors, etc. Books must be used to broaden the horizons of children who live their lives in a very limited real world. If we are successfully to help them reach out for a better world, they must be motivated to believe it is really possible for them to achieve a place in that world.

Major stress is placed upon the school to broaden the horizons of children because often parents either do not care or are unable to do very much to enrich their children's experience. The school is the one agency that touches all children and it must be used for this enrichment purpose. Some children have never been outside their own neighborhood and know only its bleakness and blight. Every effort whereby the school can transport these children to places outside their immediate surroundings; to the zoo, to a factory, to a concert, to a play, to camp, etc., will help immensely in giving these children experiences that middle class youngsters receive as a normal part of their family activity.

Another aspect of what some have come to call "compensatory education" is free summer school. In many communities tradition restricts summer school only to those children who can afford it. Though the fee is small, it is sufficient to keep many depressed-area children from attending. And it is in these areas particularly that children frequently need to make up work, to improve their background, to secure enrichment. During the summer, as well as during the other seasons of the year, the school can be a valuable instrument to help children of depressed areas glimpse the better world that can possibly be theirs.

Despite the opportunities that may be offered, some children will be particularly difficult to hold in school. The dropout rate is highest in the so-called depressed areas. Not only do many children drop out of school as soon as they become old enough to do so (usually sixteen), but the more alarming fact is that so many of them "resign" from school years before. Though they may be aware of the value of education generally, they do not see it as useful for themselves. Somehow, they have become disillusioned either with the school or with self—or with both—and they simply put in time until the age of emancipation from the world of school arrives. Then they hope to enter the world of work, but, because of lack of preparation to enter an increasingly skill-demanding labor market, these young people will meet a second frustration when they cannot find jobs or when they are not promoted or when they are laid off. The dropout or the resigned student represents a tremendous loss both to himself and to society. Here is wasted potential; here is the ingredient out of which grows disillusionment, frustration, despair; here is educational failure that leads to the failure of many children and endangers the society itself. Somehow, renewed efforts must be made to capture and hold the interest and enthusiasm of these pupils in order to educate them to the highest level consistent with their potential. This is no easy challenge, nor is it a meaningless one. All possible ideas will have to be explored. Bold and dramatic approaches relating to curriculum, to school organization, to personnel will have to be tried if we are to succeed in reducing the number of school resignations. This is one of the most basic tasks presently before us, and it is peculiarly vital to depressed areas whose children are the chief victims of such resignation.

The Teacher as a Key Figure

Perhaps the key figure in the entire educational process is the teacher. Good teachers can work miracles with children coming from any background; poor or uninterested teachers never seem to succeed, even with children of good backgrounds. It is no secret that in many cities across the country, the depressed areas have been the "Siberia" of the local school system, and those who for a variety of reasons were to be disciplined were sent to these undesired schools. Not only were the facilities inadequate, but the neighborhoods, too, were blighted, and the children, it was commonly believed, were incapable of learning. We know that almost all children are educable and that what seemed to be educational inability was simply experiential unfamiliarity, long educational disadvantage, and cultural difference. We now know it is possible and, indeed, necessary to educate these children of depressed areas. We must also by now have some glimmering of recognition that we will never do this successfully by using these areas as places of teacher punishment. The depressed area in the American city must become the place where consciously we carry out a massive and effective program of "compensatory education." Not the least of the things we must do for these areas is to guarantee that the teachers sent to teach there are persons without racial, social-class, or cultural-region prejudice. They must also be persons who have some adequate understanding of the cultural backgrounds of their pupils to be able to approach them without fear and actually attempt to teach them. Not infrequently teachers, counselors, principals assigned to the depressed-area school have been people without any real concern for these children and with the common stereotype of them as children of low ability. As a result of this low estimate of potential, the self-fulfilling prophecy went into effect. The children were not encouraged to learn very much; the teacher expended little energy on anything but maintaining order and bemoaning her lot; as a consequence, the children fulfilled the low expectation, which in turn reinforced the original assumption to prove that the teacher was right. We now recognize, however, that for teachers with ability, with devotion to good teaching, without prejudice or preconceived expectations, there is a basic challenge and deep satisfaction in working in depressed-area schools. We know, too, that unless we raise our expectations of these children, they will not achieve either an education or an opportunity in the society at large. It is no longer considered a blessing to the child to have a teacher who simply passes him from grade to grade regardless of his ability to perform at each successive stage. These children require not just teachers, but teachers of more than ordinary ability, interest, and devotion. If we are to reclaim a portion of our urban population from a dire and dismal dependency, then we must select for the schools of the depressed areas teachers and principals who want to take up the greater challenge of teaching there. We must certainly choose teachers and principals without racial or class prejudice, and we must assign them without regard to their color or religion. Every opportunity should be accorded these personnel to improve their own background through additional training, research or writing on relevant aspects of the educational process. These teachers especially should be relieved of many time-consuming, menial tasks in order to free them for the far more creative job of developing ways children can be helped to learn.

This creative job of teaching is one that is difficult at best under hospitable conditions; in the depressed schools it is a job of immense difficulty. Ultimately, no matter what else she may do, the teacher has to possess the skill to reach the children and motivate them in terms of the cultural world they are in. This skill, one is not born with; it must be acquired. But it is not acquired just as a result of the ordinary educational sequence of four or five years of college. Unfortunately, we have been training our teachers for essentially a middle-class world of white students, and many of them do not grow up to work in such a world. We must begin to reevaluate our teacher-training procedure and program. It may be that we have been turning people out as accredited teachers even though they are really ill-prepared to function in so many of the schools to which they may be assigned in the slums of the city. We have made the mistake of thinking that teachers are born and not made. We have been unaware that a population revolution has been occurring within our cities that has transformed them into severely stratified places with many kinds of problems. We have been guilty of maintaining the situation as normal, when a serious crisis has been brewing. Not only in the community, but in the college and university as well, we must prepare to equip our new teachers with the depth of cultural understanding and the range of necessary skills, methods, and techniques to enable them to do the very urgent teaching job of preparing these students, not just for American citizenship, but for urban citizenship in a highly complex, heterogeneous, and specialized social order.

Reservoir of Potential

It should be clear that these children under discussion here—these disadvantaged children who live in the depressed core of the city—have the same intellectual potential as other normal children. They are not inherently dull or stupid; many are, or would be, bright and alert, if their basic physical needs were met, if they were given experiences that would encourage them to want to learn the ways of the middle-class world, if they were carefully and devotedly taught by able teachers who believed in their potential and sought to release it through all the many means of excellent education.

Even with the accomplishment of all the educational aims enumerated and elaborated above, it is a gamble whether these children can be saved and assimilated. Indeed, there is no clear certainty that any community is really committed to assimilating them. If it were, then that community would be interested not only in taking major steps to improve their schooling, but it would also be concerned with the quality of their housing and their neighborhoods; it would be determined to do something constructive and comprehensive about the fundamental economic, educational and psychological plight of their parents. So long as these people live in poverty at the margin of despair and in a community that has fewer and fewer jobs for the unskilled, so long will the task of assimilation be retarded. If these parents can be effectively trained and related through the job to the main axis of an industrial community, then there is hope of speedy assimilation of both them and their children. If it is not possible to make the fundamental necessary changes in the economic structure to admit these able-bodied men to the world of productive work, then it is probable that much that may be done for their children will be wasted. The basic issue is the assimilation of a whole category of people; those who attempt to do so must want to assimilate them without destroying the cultural dimensions they can contribute.

To say that one wants to assimilate people without supporting that statement with community funds and action will be simply to disillusion those who are not already disillusioned. If urban residents are truly concerned about crime and delinquency in their community, if they are serious about their intention to produce skilled scientists and technicians for societal survival, if they want an over-all peaceful, integrated community with well-trained and concerned citizens, then they must understand that the small price to be paid is that of more-than-ordinary education, assistance, and involvement of this disadvantaged population of the city.

The third instrument to encourage assimilation is involvement of the people affected. If there is one thing essential to realize as efforts are made to aid these people to attain some urban and middle-class values and attitudes, it is that they cannot be told unilaterally what they must do. To be sure, they have problems, but they also have pride, and both the problems and the pride must be appreciated if the sensitive job of helping them become contributing citizens of a democratic community is to be done.

A basic structural development any governmental agency or board of education might well make is to establish a network of community councils. Each appropriate-sized district should have such a community council composed of people who live and work in the area. Such an organizational structure would make clear to the people that their advice, suggestions and ideas are actively sought. It would offer the opportunity for effective two-way communication between citizens of a community and the schools and agencies therein. Problems of the people could be taken to the community council; school or agency-related problems would be referred to school personnel or the personnel of appropriate agencies. Most important, the means of reaching the people and securing their participation would exist. Indeed, before any attempt is made to modify curricula or make any policy changes in school administration, it is elementary wisdom to establish such a citizen council and to work with and through it for the benefit of the total community. Though there are some technical aspects of education, of social work, of planning, and of government which cannot be submitted to citizen vote, there are other aspects on which organized citizens can react intelligently and meaningfully, and their invited participation from the beginning can spell the difference between success and failure of new proposals. To facilitate cultural assimilation and to teach the democratic process, there is no action more fundamental nor more immediately necessary than the creation of a genuine community council in each appropriate-sized district.

These comments outline the broad dimensions of an important community problem facing American cities and schools. It is nothing less than the problem of cultural assimilation on a large scale. It is a profound problem affecting many aspects of urban life: education, housing, family life, employment, the very cohesion of the community itself. It is a problem that will not be solved by speeches, slogans, or gimmicks. Its solution requires some genuine perception of the scope and depth of the problem, as well as the intelligent and imaginative use of the instruments of education, assistance, and involvement. Failure to solve this problem will further divide each community and will leave it increasingly in the hands of those with the least knowledge of how to run it, as those with greater knowledge seek more cohesive communities in which to work and live. Solution of this problem of assimilation will produce a stronger, healthier community with a justified pride in its concern for its most significant resource: the many millions of human beings who choose to live in them.

Robert J. Havighurst | Urban Development and the Educational System

Americans are becoming an urban people.[1] Sixty-one per cent of the population lived in metropolitan areas in 1960, and it is estimated that, by 1980, 70 to 75 per cent of the total population will be living in cities of fifty thousand or more or in the areas which feed into these cities.

In the past, urban evolution has on the whole been advantageous. But it has some disadvantages that are now forcing massive and costly urban renewal programs aimed at making metropolitan areas more fit for human living and more conducive to human values.

Metropolitan growth presents two major concerns. First, it has led to increased segregation on the basis of income and race. This segregation is a threat to democratic unity and educational opportunity, for slums or gray areas of the central cities breed political and social divisiveness and discontent. Second, space is not used properly. The location of industry, business, and dwellings have made the daily journey to work longer and more difficult than is really necessary for a large part of the population. The distance from residential areas to centers of leisure and cultural activity—theaters, museums, concert halls—is too great. Open space for recreation and for the enjoyment of nature has not been distributed so as to be available to the majority of the people.

Metropolitan developments have produced or intensified many social problems, most of which have had repercussions in education. The net effect has been to make the educational system less efficient and less effective in achieving its democratic goals.

One major problem is increased socio-economic and racial segregation of the population. As the total population of a megalopolis grows, the slum belt around the central business district becomes thicker. This is a result not only of the growth in total population but also of the concentration of lower-class people in areas of poorest housing, which are usually in the oldest parts of the city. Those who can afford to do so move away

[1] This paper draws on four previous writings of the author (2, 3, 4, 5).

24

from the city as their economic circumstances improve. In general, working-class people whose income permits it move out of the slum district and take up residence farther from the center of the city, while people in middle-class districts of the central city move out to middle-class suburbs. Thus the ever-growing total population divides itself into a lower-class conglomerate at the center, with successively higher socio-economic groups at greater distances and the upper-middle class and the upper class largely in the suburbs.

Data from the Detroit area illustrate this generalization, which applies to most, if not all of the other great cities. In the Detroit Area Study of the University of Michigan, information was collected on the incomes of families in Detroit and its suburbs. According to a report on this research, which covered family income from 1951 to 1959, the median income per family in the Detroit metropolitan area was related to the distance the family lived from the central business district. For families living within six miles of the central business district, the median income rose 3 per cent between 1951 and 1959, while the cost of living rose 12 per cent; thus during this period the median family in this area lost real income. Families living farther out, between the six-mile radius and the city limits, gained 5 per cent in median real income. Meanwhile, families in the Detroit suburban area gained 37 per cent in median real income. Thus, during these years the people in the central part of the city grew poorer, while the people in the suburbs grew richer. In other words, the central part of the city became more solidly lower class in composition, while the suburbs became more middle class.

As a result of the growth of low-income areas in the cities, *the urban lower-class school* has become a common and disturbing phenomenon. It is a school with a clear numerical predominance of pupils from working-class homes.

Such a school can be defined by its *status ratio* which is the ratio of middle-class pupils to lower-class pupils. A useful form of this ratio is obtained by weighting the numbers of upper- and upper-middle-class pupils twice as heavily as the number of lower-middle-class pupils, and by weighting the lower-lower-class pupils twice as heavily as the upper-lower-class pupils. The ratio is $2(U + UM) + LM$ divided by $UL + 2LL$. The justification for giving greater weights to the upper and upper-middle classes and to the lower-lower class is that they express educational differences more clearly than the lower-middle and upper-lower classes do.

As an example of the calculation of the status ratio, let us look at School A—a middle-class school. Of the children in this school, 30 per cent are from upper-middle- or upper-class families, 35 per cent are from lower-middle-class families, 25 per cent are from upper-lower-class families, and 10 per cent are from lower-lower-class families. Its status ratio is $^{95}\!/_{45}$ or 2.1. This kind of school can be found in a "good" area of a large city or in a dormitory suburb.

School B—a mixed-class school. The children in this school are 15 per cent upper-middle and upper-class, 35 per cent, 35 per cent and 15 per cent lower-middle, upper-lower, and lower-lower class, respectively. Its status ratio is $^{65}\!/_{65}$ or 1.

School C—a lower-class school. In this school, the children are 5 per cent upper-middle-class, 20 per cent lower-middle-class, 45 per cent upper-lower-class, and 30 per cent lower-lower-class. Its status ratio is $^{30}\!/_{105}$ or 0.29.

For the purposes of this paper we shall group schools into these three categories. Middle-class schools will be those with status ratios of 2 or more. Mixed-class schools will be those with status ratios between 0.5 and 2.0. Lower-class schools will be those with status ratios below 0.5.

Urbanization and the Status Ratio

As North American cities grow bigger, they tend to become stratified by income, socio-economic status, race, and other social characteristics. A process of segregation takes place through the moves that families make in search of "better" living conditions. People who can afford it move to a "better" section of the city, or to a suburb, and their places are taken by people below them in social status. Thus, unless something happens to reverse the process of aging and downgrading of sections of the city, the lower-class areas of the city expand into large economically segregated districts.

A major reason for people's moving is to find a "good" place for their children to live. A "good" place for children includes a "good" school, and for most middle-class people a "good" school is one with a status ratio which places it in the middle-class or in the mixed-class category.

There is a *critical ratio* for a school, of such a size that middle-class parents are likely to become anxious and to think of removing their children from the school when the status ratio drops to this point or below it. This critical ratio is subjective, depending upon the attitudes and experience of a particular parent, and depending also on such things as the tradition of the school, the racial composition of the school, the type of curriculum, and the quality of the teachers. However, there is enough of a consensus of middle-class parents about the critical ratio that they tend to agree on the question of moving out of the school district when the status ratio reaches a certain point.

Growing Economic Segregation in American Schools

There has probably been a growing amount of economic segregation in American public schools since 1940. That is, there has been a growing percentage of middle- and lower-class schools, and a decreasing percentage of mixed-class schools. To put it more exactly, the proportion of American children attending schools with status ratios above 2 and below 0.5 has increased since 1940. This is true in spite of the growth of mixed-class suburbs and in spite of the increased birth rate of middle-class people since the Second World War.

This process of economic segregation can be seen in detail by looking at what happened in a particular elementary school in a northern industrial city between 1955 and 1960.

Leibnitz School in 1955 was attended by 1,250 pupils coming mainly from lower-, middle-, upper-middle-, and upper-lower-class families of German, Dutch, and Swedish origins. It had a status ratio of about 1. The district was situated about seven miles from the city center, close to transportation lines. Parents of some of the pupils had attended the same schools. Then came a period of rapid change. Some of the three-storey apartment buildings were cut up by their owners into smaller units and rented to an influx of southern white and Negro families. By 1960 the school enrollment was 2,400. The school was running on a double-shift schedule, with one group of children coming for four and a half hours in the morning, and another group coming for an equal time in the afternoon to a new shift of teachers. The status ratio dropped to 0.06. Transiency is calculated at 79 per cent, which means that 1,900 pupils transferred in or out of school during the year from September 1960 to June, 1961. At times of heavy turnover the children waiting to transfer in or out are seated in the auditorium with their parents in some cases, and without them in others, while one clerk sits at a desk on the stage and processes transfers and records from incoming children while another clerk sits on the opposite side of the stage and processes papers for the outgoing children. The records of transfers out during the past several years show that most of the children leaving the school have gone to schools further out from the city center, or in the suburbs. The campus of Leibnitz School was at one time beautifully landscaped, but this area has been filled with gravel, to accommodate the hundreds of pupils who arrive at noon and mill around while waiting for their shift to begin.

While Leibnitz changed from a mixed-class to a lower-class school, many of its former middle-class pupils moved out to middle-class suburbs or to middle-class areas on the edge of the city, and entered middle-class schools.

In the suburbs, also, the process of shifting from mixed-class schools to middle- and lower-class schools has gone ahead. This is illustrated by the Madison Township High School. Madison is a small semi-industrial city which has been surrounded by dormitory suburbs since the Second World War. Several of these small suburbs have elementary schools of their own but send their high-school-age pupils to Madison High School. Until recently the high school had a status ratio of approximately 1, with a cross-sectional student body including about ten per cent Negroes. About five years ago a dormitory suburb five miles from Madison which sent its pupils to Madison High joined with a new suburb further out to set up its own high school, which has a high-status ratio. This was somewhat disturbing to people in Madison, but just then a new dormitory suburb on the outskirts of Madison was being built, and it supplied a number of middle-class students who practically made up for the loss of the other students. This new suburb, Elmwood, continued to grow and just last year established its own high school, which took away about one fourth of Madison High students and reduced the status ratio of Madison to 0.40. There is a Negro working-class suburb which sends its students to Madison and appears to be content with this arrangement. But the faculty and the dwindling group of middle-class parents in Madison High are now fearful that their school will become a lower-class school, and they argue that the behavior of the Elmwood group was undemocratic.

Probably economic segregation in the schools goes farther in big cities than in small cities and towns. The writer has explored this proposition by making some crude calculations concerning the schools in several cities for whom a certain amount of data are available. Table 1 shows the proportions of schools (and, presumably, of pupils) of the three types in Prairie City, a town of 6,000; in River City, a medium-sized city of 45,000; and in Kansas City, Detroit, and Chicago. The figures in Table 1 are based on a knowledge of the occupations, income, education, and other social characteristics of the districts in which the elementary and secondary schools are located.

Prairie City has two small, four-grade elementary schools, one in the factory district and the other on the opposite side of town in the upper-middle-class residential district. There is also an eight-grade elementary school in the center of town, serving its own area for the first four grades and the whole town for grades 5 through 8. Since there is only one high school, this school is a mixed-class school.

River City has fourteen public elementary schools, five in the lower-class areas, five in mixed-class areas, and four in middle-class areas. Since there is only one high school, it is a mixed-class school.

Table I. Economic segregation in schools, related to size of city
(per cent of schools, approximating per cent of youth).

Class and Type of School	Cities				
	Prairie City	River City	Kansas City	Detroit	Chicago
Elementary					
Middle class	15	30	18	16	19
Mixed class	70	35	44	52	35
Lower class	15	35	38	32	46
Secondary					
Middle class	0	0	19	30	39
Mixed class	100	100	50	40	22
Lower class	0	0	31	30	39

Kansas City's elementary-school distribution is not much different from River City's, except that there are relatively fewer middle-class schools, since the middle-class suburbs are not included in the Kansas City School District. Kansas City has sixteen junior and senior high schools, and only half of these schools are of mixed-class type. Detroit estimates are not so reliable as those from Kansas City and Chicago as they depend only on data on average income by school district (7). According to the writer's estimates the distribution in Detroit is very similar to that of Kansas City, with 52 per cent of elementary school pupils in mixed-class schools, and 40 per cent of high school pupils in mixed-class schools.

In Chicago, the proportion of children in lower-class elementary schools is estimated at 46 per cent, and the proportion in middle-class schools at 19 per cent. In the public high schools these proportions are 39 per cent in lower-class schools, 39 per cent in middle-class schools and 22 per cent in mixed-class schools.

To get a closer look at an urban lower-class school we may return to the Leibnitz School and look at one of its fifth-grade classes. All the forty-two pupils in this class were Negro. Of this number fifteen were supported by Aid to Dependent Children and two by General Assistance. The remainder, twenty-five, were supported by one or both parents working at unskilled or semi-skilled occupations. The majority of these children were found to be below grade in achievement (as measured by standard tests) in reading or arithmetic or both. Eighteen were over-age for the grade; eight of these over-age students were 13 (10 is the average age for fifth grade). The majority of these over-age students presented behavior problems. This particular room reflects the socio-economic racial composition and achievement level for the remainder of the classes in the school. Very often students with ability will not or cannot produce in such an environment.

The principal, the assistant principal, the adjustment teacher, the psychologist, and three of the classroom teachers are white. The rest of the teaching staff is Negro. The faculty is relatively stable. The teaching staff as a whole tries to do a good job of teaching. Many of the Negro teachers have had personal experience with changing neighborhoods and are familiar with the conditions under which the children live. The teachers are anxious to help their students to raise their achievement levels. An attempt is made to use materials such as the SRA reading kits which enable the children to deal with reading materials at their own ability level. Each classroom teacher finds it necessary to adapt curriculum materials for the many achievement levels found in any given class. The lower class behavior of many of the students makes it hard for some of the teachers to be as sympathetic as they might like to be. Many parents who come to school voluntarily or by request tell the teachers, "I can't do nothin' with him either, I whip him but it don't do no good." Very few parents visit the school. This may be due to work schedules, indifference, or to the feeling that the school people will handle situations involving their children correctly.

Facts such as these join together to produce the situation reported by Patricia Sexton for "Big City" schools (7). Table 2 (A and B) summarizes a set of data about the elementary and secondary schools in this northern industrial city. The children of poor families are concentrated in certain areas of the city, and they do poor work in school.

Social Consequences of the Urban Lower Class School

In the judgment of the present writer, the urban lower-class school has some serious damaging consequences for the democratic development of our society.

1. The pupils of a lower-class school achieve less well than they would if they were in a mixed- or middle-class school. As an example of this we may compare the records in the junior high school of River City which were made by pupils who came from contrasting elementary schools— one a middle-class school and the other a lower-class school. The pupils from the lower-class school averaged slightly more than one failure per pupil in English, history, mathematics or science in the eighth grade while no child from the middle-class school failed a subject in the eighth grade. The grades made in the ninth grade by the two groups (after some of the lower class pupils had already dropped out of school) in English, civics, mathematics, science, Latin, and journalism are shown in Table 3.

Table 2. Income level of big-city schools in relation to characteristics
of pupils[a]

(A)

Average family income, 1957	Composite score Iowa Achievement Test—6th grade	IQ rating	Pupils sent to detention school (per 10,000)	Condition of school building (Perfect= 1000)
Group I ($3,000 to $4,999)	5.23	2.79	31.3	574
Group II ($5,000 to $6,999)	5.61	3.31	21.7	578
Group III ($7,000 to $8,999)	6.47	4.55	6.9	688
Group IV ($9,000 or over)	7.05	5.09	2.7	779

(B)

Average family income, 1957	Number chosen as "gifted" (per 10,000)	Per cent of high school students with failure in English	Per cent of drop-outs 1957-8	Per cent of graduating class requesting transcripts for college
Group I (Below $6,000)	1	16.8	19.2	23
Group II ($6,000 to $6,999)	6	10.9	15.8	34
Group III ($7,000 to $7,999)	20	9.3	7.9	46
Group IV ($8,000 to $8,999)	36	8.5	7.2	61
Group V ($9,000 or over)	77	6.6	3.6	81

[a] Data from Patricia Sexton (7, pp. 28, 39, 60, 72, 127, 163, 182, and 202).

Table 3. School-grade distinction by social class.

Grade	Middle-Class School	Lower-Class School
A	45%	0%
B	20	10
C	25	19
D	10	27
E	0	44

By the end of the tenth grade, two-thirds of the pupils from the lower class school either had dropped out of school or had failed and dropped behind a year. Only two pupils of this school reached a C-plus, or average school grade. Of the pupils from the middle-class school, more than a third had A or A-minus averages, and only two pupils had averages below C-minus, indicating a near failure.

Of course it would not be true to say that the lower-class school *caused* the low school achievements of the pupils in that school. Their low achievements were due to a number of causes. One of these causes certainly was lack of intellectual stimulation in their homes. Another cause may have been an inherited inferiority in intelligence. But the consensus of students of the sociology and psychology of education is that the fact of attending a lower class school does have something to do with the lower academic achievement of the pupils from that school.

The research reported by Wilson from secondary schools of the San Francisco Bay-Oakland area supports this conclusion (8). Wilson studied the boys in eight high schools, three of which were lower-class schools, two of mixed-class composition and three of middle-class composition. Their average status ratios were 0.45, 1.2, and 4.4 respectively. Knowing the fathers' occupations, Wilson was able to find the relation between the fathers' occupations and the boys' school marks in the three groups of schools. The boys whose fathers were professional or white collar workers got lower grades if they were in lower-class schools than boys in middle-class or mixed-class schools whose fathers were in these occupations. Furthermore, the sons of manual workers who were in the middle-class schools got better school marks than the sons of middle-class parents in the lower-class schools.

This fact may be attributed partly to a selective factor—manual workers with educational ambitions for their children may have made special efforts to live in middle-class areas, while middle-class people who did not care much about education may have tended to live in lower-class areas. Still, granting some plausibility to this explanation, the conclusion appears to be inescapable that a kind of "academic climate" existed in each school that affected the attitudes of the students toward study and affected their educational aspirations.

2. The pupils of a lower-class school have lower educational aspirations than they would have if they were in a mixed or middle-class school. Wilson's study supports this proposition. Aspiration for a college education was related to the type of school as well as to father's occupation.

Wilson also found that a boy with a given IQ is more likely to want to go to college if he is in a middle-class school or a mixed-class school than if he is in a lower-class school.[2]

3. The pupils of a lower-class school show less "talent" than they would

[2] These findings of Wilson are supported in an extensive study of high-school seniors made at the Bureau of Applied Social Research of Columbia University. John A. Michael, the researcher, divided 518 high schools into five "climate groups" which are very similar to our social-class groups. He found that scores on a scholastic aptitude test and plans to enter college, were both *related to family* social status and to the high-school climate (6).

if they were in a mixed or middle-class school. Somewhat related to the preceding propositions is this one that the lower-class school contributes to the waste of talent. As an example, we shall take the production of "academically superior high-school seniors" in an American city of a half-million population, with eight senior high schools. Two of these schools were middle class, three were mixed class, and three were lower-class schools. These schools engaged in a "talent search" to identify seniors who were academically superior. Roughly 7 per cent of the seniors of the city were identified as "academically superior" through intelligence tests, school grades, and recommendations by teachers. Table 4 shows how these students were distributed among the various schools. The two middle-class high schools produced 63 per cent of the talented students, with 29 per cent of the city's high school enrollment. The three lower-class high schools produced 10 per cent of the talented students, out of 43 per cent of the city's high-school enrollment.

Table 4. Efficiencies of schools of various socio-economic levels in producing academically superior high-school seniors (data from an American city of 500,000 population).

High School	A	B	C	D	E	FGH	Total
Number of graduates:	412	392	325	71	400	1,203	2,803
Number of superior students in graduating class	77	45	30	5	17	20	194
Per cent of superior students	19	12	9	7	4	1.5	6.9
Rank in socio-economic status	1	2	3	4	5	7	
Number of superior students if A ratio prevailed	77	74	62	14	76	229	532

4. The lower-class school reduces the democratic quality of our society. Several of the characteristics which we regard as essential for a democracy are systematically undermined by socio-economic segregation in lower-class schools. One of these is the opportunity for upward social mobility. This depends in our society on opportunity for success in secondary and higher education, and we have seen that this opportunity is less in lower-class schools than it is in mixed-class schools.

Another experience which we believe contributes to democracy is the mingling of youth of all social backgrounds in the same school. For this reason the comprehensive high school (comprehensive in the sense that it is a mixed-class school) has been regarded by American educational leaders as the best possible kind of school. Thus James B. Conant said:

> Our schools have served all creeds and all economic groups within a given geographic area. I believe it to be of the utmost importance that this pattern be continued. To this end the comprehensive high school deserves the enthusiastic support of the American taxpayer. . . . We Americans desire to provide through our schools unity in our national life. . . . Unity we can achieve if our public schools remain the primary vehicle for the education of our youth, and if, as far as possible, all the youth of a community attend the same school irrespective of family fortune or cultural background (1).

Mr. Conant's more recent book, *Slums and Suburbs,* deals with the problems of lower-class schools and middle-class schools as realities which exist in a metropolitan area, and attempts to show how we may improve them without making them mixed-class schools.

Can We Have Equality of Opportunity in Economically Segregated Schools?

The United States Supreme Court by a unanimous decision in 1954 declared that racial segregation in the public schools is contrary to the United States Constitution. It said, "Segregation of children in the public schools solely on the basis of race, even though the physical facilities and other 'tangible' factors may be equal, deprives the children of the minority group of equal educational opportunities." The Court went on to say that "separate educational facilities are inherently unequal." While this statement was made with regard to race, the evidence on which it was made applies with great force to separate educational facilities on any basis where one group is regarded as superior and another group as inferior. Separation on the basis of socio-economic status is as much a separation of superior from inferior in the United States as is separation on the basis of skin color.

The de facto segregation by socio-economic status that exists in our public schools, and especially in the big cities, is not due to a conscious act on the part of our society, whereas de jure segregation would be. Therefore, some of us tend to accept de facto segregation as "a fact of nature," "a part of social reality," or "a result of the action of natural laws," and consequently we do not feel guilty about it.

The following account of an elementary school which changed from a mixed-class integrated school to a lower-class Negro school illustrates the process of de facto segregation.

Thirty years ago the Poplar neighborhood was a Negro island surrounded on all sides by white neighborhoods. All social classes were represented in the community from lower-lower through upper-middle. Many Negro doctors, lawyers, and teachers lived in the community as well as many government and railroad employees whose steady incomes protected their families from want during the lean depression years. Negroes who lived in the older Negro neighborhoods to the north spoke of Poplar as a good place to live on a non-crowded basis. The people of this neighborhood felt themselves to be a cut or two above the average Negro from the ghetto.

The neighborhood school reflected the multi-class character of the neighborhood. The middle-class children were favored by the predominantly Irish Catholic faculty of the school. During the eight-year period from 1934 to 1942, the number of Negro teachers rose from zero to twelve in a school faculty of forty. The Negro parents did not want Negro teachers on the faculty. They felt that the white teachers were better prepared and that their children would receive better teaching from them. At one time petitions were circulated in the neighborhood in an attempt to bar assignment of Negro teachers to the school.

In this atmosphere, even though it was somewhat unfriendly to them, the relatively few lower-lower and more numerous upper-class children had an opportunity to observe and copy middle-class behavior. Those who did try to please middle-class teachers and schoolmates were rewarded by being accepted into the formal and informal club and friendship groups of the middle class. During the elementary-school years formally organized clubs were formed which persisted through high school and college. Each of these clubs had at least one or two lower-class girls in their membership. At this time the two leading Negro sororities maintained high-school interest groups whose purposes were to encourage high-school girls to go on to college and thus into the sororities. The district high school contained all social classes for the Negro group; however, the white population of the high school at that time (1942) went no higher than lower-middle-class, with most of the students coming from the lower-middle and upper-classes.

In 1942 the character of the neighborhood started to change. Many of the middle-class residents of Poplar moved farther out from the city center, to an area where vacant property was available to Negro professionals who started to build homes that were considered to be show places by the members of the larger Negro community. The influx of Southern Negroes who had come to the city to work in the war industries started putting pressure on the facilities of the old ghetto. The ghetto could not hold them all and they pushed into Poplar. All the whites and most of the Negro middle-class people moved away, and the status ratio dropped. Now there are only two white teachers on a faculty of over fifty teachers. The Negro teachers who have lived and taught in the area for more than twenty years sadly note the changes in the student body. "These children are so hard to reach, they don't care about bettering themselves, teaching is no longer a pleasure," are phrases that are heard again and again in conversation with these teachers.

Proposed Educational Policies and Practices

Educators and social scientists who are disturbed by the existence of lower-class schools must choose one or both of two policies for action.

1. Accept the existence of such schools and work to improve them within these limits. Many people in effect resign themselves to the fact of economic segregation, and say that we must make the best of it. In particular, they say that the schools should not be used to influence the structure of the city; what the structure of the city presents to the schools is a reality with which the schools must live, they believe.

2. Work through the schools as well as in other ways to reduce economic segregation. That is, work for mixed-class schools by working for mixed-class communities. The enormous material resources now going into physical urban renewal offer a physical base for social urban renewal, and the group of people who want to reduce economic segregation see a chance to do so through urban renewal programs.

The present writer believes that *both* policies are desirable.

Improving the Lower-Class School

Efforts at improving the lower-class school should be applied at the elementary- and secondary-school levels, with major emphasis on the elementary school. A great deal of energy and ingenuity is now going into this effort, especially in the larger cities. Some of the procedures that seem to be indicated are:

1. Enrichment programs for culturally deprived children at the kindergarten-primary level. A number of large cities are trying out a type of program that gives special assistance to the primary grades in the slum schools, on the theory that many of these children lack parental examples and stimulation from parents to read and to achieve well in school. They fail to master the task of reading and stumble along for the first few years in school, after which they become confirmed non-learners and social misfits during their adolescence. Through putting specially trained teachers into relatively small classes, through using a social worker or visiting teacher

to bring the home and school into contact, and through giving the children a variety of enrichment which middle-class children are more likely to get in their homes, these children will get a better start in school and thus a better start in life.

2. Enrichment programs for lower-class children in the elementary school. A systematic attempt can be made to give lower-class children some of the intellectually stimulating experience that is fairly common in middle-class families. The Higher Horizons program of New York City is an example. Through the school the children are given access to museums, libraries, theaters and concerts. The lower-class school is given additional staff for planning and conducting this program, and for working with parents. Things are done to make this kind of school more attractive to experienced teachers.

3. Nursery school programs especially designed for lower-class children. There is an interesting area of research just developing on the cognitive development of young children, which may suggest the extension of public schooling down to age 3 or 4 in lower class districts, as a means of giving intellectual stimulation at a crucial point in the child's life. At this age basic language patterns are learned which probably go a long way toward structuring the mind. And studies of the language used in lower- and in middle-class homes indicate that the typical lower-class home gives the child a language experience that is much different from that of a typical middle-class home. The lower-class language patterns are simpler, with fewer attempts at explanation of the world, fewer qualifying adjectives and phrases, fewer complex sentences. If the research now going on proves that lower-class children can be given a permanent boost of intelligence and of learning ability at the age of 3 or 4, we will see the development of public nursery schools with this aim.

4. Talent discovery and development programs at the junior and senior high-school levels. Probably a good deal of potential talent among lower-class pupils goes undiscovered by the usual testing programs. These boys and girls do not show up as well as their middle-class equals, and they are overlooked as candidates for honors courses and college entrance programs in high school. They are likely to be found within the IQ range of 100 to 120. A program of this sort is commencing in the Kansas City public schools, assisted by a substantial fund for scholarship aid. The youth who are being picked about the eighth- and ninth-grade levels have done average school performance, but are seldom outstanding. They need counseling and stimulation to think of college as a possibility for them. Their parents need information about the importance of a college education.

5. Work-study programs for maladjusted youth at the junior high school level. Under present conditions some 15 per cent of boys and girls fail to grow up successfully through the avenue provided by the schools. They become non-learners, and react either with hostility and aggression or with apathy to the school after about the sixth grade. In slum areas this proportion is likely to reach 25 or 30 per cent. They are alienated from the values and ways of behaving of the school and other middle-class institutions. It is these boys and girls who make school teaching so difficult at the seventh, eighth, and ninth grades, and who make the junior high school and the early years of senior high school so difficult for academically motivated youth, in schools where the status ratio is below the critical point. For alienated youth, especially for the boys, there is a good deal of experimentation with work-study programs which aim to give the youth a chance to grow up satisfactorily through the avenue of work. Most such programs commence with youth at the age of 16, when they are allowed to drop out of school if they wish to do so. Such programs appear to be having some success. Possibly better results will be achieved in programs commencing work-experience as a part of a school program as early as 14, or the eighth grade.

A parallel type of program for girls who are the sociological sisters of the boys for whom a work-study program is desirable might be centered around the role of wife and mother which these girls will soon assume. Teen-age girls who fail and drop out of school are very likely to marry early. This is the "natural" thing for them to do, and the most direct path to womanhood. Yet they are poorly prepared for keeping house and rearing children.

For such girls, who can be identified by the time they reach the eighth grade, a modified school program might be established with teachers who combine home economics knowledge and skills with ability and training of the sort which characterizes a social group worker. The teacher would organize the girls into a social group which could give them satisfaction and emotional support, while they learned what they could from the school. They would be encouraged to take part-time jobs as baby-sitters and other jobs which interested them, though jobs would not be regarded as of first importance. Primarily, they would be learning from their teacher who would be both a model and a guide to them. As they grew older, and some of them dropped out of school, they would continue to meet as a club under the leadership of their teacher, in YWCA or settlement house quarters if they did not care to meet in school. They would hold engagement parties and "showers" for prospective brides and mothers. Their club leader would be available to them as a counselor, who would help them with individual counsel and with group study of the problems that concerned them most.

This type of program is just as important, socially, as a work-study program for boys, though it does not get as much attention because girls who need this kind of help are not so obviously dangerous to society and to themselves as are the boys. A few cities are working in this direction. The "Wings" project in Philadelphia is an example.

Increasing the Proportion of Mixed Class Schools

Limiting the school program to improvement of lower-class schools while the process of economic segregation goes on in our cities is a tacit admission that "separate-but-equal" education is enough for lower-class youth. There are two groups of people who accept this proposition. One group consists of apathetic educators and social scientists who believe that we are caught in the working of social laws which will have their way, no matter what we do. They see economic segregation as inevitable. If they do anything at all, they try to improve the lower-class school in some of the ways indicated above.

Another group consists of educators and social scientists with a keen social conscience and a desire for action, who have fundamental doubts about the success of a middle-class society in meeting the challenge of urbanization and industrialization. They seek to organize a working-class community to defend its way of life and to increase its standard of living. Even though they do not like the idea of economic or racial segregation, they accept this as a part of reality and attempt to build a strong militant lower-class community which knows how to cultivate its own interests in the modern city. In their view, the lower-class school needs improvement, but they would not trade it for a mixed-class school.

The present writer subscribes to still another group, believing that we should increase the number of mixed-class schools and reduce the amount of economic and racial segregation in the schools and in the community, that the schools should be used as instruments for *social urban renewal.*

The members of this group are working to achieve all-class or mixed-class communities as the building blocks of the metropolis to come. They, in common with most city-planning specialists, believe that, by means of the vast expenditures to which our big cities have committed themselves for urban renewal, the new megalopolis may consist of a set of subcommunities of 50,000 to 200,000 population which are relatively complete in themselves for the ordinary needs of family and cultural life. They believe that many of these communities should be cross-sections of the social structure of the larger society, with people of the upper, middle, and working classes living in the same area. In particular, they want to rebuild the present slum areas to suit a population of middle-class as well as working-class people.

This group does not believe that the city of the future will do away with all selection of one's neighbors and the playmates for one's children. There will always be subsegregation of people who want to live near one another. Thus there will be segregation not only in homes and apartment houses, but also in blocks and small groups of blocks. But economic or racial segregation by larger units of 20,000 or 50,000 or more is neither inevitable nor desirable. Smart city planners, wise community leaders, and creative educational administrators can find the way to the all-class community and the mixed-class school.

The community in which the present writer lives is an example of a partial attempt to create an all-class community. This attempt may or may not succeed. It would succeed if the citizens of the community deliberately decided to work for this goal. In this community there has been urban renewal of the physical sort—tearing down slum buildings and putting up the kind of houses middle-class people like and can afford. For instance, the process of urban renewal erased from sight a 60-year-old, five-story, walk-up apartment house that had been cut up into so many small slum units that the place became known as Bedbug Manor. On some of the ground where Bedbug Manor stood, there is now a large modern air-conditioned apartment building, with busy traffic-ways on all sides of it, which is more-or-less affectionately becoming known as Monoxide Manor, in recognition of the many cubic feet of automobile engine exhaust gases released on all sides of the building at all times.

We certainly are not sad because Monoxide Manor has replaced Bedbug Manor, but we should be sad if the schools of this community lost all the children of Bedbug Manor and had only Monoxide Manor children in their place.

Through low-cost public housing as well as through the natural obsolescence of housing in that community, it is socially desirable that there be about as many homes for working-class families as there are homes for middle-class families.

Probably we cannot expect every elementary school in the local community to be a mixed-class school. Some areas of the local community will have older houses with lower rents, and will be inhabited mainly by working-class people. Other areas will be mainly middle class. But the high school serving this local community can be a mixed class school, the local public library can serve all kinds of families, the churches can draw all kinds of families, and the community can deliberately work to maintain itself as an all-class community.

The arguments for the all-class community and the mixed-class school may be summarized as follows:

It is desirable that working-class and middle-class children should attend the same schools so as to:

1. Give each group more understanding and liking for the other.

2. Give working-class children the stimulation of competition and co-operation with middle-class children.

It is desirable for Negro and ethnic and old-American white children to attend the same schools so as to:

1. Help all groups develop feelings of equality and mutual trust.

2. Avoid deep-seated suspicion and hostility by the minority groups, which suffer from discrimination in the past and often in the present.

None of these results is likely to come from schools in which whites are in a vastly preponderant majority or a very small minority. A *viable* proportion of the various groups must be established and maintained.

The Crucial Situation of the Public Schools in the Maintenance of Mixed-Class Communities

At present every big city is becoming more segregated economically and racially, through the moving of middle-class people to suburbs or to middle-class areas in the city, while lower-class in-migrants take over the houses deserted by their former middle-class residents. If mixed-class local communities are to be retained in these cities, the middle-class people must quit moving out. And middle-class people are very sensitive to the status ratio of the school to which their children go. As the status ratio goes down toward the critical point, they get ready to move out. Only a school policy aimed at maintaining a status ratio well above the critical point can reassure them sufficiently to induce them to stay. The following parable illustrates what too often happens in this kind of situation.

In a community called Ferndale there was a neghborhood of about 500 families who lived in pleasant one-family homes in an area that had been built up since the Second World War. These people were mostly middle-class people, with a few skilled workers. There was a small number of Negroes in this area—also middle-class people—and they were well accepted. Their children attended the local elementary school, the parents belonged to and were active in the Parent-Teacher Association, and the climate was favorable for a slow increase in the proportions of Negro middle-class families, but no sharp change was desired, because the white residents were satisfied with the situation and did not expect to move out.

The children from Ferndale attended the Franklin High School, which served eight elementary schools, and had been a mixed-class school for the past 20 years. However, recently an older part of the Franklin district changed rapidly from all-white to all-Negro, and so many of the houses were broken up into smaller units that the school enrollments increased rapidly and the status ratio dropped considerably in several of the elementary schools. This process was repeated until the only elementary school that was not entirely Negro was the Ferndale School. Thus the Franklin High School became predominantly Negro and more and more working-class in composition. When Franklin High became 85 per cent Negro, and as the status ratio moved down, middle-class residents of Ferndale became dissatisfied with the high school and began to talk of moving out.

However, some of the leaders of Ferndale studied the situation and concluded that if their children could have access to a mixed-class high school that was also mixed racially, they would prefer to stay in Ferndale. Then they studied various possible educational plans, and finally worked out a plan for putting Franklin and three other high schools into one large high-school district, with at least one of the four high schools operated as a college-preparatory high school and open to children throughout the enlarged district, if their elementary school work was average or better. These people expected that under these conditions the great majority of their children would go to the college-preparatory high school, which would be a mixed-class and integrated school.

The Ferndale group presented their proposal to the Board of Education, but it was ignored. Privately, members of the Board and administrators in the school system said that there were two objections to the Ferndale proposal. One was that it would be very difficult to administer an enlarged high-school district with four high schools serving different kind of pupils in different ways. They could see many problems in such an arrangement, and they preferred the time-tested tradition of one high school to a definite geographical district. The other objection was that the proposal of the Ferndale people would involve the Board of Education in the process of urban renewal, which was none of their business. They said that their business was to give the best possible education to the children that came into the schools, regardless of their race, creed, or color.

Then the residents of Ferndale said one to another, "There is nothing more to do. We shall have to move away so as to get our children into the kind of high school we want for them." The white residents sold their homes and moved out. Their places were taken by Negro middle-class people who were sad to see their white neighbors disappear, but were glad to live in such a nice area, and to inherit the Ferndale elementary school which continued to be a middle-class school. But the Negro middle-class parents were also unhappy about Franklin High School, which was a lower-class school. Some sent their children to a private non-denominational school. Others sent their children to a Catholic parochial high school that was mixed-class in composition. And a good many sought an opportunity to move out to a suburb or to a neighboring area which was mainly white and had a middle-class high school.

Ferndale gradually decreased in attractiveness as a residential area, as the houses grew older and the middle-class people left to go "next door" into the middle-class area of Southdale, where the high school was more to their liking. But Southdale high school began to change as two of its tributary elementary schools became slum schools, on another edge of the district, and the status ratio began to fall. Some of the Southdale community leaders asked a social scientist who was a specialist in community analysis to help them to understand their community, and to help them create a stable mixed-class, integrated community. The social scientist gave them a report on the trends that were under way, and predicted that within five years Southdale would be an all-Negro community, and one most attractive to Negro middle-class people. When some of the leaders asked him for advice on an active program to prevent this from coming to pass, he advised them to learn to live with the inevitable.

Meanwhile the school administrators and the Board of Education presided over the schools in a city which passed the 50 per cent mark in its proportion of Negroes, and became two-thirds working class in composition. They worked unceasingly and unselfishly to make the schools as good as possible for all the children, regardless of economic status, creed, or color, but the schools became increasingly lower-class and Negro.

Schools and Urban Renewal

If the process described above is to be prevented from occurring again and again in our big cities, certain educational policies will have to be worked out and adopted for a transitional period of perhaps 20 years. The goal of these policies should be to stop the flow of middle-class people from the central city, and to encourage the formation of mixed-class and integrated communities of 50,000 to 200,000 in population.

The procedure for defining and establishing such policies might well be a citizens' committee or round-table in each local community area, which would study the community and work with the school administrators in devising appropriate educational policies. Such a citizens' organization would be essential for establishing mutual trust and understanding between the different racial and economic groups making up the community. Groups like this might work together to support the following types of educational programs.

1. A set of regional high schools generously selective on the basis of intelligence and school achievement so as to be open to the top third of the high-school-age group. Admission to these high schools should be controlled so that no school would have less than 60 per cent white students and every school would have a status ratio higher than 0.6. By the end of the transitional period these schools would probably become comprehensive high schools serving local communities and open to all high school students.

2. A set of work-study centers at the junior-high-school level for boys and girls who have demonstrated that they cannot profit from the regular academic high school program. These centers should be located in junior and senior high schools but run on a separate schedule. They should enroll 10 to 20 per cent of the school population between the ages of 13 or 14 and 16, but enrollment should drop as the elementary schools improve their kindergarten-primary programs.

3. A set of general high schools with strong commercial and vocational training programs for young people who are not attending other types of schools. By the end of the transitional period they would probably merge with the selective schools into comprehensive high schools serving local communities.

4. Special attention at the kindergarten-primary level to children from culturally and emotionally inadequate homes so as to give these children as good a start in school as possible, thus reducing the number who would later go to the work-study centers.

5. A set of pre-school centers in areas where many children live under conditions of emotional and intellectual deprivation. These centers would supplement the homes in an effort to give children a better start in school.

6. A set of regional junior colleges so located that there would eventually be one in each local residential community.

7. An adult-education program on an area-wide basis, a program that uses junior colleges and branches of the public library, a program that exploits the educative potential of the metropolitan area and seeks to make adult education available to all kinds of people.

A program such as this is an essential part of any rational plan for urban renewal. The educational system is inextricably bound up with the fate of urban renewal. And urban renewal is necessary to make our democracy work.

REFERENCES

1. Conant, James B., *Education and Liberty,* Cambridge, Mass.: Harvard University Press, 1953, pp. 81 and 85.
2. Havighurst, Robert J., "Metropolitan Development and Its Implications for Education," in *A Seminar on Dimensions of American Society,* Washington, D.C.: American Association of Colleges for Teacher Education, (in press).
3. _____, "The Urban Lower Class School," paper presented at the Human Development Symposium, University of Chicago, April 1962.
4. _____, "Metropolitan Development and Educational Problems," in Robert J. Havighurst and Bernice L. Neugarten (Eds.), *Society and Education,* 2nd ed., Boston: Allyn and Bacon, 1962, Chapter 13.
5. _____, "Metropolitan Development and the Educational System," *Sch. Rev.* 1961, 69:251-269.
6. Michael, John A., "High School Climates and Plans for Entering College," *Pub. Opin. Quart.,* 1961, 25:585-595.
7. Sexton, Patricia, *Education and Income,* New York: Viking Press, 1961.
8. Wilson, Alan B., "Class Segregation and Aspirations of Youth," *Amer. sociol. Review,* 1959, 24:836-845.

Sloan R. Wayland | Old Problems, New Faces, and New Standards

For some reason, the city has had few strong and articulate supporters among the intellectuals. The good life and city life are seldom seen as having a close relationship. Even such urban apologists as Lewis Mumford and Jane Jacobs are nostalgic for an earlier form of city life and are deeply concerned about the present city. The only supporters of the city are the tens of millions of people in every country of the world who have chosen, and continue to choose to live in the city. Perhaps a death wish is attracting them to their ultimate doom, or perhaps the intellectual has not fully understood the city.

The early history of sociology was characterized by repeated attention to a polarity in social organization which tended to convey a negative evaluation of the city. Although each sociologist developed his own concepts, and emphasized somewhat different aspects of the problem, the differences between them were largely in detail, not in kind. Toennies used the concepts *gemeinschaft* and *gesellschaft;* Durkheim, "Mechanical" and "organic solidarity"; Spencer, "military" and "industrial"; Becker, "sacred" and "secular"; MacIver, "community" and "society"; Sorokin, "traditional" and "atomistic"; and Cooley, "primary" and "secondary groups." In these polarities, one type of social organization was characterized by relative smallness in size, by a high rate of interaction between members, by association of members around a number of different points of interest, by affective contacts, and by relative independence of other social systems. The second type of social organization was characterized by a high division of labor, impersonality and contractuality in social contacts, single purpose association, rationalism and bureaucratization, low dependence on tradition, and lack of autonomy of units within a larger system.

These concepts were presented as analytic tools, to be used in historical, cross-cultural, and intra-societal studies; and the movement from the first type of social organization to the second was seen as the direction of history and the wave of the future. Although the tone communicated in the references to the second pattern of social organization was not as explicit as may be found in the writings of the agrarian fundamentalists, it is clear that a valued type of society was giving way to a much less desirable system.

Other writers of this period were quite explicit as to the ultimate outcome of this historic trend. Scott Greer summarizes the positions of Ortega and Spengler as follows: "Ortega saw the hierarchial orders crumbling beneath the waves of economic and political democracy, and prophesied the state of the masses; western culture would perish under the onslaught of the vulgar. Spengler spoke of the death of culture in the cities of the Autumn, social products of a loss of nerve that would lead, in the end, to Caesarism and the deification of massive power." (1).

None of these scholars chose to use the concepts of rural and urban to convey what they wanted to say, but their detailed analyses are full of explicit references to rural-urban differences. In a sense the new city was the clearest expression of the society which was coming into being. Among more contemporary writers, the suburb has been the concept more frequently used as a synonym for the mass society.

It is in this context that the demographic reports, showing slow rates of growth or even decline in total population for some of the larger legal cities, have been received with a certain sense of satisfaction by those who have not been able to emotionally or intellectually accept the city. Usually ignored is the fact that the reported stabilization or decline is an artifact of the choice of the unit which has been selected for the reporting of data. In fact, many of the purported problems of the city are functions of the concepts which are available for us in considering the city.

One of the assumptions of the present paper is that we are in great need of a new conceptual framework for use in considering the social unit which we loosely call the city. Existing concepts which have largely grown up in context discussed above have been demonstrated to be inadequate for purposes of research, as well as for discussion of interested citizens and those involved in public action. Such terms as neighborhood, community, city, urban, rural, suburban, exurban, rurban, satellite cities, urban regions, metropolitan areas, and megalopolis do not provide a common framework for discourse. For example, a political decision reached in one area, to extend the boundaries of a legal city to incorporate adjacent areas, results in reported growth of a city; whereas a city such as New York, where no such decision has been reached, is reported as declining in population.

The problems we are now facing in urban areas are essentially current expressions of the same problems we have been facing for a century or more. However, the new standards which we have developed have made us discontent with our existing programs, and we are seeking new courses of action which are adapted to the special characteristics of the new population groups which make up our cities. The problems about which we are concerned are no less real nor urgent if they are current expressions of old problems. The new standards are no less appropriate because they are new, and the needs of the new migrant groups are as worthy of public attention as their predecessors. The major intent of the present writer is to shift the focus of attention from what are sometimes thought to be new problems to the new element in the situation—the new standards. This proposition is believed to obtain for many dimensions of city life. Our attention is of course focused on education, but other areas will be considered as they are relevant.

As a framework within which to consider education in the city, the three major approaches to the study of the city which have characterized American sociological thought will be used. These three have appeared at somewhat different periods in time and are still employed by different scholars in varying degrees. These three are ecology, social structure, and social process. The social survey approach is not included, although it played an important role historically, since its theoretical character was very limited and since it is not believed to be of importance in the analysis of education in the city. In a sense, studies such as Conant's *Slums and Suburbs* are in this tradition and are believed to have limited utility in advancing our understanding of the problem.

Ecology

This is not the place for an analytical and evaluative examination of the ecological approach. However, certain key elements need to be identified in order that the implications for education may be more readily understood. In essence, the ecologist is interested in the identification of personal attributes and patterns of social interaction as they are located in space. The sociologists are generally interested in the identification of regularities in human behavior, and to this concern is added the material setting. Hypothetically, this may apply to all levels, from primary groups to international relations. In practice, this approach has been used most extensively in the study of cities and their environs, and the majority of such studies have used American cities as their units of study.

From the studies which have been made using this approach, a series of conclusions have been reached which are largely descriptive in character:

1. Segments of cities may be identified which are relatively homogeneous in character.

2. These segments have a patterned relationship to each other, including concentric zones, sectors, and multiple-nuclei.

3. These segments have a functional relationship to each other within the larger context of the city as a social system.

4. These segments are not fixed but are in a constant process of change. The processes involved have been described through the use of such concepts as invasion, succession, assimilation.

5. The attributes which are socially relevant in the determination of the homogeneous character of a segment are a function of the values of a particular population. The color of one's hair is not a factor, since this is not a value which expresses itself in human behavior. Over time, religious identification may decline as a discriminating variable and be replaced by social class.

6. The location of individuals in a city has not been historically a consequence of explicit public control but is largely a self-selective process based on manifest and latent structures.

7. Legal boundaries of cities are of limited sgnificance in the separation of one segment from another, except where such boundaries introduce significant structural differences. Quinn's hypothesis of median (location) is an expression of the operating principle. This generalization attempts to account for location of urban activities at those points which involve the least cost and effort to the persons involved.

This approach to the study of the city is more than four decades old, and although its limitations as a complete framework for studying the city are generally recognized, its utility is accepted by urban sociologists. With this brief statement in mind, attention may now be given to current discussions of the city and education.

One of the themes of the alarmist is that the city is dying and that it is in urgent need of rather drastic attention if it is to survive. In this connection, one of the facts referred to is the decline of population in the central segment of the city and the identification of other segments as gray areas. The facts of the case are just the opposite. It is the vitality of the city which has given rise to the population change. The problem is in the definition of the city. If one ignores the city boundaries, as most people do when they move, we see that all of the larger cities of the country have continued to grow, and to grow rapidly during the past decades. The logic of the case of those who are concerned about the decline of population in the central segment of the city is apparently that specialized, non-residential functions, such as offices, stores, industries, and service units—all of which require space, ought to continue to expand as they have and, at the same time, that the residential population ought to continue to grow. In other words, the central segment ought to experience endless increases in density. This can only mean one thing: in the smaller and smaller residential areas which are left as more property is used for non-residential purposes, the density of population ought to increase. This is, of course, technically possible; apartment buildings the size of the Empire State Building could be erected, but this is not the only alternative. In fact, the historic tradition as shown by the ecologists is that the alternative of movement from the central core out to one or the other segments will be taken by former residents of the core. But have such movers left the city? Obviously not. They may have left the legal city, but not the sociological city. If one considers the full range of human activity from family life, to religious, recreational, and economic activities, it is clear that political identifications and activities constitute only a small segment of the total concern of most people. One may still behave as if he lived in New York City, even though the neighborhood where he lives is some distance removed from Times Square, whether in Bronx Park or across the city line in New Rochelle.

If the legal boundaries of cities can be ignored by the analyst as they are by the people he is studying, it becomes clear that the processes of movement which the ecologist first studied inside the legal boundaries of cities are continuing to open in much the same fashion. The flexibility which the automobile provides has made possible less dense settlement than was true earlier, and has also facilitated movements laterally within rings, rather than only toward the central city. Again, this is simply an extension of a process which has been present before.

Assimilation of Migrants

It is unnecessary to discuss in detail the extensive experience of American cities in absorbing new immigrants into the life of the city, and, in time, moving them from the original points of settlement outward from the central core. Obviously, our cities have been made up of foreign and rural immigrants since such immigration began. With the restrictions on foreign immigration for the past forty years, and with the decline in the opportunities in rural areas for gainful employment, the cities have increasingly relied on the rural migrant as the major source of unskilled workmen. Millions of such rural migrants have been absorbed into the urban population in the past, and will continue to be absorbed in the period ahead. Those of us who are one generation removed from such a status do not always look with hope on the prospects of the new rural migrant, but there is no change in our social structure which stands in the way of such absorption.

For the first time in our history we are facing the very real possibility of a drying up of the sources of the new lower class for our cities, since we are not likely to open our doors again to foreign immigrants. The number who can come in under the existing quota system becomes decreasingly significant as the total population of this country expands. Political refugees, such as the Hungarians and the Cubans, and in recent days, the Chinese, are special cases of short-term influences, but their impact on the total population is minor. At the same time, the traditional internal source—the rural migrant—is becoming a smaller and smaller pool while our existing urban population is assuming greater magnitude. A surplus rural population will continue to exist for a period ahead. Areas of subsistence agriculture still exist, and cities will continue to receive both the parents and the offspring of such families. Increased efficiency in agriculture will be achieved at the price of squeezing the marginal farmer off the land, and the remaining farm families will have some children who cannot find a place in agriculture. However, the migrations of the past two decades have taken a significant proportion of this population.

The educational level of the rural population has been rising rapidly in the past two decades. The adjustments involved for such migrants will become less difficult in the future than they have been in the past. This is true for the Negro and the Puerto Rican migrants, as well as the hillbilly.

Negro migrants. Special attention needs to be given to the Negro migrant to the larger cities, whether coming from rural areas or southern cities. It is evident that his absorption into the urban pattern will not be as easy as that of some other groups with less visibility. We do face the possibility that the new lower-class segment of our cities in the generation ahead will be largely Negro for a generation, and one of our democratic tasks will be to live through this period in such a manner as to avoid the stabilization of the class structure with a predominately Negro lower class.

In the framework which has been used thus far, the question is whether the new migrants, particularly the Negro, will experience the same pattern of residential and social mobility which has characterized the earlier streams of migrants to the cities. Unfortunately, we have not had enough carefully done studies of the middle- and upper-class Negro. Even so, past experience may not be a fully adequate guide to the future, since legal structures have been established which did not exist earlier. In addition, the political strength of the Negro, associated with his ecological position, constitutes new elements in the situation.

A comparison of the present and future Negro urban population with other immigrant groups cannot be made as exact parallels. The case of the Irish may, however, be instructive. The Irish peasants who were forced off the land were an unlikely lot, who came to the cities of the United States in large numbers over a relatively short period. Their assimilation proceeded at a slow pace; they had no useful skills at the outset and were not interested in education. For a generation or more, they were considered to be a very low form of human life, without much prospect of change. Their areas in New York City were characterized by lawlessness, juvenile gangs, great poverty, and very poor health. The public image which they created was far worse than the current references to the slums of our present cities. For many other immigrant groups, one generation was enough for changes to begin to occur. However, the change was much slower for the Irish. By the time of the large immigrations of the eastern and southern Europeans, at the end of the nineteenth and the beginning of the twentieth century, the Irish had begun to move up, but their identity persisted during the period in which the Italians, Poles, and Russians were becoming established. After a relatively slow start, they have achieved a state of great respect, as may be seen on St. Patrick's Day when the green is worn by persons of almost all backgrounds.

Our melting-pot image of the assimilation of the new immigrant has not been characteristic of the experience of several groups. Their differences have been matters of pride, and they have not chosen to be assimilated, even when the way was open for them. Many Jews, Chinese, Japanese, and other ethnic and religious groups have retained their identity over a long period of time in the American society. Within such groups there may be well-established class differences. There is no necessary reason to believe that the Negro must lose his identity as a Negro in order to be assimilated.

The increase in the non-white population in the central core of the larger cities has, of course, been dramatic during the post-war period. However, the rates of increase in the areas outside of the cores have been substantial also. During the decade from 1950 to 1960, the percentage increase in non-white population in the inner and outer rings of New York City has been substantially greater than for the white population, and this has been the experience of every county in both rings. It is not assumed that these increases are made up entirely of middle- and upper-class Negro families who have moved to the suburbs. However, part of this increase is precisely this, and a careful analysis of the detailed characteristics of such areas, which will soon be available from the U.S. Census, ought to provide a clearer picture of this migration.

Educational Issues and Ecological Analysis

A number of educational issues of varying degrees of significance are illuminated by the ecological approach to the study of urban life. Some of these are listed below with brief comments.

1. A central administration is faced with the fact that differing levels of interest in education are not randomly distributed throughout the city but will vary from zone to zone. Because of this, the administration is likely to be subjected to substantially different levels of pressure from the zones in terms of their levels of interest in education. Those areas from which the least organized parental pressure comes are the areas in which the educational level of parents is low, and the commitment to education on the part of the pupils is least.

2. A counterforce to this grows out of the fact that all the zones are part of an integrated system under one administration, and standards which are set for the system will, in a measure, apply to all. In this way the lower-class zones, or those areas in which subcultural groups live who have a lower commitment to education, will likely receive a higher level of educational service than would be the case if such groups were an independent group in a small town with responsibility for its own administration. To the extent that this obtains, its ecological position may be seen as a determining factor.

3. Since teachers also make choices as to their residence in terms of values shared by the community, it is to be expected that teachers will not live in either the high-income or the low-income areas of the city nor in areas which are populated by subcultural groups different from their own. This, in turn, limits the extent to which they may become significant persons in areas of experience other than the school activities.

4. An area served by a particular school is likely, over a period of time, to experience ecological succession, and the changing character of the population makes difficult the development of local leadership for support of educational as well as other local activities. Similarly, a rapid turnover of students creates a very real problem in the planning of a school curriculum designed to serve a particular group of students. This becomes especially difficult when the new students coming in are of a different racial or language group.

5. A related problem is the determination of a basis for establishing the boundary lines which a particular school is to serve. Since the process of invasion and succession is a continuing one, any basis on which the boundary lines are drawn will result in changes in the composition of the

student body. Even if one wanted to maintain a mixed student body as a matter of policy, this would in many instances involve shifts in the boundaries, since mixture in housing would only by chance happen to match the mixture desired in the school.

6. Since city boundaries are usually not adjusted to correspond to the continuing out-movement of families, the large city district finds itself surrounded by a number of small districts. The school systems which are adjacent to each other, but across city boundary lines, may be serving very similar students.

7. Particularly acute problems come when the ecological pattern of a city is characterized by sectors, or multiple nuclei, which throw families of widely different class levels into the same school district. This is likely to occur near the central part of the city where luxury apartments are near tenements. Although the families in luxury apartments are likely to have fewer children of school age, they will, nevertheless, have some children to be educated. Many such families may choose to send their children to private schools.

8. Implicit in several of the previous issues is the question as to whether any particular school is to be viewed as an integral part of a particular neighborhood, and to serve as a community center. Conflicting tendencies are to be found in the philosophies and practices of large city schools. In some instances, a number of actions are taken which are designed to facilitate identification of a school with the area it serves. In order to give expression to this point of view, an effort is made to locate the school with boundaries that roughly correspond to a neighborhood. Then the neighborhood changes, or under pressure for mixed student bodies or for open enrollment, the concept of the community school begins to break down.

9. The issue of open enrollment may be seen in the ecological framework as a form of invasion in one institutional area—education—which is not reinforced by other dimensions of social behavior. As was noted in the first of this series of comments, areas of a city differ in the degree to which parents and students are committed to education, and the quality of the educational experience differs accordingly. The policy of open enrollment has been expressed primarily in terms of access of Negro students to schools which are judged to be better schools than those which they have been attending. The same principle might well apply to white families in lower-class areas, who might want their children to go to schools which are in middle- or upper-class areas. It is likely that the Negro parents who choose to send their children into another school district are upward mobile parents whose opportunities for living in areas commensurate with their class position has not been limited.

Social Structure

Attention will now be turned to the second approach which sociologists have used in studying the city. Since these approaches are not entirely mutually exclusive, some of the observations made earlier will apply here as well. During the period from about 1925 to 1950, a series of studies were made of American communities, in which the focus of attention was on broadly structural characteristics. In general, this involved the identification and description of the social class and sub-cultural dimensions of the unit under examination. The first major study of this type was the Robert Lynd study of Middletown, in which he identified two major units: the business class and the working class. These groups were described in terms of the behavior in the community context within major institutional areas—family, religion, economics, politics, recreation, etc. Over a period of time, additional studies appeared by Warner, Davis, Hollingshead, Dollard, Cayton and Drake, and others.

It should be pointed out that this approach was never used in studies made of large cities. Cayton and Drake studied the Negro in Chicago, New Haven, and Newburyport, Massachusetts. However, the conclusions reached in these studies have been widely, and, it is to be feared, loosely used in describing large cities.

As in the case of the ecological analysis, no effort will be made here to describe in detail the conclusions reached through the use of this approach. In general, the scholars who used this approach found:

1. Within American cities, a number of distinguishable strata (usually five or six) were found, whose basic styles of life were judged to be different.

2. Class membership expresses itself in social interaction patterns in the various institutions of the community.

3. Associated with class membership is a set of attitudes and values.

4. Mobility usually involves movement from one class level to an adjacent class level over one generation, but on occasions, movement may take place over two or three class levels.

5. Although wealth and income are usually good indicators of class position, the more important indicator is the way in which one makes his living. Since education is associated with occupations, educational level is another good indicator of class position. In addition, educational level may be associated with values, aspirations, and general style of life. In situations where reputational data are not available, such factors as occupation, income, education, and type and location of residence may be used to estimate the class position.

6. The class strata function in a complementary fashion to each other in a community social system. This necessitates the existence of at least a minimum set of common values shared by all.

A number of good critiques on the research of social class have been made in recent years. These critiques have dealt with methodological difficulties, as well as theory and interpretation. As noted earlier, one major unanswered question is the extent to which the class approach has meaning in the large city. That social differentiation exists in the city is quite clear, but the appropriateness of social class as the important variable is another matter. Another major difficulty is the tendency toward reification of the concepts. As the term "middle class" is used, for example, it is not always clear whether the user is thinking of it as a concept, an analytical tool, or as a thing. Whether used as a conceptual tool or as a term with an existing referent, the grossness of the categories is frequently forgotten so that lower class or middle class is assumed to refer to a very homogeneous set of attributes. There is certainly nothing in the research literature to suggest this. However, in the process of reporting the central tendencies of the characteristics of various classes, the researchers have conveyed to the uncritical reader an impression of very discrete categories, rather than a continuous distribution.

Educational Implications of the Social-Structural Approach to the City

One of the cliches in educational circles is that teachers are middle class, and that this personal attribute constitutes a difficulty in the achievement of educational goals, particularly for lower-class children. This point is usually made with reference to the urban teacher who is working with lower-class children. Several aspects of this proposition warrant more serious attention than is customarily given, since it is my belief that a number of the underlying assumptions of such statements are subject to question.

The first aspect of this question is the class position of the teacher. As noted above, the categories of class position are, at best, crude and extremely gross. The teacher's educational level tends to be relatively high, prestige in occupational ratings relatively high, but income only average. The social origins of teachers cover a wide range, particularly among women. One may choose to say that the general style of life and the value systems of teachers are like those in the society with a similar education, income, and occupation. However, at best this is a gross statement, and the variation among teachers on personality factors may turn out to be of much greater significance than structural position.

Of greater significance in structural terms is the nature of the social system of which teachers are a part. If each teacher were to recruit his own students, devise his own set of activities for a particular group of students, set his own educational goals and evaluate them in his own terms, the special values of the teacher might be of great importance. This, of course, is not the case. The teacher is a member of a bureaucratic system in which the basic content which he teaches, the norms of behavior of students and teachers, the goals of teaching, and the evaluation of students, are established for all to follow. And these are, by and large, not established locally, although each school system varies in detail. Individual teachers do from time to time reject these norms, but the system functions as it does because these are the exceptions. In other words, school systems are organized to achieve goals which are thought to be relevant to all those served, and the system is designed to protect the individual student against the caprice of the individual teacher.

But, it is argued, the whole school system is middle class in its orientation, and so the very system referred to above simply reinforces the middle-class bias. Under examination, this point of view may be more accurately seen as arguing that the organization, content, and goals of school systems are not, among other attributes, lower class in character. To this point of view, there can be no disagreement. That middle- and upper-class people in our society place more value on the content of the school curriculum than many lower-class people do is quite a different matter from saying that the school curriculum is middle class. (Note that most statements of this sort do not say both middle and upper class.)

The consequence of the operation of an educational system has been historically to move many members of the lower-class population to higher strata. The development of the large strata that is called middle class is closely related to the successful functioning of an educational system in a free society. However, the negative connotations which are assumed when the statement is made, "the schools are middle class oriented," and the assumption that this is an adequate, complete, and exhaustive statement in describing school systems are points of view which seem to me to be unsupported in fact and a substitution of slogans for critical examination.

An illustration of the difficulty in the misuse of sociologically derived social class data may be found in the arguments centering around the use of the IQ. In the recent book by Patricia Sexton (5), the author argues that school systems ought to abandon completely the use of the IQ measure, since the test is not free of cultural influence in its content. Again, the term "middle class" is used to refer to the bias which such a test in an insidious way is supposed to contain. The IQ measures have been used in in ways which are quite at variance with their qualities. But the fact that they *do* measure abilities in those areas around which school systems are organized seems to be well established. It is worthy of note that Dr. Sexton does not seriously question these purposes of the school system, but, in fact, wants to insure that lower-class students are not denied the opportunity to take part in them as fully as all other students.

The sociologist in his emphasis on the social structure of communities has served both a clarifying and a confusing role. By emphasizing the social class character of American communities, he has brought to the attention of educators a dimension which is of great importance. He has helped teachers to see that individual differences among their students are not simply idiosyncratic personality variables, but are also functions of structural aspects of a social system. The shock which this literature has created in student teachers, and their strong feelings that social class differences ought not to be tolerated, is testimony to the educational value need which this approach has provided. Unfortunately, the underlying theoretical approach for which social class is one expression has not been as fully understood. The significance of social structure for the behavior of students and educators is only dimly seen by many. In the process, social class has been used most extensively in the consideration of population groups in the large cities, in spite of the fact that the research to date has not been done in these cities. Whether, in fact, social class is as important a variable in the large city as in the smaller cities and towns is yet to be determined. Certainly, ethnic, religious, and subcultural groups in the large cities are of great structural significance, and the relationship between this order of variable and social class awaits intensive exploration.

A good illustration of the significance of factors in educational achievement, other than social class, may be seen in the recent report of the colleges which have been most productive of graduates who subsequently completed Ph.D.'s (7). The colleges with the highest rates were City College, Brooklyn College, and Queens College, of New York City, and Brigham Young University and the University of Utah in Utah. In each of these instances, a high proportion of the students enrolled in these colleges were members of religious groups who place a very high value on education. In fact, in both instances, the occupational backgrounds and other traditional measures of the class positions of the parents of these students were of an order which is generally associated with much lower educational aspirations. This same point was clearly shown in the analyses of differential patterns of educational attainment in the various states of the Union in 1950.

In the earlier section dealing with ecology, the structural position of the Negro was referred to. As was noted there, the problems of residential mobility and of social mobility need to be seen as different problems. Restricted housing policies tend to blur the differences. In addition, there is a question as to whether the middle- and upper-class Negro has the same sense of identification with lower-class Negroes which characterized earlier immigrant groups in the process of their assimilation into the class structure of our cities. Having placed a value on desegregation, those who arrive at a position where it is easier for them to live in a desegregated fashion seem to find it difficult to furnish leadership for those who are still living in a situation of segregation. On Long Island, during the period of election to local school boards in the spring of 1962, Negro candidates were present on the tickets in five different suburban communities. Negroes are on several school boards in suburban schools in New Jersey and New York. Whether there is as great a concern about the educational advancement of Negro youth in the city by middle- and upper-class Negroes is not clear.

Social Structure and Educational Issues

In the preceding discussion, some general problems of the relationship of social structure analysis of the city have been identified. In the section below some of the more concrete issues are listed.

1. The distinctive strategies which are necessary in order to take into account the varied cultural backgrounds of students in a large city pose special problems for a large bureaucratic system. One manifestation of this difficulty is apparent in the recent negotiations between the Board of Education in New York City and the representatives of the teachers. The Board wanted to provide a special system of recognition for those teachers who were working with special groups of students, but the teachers' representatives insisted upon the maintenance of a uniform salary schedule.

2. The existence of a widely differential social structure, such as is usually found in large cities, creates an almost irreconcilable strain between alternative approaches to the curriculum. For example, Mr. Conant wants an extensive vocational program for those students from the slums, even at the risk that this may extend the already existing differences, and a Higher Horizons type program seems to work on the premise that any existing differences as products of the cultural backgrounds of students ought to be evened out through deliberate actions by the school system. This strain between these two approaches is also evident in the study of Big City by Dr. Sexton, who advocates both approaches at different places in her book, without fully appreciating the different premises on which they are based.

This strain may be seen in an analogous setting outside of the city. Rural schools have been faced with the dilemma of providing an education which will serve the purposes of those who choose to stay in agriculture and those who migrate to the city. If the choices were made by rural youth early and were fixed for life, the development of the curriculum might be easier. However, the choice may not be made until after the completion of high school. In a sense, the urban school has to prepare for social mobility, but for those who are not interested, or do not have the competence, the school must also provide a relevant program. However, this choice is not one which the school can make for the student, and the timing of the choice may, or may not occur during the period when the student is under the care of the school.

3. By virtue of the sheer largeness of the population in a big city, there are enough deviant groups to make possible and even to encourage the establishment of special units to meet the special needs of such groups. To the extent that such deviancies are functions of the social structure, these special units may be seen as class based. In smaller systems, it is more difficult to segregate the deviant.

4. Similarly, the population size facilitates the establishment of alternative educational structures to the public school system if there exists in the city significant numbers of subcultural groups who want to maintain their separateness. For example, large cities make possible highly developed parochial systems, even to the point of special teacher-training institutions, and other supporting services. The public school becomes a residual unit for such groups in that those students who are excluded from the parochial system are in the public school.

5. Since the character of the social structure has been changing over our history from a pyramid with a rather broad base to a diamond shape with heavier concentrations in the middle ranges, our "old problem" of reaching the lower-class segment is seen as if it were a new problem. We no longer take it for granted that a large number of children will receive little education. In an earlier generation we were concerned about increasing the proportion of children who were enrolled in school. Our current problem is a much more refined one—how to keep the student at the upper secondary level from dropping out of school. A full length book, reporting on a special research study of this problem, has just been published. In essence it is the old problem in its modern form, but with our new standards, we are no longer comfortable with the norm of a previous day. John Gardner, in his annual report of the Carnegie Foundation, and more recently Mr. Conant, have been urging schools to extend their responsibility for vocational guidance until students have reached the age of twenty-one.

Higher standards of educational service are thus being proposed, going much beyond earlier practice.

Social Process Approach to the City

The most recent emphasis in community study has been on the dynamics of the community as a social system. This is not to imply that the earlier approaches ignored this dimension. Lynd in his second book, *Middletown in Transition,* continued his earlier structural emphasis but gave much more attention to the processes within Middletown. However, a new set of questions has been raised in recent years. The major focus, and the one to which specific attention will be given here, is that of the decision-making process in the cities. During the past decade there has not been a study which falls clearly in the category of social structures as used above, but there have been a number dealing with decision making. Many of these have dealt with cities of substantial size.

Hunter's studies of Atlanta, Georgia, and Salem, Massachusetts; Kimball's *Talladega Story;* Rossi and Dentler's study of decision making around urban renewal in Chicago, and other studies in Syracuse, New Haven, and El Paso, have explored decision making as a community process. Murray Ross in his book, *Community Organization,* and James Coleman, in *Community Conflicts,* have explored this process on a more theoretical level.

In general, two different patterns have been identified. Whether, in fact, there are two patterns or simply two different results as artifacts of the different methodologies is still a matter of debate. Hunter in his two studies has advanced the proposition that a small group of residents serve as multiple-issue leaders. All issues of any significance for the community must receive their attention before action can be effectively taken. Although they may not initiate the directions of action, their support is necessary for such actions. And so the community power structure is characterized by a small group at the top who serve as the focal point for community decision making in all important areas.

An alternative proposition holds that each major institutional area in a community has its own distinctive group of opinion leaders and decision makers. Some overlap may occur, but the degree of overlap is small and tends to occur in those institutional areas which are closely related. Through an approach which is essentially event analysis, the decision-making process is traced, and the significant persons involved are identified. Since this approach differs from the reputational ones used by Hunter, the difference may be due to the methods.

A by-product of this approach is the interesting light which it sheds on some of the assumptions of the social structure approach. Under that approach, the implicit assumption tended to be that the upper-class was in the most powerful position in the community. This may have been true in the smaller communities which were studied, but data are fairly clear that the social elite may not be the same as the community decision makers. This is particularly true for the situations in which the single-issue segmented leaders seemed to be functioning. In Syracuse, where thirty-nine community problems were considered over a two-year period, some nineteen different leadership groups were identified, and there was very little overlap in their membership.

Rossi, in one such study of decision making with reference to schools, found that those who were in what he called the school public, that is, those who were very actively concerned about school decisions, differed in several ways from other political publics. Women were more likely to be in school publics, and position in one family cycle was also more important.

Since the social process approach is relatively recent in its appearance, the body of data here are not as extensively developed as the other areas, and the implications for education in the large city are not so apparent.

Social Process Approach and Education

A few of the possible implications of this approach for the problems of education in the large city will be considered. These will take the form of problems for which more research is needed.

1. In the Hunter materials, it is clear that the professional worker is not included in the decision-making group. He may initiate action which will go up to the power group, but at best he is in a staff position to the leadership. In the segmented leadership approach, the top professionals and certain laymen who have earned a position of leadership in the particular institutional area have a much more potent position. As the public sector becomes more important in American life, and particularly in the large cities, public bodies such as city councils may become more significant units as the integrators of the public and the private sectors, and, in turn, may facilitate the development of segmented leaders who bargain among themselves, the public, and the officially constituted bodies for access to scarce resources.

2. The educational enterprise may be fruitfully considered as functioning in a staff relationship to the community, in that it provides a common service to all but is outside of the line structure. Schools serve the weakest segment of the community in terms of direct political power—the children —and although administrators do have jobs to fill and contracts to let,

they are in an institution which must maintain an apolitical stance. Perhaps this is related to the difficulty of meaningful location of the teacher in the class structure of a community and in the decision-making process. On occasion, in situations which are characterized either by social disorganization or deviance from general norms, administrators and teachers have operated effectively in a line position, that is, they have been able to give leadership to the community. However, these situations are relatively rare, and once disorganization has given way to organization or deviancy has diminished with closer approximation to norms for communities, the leadership role of the educator tends to assume the more normal position.

To the extent to which this approach is a valid one, the revival of the earlier idea of the school as the focal point for area development may prove to be as unfeasible now as it has been when promoted at earlier times in history. Several questions of fact and of policy are involved.

a. Is the area served by the school one which is, or potentially might become, a viable social unit? Is there a genuine school-community or is the community simply that arbitrary area which is the attendance unit?

b. Is it reasonable to assume that a school staff will have the competences and interests which are required for leadership roles in a community, since their recruitment, training, and work experience has been directed to a very special segment of the community—the youth?

c. Under what circumstances will the community or other agencies with official or assumed responsibilities in the area accept leadership from the school? This is particularly crucial in view of the issues raised in (b) above.

d. Isn't the task of the school, even with a relatively narrow definition of its goals, so complex that any additional tasks may jeopardize the achievement of those goals which it is best qualified to fill? To what extent is the prestige of the school gained from its staff relationship to the system being exploited, to attempt to make up for the inadequacies of institutions which are in the line? It is one thing to argue that education can assist a community to real sound decisions on problems which it is facing, but it is quite another matter to argue that educators ought to make and implement decisions which have many non-educational dimensions.

3. The problem of fiscal dependency or autonomy is one to which greater understanding of the decision-making process in large cities could contribute directly. Who, in fact, makes decisions now regarding amounts

of financial support and utilization, and to what extent is this a pattern which would actually be altered if a change in legal arrangements were made? With the substantial amounts of money now coming into the large cities from state appropriations, a fiscal independent arrangement might sever the political tie which is necessary in order to participate effectively in the decision-making at the state level.

4. In the area of education, as in a number of other areas, the decisions which are in practice within the control of a city are increasingly circumscribed by both manifest and latent structures. The increased reliance on state legislatures for funds is matched by corresponding legal specifications in many areas of educational operations. Financial assistance from the Federal Government is also increasing, particularly in the support of specialized types of programs. The effect of this financial assistance has been in the intended direction; school districts have instituted programs in line with the purposes of the grants. As our educational system takes on more and more of the aspects of a national educational system in its latent structure, the realistic alternatives for local decisions are reduced. National conferences, such as this one on the education in large cities, are one such mechanism by which the experiences in different situations are communicated to interested persons, and common values and understandings are developed.

One latent function of this development seems to be the increased importance of individuals and groups in local communities who have ties with state and national bodies. Multiple-issue leaders are no longer able to maintain the extra-community contacts involved in each of a number of different areas of community concern. As a consequence segmented leadership is strengthened.

Interrelationship of Different Sociological Approaches to the Study of the City

In the sections above, the approaches of ecology, social structure, and social process have been briefly discussed as means of illuminating the problems of urban education. As has been indicated earlier, these are not competitive approaches, but are essentially complementary in character. Any one alone highlights certain dimensions and takes on other given aspects. Furthermore, the contributions of other disciplines, such as political science, economics, and psychology, have not been considered although they are as relevant as the sociological approach.

It should also be emphasized that the approaches which have been used by sociologists historically are not the only ones which may be used. They represent the work of sociologists at this stage in the development of the discipline, and as the discipline continues to mature, other, and hopefully, more meaningful approaches will be developed.

New Standards

In the preceding discussion, attention has been given to two aspects of the title of this paper·—old problems, and new faces—but only passing attention has been given to the third part—new standards. Through the employment of sociological concepts, the large city has been examined, with the conclusion that most of our current problems are, in essence, current expressions of basic characteristics which have a long history. One new element in the picture is the proportionately large Negro population. And whether this is, in fact, fundamentally new or simply a current form of a traditional feature of our large cities, is yet to be proven. Clearly, many of the characteristics which are commonly referred to in discussing the new Negro migrant sound very familiar in historical perspective. Juvenile delinquency, broken homes, cultural deprivation, inadequate community organization, and low educational aspirations have been reported by our journalists, fiction writers, reformers, historians, and social scientists for a century.

One of the persistent themes, among those who take the position that the urban Negro migrant is different, is the structure of the family. Current reports emphasize the important role of the mother and attribute this to the persistence of a cultural pattern having its origin in the period of slavery. The following description reported from one community study seems to fit this image. "The husband-wife relationship is more or less an unstable one, even though the marriage is sanctioned either by law or understandings between the partners. Disagreements leading to quarrels and vicious fights, followed by desertion by either the man or the woman [and/or] possible divorce, is not unusual. The evidence indicates that few compulsive factors, such as neighborhood solidarity, religious teachings, or ethical considerations, operate to maintain a stable relationship. On the contrary, the . . . culture has established a family pattern where serial monogamy is the rule. . . . The burden of child care, as well as support, falls on the mother more often than on the father when the family is broken. The mother-child relation is the strongest and most enduring family tie." (2) However, this set of statements does not refer to the urban Negro migrant but to Class V families in the small town of Elmtown, Illinois, on which Hollingshead reported. Similar data came from other studies which, as in the case of Elmtown, involved few if any Negro families.

In addition, the impact of immigration on family structure needs also to be taken into account. The assumption is frequently made that since the European migrants come from a culture with a strong family system, they did not display the characteristics which are attributed to the Negro with his slave background. A reference to the very extensive study of the Polish peasant (6) as he migrated to the United States, will raise a serious question about this assumption. In volume V of the classic study by Thomas and Znaniecki on the Polish peasant, the table of contents of the second half of the book reads as follows: "Demoralization," "Economic Dependency," "Break of Conjugal Relations," "Murder," "Vagabondage and Delinquency of Boys," and "Sexual Immorality of Girls." In the chapter on "Break of Conjugal Relations," the authors state: "The looseness of mores which prevails among Polish immigrants, and astonishes the American social worker, is thus easily explained. Sexual indulgence, as such, has no meaning of 'wickedness' attached to it. . . ." (6). The forty-three cases which are briefly described could very easily be accepted as current cases of urban Negro migrants, if the Polish names did not appear, and if the dates were 1962, and not 1910.

The burden of the argument which has been presented above is not that all immigrant groups are alike in every detail. However, more careful analysis is needed to sort out those features which are functions of class position and of immigrant status from those features which are uniquely a function of the Negro subculture. It is believed that a great deal which has been attributed to the subculture of the Negro will turn out to be associated with factors which are not uniquely Negro.

The genuinely new dimensions in the total picture are our new standards. The problem is not due to our past deficiencies and inadequacies so much as to our past successes, with resulting aspirations for the future. The assimilation of past immigrant groups and the building of a large middle class with high educational attainment in a relatively short period of time makes us even more sensitive to the presence of groups in our society who are not participating fully in this new society. Earlier norms are now considered deviations.

This shift may be seen in the emergence and wide usage of the concept of cultural deprivation. The tone of some of the writing on this subject suggests that this is something new and is a unique product of the large city. Low verbal ability is described as though it could only happen in an urban slum. This myopic and anti-historical approach to the problem may be politically supportable, but it does not represent good scholarship. The historic task of formal education has been an attack on cultural deprivation. In the sense in which cultural deprivation is used, all but a very small fraction of mankind has been in this category. Cultural deprivation becomes a point of concern and a focal point of attention only because of the current and very recently achieved status of a society in which most young parents have received a high school eduaction and a significant proportion have had some post-high-school educational experience.

It is not necessary to identify the new standards in detail. Whatever they are today, they will be higher tomorrow. They may be summarized in the following way:

Start the child in school earlier; keep him in school more and more months of the year; retain all who start to school for twelve to fourteen years; expect him to learn more and more during this period, in wider and wider areas of human experience, under the guidance of a teacher, who has had more and more training, and who is assisted by more and more specialists, who provide an ever-expanding range of services, with access to more and more detailed personal records, based on more and more carefully validated tests.

Our past successes have made it possible for these new standards to become operating principles, rather than dreams. And an educated society increases the capacity of its members, since a high level of learning occurs outside of the conventional school as well as within it. The tail will never catch the head; and, as all move ahead, the tail may even lag further behind. Our problem is to make sure that those who find themselves at the various levels in the educational structure are there by virtue of achievement rather than ascription.

REFERENCES

1. Greer, Scott, *The Emerging City*, New York: Free Press, 1962, p. 14.
2. Hollingshead, August B., *Elmstown Youth*, New York: Wiley, 1949, pp. 116-117.
3. Lichter, Solomon, Rapien, Elsie, Seibert, Frances, and Slansky, Martin, *The Drop-outs*, New York: Free Press, 1962.
4. Quinn, James A., *Human Ecology*, Englewood Cliffs, N. J.: Prentice-Hall, 1950, pp. 86-94.
5. Sexton, Patricia, *Education and Income*, New York: Viking Press, 1961.
6. Thomas, William I., and Znaniecki, Florjan, *The Polish Peasant in Europe and America*, Vol. V. Boston: The Gorham Press, 1920, pp. 221-271.
7. Wayland, Sloan R., and Brunner, Edmund deS., *The Educational Characteristics of the American People*, New York: Bureau of Publications, Teachers College, Columbia University, 1958.

Miriam L. Goldberg | Factors Affecting Educational Attainment in Depressed Urban Areas

In the United States, the cities have historically provided the loci for integrating immigrants into the American culture. Newcomers could move from exclusive contact with compatriots to increasing participation in the broader culture as they and their children acquired the skills of language and learned and accepted the mores demanded by the new life. Thus, the cities provided each newly arrived group with opportunities for some of its members to move from the status of alien slum dwellers to that of middle-class citizens in the course of one or two generations.

The old cities have grown in size and in complexity, spilling over into ever-widening metropolitan areas while their centers, continuing to provide employment, no longer sufficed in size and in amenities to provide adequate living space for the increasing middle class. The expansion of the geographic area serviced by the city and the deterioration of the central core have within recent decades reached such proportions as to prompt the emergence of a sizable literature of inquiry and opinion dealing with problems of urban development and redevelopment.

The nine-volume *New York Metropolitan Region Study,* undertaken by Harvard University's graduate school of Public Administration under the directorship of Raymond Vernon (25), described and analyzed the population, business, finance, housing, and government of the area, as well as the relation of the core to the rest of the region and of the total complex to surrounding areas and to the nation as a whole. In more general terms and on a far smaller scale, *The City in Mid-Century* (5) presents a series of papers dealing with architecture, politics, automation and social problems of the urban areas. A variety of articles and numerous books dealing with problems of urban renewal and redevelopment have come from sociologists, architects, city planners and interested laymen. Patterns of urban renewal, which formed the basis for many recent housing and business building projects, have come under sharp attack in Jane Jacobs' *The Death and Life of Great American Cities* (9). Lewis Mumford, in his most recent volume *The City in History* (17), traces not only the historical development of cities but also introduces comparative analyses of cities in different parts of the world, attempting to explain their functional similarities and differences. Most recently, a psychological approach to the study of the city population resulted in *The Midtown Manhattan Study,* of which the first volume, *Mental Health in the Metropolis* (23), appeared this year. Even more extensive and of older origin is the literature dealing with delinquency. Serious increases in the rate of juvenile crime in large cities during the years following the Second World War have prompted sociologists, psychologists, and social workers to produce an extensive body of theoretical and empirical considerations of the problem, its causes and cures.

But, in this great outpouring of concern with the problems of urban life, one area has been shockingly conspicuous by its absence—namely, education. None of the sociologists, planners, psychiatrists, or welfare workers have made more than passing references to the increasingly complex and varied educational problems of the metropolis or to the relation between education and such other aspects of city life as jobs, housing, health, delinquency, and cultural resources. Only Queen and Carpenter in *The American City* (19) include a chapter on education as related to urbanization and social mobility.

While the various disciplines concerned with urban problems have paid scant attention to education, the urban schools, in attempting to cope with the increasingly complex factors which affect their day-to-day operation, have too often failed to turn to the social sciences for theoretical and empirical bases upon which to construct their programs. The various efforts now under way (Higher Horizons, Great Cities Project, the Banneker schools in St. Louis, the Amidon School in Washington, D.C., etc.) have operated generally on the theory that what the present situation calls for is an expansion of services which had proved effective in past generations or with middle-class children who had learning difficulties. Characteristic of these programs are increases in such services as guidance, remedial instruction, individual psychological testing, and counseling. Increased demands on the pupils in terms of higher standards and greater effort are also typical.

Thus, efforts within the educational enterprise of large cities have run parallel to rather than intermeshed with the theory and research from the social sciences and from professional groups concerned with studying urban life.

In order that the big cities may continue to play their historical roles of integrating newcomers into the broader culture, of stimulating upward mobility among present in-migrants, of preparing each new work world, the schools must be viewed as one, if not *the,* central agency through which these goals can be achieved. And the schools, in turn, must make increasing use of the knowledge and insights available from the social sciences and their professional counterparts in examining and modifying their organizational forms, approaches to teacher education, materials, and procedures.

Although the total metropolis must be viewed as an essentially interdependent complex, no part of which can solve its problems alone, the central core of the city, with its great masses of financially and culturally disadvantaged people living in severely blighted and gray areas, demands particular emphasis and first priority in any attempt to study and improve education and total living patterns in the rapidly enlarging metropolitan areas of the country.

Who Lives in the City?

The most dramatic change in the make-up of urban population in the last several decades relates to the movement of middle- and upper middle-class families from the city itself to the surrounding suburban and exurban areas. As a result, the metropolitan areas have increased in population while many of the older cities themselves have shown either little change or a decline in population (25). This has occurred despite the continued in-migration of people from rural areas, young women looking for career opportunities and small-town people in search of employment.

Resident in New York City, for example, is a small group of upper-income families who prefer the convenience of accessibility and the advantages of urban living to the greater spaciousness and isolation of the further suburbs. This group produces a very minor part of the public school population, since most of its children go to independent day or residential schools. A second group, the "clerical workers" (25), those immediately below the professional or managerial level but above laborers and service workers, represent a considerable portion of the city's residents, living, mainly, within the city limits in the areas surrounding Manhattan. Within Manhattan and the neighboring portions of the other boroughs, in the most decayed areas of the city, whether in obsolescent structures or in low-cost public housing, lives the great mass of low-income families. In fact, according to the U.S. Census of Population about 70 per cent of all residents of the New York metropolitan region who earned less than $1500 per year lived in the core of the city, whereas only a little better than half the people who earned between $7000 and $10,000 lived within the city limits. Analyses of the population statistics of other cities would probably reveal similar patterns.

While the last several decades have witnessed the exodus of middle- and upper-class families from the city to the suburbs and exurbs, they have also witnessed the in-migration of large numbers of low-income families from the rural South, the Kentucky and Tennessee mountain areas, Mexico and Puerto Rico. The southern Negroes settled in most of the great Eastern and middle Western cities, the other groups tended to concentrate in one or another locality. These in-migrants swelled the ranks of the low-income population, taking over the decaying housing vacated by the somewhat higher-income "natives" of the cities—natives who, one or two generations before, were themselves immigrants.

These population shifts had a marked effect on the school population. The middle- and lower-middle class still account for a sizable proportion of the school children, but mainly in the outlying districts of the city. In the core areas the school population is composed in part of the residues of former migration waves who, though long resident in the cities, did not move too far up the socio-economic ladder as did their brighter or more ambitious or more fortunate compatriots. For the rest, the school children come from families of recent in-migrants who are not only economically disadvantaged but, because of their ethnic and/or racial membership, present rather unique problems even within the general designation of low socio-economic status. It was largely due to the great increase of these latter groups in the city population that city schools were prompted to take a harder look at their educational procedures.

The Changing City Population

The problems confronting our large city school districts today are complicated not only by sheer size and general heterogeneity of population, but also by the changed nature and mobility patterns of our present and incoming city dwellers. Neither the immigrant nor the slum is a newcomer to the city. Especially in the northeast, and somewhat later in other urban centers, immigrant groups formed a sizable proportion of the total school population. Each of these, in turn, moved into the slum areas of the great cities and each, in turn and often in combination, presented specific educational problems to the city schools. The effects of residence in the American city, largely through the auspices of the school, were more or less rapid in acculturating these various incoming groups to the broader American culture. In some instances, the internal organization of the ethnic group tended to support a feeling of social control which facilitated the development of indigenous middle-class groups. While perpetuating aspects of their own cultures, these migrant groups did not prevent their members from moving out into the broader spheres of American life and becoming quite indistinguishable from the surrounding inhabitants. In other instances, where the general level of education of the immigrants was exceptionally low, and where mutual controls were limited, the movement out of the slums into better working and living conditions took somewhat longer (19).

The in-migrant groups with which the large population centers are most keenly concerned today differ in several respects from their predecessors. And what is perhaps more important, the mobility patterns of the resident groups are today quite different from those of four and five decades ago.

Changing mobility patterns. While the immigrants of the late nineteenth and early twentieth century could, as their status improved, move out of the "downtown" slums of the city into the surrounding "uptown" areas, they all remained within the city limits and thus within the limits of the city school district. As the more capable and/or ambitious members of each group moved up on the social ladder and became acculturated to the values and attitudes of the middle-class culture, they still remained a part of the parent body of the city schools.

Thereafter, just prior to the Second World War, and at a geometrically increasing rate, the mobility of the city dwellers was not to the outskirts of the city, but rather to the suburbs which lay beyond the limits of the city school district. As the new migration waves of Negroes, Puerto Ricans, Mexicans, hillbillies, etc., took up the slum and gray areas of the major cities, the middle-class groups began to move beyond the city limits into the newly developing surburban communities which had their own school authorities as well as local governments. Even middle-income housing which was close to the city center began to be viewed as a less desirable place in which to live, especially for families with children. An increasing number of middle-class families left the city and in-migration continued the proportion of school children from disadvantaged families increased markedly.

Changes in School-Leaving Age and in Promotional Policies

Although, by 1918, every state had enacted a compulsory-school-attendance law and thirty-one of the forty-eight states legally required school attendance through 16 (the remaining seventeen varied from age 12 to age 15), the firmness with which such laws were enforced differed greatly from state to state and from one local school district to another. As a result, many children began to work at age 12 and school drop-out at the end of the fifth or sixth grade was not unusual.

Enactment of state and federal child-labor laws and increasingly strict enforcement of school-leaving age resulted in an ever greater percentage of pupils age 5 through 17 enrolled in school. In 1900, for example, only 79 per cent of children of this age were in school; by 1958, 97 per cent were attending school.

The effect was most keenly felt by the secondary schools. Whereas, in 1900, only 8 per cent of all children age 14 to 17 were in public secondary schools, by 1958 the percentage had risen to 77. This increase in secondary school enrollment was spurred by the adoption of "social promotion policies" by which pupils moved from grade to grade on the basis of age rather than academic achievement. Where such a policy is enforced, high-school populations today can include total illiterates as well as large numbers of pupils with primary level academic skills and minimal educational motivation.

Although the city schools have, over the years, been confronted with all pupils in the early grades, the presence of hundreds of thousands of academically ill-prepared and unmotivated students in the high schools is a relatively new phenomenon which did not exist in the late nineteenth and early twentieth centuries. In New York City, for example, school attendance is mandatory through age 17, and only under special circumstances may a student leave at the state-mandated age of 16. Since a strict annual promotion policy was followed until 1960, the great majority of the 15- to 17-year-olds were in the high schools.[1] But generally, neither the academic nor the vocational city high schools had evolved curricula suited either to the times or the learning abilities and educational drives of the increasing number of poorly equipped and uninterested students.

Ethnic group differences. Despite many similarities, there are significant ways in which the present in-migrant populations differ from past immigrant groups into the United States. In the first place, the Negro migrants from the rural south into the northeastern and midwestern cities present unique problems. Their very color prevents them from moving into the general culture and becoming undifferentiated from the rest as was true for so many of the groups which came before. In addition, a great many social restrictions prevent even those of them who have attained the requisite financial and cultural status from moving into either highly desirable residential areas within the city or into suburban areas. By and large, even in the northern cities, the Negroes remain largely dependent upon white employers and their employment has, in most cases, been restricted to unskilled, unpleasant, and poorly paid occupations. In discussing the differences between the Negro in-migrant population and

[1] U.S. Office of Education Circulars, State Legislation on School Attendance. Circular No. 615, January 1, 1960, pp. 1-30.

previous waves of migration, Queen and Carpenter (19) point out the following: unlike the European and Asiatic immigrant, the Negro comes into the urban center with a knowledge of the language and, to some extent, of American culture. He does not perceive himself as a foreigner. Although he must make the adjustments from rural to urban dwelling, the transition from agricultural to industrial work, he, unlike other groups, confronts a special case of restriction and prejudice. The Negroes settle near the heart of the city, as did all other newly arrived groups, but their outward movement is quite different; they cannot skip over the intervening spaces and thus must push out on a continuous line within the city limits. Whereas many groups in the past retained their ethnic identity through close living in what were often separate communities, these were by and large voluntary associations. For the Negro, segregation is largely compulsory; he cannot withdraw from his own ethnic group even after two or three generations. What is of special interest is the fact that group solidarity seems to be less developed in the Negro community than in most of the other immigrant or in-migrant communities in the past or even today. Most of their institutions tend to be weak in social control and power over their own membership and those who rise to higher status too often no longer feel a sense of responsibility toward members of their group.

The rapid and sizable increase in Negro population in the northern cities can be seen from a comparison in Table 1, of figures for 1900, 1950 and 1960.

Each of these great cities has, since the Second World War, been the haven for Negro in-migrants seeking jobs, and, more significantly, seeking a release from the legalized inferior status which they suffered in their southern communities. But having arrived in the northern cities, they meet with prejudice and segregation no less powerful because of its de facto rather than its de jure nature.

Table I. Approximate number of Negroes resident in selected northern cities in 1900, 1950 (19), and 1960 (28).

City	Population Size		
	1900	1950	1960
New York	60,000	750,000	1,100,000
Chicago	30,000	500,000	800,000
Philadelphia	60,000	400,000	530,000
Detroit	4,000	350,000	500,000
Washington, D.C.	85,000	300,000	400,000

Like other in-migrants, the Negroes bring with them the customs and living patterns of their former milieu, which are often non-adaptive to urban living. Of particular importance from an educational point of view is the unstable family pattern and the strong female dominance in the home, characteristic of disproportionately large numbers of Negro families. In one study (3), comparing Negro and white lower-class school children, Deutsch found that the number of broken homes (generally fatherless) in the Negro population studied was equal to the number of intact homes in the white population; and the latter had too few broken homes to enable a comparison within the white sample.

The Puerto Ricans, with their mixed Spanish, Indian, and Negro ancestry, range in appearance from "white" through "indios," those with copper-colored skin, "grifos" those with light complexion but kinky hair, to others who are indistinguishable from Negroes. Since many of them come from towns rather than from rural areas, they have some familiarity with city life, but too often their usual living patterns are not adaptive to life in the American city. Though they are American citizens upon arrival they are looked down upon as foreigners because they speak a foreign language; and, although most of them are not Negroes, they are further looked down upon as colored. There has been considerable speculation about the possibility that the Puerto Rican school children and youth speak Spanish among themselves as well as at home in an effort to retain their identity and avoid being taken for Negroes. The conscious retention of a foreign language as the major vehicle of communication even among second generation members of the group impedes the acculturation process.

Unlike previous immigrants, the Puerto Rican does not have to prepare for American citizenship. It is his birthright. Nor does the journey from the "old country" require a complete rupture with the former life. The Puerto Rican migration lacks the finality that resulted from the long and often arduous trans-oceanic journey of past waves of immigrants. The short and relatively inexpensive plane journey allows for actual return to the island, or what is equally significant, for the feeling that one can go back if one wishes. This factor, too, impedes rapid acculturation as the in-migrant need not see himself as so completely dependent upon the new siutation as to have to succeed in it or be lost.

Like the Negro, the Puerto Rican family is largely mother-dominated. The Puerto Rican woman more often than the man makes the initial trip to the mainland and then sends for other members of the immediate or extended family (15). In 1950 in New York City the sex ratio was sixty-three males to one hundred females. Marital relations tend to be unstable with a high rate of separation and divorce both prior to and after coming to the mainland. In 1948 there were approximately 200,000 Puerto Ricans in New York City (19), and the increase (since 1946) has been about a third of a million per decade (25).

Until very recently, the Puerto Rican community lacked any of the strong leadership or formal associations so characteristic of former immigrant groups. Although their integration into the metropolitan areas has proceeded more rapidly than for the Negro in-migrants, their ". . . status is very unclear and insecure. They are at the same time Americans and foreigners, white and colored, urban and colonial" (19).

The characteristics and incidence of other recent in-migrant groups which present special problems in some of the larger cities will not be discussed here.

Changes in Employment Opportunities

Not only has the composition of "the poor" changed since the early decades of the century, but the economic relation of the poor to the system has changed. As Goodman (7) points out, earlier minorities poured into an expanding economy that needed people; the present in-migrants come into an expanding economy which does not need people. This statement becomes especially true if the need for "people" is translated into the need for "hands."

With increased and refined mechanization of production the entire country has seen a shift in the relative employing potential of manufacturing as against services. Whereas in earlier decades industrial production employed a greater share of the working public than did the auxiliary services, today there are more white- than blue-collar workers.[2] And this trend is continuing. In the New York metropolitan region manufacturing now employs about 30 per cent of the working population (and this figure is expected to fall by at least 2 per cent by 1985), while consumer trade and services, business and professional services, finance, government and "other" non-manufacturing jobs account for 70 per cent of all jobs. By 1985 the greatest increase (about 6 per cent) is anticipated in business, professional and financial services; and another 2 per cent increase in government services (25).

These figures were projected with no attention to the coming of increased automation. As more and more industries turn to automated processes—a trend now held in check by strong opposition of organized labor and groups of small businessmen—fewer jobs will be available to those with minimal education. For example, the electronic data processing

[2] Bureau of Labor Statistics, 1962.

industries anticipate by 1970 the need for an additional three million workers to operate the machines.[3] There is no estimate of the number of existing jobs which the machines will replace, but the skills and abilities of the men who run the electronic "brains" are not the same as those of the men who now do many of the jobs which the machines will make obsolete. There will be increasingly less room in the job market for the unskilled or even semi-skilled worker, whether in manufacturing or in service. But there will be more need for people with the ability and education to meet the increasing demands for specialized professional, business and government services.

The effect of the shifting economy on the future job market presents perhaps the most significant difference in the opportunities available to previous immigrants and present in-migrants. The plight of the unskilled and uneducated presents a more pressing social problem than ever before. And because the cities harbor the greatest numbers of such people, especially young people, the city schools must find ways to educate large masses of pupils who, so far, have not been amenable to learning what the school has taught and who, consequently, swelled the ranks of unskilled labor. As the demand for unskilled labor dwindles, these minimally educated youth, especially the Negro youth for whom discrimination limits even existing job opportunities, face a hopeless future. Conant (1) in viewing this situation contends that " . . . we are allowing social dynamite to accumulate in our large cities," and views the continuation of this situation as "a menace to the social and political health of the city."

In summary, several simultaneous occurrences in recent decades have created unique and urgently pressing problems for the schools of large cities:

1. The changing nature of the city population resulting from the out-migration (to non-city school districts) of middle-class families and the in-migration of low-income groups.

2. The raised school-leaving age and the need for adequate secondary school provisions for presently unmotivated and uninterested pupils.

3. The ethnic and racial membership of the present in-migrants, which create problems of caste as well as of class that affect both educational aspirations and employment opportunities.

4. The changing job market with its decreasing demand for unskilled and semi-skilled labor and its increasing need for people who can fill occupations which require higher levels of educational training.

[3] Speech by John Sullivan at the Electronic Data Processing Conference, held at Teachers College, June, 1962.

Although the city schools have, historically, worked to integrate the newcomers into the broader culture, the combination of circumstances confronting education today are sufficiently different from those met in the past, and so much more urgent, that schools must reappraise their present concepts and procedures and expose to investigation some long held assumptions. Whether the general tenets of the "social uplift" movements of the late nineteenth and early twentieth centuries are applicable today is a moot question. Much of the sentimental description of the ethnically diverse, rich lower-class culture of past eras fails to carry much conviction vis-à-vis today's slums. Changes in the physical living and learning conditions through improved housing and improved school buildings have not proven as effective in changing attitudes and mores as their early proponents had anticipated. The settlement houses and other community agencies have found many of their older techniques and approaches inoperative with the new populations which they must service. And education for citizenship—a powerful means of bringing the earlier newcomers into the American culture—is, ipso facto, meaningless for newcomers who are already citizens.

What are some of the specific problems which confront the school and what are some of the assumptions which must underlie school efforts? For tentative answers we must turn to the research of the social sciences rather than to the inspirational teachings of "social uplift" or to school procedures which proved unsuccessful in the past.

Class Status Differences as Related to School Performance

The city schools today deal with pupils who represent the total range of academic ability and educational motivation. In all cities there are "good schools" and "difficult schools." The former are generally located in the areas away from the city centers, beyond the "gray" belt, or where there is a large concentration of higher-income families in cooperative houses or in middle-income housing projects in downtown sections. The "difficult schools" are concentrated in the blighted and gray areas.

In general, the "good schools" differ little from schools in suburban areas, either in pupil population, stability of teaching staff, or parental drive for higher education. Largely fed by middle-class white families, these schools deal with pupils whose abilities and academic performances, as measured by intelligence, aptitude, and achievement tests, are above the national average. Although these schools have their share of retardates, slow learners, and even an occasional discipline problem, these are the exception rather than the rule.

The "difficult schools," on the other hand, generally service pupils from economically and culturally disadvantaged homes. Some are exclusively Negro; others, as in New York City for example, enroll mainly Puerto Rican pupils; still others draw from low-income white families as well. Both the pupil and teacher turnover is great. Three "difficult" elementary schools in New York City (11), for example, had a 100 per cent turnover in pupil population from the beginning of the school year 1959-1960 to the end; and in 43 schools the turnover was between 70 and 99 per cent. For the 91 elementary schools in the borough of Manhattan, the median turnover was 51 per cent, for the 25 junior high schools in the same borough, 47 per cent. In general, this turnover represents inter-school but intra-city mobility. No comparable figures on teacher mobility are available but one of the great concerns consistently voiced by principals of difficult schools is their inability to keep teachers. In an all-Negro school studied by Deutsch (3), one class had six teachers in a single term. On the average, the pupils fall consistently and significantly below the national average on all tests of intellectual or academic attainment.

Many studies have compared the IQs and achievement records of lower- and middle-class pupils. In most cases, groups of pupils from higher-income families scored higher on all cognitive measures, even when these were ostensibly "culture fair" (6). This remained true even when special practice sessions and rewards were provided to overcome initial unfamiliarity with test-taking and lack of motivation to do well on such tests (8). Although some students of the problem contended that class-status differences were more marked on verbal than on non-verbal items (6), others (24), in reanalyzing the data, found that differences between verbal and non-verbal items were a statistical artifact. However, differences between an abstract and a contract mode of approaching problems persisted.

These latter differences were highlighted by Miller and Swanson in their discussion of expressive styles (14). When the child-rearing practices favored psychological discipline, symbolic reward, and maternal self-control (the patterns most often associated with middle-class families), the child tended to develop a *conceptual style*. When the discipline was physical, the rewards tangible, and maternal self-control limited (more typical of lower-class homes), the child more often developed a *motoric style*. Further support for these varied ways of approaching problems come from Siller's study (22). He found significant social-class differences in pupil selection of abstract as opposed to concrete explanations and definitions. But, in the main, the greater part of the difference was accounted for by a small group of consistently low scorers in the low-status group.

In general, the expressive style of the lower-class child can be described as more often motoric, concrete, "thing-oriented," and non-verbal. The middle-class child, on the other hand, is more often conceptual, abstract-symbolic, "idea-oriented," and verbal in his style of expression.

Perhaps the most significant area of difference between lower- and middle-class school populations relates to their differences in motivation toward school and their perception of the purpose and meaning of schooling. In their study of working-class and middle-class children's conflicts and psychological defenses, Miller and Swanson (14) contrasted the values of the two groups as follows: The middle-class family members believe that their economic position can be improved through effort and sacrifice. They are willing to postpone gratification for greater future reward. They need to maintain a reputation for honesty, responsibility and respectability. They must accumulate money and social graces, develop abstract thinking ability needed for advancement in their work. The focus on individual advancement, self-denial, and competent performance leads to esteem for formal education, rationality, controlled and respectable behavior, hard work, and, above all, " . . . mastery of self by rational means as a prelude to mastering the world . . . " In resolving conflict, the middle-class individual has severe standards about aggression, is likely to brood rather than act, and tends more often to internalize blame than to turn it outward.

The working-class individual recognizes his limitations in economic power and advancement and creates values and behavior which further limit mobility. Because he sees success and security as uncertain, he is more "present-" than "future-oriented." Although some may view formal education as desirable, it is not vital for job getting or retention; physical strength and manual skills are more highly valued. In general, self-control and responsibility are less evident and there is more concern with the pleasures of the moment than the unknown rewards of the future.

These diverse *weltanschauungen* find direct expression in school behavior. The middle-class child is "good" because from the earliest years he is taught to control expressions of anger and to inhibit direct aggression. He responds to appeals to internalized standards of right and wrong since he has learned that one cannot transgress against social demands if one wants to "get ahead." The lower-class child has been brought up on direct expression of aggression in the home and in the street. Since control of such behavior is seen to have little relevance to social positon or job maintenance, there is no need to teach the child the skills of control.

Although there is considerable disagreement as to the attitudes of the middle-class toward education, there is little argument about its strong belief in and support of formal schooling. Years of schooling are the rungs of the ladder upon which upward mobility proceeds. Although there are great individual differences in the degree to which the middle-class child wants to do well or wants to go on to higher education, the group, as a whole, sees its future bound up with extended schooling.

The lower-class family, even when it would like to see its offspring achieve a higher status than its own, cannot provide the model of attitudes and behaviors which underlie a perception of the world as open, and schooling as a means of moving out and up into the open world. Only when the family is dissatisfied with its status and consciously wishes to move up or at least to insure that their sons will move up, do the boys view school success as important (10).

Despite consistent differences in demonstrated intellectual and academic ability, attitudes, motivation, behavior patterns, and expressive styles between lower- and middle-class pupils, there is a great deal of overlapping. In all studies there are some in the one group who resemble the other group far more than their own. And in all comparisons of lower- and middle-class children there is a sizable though smaller proportion of the former who score high on tests, do well in school, plan on advanced education and show a high degree of similarity to the school performance of middle-class children. Conversely, there are middle-class children whose motivation and performance are poor, indeed.

The extent of the overlap is demonstrated in Table 2 by a comparison of the percentages of pupils from *high-status old American* families, *low-status old American* families, and identifiable *ethnic groups* (other than Scandinavian) who scored above given IQ points (6). Despite great differences in the percentages scoring above given IQ points, there are almost a fourth of the younger group and a sixth of the older group of low-status old American pupils who score above IQ 110 and a few pupils in both low-status groups who achieve IQ scores above 130.

Table 2. Percentage of pupils (age 9 to 10 and 13 to 14) from high- and low-status families scoring above given IQ points.

Above IQ Point	High-Status Old American		Low-Status Old American		Ethnic	
	Percentage, Age 9-10[a]	Percentage, Age 13-14	Percentage, Age 9-10	Percentage, Age 13-14	Percentage, Age 9-10	Percentage, Age 13-14
130	19	13	0.02	0.8	0.02	0.7
110	64	68	24	15	22	11
100	17	13	55	65	48	66

[a] Percentage columns added for this paper.

Negro and Puerto Rican Pupils as a Special Case of Lower-Class Pupils

While in general, middle-class and lower-class children differ from each other in the various ways noted above, Negro lower-class children differ even more from the typical white middle-class child than do white children from low-income families. The Negro child is heir not only to the characteristics of lower-class status, but as a member of a minority group which has historically been considered inferior, he carries the scars of every kind of discrimination, forced segregation, and limited channels of mobility.[4] Differences in personality and school achievement due to ethnic group membership over and above those related to class status must, therefore be considered.

Negroes and other severely disadvantaged cultural groups account for increasing proportions of the large city school populations. In many instances the proportion of school children from these disadvantaged groups exceeds the proportion of the group itself in the city population. For example, in New York City (18) as of 1960, the Negroes represented 14 per cent of the total population. However, their children represented almost 22 per cent of all children in the public schools. The Puerto Ricans, who numbered approximately half a million, thus about 7 per cent of the city dwellers, accounted for almost 16 per cent of children in the public schools. Together, these two groups, though only about one-fifth of all New York City residents, accounted for almost two-fifths of the city's public school children. (Projected figures based on anticipated in-migration to the cities and birth rates suggest that by 1970 one out of every two pupils in large city schools will fall into the category of culturally disadvantaged.) (21, p. 1)

While mobility out of the city is more often associated with the white middle-class population, intra-city mobility is more often associated with Negro and other disadvantaged groups. All three schools in New York City which had a 100 per cent mobility (11) were almost completely Negro, and among the 41 schools which had a turnover of 70 per cent or more of its pupils, the majority were either preponderantly Negro or Puerto Rican.

Scores on intelligence tests also differentiate ethnically disadvantaged groups from white groups even when the latter are themselves in-migrants to the city or of lower socio-economic status. A study of the IQs of in-migrant and indigenous (born in New York City) Negro, Puerto Rican and "other" pupils (16) found significant differences among the groups, (Table 3).

[4] American Indians and, to a somewhat lesser degree, Puerto Ricans and Mexicans probably fall into the same category.

Table 3. Third- and sixth-grade mean IQ scores of in-migrant and indigenous Puerto Rican, Negro, and "other" pupils in New York City schools.

| | Mean IQ Scores | | | | | |
| | In-Migrants | | Indigenous | | All | |
Group	3rd grade	6th grade	3rd grade	6th grade	3rd grade	6th grade
Puerto Rican						
Boys	84.3	78.4	87.0	82.4	85.8	80.0
Girls	85.8	79.5	88.8	86.6	87.6	83.0
Total	85.0	79.0	87.9	84.5	86.7	81.2
Negro						
Boys	87.9	84.4	91.8	88.1	91.1	87.1
Girls	88.9	87.3	90.9	91.7	90.5	90.7
Total	88.4	85.8	91.4	90.0	90.8	89.0
Other						
Boys	99.7	100.1	104.3	107.6	103.8	106.5
Girls	101.3	101.2	104.6	112.5	104.3	110.5
Total	100.4	100.7	104.4	109.9	104.0	108.4
All Pupils						
Boys	87.3	85.5	95.7	98.6	93.7	94.8
Girls	88.9	87.3	96.0	101.8	94.4	97.5
Total	88.1	86.3	95.8	100.2	94.0	96.1

Lower scores on the sixth-grade tests as compared to the third-year tests may be explained, in part, by the non-verbal nature of the lower grade tests and the high reading component of the higher grade tests. Even in schools where Negro and Puerto Rican in-migration was light, schools generally located in higher-income areas, the IQs of both Negro and Puerto Rican pupils, in-migrant or indigenous fell well below that of the "others."

Although at the third grade level there were no significant sex differences in IQ scores, the sixth grade girls of all three groups scored higher on IQ tests than did the boys.

For Puerto Rican and Negro pupils, both indigenous and in-migrant, IQ scores were generally higher in schools where the number of in-migrant pupils was relatively low than in schools where the number of newcomers was high. For the "others," however, scores were higher in both heavy and light in-migration areas than in those which had moderate rates of "other" in-migration.

Residence in large northern cities has an upgrading effect on the IQs and achievement levels of Negro pupils, and those born in these cities generally score higher than those who arrived after elementary school age.

Klineberg (12) reported in a 1935 study that IQs of Negro in-migrant children increased with length of residence in New York City but that, in general, there was a leveling off after five or six years. In the New York City study cited above (16) all three indigenous groups had higher IQ scores than the respective in-migrants and the lower the grade at which the in-migrants entered, the greater was the difference.

In a study of Negro in-migrants to Philadelphia (13), Lee found a steady improvement in IQ scores as length of residence in Philadelphia increased. For all those entering before fifth grade, there was a significant difference between first score and the score attained at ninth grade. When pupils entering in first grade were compared to Philadelphia-born pupils on first testing, the scores were significantly higher for the indigenous pupils (even those who had not attended kindergarten) but were no different by ninth grade. Of interest is the finding that Philadelphia-born Negro pupils who had attended kindergarten scored higher at each grade level than those who had not attended. These differences may have been due to selective attendance, with higher income families more apt to send their children to kindergarten, or the effects of the extra year of schooling.

However, although birth or extended residence in northern cities does tend to raise the IQ scores of Negro children, these still remain below or at the lowest end of the national average. In the Philadelphia study (39) even those born in the city had average IQs of 92.1 in the first grade and 93.7 in the ninth grade. Only those who attended kindergarten reached a mean-IQ status of approximately 97—thus approaching the national norm.

Although Negro pupils show increases in IQ, they do not necessarily show superior reading achievement with increased residence in the city. In the New York City comparison of the reading scores of indigenous in-migrant sixth-grade pupils (15), the indigenous Negro children read no better, on the whole, than did the in-migrant group, whereas both Puerto Ricans and "others" born in the city read better than the respective in-migrants in all types of schools (Table 4).

In comparing the achievement scores of fourth, fifth, and sixth graders in a 99 per cent Negro school and a 94 per cent white school of nearly comparable socio-economic levels, Deutsch (3) found that both groups were retarded when compared to national norms, but that the Negro pupils showed twice as great a degree of retardation as the whites. Average gains for the Negro pupils in a year were less than one month with a maximum observed gain of 2.7 months in one class. Deutsch concludes that "with more schooling there is proportionately decreased learning over time."

What factors account for the consistently lower academic status of

Table 4. Third- and sixth-grade mean reading scores of in-migrant and indigenous Puerto Rican, Negro, and "other" pupils in New York City schools.

| | Reading Grade Equivalents | | | | | |
| | In-Migrant | | Indigenous | | All | |
Group	3rd grade	6th grade	3rd grade	6th grade	3rd grade	6th grade
Puerto Rican						
Boys	2.3	4.1	2.6	4.6	2.5	4.3
Girls	2.6	4.3	2.8	4.7	2.8	4.5
Total	2.4	4.2	2.7	4.6	2.7	4.4
Negro						
Boys	2.8	4.9	2.8	4.9	2.8	4.9
Girls	3.1	5.0	3.2	5.2	3.2	5.2
Total	3.0	4.9	3.0	5.0	3.0	5.0
Other						
Boys	3.4	6.5	4.0	7.0	3.9	6.9
Girls	4.0	6.4	4.2	7.3	4.2	7.2
Total	3.6	6.5	4.1	7.1	4.0	7.0
All Pupils						
Boys	2.6	4.9	3.3	6.0	3.1	5.7
Girls	2.9	5.1	3.5	6.2	3.4	5.9
Total	2.7	5.0	3.4	6.1	3.2	5.8

children from disadvantaged ethnic groups, especially the Negroes, than of children from lower class white families living in the Northern cities?

One theory which is frequently used to account for the lower intellectual or academic status of children from low socio-economic backgrounds proposes that in an open society, such as ours, with many available channels of mobility, the brighter and more ambitious move up in social status while the less able retain their lower-class membership. Further assuming that intelligence is largely hereditary, it would be expected that the offspring of those who moved up in socio-economic status would be, on the average, brighter than the offspring of those who remained behind.

Even if the theory of social sorting on the basis of intelligence or ambition or the interaction of both has operated for some groups, the Negro population has not yet been exposed to this kind of sorting. For centuries their access to higher status in education, in vocational choice, in living site and in social intercourse with the broader society has been severely limited, and historically they have been relegated to inferior status despite individual attainment.

From a review of the literature on the personality correlates of class and minority group status Deutsch (3) concludes that " . . . The more constricted an individual's social frame of reference and the greater its distance from the cultural mainstream, the less meaningful and the less effective are the dominant cultural values that impinge on him in the schools and other social institutions." Certainly the Negro group is the one most consistently barred from the "cultural mainstream" and thus, the least amenable to the values and teachings of the school.

From his study, Deutsch found that 65 per cent of the Negro children had never been more than twenty-five blocks away from home, that half reported no pen or pencil at home and the majority of homes had no books (comic books, and magazines were available in some of the homes and 60 per cent had television sets). Many of the children had to fix their own meals and a large number came to school without breakfast. When compared to the white pupils, the Negro group not only showed greater academic retardation and less adequate yearly gains in achievement, they also regarded their home environment less favorably despite equal socioeconomic level and despite greater crowding in the white homes. The greatest differences between the groups were in the incidence of broken homes—generally without a father—and on measures of self-image. The groups also differed in their ability to concentrate and persist when confronted by a problem. While those who came from intact homes did better academically than those from broken homes, the former did not view their homes or themselves more favorably. A negative self-image was not related to achievement, but was strongly related to being a Negro. By the fourth grade, school experience appeared to exercise little influence on developing self-attitudes.

Even more than the white low socio-economic status group, the Negro pupils lacked any "future" orientation since the home failed to create expectation of future rewards for present activities. Deutsch (3) suggests that " . . . This inconsistency between the lack of internalized reward anticipations on the part of the Negro child and his teachers' expectations that he does have such anticipations, reflect the disharmony between the social environment of the home and middle-class oriented demands of the school."

Differences in personality and school achievement between the sexes was very marked in the Negro group. In fact, the Negro boys' performance contributed most to the differences between the Negro and white pupils. The Negro girls had higher achievement scores, a longer attention span, less often reported negative family atmosphere, and were more popular with classmates. In the white group the girls excelled the boys only in reading.

It is in the comparisons by sex that the excessive proportion of broken homes in the Negro group showed the most marked effects. As stated earlier, the number of broken homes among the Negro pupils was equal to the number of intact homes in the white group. Because there is no father in the home, the boy lacks a successful (or any) male model; the girl, on the other hand, has an adequate model in the mother. Also, there are more girls who can aspire realistically to relatively higher status jobs such as secretary, nurse, and teacher; for the boys, aspirations for higher status jobs are less realistic.

From various achievement, background and personality measures and from continuous classroom observations Deutsch concluded that "seemingly, the weight of the whole complex of negative factors . . . is depressing the scholastic functioning of these children as well as distorting personality growth ... . When the home is a proportionately less effective socializing force, the school must become a proportionately more effective one, ..."

A Summary Portrait of the Disadvantaged Pupil

Beginning with the family, the early pre-school years present the child from a disadvantaged home with few of the experiences which produce readiness for academic learning either intellectually or attitudinally. The child's view of society is limited by his immediate family and neighborhood where he sees a struggle for survival which sanctions behavior viewed as immoral in the society at large. He has little preparation either for recognizing the importance of schooling in his own life or for being able to cope with the kinds of verbal and abstract behavior which the school will demand of him. Although he generally comes to first grade neat and clean and with his mother's admonition to be a "good boy," he lacks the ability to carry out those tasks which would make him appear "good" in the eyes of his teacher.

Early difficulty in mastering the basic intellectual skills which the schools and thus the broader society demands leads to defeat and failure, a developing negative self-image, rebellion against the increasingly defeating school experiences, a search for status outside the school together with active resentment against the society which the school represents. The child early finds status and protection in the street and the gang which requires none of the skills which are needed in school but makes heavy use of the kinds of survival skills which he learned in his early home and street experiences.

Unlike the small town or suburban delinquent who becomes a member of an out-group by transgressing against the laws of the school or society, delinquency aids the slum child in becoming a member of the in-group and protects him against isolation and a sense of unacceptability.

Into this pattern of rebellion against defeat in school—the major accepted societal enterprise with which the child is involved—other social forces enter. Different ethnic perceptions of what life has in store for their group act to complicate the problem further by reinforcing the cohesiveness of the in-group. Other equally disadvantaged groups provide a kind of scapegoat against whom to express the hostility intended for the broader society. Realistic or perceived barriers to social mobility through legitimate channels, one of which is longer years of schooling, weakens the drive to succeed at school, especially since success requires skills which the disadvantaged youth has often been unable to master. These perceptions reinforce the search for activities which lead to actual immediate gain or to fantasies of "easy money" in the future.

Added to these problems are those related to the orientation to present as against future gratification. The inability to view schooling as a necessary preparation for later reward, especially when it is perceived as interfering with present gratification in terms of peer status, earning power or independence, leads to early drop-out, to involvement in activities leading to gratification of sexual and power needs, to a search for "kicks" and excitement or to illegal activities for immediate gain.

Statistical information about limited job opportunities and even more limited chances for mobility for those without a high school diploma is not enough to affect the individual's realization of what these statistics mean for him. Even more remote and external to the individual are the facts of a changing economy—the decrease in menial or even manual jobs and the increased demand for academically trained people.

The general academic inadequacy of the majority of disadvantaged pupils and their belief that worthwhile life activities can be found only outside the school create difficulties for those disadvantaged individuals who, for whatever reasons, are able to cope successfully with school tasks and would wish to identify with the values of the school and the broader society. Because there are few such individuals they find that excessive success in school is fraught with dangers. When the school population is composed entirely of a single ethnic group or an ethnically mixed but culturally disadvantaged group, there are not enough academically successful students to form a sufficiently strong subgroup to withstand the pressures of the street and the street gang which are often felt as physical hurt. Where the school population is mixed, and there is a group of white, middle-class children who conform to school expectations, the Negro or

Puerto Rican slum child is barred from social membership in such groups and thus may find the risk of identifying with its values too great.

Focus on the School

At some point the circular negative reinforcement has to be attacked. Perhaps the most accessible place is the school itself. One of the major issues confronting education today is to discover the means by which the school can compensate for the lack of readiness for learning which lower-class children, in general, and the Negro and other discriminated-against groups of children in particular, bring to their school work. The issue is not whether to imbue these children with middle-class values or to strengthen the positive aspects of their own unique cultural forms. The issue is, rather, to provide these children with the skills and knowledges which will enable them to select their future direction rather than be hemmed in by the increasingly limited sphere of operations left to those who lack these skills.

How then can modifications in school organization, curriculum, staffing, etc. shift the climate from one of failure and its consequent sense of inadequacy and antagonism to one of success? Where must the school begin? Can the school itself effect sufficient change in attitude and learning behavior to modify the social patterns of the disadvantaged children without a simultaneous frontal attack on the total social situation?

On the following pages are some suggested directions for research and school experimentation to test the hypothesis that the school can compensate for the early attitudinal and intellectual "unreadiness" for learning of culturally disadvantaged pupils. Because of the importance of the early years in the development of basic values and behavioral and cognitive modes, the emphasis in the suggestions for school modifications will be largely on the pre-school and elementary years.

Research Problems

Although a good deal is known about the nature of the learning problems in disadvantaged areas, there are still many questions which remain unanswered and require systematic research efforts:

1. One source of clues to compensatory school efforts which might prove effective can be found through an understanding of the *deviate* in the disadvantaged groups—the "good" learner. What accounts for the boy or girl who does well in school, is interested in pursuing higher education, enjoys reading and other schoolish activities even outside of school? The work of Reckless and his associates (20) suggests that there is a great difference in the self-image of the delinquency-prone boy who does

not actually come into conflict with the law and the boy from the same general level environment who does engage in delinquent acts. Although Deutsch (3) did not find any direct relationship between self-image and achievement, this might have been due, as he suggests, to the fear motivation for learning. Certainly, some pupils, even from the most disadvantaged homes, have successful school experiences with teacher who reach them through positive motivation. Who are these pupils, in what ways do their home relations differ from the rest, what was the image of school which they had before entering, what kinds of attitudes toward their own status and toward education do their parents have? All of these and other pertinent areas of investigation may shed light on pre- and in-school procedures which might raise the educational sights of disadvantaged children.

2. Because of its complex nature the city services many groups which differ socially, economically and ethnically. Although a good deal is known about the general educational aspirations of middle-class families, little systematic information is available about their attitudes toward their child's attendance at schools which service children of widely diverse backgrounds. Conversely, a systematic study of the attitudes of parents from disadvantaged groups is needed. This information becomes crucial when plans for cross-district or "open enrollment" are contemplated. Since many city neighborhoods tend to be highly homogeneous by class and ethnic group membership, artificial measures must be introduced to bring children from various backgrounds together, especially at the elementary and junior high school levels. The school expectations of the diverse groups may play a crucial role in determining the success of various "integration" measures.

3. The effects of the schools themselves on fostering or depressing achievement has been given minimum study. In some schools, even in depressed areas, pupils, in general, learn more, like school better and present fewer disciplinary problems. And within a single school some teachers are more successful than others. What combination of administration, supervision, personnel policies and parent involvement create these school to school differences? What personality characteristics, teaching styles, class-room organization or instructional methods discriminate between more and less successful teachers? Do teachers from lower-class backgrounds relate better to disadvantaged pupils than teachers raised in middle-class homes? Do Negro or Puerto Rican teachers work more effectively with children from their respective groups than do white teachers? There is little systematic evidence on any of these questions.

Nor is there sufficient understanding of the effects that various school climates have on raising or lowering pupils' educational and vocational aspirations. The work of Wilson (27) suggests that, in the predominantly lower-class school, middle-class boys do less well than do comparably able boys from similar families in predominantly middle-class schools. For example, of those whose fathers were either professionals or white collar workers, 66 per cent in middle-class high schools as against 39 per cent in predominantly lower-class high schools aspired to professional occupations. By the same token, 44 per cent of the children of manual workers who attended middle-class high schools as opposed to only 27 per cent from similar backgrounds in the lower-class schools aspired to professional vocations.

Differences in achievement were also influenced by the general school climate. For example, in the middle-class schools, half of the pupils from white collar families and 35 per cent from families of manual workers achieved median grades of "A" or "B" while only 18 per cent and 11 per cent, respectively, of the pupils of comparable background achieved those grades in the lower-class schools.

In view of the above findings, questions regarding the most desirable population composition of schools takes on special importance, especially where specific plans for moving pupils across neighborhood school lines are under way. But in addition to the general problem of the social class climate of the school, there is the question of the ethnic make-up. Does the proportion of Negro pupils transported into a predominantly white, middle-class school make a difference? Or is the caliber of the students perhaps more important than the number? The scant evidence available to date suggests that the positive social acceptance effects presumably associated with interracial contact do not necessarily materialize. In one city, where Negro pupils were moved into predominantly white schools, sociometric ratings found that the Negro pupils rated the white pupils higher than they did each other, while the white pupils rated each other higher than the Negroes. Thus, the Negro pupils showed lower acceptance of self as well as lower acceptance by others.[5] In a California (26) study, where white and Negro pupils from racially segregated elementary schools were placed in a newly integrated junior high school it was found that, for the white pupils, willingness to accept members of a Negro group was very low before integration and decreased during a year of contact. The willingness of the Negroes to accept white pupils was high on the pre-test and increased slightly after a year of integrated schooling.

Such results as those cited above raise some very important questions regarding pupil selection, pupil and parent preparation, and school per-

[5] Personal communication.

sonnel attitudes in planning for integration in those areas where *de facto* segregation is the rule.

Implications for School Experimentation

Many large cities have made deliberate efforts to study and improve the education of disadvantaged youth. Some of the suggestions for experimental programs which follow derive from various sources in the literature and to some extent overlap those already in operation.

1. **Pre-school education.** To compensate for the lack of "learning readiness" experiences characteristic of the pre-school years of the disadvantaged pupil, the school should experiment with carefully designed programs beginning no later than age three which will provide the child with verbal and symbolic experiences which lay the foundation for later academic achievement and which the middle-class pre-school child so often has at home. In addition, the pre-school years can provide opportunities for consistent success in the school setting and thus help develop positive attitudes toward school attendance. Such programs might differ considerably from the standard nursery school program, with a greater emphasis on experiences preparatory to school learning.

2. **The primary grades as preparatory to formal instruction.** As an extension of the concept of building up positive attitudes through a series of successful school experiences experimentation with the postponement of the introduction of formal school subjects (for those who have not had pre-school experiences) would be desirable. Because of their lack of background for dealing with symbolic material, it might be effective to consider the first two years of the elementary school as preparatory to the formal learning of the three R's (though arithmetic may be more readily introduced at an earlier age). In one long established independent school in New York City it was found that postponement of formal reading instruction until second grade resulted in the virtual elimination of the need for remedial reading instruction. Although the population of the private school differed greatly from the disadvantaged groups, the concept of postponing exposure to potentially defeating experiences is applicable. The first two years can be used to build up a reprtoire of verbal experiences, both speaking and listening;[6] to acquaint pupils with literature through story telling and records; to expose them to the resources of the city; to provide opportunities for self-government. But what is equally important, these learnings can proceed in the absence of the continuously

[6] In this connection Deutsch (3) found that in many instances pupils were not following directions because they did not hear what was asked since they had had so little exposure to spoken language beyond terse commands.

defeating experiences of being *wrong*, of not knowing the correct answer, of being viewed and viewing oneself as "stupid."

It could be hypothesized that after two or three years of preparation for learning in a stimulating and encouraging climate, disadvantaged pupils would be more successful in mastering formal learning.

One note of caution: to be meaningful, such programs would have to be rich in content and allow the pupils to feel that they are learning significant material. Both pupils and parents would be highly resistant if the first two elementary grades were no more than an extension of kindergarten, and were viewed as demeaning rather than as upgrading.

3. Male teacher. The lack of adequate male identification models in the homes of many of the disadvantaged boys suggests the need for male teachers even in the very early years. Since it is not possible to staff a sufficient number of classes with qualified male teachers, the use of male assistants or student teachers might be desirable. The long-term effects of contact with male models in the classroom should be studied.

4. Separation by sex. In view of the evidence on the significant differences in attitudes, self-concepts and achievement patterns of boys and girls, particularly in the Negro groups (and possibly in other ethnic populations which suffer from broken homes) separate classes for boys and girls might prove desirable. The lack of competition from apparently more successful girls might provide a more encouraging classroom climate for the boys. Since so many disadvantaged boys are surrounded by female authority both at home and at school, they may need to assert their "maleness" through transgressions against the female domination. Elementary school classes for boys with men teachers may provide an antidote to the largely female world in which so many of the boys live. It would also be desirable to test the effects of exposing them to male teachers of their own ethnic group which, theoretically, should increase the possibility of personal identification.

5. Changes in materials. The controversy over the kinds of materials appropriate for lower class pupils has raged for many years. Some contend that the texts should exemplify values which will "uplift" the pupils. Further arguments center around the desirability of focusing materials on the ethnic group from which the pupils come.

Perhaps some of these arguments could be settled by a shift from the suburban content and illustrations typical of most early text books to urban oriented material. The city apartment house rather than the one family house surrounded by lawns and flower beds; public transportation as well as the private automobile; fathers of many occupations rather than the typical businessman; all of these could form a part of the teaching materials of city children. Furthermore, if the material is truly derived from the life of the city, its content would have to be interracial and interethnic. The focus of the materials need not be limited to the present experiences of various groups of city dwellers, but could also include portrayal of the future opportunities which the city holds for them. Thus, the "either-or" nature of the controversy regarding teaching materials could be obviated.

Consideration might also be given to the development of textbooks without grade labels, providing at each reading level a series of books graded in content. With such materials, older pupils whose reading level may be low would be dealing with content appropriate to their age and interests.

6. The application of special methods. The social psychological research literature allows for several inferences regarding classroom procedures which might lead the disadvantaged child from this typical approach to problem solving to approaches which are more adaptive to academic success.

a. *Motor-oriented teaching.* From their study of expressive styles Miller and Swanson (14) concluded that ". . . if the teacher enables them [lower-class pupils] to express themselves with the large muscles of the torso and limbs, her students may make surprising educational progress." (p. 397). Other researchers have noted the emphasis on the concrete rather than symbolic approaches to problem solving, the great admiration for physical prowess, the tendency to respond physically or by physical conversation symptoms in psychological defense situations.

To what extent can approaches and materials be designed to allow the pupil to use his whole body in responding to problems? Can "acting-out" be substituted in the early stages for "talking about" or "writing down"? Can early dramatic play and later role playing be utilized as means for inducting the physically-oriented child into symbolic, verbal learning?

Reissman's contention that "teaching machines are likely to appeal to the deprived child" (21) because of his preference for a "doing" operation merits investigation in this connection. In fact, any technique which will allow those who can express themselves more effectively through motor than through verbal responses should be developed and introduced experimentally, accompanied by carefully controlled evaluation both in terms of immediate gains in achievement as well as in terms of attitudes toward learning and their effectiveness.

b. Use of tangible rewards. Many studies have pointed to the "present" as opposed to the "future" orientation of lower-class pupils. Their response tends to be more positive and their involvement greater when they are rewarded not only immediately but also tangibly (4). The symbolic type of reward of "right" or "that's good" such as the teacher may use or which acts as reinforcement in programmed instruction, is though immediate, too intangible to act as a motivating force for many disadvantaged pupils. In view of Deutsch's (3) inference that much of the learning that does take place is motivated by fear, perhaps the substitution of tangible, material rewards would produce a less fearsome and happier climate.

Again, such techniques would be worthwhile if they can be used transitionally, to provide the initial motivation to engage in the learning experience on the assumption that engagement will lead to successful accomplishment, and that this, in turn, will motivate future involvement.

c. Increasing the attention span. Discrepancies in attention span between middle-class and disadvantaged pupils of the same age have been found consistently. In his study, Deutsch, (3) for example, found that the Negro pupils tended to drop a problem when it became the least bit difficult and responded with "so what" to teacher-prodding. However, when engaged in work relating to Negro History week, these same pupils showed a level of involvement and concentration not observed in connection with other content. Reissman (21) suggests that although the "deprived child does not easily get into problems . . . once he does become involved, he is often able to work tenaciously for long stretches at a time." (p. 67). Such findings suggest the need for experimenting with learning tasks graduated in length and focused on content which will engage the learner. The development and experimental use of such material is strongly indicated.

7. Teacher education and reorientation. One of the most important areas for study relates to teacher education and reorientation. On the basis of investigations of the characteristics and procedures of more successful teachers, both the selection of teachers and their in-service education can be based on evidence of effective work with disadvantaged pupils.

a. Use of class time. The various purposes for which class time is used needs to be carefully analyzed. Deutsch's (3) finding that 50 to 80 per cent of all class time in the Negro school as compared to 30 to 50 per cent in the lower class white school was devoted to non-academic tasks suggests the need for reappraising the actual functioning of the teacher in the classroom. Perhaps there is a need for a series of precise "time-motion" studies of the teacher's day in order to discover how a greater portion of it might be devoted to actual teaching.

It would also be well to study the relative efficiency of devoting large blocks of time early in the year to the establishment and practice of routines as compared to using short periods over a longer time span for such purposes.

b. Modes of discipline. An analysis of the kinds of disciplinary actions which prove most effective could form part of a teacher reorientation program. Since most of the disadvantaged pupils are accustomed to responding to physical discipline and not to appeals to "goodness," or social acceptability, what techniques can the school use which will help reorient the pupil to respond to non-physical discipline? Or, are there forms of physical discipline which do not hurt the child but which he can accept and respond to? How can discipline be maintained in the class without developing a climate of fear and resentment? Some answers can be derived from observation of teachers who have minimal disciplinary problems; other insights might come from a systematic analysis of these activities in which the pupils tend to be more unruly and difficult to manage and those in which their involvement with the task is sufficient to keep them "out of trouble."

c. Accepting the disadvantaged child. There is some evidence to indicate that teacher ratings of pupil acceptability are related to the pupil's social class status. In a study of pupil self-ratings, and of how they believed their teachers saw them as well as teacher ratings of achievement and personality characteristics, Davidson and Lang (2) found that the more favorably a pupil viewed himself, the more favorably he expected to be viewed by the teacher; and that those who were rated higher on achievement, more often had a more favorable self-perception and anticipated a more favorable teacher rating. Although lower class pupils more often received unfavorable achievement ratings, differences in behavior ratings were not significantly different by social class. In general, favorability of teacher rating, though independently related both to social class and to pupil achievement, was more highly correlated with the latter than with the former. These findings suggest that a pupil's school performance affects his teacher's view of him more consistently than does his social class membership. However, it is highly probable that the lower-class poor achiever is viewed more negatively than the middle-class low achiever.

How can teachers be helped to accord pupils acceptance when they fail to meet desirable achievement standards and present behavior problems typical of disadvantaged children? To the extent that the child's feeling of acceptance by the teacher raises his estimate of himself, teacher responses to pupils might play a stronger part than expected in the development of the pupils' self-concepts.

d. *Openness to new teaching styles.* While the problem of accepting new methods and styles of teaching is common to many teachers, the need for trying totally new ways of working, which may well be indicated for the disadvantaged pupils, can create considerable teacher resistance and confusion. For example, teachers would need help with accepting such procedures as the postponement of formal reading instruction, the use of "acting out" procedures, the change from group to individualized instruction, etc. and would require concrete assistance in implementing such techniques.

The Need for Controlled Research

There are many areas in which changes in existing procedures should be tried and examined. The above are only examples. The advantages of individual versus group instruction; the role of guidance and psychological services; procedures for parent involvement and re-education; the relationship between the school and other social agencies; the problems of delinquency and the school's relation to law enforcement personnel and to the courts as well as many others need to be studied.

But in undertaking the development of new programs it is important to guard against the shortcomings which have characterized so many well intentioned programs. Unfortunately, in their zeal to do their very best for the disadvantaged pupils, schools have developed pilot programs which introduced many modifications simultaneously. For example, some cities have included increased guidance, remedial teaching, exposure to cultural resources, parent involvement, and many others. Such programs are expensive and require large numbers of specialized personnel so that, even if they prove successful, it is most difficult, if not impossible, to replicate the total program on a city-wide scale. But as they are generally organized, there is no way of discovering which of the modifications and in what combination are most effective. It is possible that one or two new approaches do as much as a whole host of changes. But how is one to know, except by testimonial—which is at best a questionable technique—which procedures really effected a change in the pupils.

Whatever additions or modifications a school undertakes should be so developed as to enable careful evaluation of the effectiveness of the particular procedures. Only in this way will we have sufficient evidence to plan adequate programs for disadvantaged pupils.

REFERENCES

1. Conant, James B., *Slums and Suburbs*, New York: McGraw-Hill, 1961.
2. Davidson, Helen H., and Lang, Gerhard, "Children's Perception of Their Teacher's Feelings Toward Them Related to Self-Perception, School Achievement and Behavior," *J. exp. educ. Psychol.*, 1960, 29:2:107-118.
3. Deutsch, Martin, *Minority Group and Class Status as Related to Social and Personality Factors in Scholastic Achievement*, Monograph No. 2, Ithaca, New York: Society for Applied Anthropology, 1960.
4. Douvan, Elizabeth, "Social Status and Success Strivings," *J. abnorm. and soc. Psych.*, 1956, 52:219-223.
5. Dunham, H. Warren (Ed.), *The City in Mid-Century*, Detroit: Wayne State University Press, 1957.
6. Eels, Kenneth, Davis, Allison, Havighurst, R. J., Herrick, Virgil E., and Tyler, Ralph, *Intelligence and Cultural Differences*, Chicago: University of Chicago Press, 1951.
7. Goodman, Paul, *Growing Up Absurd*, New York: Random House, 1960.
8. Haggard, Ernest A., "Social Status and Intelligence: an Experimental Study of Certain Cultural Determinants of Measured Intelligence," *Genet. psychol. Monogr.*, 1954, 49:141-186.
9. Jacobs, Jane, *The Death and Life of Great American Cities*, New York: Random House, 1961.
10. Kahl, Joseph A., "Educational Aspirations of 'Common Man' Boys," *Harv. educ. Rev.*, 1953, 23:186-203.
11. Kasindorf, Blanche Robins, *Pupil Transiency in the Elementary and Junior High Schools, School Year 1959-1960*, Pamphlet No. 166. Board of Education of the City of New York. Bureau of Educational Program Research and Statistics.
12. Klineberg, Otto, *Negro Intelligence and Selective Migration*, New York: Columbia University Press, 1935.
13. Lee, Everett S., "Negro Intelligence and Selective Migration," *Amer. sociol. Rev.*, April 1951, 16:2:227-233.
14. Miller, David R., and Swanson, Guy E., *Inner Conflict and Defense*, New York: Henry Holt, 1960.
15. Mills, C. Wright, Senior, Clarence, and Golden, Rose K., *The Puerto Rican Journey*, New York: Harper, 1950.
16. Moriber, Leonard, *School Functioning of Pupils Born in Other Areas and in New York City*, Pamphlet No. 168, Board of Education of the City of New York, Bureau of Educational Program Research and Statistics, May 1961.
17. Mumford, Lewis, *The City in History*, New York: Harcourt, Brace and World, 1961.
18. New York City Board of Education. *Special Census of School Population, October 31, 1961, Summary Tables*, Pamphlet No. 189. The Board, Bureau of Educational Program Research and Statistics, May 1962.
19. Queen, Stuart A., and Carpenter, David B., *The American City*, New York: McGraw-Hill, 1953.
20. Reckless, W., Dinitz, S., and Murray, E., "Self-Concept as an Insulator Against Delinquency," *Amer. sociol. Rev.*, December 1956, 21:744-746.
21. Riessman, Frank, *The Culturally Deprived Child*, New York: Harper, 1962.

22. Siller, Jerome, "Socioeconomic Status and Conceptual Thinking," *J. abnorm. soc. Psychol.,* November 1957, 55:3:365-371.
23. Srole, L., Langner, T. S., Michael, S. T., Opler, Marvin K., and Rennie, T. A. C., *Mental Health in the Metropolis: the Midtown Manhattan Study,* Volume 1, New York: McGraw-Hill, 1962.
24. Tyler, T. T., "Comments on the Correlational Analysis Reported in Intelligence and Cultural Differences," *J. educ. Psychol.,* 1953, 44:288-295.
25. Vernon, Raymond, *Metropolis 1985,* Cambridge, Mass.: Harvard University Press, 1960.
26. Webster, Staten W., "The Influence of Interracial Contact on Social Acceptance in a Newly Integrated School," *J. educ. Psychol.,* 1960, 52:6:292-296.
27. Wilson, Alan B., "Class Segregation and Aspirations of Youth," *Amer. sociol. Rev.,* December 1959, 24:6:836-845.
28. *World Almanac and Book of Facts for 1962,* New York: World Telegram and Sun, 1962.

PART II

Psychological Aspects of Education in Depressed Areas

In its *Master Plan for Human Redevelopment,* the Baltimore Area Health and Welfare Council describes the recognizable characteristics of its "hard core," "multi-problem," "culturally-deprived," "disorganized" families in the depressed areas of the city as follows:

Many do not understand, or are not in contact with, modern urban living;

Many are participants in subcultures, the values and customs of which are different from urban middle class values and experiences;

Many, particularly children and youth, suffer from the disorganizing impact of mobility, transiency, and minority group status;

Many have educational and cultural handicaps arising from backgrounds of deprivation;

Many are members of families with many problems: divorced, deserted, unemployed, chronically sick, mentally ill, retarded, delinquent;

Many lack motivation or capacity to cope with their problems or to improve their situations;

Most lack opportunities or motivation to become responsible citizens for the maintenance or improvement of their neighborhood or community.[1]

How pervasive is the psychological impact of conditions in America's grey areas on the educational performance of children and the development of their individual potential? The full extent is difficult to assess. Concentrating on bare economic survival, parents in depressed areas can give little attention to stimulating their children's intellectual growth, planning for the educational future, or even preparing them for the demands of the classroom. Academic retardation and non-promotion; discipline

[1] Health and Welfare Council of the Baltimore Area, Inc. "A Letter to Ourselves: A Master Plan for Human Redevelopment," mimeographed report, Baltimore: the Council, January 18, 1962, p. 3.

and behavior problems; poor test performance, especially on tests of general intelligence and scholastic aptitude; poor motivation for academic work; apathy, withdrawal, and contempt for assignments and classroom activities; open hostility or conflict with teacher and school norms; high drop-out rate—these are some of the problems faced by a school having large numbers of children from homes in depressed areas. These problems vary in nature, extent, and intensity among different cities and different ethnic and racial groups.

There are large variations in the scholastic performance of different groups; not all minority or in-migrant groups present the same educational problems. Moreover, and perhaps more significantly, the variations within the group are as great as the inter-group diversity. This range of differences underscores the need for better delineation of the nature and meaning of "cultural deprivation." What are the salient characteristics of disadvantaged children to consider in educational planning? In what ways, if any, is disadvantaged status related to race, to ethnic origins, to point of origin of in-migration, to socio-economic class, to recency of arrival in the slum area? What are the psychological effects of discrimination and segregation in housing, employment opportunities, and education on the children and what accounts for the different ways that individuals respond to these barriers? Why do individuals and groups react differently to the discrepancy between personal aspirations for culturally defined success goals and the realistic possibilities for attaining these ends by legitimate means? Which specific aspects of the "culture of the slums" account for the easy abandonment of basic scholastic goals? Which aspects affect the alienation from the dominant forms of a middle-class society? Are there specific aspects of life in a disadvantaged neighborhood which shape personality, attitude, and motivation? What are the differences between the achievers and the non-achievers and what accounts for these variations from seemingly similar family structures, neighborhoods, and racial or ethnic groups? What are the "positive" aspects of life in disadvantaged areas that have meaning for educational planners?

Dark skin color and its psychological impact on the child's perception of his social status, his personal worth, his self-esteem and his educational and vocational aspirations are examined in the first paper. The problems call for varied family, school, and community measures to upgrade the child's aspiration level and standards of achievement so that he will be able to seize new opportunities in education, employment, housing and other areas of life as these are opened to him. The second paper re-emphasizes the historical role of education as one of the most effective means for social mobility; challenges the schools to modify curriculum and materials and create the conditions for building "a positive self-esteem to supplant the feelings of inferiority and sense of hopelessness which are supported by an all too-pervasive pattern of social realities." The third paper deals with the effects of impoverished circumstances on reading and learning disabilities, as well as general adjustment to life. The combination of factors in the early formative years serves these children poorly for academic life, while it diminishes the effectiveness of the school as a major institution for socialization and acculturation.

Professor and Mrs. David Ausubel review the psychological research on the personality development of children from economically and racially segregated families. They examine the nature of and bases for individual behavioral differences within disadvantaged groups and consider the implications of these studies for school policies and practices. Their focus is on the factors affecting ego-development—the growth of the individual's self-image, motivations, and personality traits as these affect his aspirations and his drive toward goals. Educational problems of segregated Negro children, the Ausubels observe, are bound up with other cultural forces which negate opportunities for status—forces which mold "significant differences in self-esteem, in aspirations for achievement, in personality adjustment, and in character structure." These same family, school and subcultural patterns retard academic progress, depress educational goals, and lower vocational aspirations.

The Ausubels contend that significant changes in the ego structure of Negro children are needed and that these can be brought about in two complementary ways: the elimination of all aspects of inferior and segregated caste status and the initiation of various measures in the family, school, and community to build self-esteem and to enable the Negro to take full advantage of the new opportunities open to him. While no panacea in itself, the desegregated school is seen as "an important and indispensable first step in the reconstitution of Negro personality, since the school is the most strategically placed social institution for effecting rapid change both in ego structure and in social status." Professor Ausubel counsels "natural" desegregation of schools through changing housing and neighborhood patterns, rather than through "artificial" administrative means—assuming that district lines have not been gerrymandered. Since ego-development is the product of interpersonal relations (in family, neighborhood, and school), real desegregation grows out of relations in daily situations where children can interact positively.

Since counselors in depressed urban-area schools act, to a large extent, *in loco parentis,* Ausubel suggests that there may be some advantage to Negro counselors for Negro children. The counseling role is one of dealing, primarily on an individual or small group basis, with adaptive and value problems—raising aspirational levels, helping with personal adjustment, bridging school-neighborhood cultural gaps, assisting with development of transitional and coping mechanisms, and working with parents to raise the level and stability of the home. There appears to be some evidence that the Negro child can identify better with persons of his own race, can be less suspicious of the counselor's motives. A Negro counselor, having presumably overcome many of the minority-group ego problems himself, may be more sensitive to the child's problems and therefore, may reach rapport with the child more quickly. However, other aspects of the intricate pupil-counselor relationship rule out automatic matching of races and groups.

Realistic vocational guidance considers individual interests, aptitudes, skills, and job opportunities without repressing aspirations on the basis of present employment restrictions. Sociological and technological trends challenge the young Negro, requiring him to alter his ego "so that he desires and is able to achieve a level of educational and vocational training that would make it possible for him to compete successfully with whites in modern industrial society." The problem of raising aspirational and achievement levels among minority groups is especially acute because "comfortable adjustment" to segregated caste status is no longer possible and because automation has eliminated many unskilled jobs.

Professor Kenneth B. Clark underscores the crucial role of the school in determining the level of scholastic achievement, arguing that standards and quality of education need not be lowered by the limitations of the home and the immediate neighborhood from which the children come. Far more significant in determining level of academic achievement are the general attitudes of teachers toward their students and the manner in which these are communicated. Too many teachers, Clark suggests, maintain "the pervasive and archaic belief that children from culturally deprived backgrounds are by virtue of their deprivation or lower status position inherently uneducable."

Professor Clark proposes that schools "break through the barrier of IQ depression," since many ideas about the IQ are more relevant to assumptions about class than about education. He sees the IQ scores setting ceilings which serve as self-fulfilling prophecies: "when a child from a deprived background is treated as if he is uneducable because he has a low test score, he becomes uneducable and the low test score is thereby reinforced." To Professor Clark, homogeneous grouping burdens children with resentment and humiliation, while masking significant individual differences in aptitudes, interests, and abilities among children of the same IQ range. Grouping by ability, Clark maintains, may create as many problems and stigmas as segregating by race.

Schools must provide extra stimulation and encouragement for children from lower status groups to compensate for past deprivations and to build positive self-esteem, supplanting feelings of inferiority and hopelessness. To increase motivation for scholastic attainment and to enhance self-concepts, schools must provide "a single standard of academic expectations, a demanding syllabus, and skillful and understanding teaching." Too often, Clark argues, low expectations and standards, weak educational stimulation, and poor teaching have reinforced a sense of failure among culturally disadvantaged children already vulnerable to inferiority feelings and personal humiliation. Even textbooks and instructional materials may "directly or indirectly add to the burdens of already psychologically overburdened, disadvantaged minority-group children." It is harder to suggest the dimensions of new and more appropriate materials than to recognize the deficiencies in the present textbooks.

Clark cautions against fragmentary approaches to improving the effectiveness of education for children in depressed urban areas. He urges bold, imaginative and comprehensive planning—characteristics he ascribes to New York City's Demonstration Guidance Project. The two essential ingredients of successful education for these children are belief in their educability and respect for them as human beings.

Professor Martin Deutsch assays the impact of social and developmental factors on the intellectual growth and academic achievement of culturally disadvantaged children in urban depressed areas. His thesis—quite different from that of Professor Clark—is that the "lower-class child enters the school situation so poorly prepared to produce what the school demands that initial failures are almost inevitable and the school experience becomes negatively rather than positively reinforced." Dr. Deutsch examines the environmental and psychological factors that barely equip children from depressed areas for the learning tasks and for the behavioral requirements that schools expect of middle-class youngsters. Stimulus deprivation, experiential poverty, and inadequate training in auditory and visual discrimination all handicap the culturally disadvantaged child for primary school. Discussing the significance of language development and the language-symbolic process in all learning, Deutsch observes that early verbal impoverishment may contribute heavily to the child's disadvantage.

Professor Deutsch recommends, in addition to considerable verbal enrichment, orienting the lower-class child to an understanding of what school is all about and why he is there. The focus should shift away from the school's problems in relating traditional curriculum and teaching procedures to this child; its fix ought rather to be the "enormous confusion, hesitation, and frustrations the child experiences and does not have the language to articulate when he meets an essentially rigid set of academic expectations." In exploring the educational factors and school conditions, Deutsch calls for clearer definition of the problems of urban education, flexible experimentation with new methods, better training and orientation of teachers and administrators to the required learning procedures. In his own research, Deutsch is studying the effects of a pre-school enrichment program for three- and four-year olds, testing the hypothesis that "early intervention by well-structured programs will significantly reduce the attenuating influence of the socially marginal environment." Deutsch would put his emphasis on working with young children, pre-schoolers and kindergarteners and their parents, on the assumption that the younger the child the greater the greater the possibilities of reversing the effects of cultural deprivation. More ways of linking the school's work with the home are needed. Parents could be of considerable help if trained to aid their children, since they are often embarrassed by their own ignorance.

These questions were outgrowths of the discussions which followed an examination of some of the psychological aspects of education in depressed areas. Do culturally disadvantaged children learn differently from other children; are they more prone to certain kinds of learning disabilities? What insights from learning theory provide clues to the problems encountered by the youngsters from depressed areas? Have the inadequacies been diagnosed exactly or has the focus been on the symptoms—poor reading and language skills, for example? What special modifications in teaching methods and materials can overcome academic difficulties? Better still, how can we systematize the selection and organization of experiences, materials, methods and services, in the context of ideas about deprivation? Certainly, there needs to be greater emphasis on many different kinds of verbal experiences. As was pointed out in the discussions, youngsters who have a limited classroom vocabulary may have an unexpected range of expressions which are either overlooked or restrained by the teacher because of its vivid, colorful nature. Starting with the expressive vocabulary and building towards more acceptable language patterns by using whatever structure is required may help overcome the verbal deficit. Instructional materials fitting the background and experiences of a particular group of children may help compensate for verbal deprivation. Of the wealth of available books, games, workbooks, specialized reading equipment, remedial devices, and other materials, which has a special appeal for youngsters with limited verbal backgrounds?

The plight of the culturally deprived youngster has been described by Professor Deutsch's Institute for Developmental Studies as follows:

Not only do they fall behind in the basic skills, such as reading and arithmetic, but they also respond minimally to the broader aspect of the function of the school: the instilling of a respect for knowledge, the fostering of the development of the cognitive skills necessary for acquiring knowledge, and that general function of equipping a child to live as a responsible citizen.[2]

What kinds of educational enrichment experiences will increase the disadvantaged child's appetite for school tasks and their accomplishment? Should he enter school earlier than middle-class children? How much stress should be placed on the pre-school variables in program planning? What kind of nursery and pre-school programs does he need? Can early curriculum enrichment foster essential cognitive skills and enhance motivation for school achievement? Can reinforcement boast the child's ability to learn those things which the school rates important? What is the nature of reinforcing experiences? To what extent must parents be involved in early educational programs? Should the school undertake parent education programs in home management, child care, and the expansion of cultural activities?

The question of assessment of individual potential among disadvantaged children was raised and explored. While there was general agreement on the shortcomings of group intelligence tests with culturally and verbally deprived children, alternative means of assessment are not readily available. How can performance be used as a symptom for prediction of potential, without setting limits on instruction?

The responses of individuals to the psychological and social conditions in depressed urban areas vary widely, for obscure reasons. Can these differences be identified early enough for the school to differentiate its offerings? Should the school adapt itself to individual variations in need gratification; how should it modify the use of rewards and reinforcement?

To what extent does the family influence the aspirations, motivations, and attitudes toward school, toward education, toward a view of life opportunities? What aspects of the home background contribute to the lack of school achievement: for example, language patterns, child-rearing methods, physical surroundings, female or male dominance, diet, family stability, play materials? What is the responsibility of the school for working with families? What members of the staff can work best with families? Does it reassure parents to have visiting teachers or social workers of their

[2] Institute for Development Studies, *Descriptive Statement.* New York: New York Medical College, 1960, p. 1.

own ethnic or racial group? What measures are needed to help recent immigrants adjust to urban life? What should be the nature and extent of their assimilation?

The psychological impact of life in a depressed area affects the motivation, the aspiration, the release of potential of the individual. Understanding the nature and perimeters of this impact could provide guides for better educational planning in the school, in the home, in the community.

David P. Ausubel and Pearl Ausubel | Ego Development Among Segregated Negro Children

Ego development refers to the orderly series of changes in an individual's self-concept, self-attitudes, motives, aspirations, sources of self-esteem, and key personality traits affecting the realization of his aspirations as he advances in age in a particular cultural setting. It obviously varies from one individual to another within a particular culture or sub-culture in accordance with significant temperamental traits and idiosyncratic experience. Nevertheless, it manifests a certain amount of intra-cultural homogeneity or intercultural difference because of culturally institutionalized differences in interpersonal relations; in opportunities for and methods of acquiring status; in prescribed age, sex, class, and occupational roles; in approved kinds of personality traits; and in the amount and types of achievement motivation that are socially sanctioned for individuals of a given age, sex, class, and occupation.

For all of these reasons the ego development of segregated Negro children in America manifests certain distinctive properties. Negro children live in a predominantly lower-class subculture that is further characterized by a unique type of family structure, by specially circumscribed opportunities for acquiring status, by varying degrees of segregation from the dominant white majority, and, above all, by a fixed and apparently immutable denigration of their social value, standing, and dignity as human beings because of their skin color. Hence, it would be remarkable indeed if these factors did not result in significant developmental differences in self-esteem, in aspirations for achievement, in personality adjustment, and in character structure. In fact the Supreme Court decision of 1954 outlawing school segregation was based primarily on considerations of ego development. It recognized that school and other public facilities cannot be "separate and equal" because enforced and involuntary separateness that is predicated on purely arbitrary criteria necessarily implies an inferior caste status, and thereby results in psychological degradation and injury to self-esteem.

In the context of this conference on the education of culturally disadvantaged groups in depressed urban areas, our interest in the ego development of segregated Negro children obviously transcends mere theoretical considerations. Recent technological and sociological changes are confronting the American Negro with significant new challenges to his traditional role and status in our society. In the past it was possible for him to achieve some measure of stable adjustment to his inferior caste position, unsatisfactory though it was. He more or less accepted his devalued social status and second-class citizenship, aspired to low-level occupational roles requiring little education and training, found work in unskilled and menial occupations, and lived within his segregated subculture shunning contact and competition with whites. But two important changes are currently rendering this type of adjustment less and less tenable. In the first place, automation is rapidly decreasing the need for unskilled and uneducated labor in America. The poorly trained and poorly educated Negro youth who drops out of secondary school as soon as he reaches the minimum legal age, or fails to acquire some post-high-school technical training, finds himself at a much greater disadvantage in today's job market than was true of his father and older brother just a decade ago. He now lives in a wider culture in which a much higher level of educational and vocational training is a prerequisite for occupational adjustment, but he still grows up in a subculture that neither fosters aspirations for such education and training, nor provides the moral and material support necessary for their realization. Second, there are many indications that the Negro is no longer content with his segregated caste status and second-class citizenship. At the same time, however, he possesses a character structure and a repertoire of educational and vocational skills that, on the whole, do not prepare him to compete adequately with whites in the wider culture. In short, he is more desirous of participating in the unsegregated American culture, but lacks the personality traits and intellectual attainments that would enable him to do so effectively.

As educators, our job is to help the Negro child fill the new and more desirable place in American society that technological change and his elders' aspirations for equality are creating for him. Essentially this means altering his ego structure so that he desires and is able to achieve a level of educational and vocational training that would make it possible for him to compete successfully with whites in modern industrial society. It is true, of course, that the Negro's ego structure is largely a reflection of the actual social and legal status he enjoys in our culture; and as citizens it is our obligation to help him achieve equality of opportunity and equality before the law. But status and its reflection in self-esteem depend as much on real achievement as on equality of rights and opportunity. A changed ego structure, as manifested in higher educational and vocational aspirations, in the development of personality traits necessary for realizing these aspirations, and in the actual achievement of higher educational and vocational qualifications, can do as much to improve the Negro's status in society, and hence enhance his self-esteem, as can amelioration of his social and legal status. If, on the other hand, the Negro community cannot obtain our support in helping to mold the Negro youth's ego structure in ways that will eventually improve his competitive position in the employment market, he can only look forward to becoming permanently unemployable and subsisting on public assistance. This latter state of affairs would not only tend to perpetuate the Negro's lower-class and inferior caste position with its attendant adverse effects on ego development, but would also increase racial tensions and encourage anti-social behavior.

In this paper we propose to do three things. First, we would like to consider the personality development of the segregated Negro child as a special variant of the more typical course of ego development in our culture. Here the approach is normative, from the standpoint of a personality theorist interested in subcultural differences. In what ways does the ego development of segregated Negro children differ from that of the textbook child growing up in the shadow of our dominant middle-class value system? Second, we would like to consider some kinds of and reasons for individual differences within this underprivileged group. Do all Negro children in the Harlem ghetto respond in the same way to the impact of their segregated lower-class environment? If not, why not? Are there social class, sex, and individual differences among Negro children? Questions of this type would be asked by a personality theorist concerned with idiosyncratic and group variability within a subcultural setting, or by a psychiatrist treating the behavior disorders of such children in a Harlem community clinic. Finally, we propose to consider the implications of this material for such practical issues as educational practice and desegregation.

Overview of Ego Development in White Middle-Class Children

Before turning to a description of ego development in segregated Negro communities, it may be helpful to examine briefly the typical middle-class model with which it will be compared. In doing this we do not mean to imply that the developmental pattern in suburbia is necessarily typical of the American scene. Obviously only a minority of America's children live in the ecological equivalent of suburban culture. Nevertheless it is still a useful model for comparative purposes because it reflects the value system that dominates such official socializing institutions in our society as the school, the church, the youth organizations, the mass media, and the child-rearing manuals. Hence, it is the most widely diffused and influential model of socialization in our culture. It is the official model that most parents profess to believe in regardless of whether or not they practice it. It is the model that would most impress foreign anthropologists as typical of American culture.

The infant in suburbia, as in many other cultures, may be pardoned for entertaining mild feelings of omnipotence (7). Out of deference for his manifest helplessness, his altruistic parents are indulgent, satisfy most of his needs, and make few demands on him. In view of his cognitive immaturity, it is hardly surprising then that he interprets his enviable situation as proof of his volitional power than as reflective of parental altruism. As he becomes less helpless and more responsive to parental direction, however, this idyllic picture begins to change. His parents become more demanding, impose their will on him, and take steps to socialize him in the ways of the culture; and by this time the toddler has sufficient cognitive maturity to perceive his relative impotence and volitional dependence on them. All of these factors favor the occurrence of satellization. The child surrenders his volitional independence and by the fiat of parental acceptance and intrinsic valuation acquires a derived or attributed status. As a result, despite his marginal status in the culture and manifest inability to fend for himself, he acquires feelings of self-esteem that are independent of his performance ability. He also internalizes parental values and expectations regarding mature and acceptable behavior.

In suburbia, derived status constitutes the cornerstone of the child's self-esteem until adolescence. Beginning with middle childhood, however, forces are set in motion which bring about preliminary desatellization from parents. Both in school and in the peer group he is urged to compete for a primary status based on his academic proficiency, athletic prowess and social skills. School and peer groups legislate their own values, impose their own standards, and also offer him a subsidiary source of derived status insofar as they accept him for himself in return for his loyalty and self-subordination. All of these factors tend to devalue the parents and to undermine their omniscience in the child's eyes. The home becomes only one of several socializing agents that foster the development of aspirations for academic and vocational success and of the pattern of deferred gratification necessary to achieve them. Nevertheless, until adolescence, parents remain the major socializing agents and source of values in the child's life. Compared to the derived status obtained from parents, the primary status available in school and peer group plays only a subsidiary role in the total economy of ego organization.

Ego Development in Young Negro Children

Social-class factors. Many of the ecological features of the segregated Negro subculture that impinge on personality development in early childhood are not specific to Negroes as such, but are characteristic of most lower-class populations. This fact is not widely appreciated by white Americans and hence contributes to much anti-Negro sentiment: many characteristic facets of the Negro's value system and behavior pattern are falsely attributed to his racial membership, whereas they really reflect his predominant membership in the lower social class. Nevertheless, these characteristics are commonly offered as proof of the alleged moral and intellectual inferiority that is supposedly inherent in persons of Negro ancestry and are used to justify existing discriminatory practices.

Lower-class parents, for example, are generally more casual, inconsistent, and authoritarian than middle-class parents in controlling their children, and resort more to harsh, corporal forms of punishment (30, 31, 70, 71, 74). Unlike middle-class fathers, whose wives expect them to be as supportive as themselves in relation to children, the lower-class father's chief role in child rearing is to impose constraints and administer punishment (74). Even more important, lower-class parents extend less succorant care and relax closely monitored supervision much earlier than their middle-class counterparts (29, 30, 35, 54). Lower-class children are thus free to roam the neighborhood and join unsupervised play groups at an age when suburban children are still confined to nursery school or to their own backyards. Hence, during the pre-school and early elementary-school years, the lower-class family yields to the peer group much of its role as socializing agent and source of values and derived status. During this early period lower-class children undergo much of the desatellization from parents that ordinarily occurs during middle childhood and preadolescence in most middle-class families. They acquire earlier volitional and executive independence outside the home and in many cases assume adult responsibilities such as earning money and caring for younger siblings. Abbreviated parental succorance, which frustrates the dependency needs of middle-class children and commonly fosters overdependence (100), has a different significance for and effect on these lower-class children. Since it reflects the prevailing subcultural norm, and since the opportunity for early anchorage to a free-ranging peer group is available, it tends to encourage the development of precocious independence.

This pattern of precocious independence from the family combined with the exaggerated socializing influence of the peer group, although characteristic of both white and Negro lower-class children, does not necessarily prevail among all lower-class minority groups in the United States. Both Puerto Rican (3) and Mexican (75) children enjoy a more closely-knit family life marked by more intimate contact between parents and children. In Mexican families, maternal and paternal roles are also more distinctive, masculine and feminine roles are more clearly delineated in childhood, and the socializing influence of the peer group is less pronounced (75).

The working-class mother's desire for unquestioned domination of her offspring, her preference for harsh, punitive, and suppressive forms of control, and her tendency to maintain considerable social and emotional distance between herself and her children are probably responsible in part for the greater prevalence of the authoritarian personality syndrome in lower-class children than in middle-class children (36, 53, 69). Lower-class children tend to develop ambivalent attitudes toward authority figures and to cope with this ambivalence by making an exaggerated show of overt, implicit compliance, by maintaining formally appropriate social distance, and by interacting with these figures on the basis of formalized role attributes rather than as persons. Their underlying hostility and resentment toward this arbitrary and often unfair authority is later expressed in such displaced forms as scape-goating, prejudice, extremist political and religious behavior, ethnocentrism, and delinquency (36, 53, 69).

Much of the significant relationship between social-class status and school achievement undoubtedly reflects pervasive social-class differences in cognitive orientation and functioning that are operative from early childhood (15). Middle-class children are trained to respond to the abstract, categorical, and relational properties of objects, whereas lower-class children are trained to respond more to their concrete, tangible, immediate, and particularized properties. This difference in perceptual disposition is carried over into verbal expression, memory, concept formation, learning and problem-solving. Hence, since schools place great emphasis on the learning of abstract relationships and on the abstract use of language, lower-class children, on the average, experience much greater difficulty than middle-class children in mastering the curriculum.

Racial factors. All of the foregoing properties of the lower-class environment also apply to the segregated Negro community. Most authorities on Negro family life agree that well over 50 per cent of Negro families live at the very lowest level of the lower-class standard (56). In addition, however, Negro families are characterized by a disproportionate number of illegal and loosely connected unions (56). Illegitimacy is a very common phenomenon and is associated with relatively little social stigma in the Negro community (20); nevertheless, illegitimate Negro children, especially at the older age levels, are significantly inferior to their legitimate counterparts in IQ, school achievement, and personal adjustment (59).

Negro families are much more unstable than comparable lower-class white families. Homes are more apt to be broken, fathers are more frequently absent, and a matriarchal and negative family atmosphere more commonly prevails (25, 28, 34, 56). Thus the lower-class Negro child is frequently denied the benefits of bi-parental affection and upbringing; he is often raised by his grandmother or older sister while his mother works to support the family deserted by the father (34). One consequence of the matriarchal family climate is an open preference for girls. Boys frequently attempt to adjust to this situation by adopting feminine traits and mannerisms (28).

Negro family life is even more authoritarian in nature than is that of the lower social class generally. "Children are expected to be obedient and submissive" (56), and insubordination is suppressed by harsh and often brutal physical punishment (28, 31, 56). "Southern Negro culture teaches obedience and respect for authority as a mainspring of survival" (51). Surveys of high-school and college students show that authoritarian attitudes are more prevalent among Negroes at all grade levels (50, 51, 108).

Being a Negro also has many other implications for the ego development of young children that are not inherent in lower-class membership. The Negro child inherits an inferior caste status and almost inevitably acquires the negative self-esteem that is a realistic ego reflection of such status. Through personal slights, blocked opportunities, and unpleasant contacts with white persons and with institutionalized symbols of caste inferiority (segregated schools, neighborhoods, amusement areas, etc.) —and more indirectly through mass media and the reactions of his own family—he gradually becomes aware of the social significance of racial membership (45).

As a consequence of prejudice, segregation, discrimination, inferior status, and not finding himself respected as a human being with dignity and worth,

. . . the Negro child becomes confused in regard to his feelings about himself and his group. He would like to think well of himself but often tends to evaluate himself according to standards used by the other group. These mixed feelings lead to self-hatred and rejection of his group, hostility toward other groups, and a generalized pattern of personality difficulties (58, p. 146).

Segregation

. . . means that the personal worth, of either a white or Negro person, is measured solely by group membership regardless of individual merit. Such a measure is realistically false and of necessity distorts the developing self-image of Negro and white children as well as their view of each other. Under these psychological circumstances the Negro child, for example, is burdened with inescapable inferiority feelings, a fixed ceiling to his aspiration level which can constrict the development of his potentialities, and a sense of humiliation and resentment which can entail patterns of hatred against himself and his own group, as well as against the dominant white group (14, p. 151).

The Negro child perceives himself as an object of derision and disparagement (45), as socially rejected by the prestigeful elements of society, and as unworthy of succorance and affection (34); and having no compelling reasons for not accepting this officially sanctioned negative evaluation or himself, he develops a deeply ingrained negative self-image (14, 123).

It does not take long for Negro children to become aware of the unfavorable implications of their racial membership. In interracial nursery schools, most children show some type of racial awareness at the age of three (115), and this awareness increases rapidly between the ages of 3 and 7 (116). Once aware of racial differences, they soon learn that "skin color is important, that white is to be desired, dark to be regretted" (68). Very significantly, racial self-recognition develops later in Negro than in white children (77, 116); in the light of doll play evidence indicating that they resist identifying with their own stigmatized racial group (23), this delay in racial self-recognition can only be interpreted as reluctance in acknowledging their racial membership.

All of the sociometric rejection and maltreatment experienced by Negro children in a mixed group cannot, of course, be attributed to their inferior caste status alone. Some of the victimization undoubtedly reflects the dynamics of a majority-minority group situation. Thus, when white children are in the minority, the values, judgments, and verbal expression of the Negro majority tend to prevail (96). Under these conditions, Negroes curse whites but the latter do not openly retaliate despite revealing anti-Negro prejudice to white investigators (96).

In addition to suffering ego deflation through awareness of his inferior status in society, the Negro child finds it more difficult to satellize and is denied much of the self-esteem advantages of satellization. The derived status that is the principal source of children's self-esteem in all cultures is largely discounted in his case since he can only satellize in relation to superordinate individuals or groups who themselves possess an inferior and degraded status. Satellization under such conditions not only confers a very limited amount of derived status but also has deflationary implications for self-esteem. We can understand, therefore, why young Negro children resist identifying with their own racial group, why they seek to shed their identities (34), why they more frequently choose white than Negro playmates (116), why they prefer the skin color of the culturally dominant caste (23, 47, 68), and why they tend to assign negative roles to children of their own race (116). These tendencies persist at least into late adolescence and early adult life, insofar as one can judge from the attitudes of Negro college students. These students tend to reject ethnocentric and anti-white ideologies and to accept authoritarian and anti-Negro propositions (114).

Ego Development in Older Negro Children and Adolescents

Social-class factors. During middle childhood and preadolescence the ego development of the segregated Negro child also reflects the influence of both general social class factors and of more specific racial factors. As already pointed out, early experience in fending for himself both in the wider culture and in the unsupervised peer group, as well as in exercising adult-like responsibilities, accomplishes precociously much of the desatellization from and devaluation of parents characterizing the ego development of middle-class children during this period.

In these developments, the school plays a much less significant role among lower-class than among middle-class children. The lower-class child of school age has fewer illusions about parental omniscience for the teacher to shatter, and is coerced by the norms of his peer group against accepting her authority, seeking her approval, or entering into a satellizing relationship with her (30). School can also offer him very little in the way of either current or ultimate primary status. His parents and associates place no great value on education and do not generally encourage high aspirations for academic and vocational success, financial independence, or social recognition (30, 54, 97). It is hardly surprising, therefore, that lower-class children are less interested in reading than are middle-class children, have lower educational aspirations, take their schoolwork less seriously, and are less willing to spend the years of their youth in school in order to gain higher prestige and more social rewards as adults (30, 54, 97).

Even if they equalled middle-class children in these latter respects, academic achievement would still be quite a valueless reward for a child who soon comes to realize that professional status is beyond his grasp (30). Hence, anxiety regarding the attainment of internalized needs for vocational prestige does not drive the lower-class child to excel in school (30). Also, because of low achievement and discriminatory treatment, he fails to obtain the current rewards of academic success available to middle-class school children (30). On what grounds could a child immersed in an intellectually impoverished environment be expected to actualize his genic potentials for verbal and abstract thinking, when he is unmotivated by parental pressures, by ambitions for vocational success, or by the anxiety associated with realizing these ambitions?

Lower- and middle-class adolescents differ markedly both in their social value systems and in their vocational interests. Middle-class youths and their parents are more concerned with community service, self-realization, altruistic values, and internalized standards of conduct (60, 112), and prefer demanding, responsible, and prestigeful occupational pursuits (88, 89, 103). They also make higher vocational interest scores in the literary, esthetic, persuasive, scientific and business areas than do lower-class adolescents. The latter adolescents and their parents, on the other hand, place greater stress on such values as money, security, respectability, obedience, and conformity to authority, and tend to prefer agricultural, mechanical, domestic service, and clerical pursuits (88, 89, 103).

The lower-class child's *expressed* levels of academic and vocational aspirations often appear unrealistically high (34), but unlike the analogous situation in middle-class children, these do not necessarily represent his *real* or functional levels of striving. They more probably reflect impairment of realistic judgment under the cumulative impact of chronic failure (99) and low social status (48), as well as a compensatory attempt to bolster self-esteem through the appearance rather than the substance of aiming high. Lacking the strong ego involvement which the middle-class child brings to schoolwork, and which preserves the attractiveness of academic tasks despite failure experience (98), he quickly loses interest in school if he is unsuccessful. Finally, since he does not perceive the eventual rewards of striving and self-denial as attainable for persons of his status, he fails to develop to the same degree as the middle-class child the supportive traits of ego maturity necessary for the achievement of academic and vocational success (30). These supportive traits include habits of initiative and responsibility and the "deferred gratification pattern" of hard work, renunciation of immediate pleasures, long-range planning, high frustration tolerance, impulse control, thrift, orderliness, punctuality, and willingness to undergo prolonged vocational preparation (30, 54, 86, 97).

Despite having less deep-seated anxiety with respect to internalized needs for academic achievement and vocational prestige, children of lower-class families exhibit more signs of personality maladjustment than do children of middle-class families (4, 6, 57, 101, 102, 111). This greater degree of maladjustment is largely a response to the greater vicissitudes and insecurities of daily living; to the greater possibility and actual occurrence of failure in an educational and vocational world dominated by middle-class standards in which they are greatly disadvantaged; to inner tensions engendered by conflict between the values of the family and those of the dominant middle-class culture; to feelings of shame about family background that are associated with impulses to reject family ties; to feelings of guilt and anxiety about these latter impulses (102); and to the personal demoralization and self-derogation that accompany social disorganization and the possession of inferior social status (5, 7, 111). In most instances, of course, the symptoms of maladjustment are uncomfortable rather than disabling; but the generally higher level of anxiety, and the more frequent occurrence of motivational immaturity in lower-class children and adolescents, also increase the incidence of such serious disorders as schizophrenia, drug addiction, and anxiety neurosis and its various complications (7, 57, 111). Proneness to delinquency is, of course, higher among lower-class adolescents because of greater family and social disorganization, the deep-seated resentments and aggressive impulses attributable to socio-economic deprivation, the influence of organized, predatory gangs, and the tacit encouragement offered by the lower-class value system and the slum-urban teen-age cult of thrills, kicks, self-indulgence, violence, and non-conformity.

Racial factors. All of the aforementioned factors inhibiting the development of high level ego aspirations and their supportive personality traits in lower-class children are intensified in the segregated Negro child. His over-all prospects for vertical social mobility, although more restricted, are not completely hopeless. But the stigma of his caste membership is inescapable and unsurmountable. It is inherent in his skin color, permanently ingrained in his body image, and enforced by the extra-legal power of a society whose moral, legal, and religious codes proclaim his equality (123).

It is proper to speak of a stigma as being "enforced" when the stigma in question is culturally derived rather than inherent in the physical existence of the mark per se (that is, a mark of inferiority in *any* culture such as lameness or blindness). Dark skin color is a stigma in our culture only because it identifies a culturally stigmatized caste. When we speak of the stigma being "inherent in his skin color," we mean that it is a stigma which the Negro inherits by virtue of being born with that skin color in a culture that places a negative valuation on it. Hence the stigma "inheres" in the skin color. But this does not imply that dark skin color is inherently (that is, apart from a particular set of cultural values) a mark of inferiority; the stigma is only inherent for the individual insofar as he acquires it by cultural definition rather than by anything he does.

Hence, since a culturally derived stigma refers to an identifying char-

acteristic of a group which has been relegated to an inferiority status position in society, the stigma can only be perpetuated as long as the culture
provides some mechanism for *enforcing* the low status position of the
group in question. In the absence of cultural enforcement the stigma
would vanish in as much as it is not inherent in the characteristic itself but
is merely a symbol of membership in an inferior caste. In our society (unlike the Union of South Africa), there are no laws which explicitly create
an inferior caste status for the Negro; even segregation statutes accord him
a separate rather than an inferior status. Hence the "mark" is enforced
extra-legally by preserving through informal social practices the social inferiority of which the mark is but a symbol.

If this situation exists despite the authority of God and the Constitution,
what basis for hope does the Negro child have? It is not surprising, therefore, that, in comparison with lower-class white children, he aspires to
jobs with more of the formal trappings than with the actual attributes of
social prestige; that he feels impotent to strike back at his tormentors; that
he feels more lonely and scared when he is by himself; and that he gives
more self-deprecatory reactions when figuratively looking at himself in
the mirror (34). He may have less anxiety about realizing high-flown
ambitions than the middle-class child, but generalized feelings of inadequacy and unworthiness make him very prone to overrespond with anxiety
to any threatening situation. In view of the general hopelessness of his
position, lethargy, apathy, submission, and passive sabotage are more
typical than aggressive striving of his predominant reaction to frustration
(95, 105).

Rosen (95) compared the educational and vocational aspirations of
Negro boys (age 8 through 14) and their mothers to those of white, Protestant Americans, French Canadians, American Jews, Greek-Americans,
and Italian-Americans. The mean vocational aspiration score of his Negro group was significantly lower than the mean scores of all other groups
except the French Canadian. Paradoxically, however, 83 per cent of the
Negro mothers aspired to a college education for their sons.[1] Rosen concluded that although Negroes have been

. . . exposed to the liberal economic ethic longer than most of the other
groups . . . their culture, it seems, is least likely to accent achievement values.
The Negro's history as a slave and depressed farm worker, and the sharp discrepancy between his experience and the American Creed, would appear to

---

[1] Another datum at variance with the general trend of the evidence is Grossack's
finding that female Negro students in the South score significantly higher on need
achievement measures than do comparable white females, and that the males of
both groups are not significantly different (52).

work against the achievement values of the dominant white group. Typically, the Negro life-situation does not encourage the belief that one can manipulate his environment, or the conviction that one can improve his condition very much by planning and hard work (95, p. 55).

. . . Negroes who might be expected to share the prevalent American emphasis upon education, face the painfully apparent fact that positions open to educated Negroes are scarce. This fact means that most Negroes, in all likelihood, do not consider high educational aspirations realistic, and the heavy drop-out in high school suggests that the curtailment of educational aspirations begins very early (95, p. 58).

Ethnicity was found to be more highly related to vocational aspirations than was social class; sizable ethnic and racial differences prevailed even when the influence of social class was controlled. These results are consistent with the finding that white students tend to prefer "very interesting jobs," whereas Negro students are more concerned with job security (106).

The relatively low vocational aspirations of Negro children are apparently justified by the current facts of economic life. Negroes predominate in the unskilled occupations, receive less pay than whites for equivalent work, and exceed the percentage figured for whites in degree of unemployment (43, 105). In skilled occupations, Negroes are excluded at all educational levels (120): higher educational qualifications in Negroes are less frequently associated with higher-level vocational pursuits than they are in the case of whites (119). Thus,

. . . from long experience Negroes have learned that it is best to be prepared for the absence, rather than the presence of opportunity—or, at most, to prepare and strive only for those limited opportunities which have been open in the past. . . . Like most other people, Negroes tend to accept the views that prevail in the larger society about their appropriate role in that society, [and aspire and prepare] for only those positions where they are confident of acceptance (110, p. 461).

Negro children and lower-class white children who attend schools with a heterogeneous social class and racial population are in a more favorable developmental situation. Under these conditions, the unfavored group is stimulated to compete more aggressively, even to the point of unrealism (16, 109), with the more privileged group in every-day contracts and in aspirational behavior (16). In their self-judgments they compare themselves with *actual* models, who in fact are only slightly better off than they are, and hence do not feel particularly inferior (34). Negro children in segregated schools, on the other hand, are not only deprived of this stimulation, but in comparing themselves to other children paradoxically feel more depressed and less able to compete adequately (34), despite the fact that their actual contacts are confined to children in the incapsulated community who share their socio-economic status. Apparently then, they must use idealized mass media models as the basis for comparison.

Negro children are placed in the same ambivalent, conflictful position with respect to the achievement values of western civilization as are the children of many native peoples experiencing acculturation and the socio-cultural impact of rapid industrialization. On the one hand, exposure to the new value system and its patent and alluring advantages makes them less able to accept the traditional values of their elders; on the other hand, both loyalty to their families and the excluding color bar established by the dominant group make it difficult for them to assimilate the new set of values (9, 11, 12, 35, 81). Resentment and hostility toward the rejecting whites, as well as disillusionment regarding white middle-class values and institutions, predispose them arbitrarily and indiscriminately to repudiate the aspirations and personality traits valued by the dominant culture. These negativistic tendencies are even manifested in speech patterns: minority group children tend to reject the accepted model of speech that is symbolic of superordinate status in a social order that accords them only second-class membership (2).

Further abetting these tendencies toward resistive acculturation are many organized and institutionalized forms of nationalism and counter-chauvinism. Among the Maori, "resistance took the form of unadaptive but adjustive messianic and magical cults, emphasis on moribund and ceremonial features of the ancient culture, and indiscriminate rejection of progressive aspects of European culture" (9, p. 221). Numerous parallels can be found among the American Negro—for example, the Father Divine and Black Muslim movements.

One of the most damaging effects of racial prejudice and discrimination on the victimized group is that it provides an all-embracing rationalization for personal shortcomings, lack of striving, and antisocial conduct.

Some Negroes use the objective injustice of [creating scapegoats] as an opportunity to relieve or ward off feelings of personal inadequacy, self-contempt, or self-reproach by projecting all the blame onto white prejudice and discrimination. For other Negroes, however, reaction-formation becomes a main defense against the negative racial image. . . . Thus they may develop extremes of moralistic, prudish, and compulsively meticulous attitudes [to disprove the stereotype] (14, p. 152).

The Negro child is offered an excuse for anti-social behavior and evasion of social responsibility through feeling deprived of the social rewards for self-denial which are part of a healthy socialization process. But since these reactions are at variance with the democratic ideal of many other teachings to which children of both races are exposed at home, at church, and at school, they arouse of necessity feelings of inner conflict, confusion, anxiety, and guilt. These constitute liabilities for optimal adjustment (14, p. 152).

A continuing set of small incidents, closed doors, and blocked opportunities contribute to feelings of insecurity and mistrust and lead to the building of faith only in immediate gratifications and personal possessions (14, p. 148).

Withdrawal from Competition. An important factor helping to perpetuate the Negro's inferior social status and devalued ego structure is his tendency to withdraw from the competition of the wider American culture and to seek psychological shelter within the segregated walls of his own subculture. Such tendencies are particularly evident among middle-class Negroes who, instead of providing the necessary leadership in preparing their people to take advantge of new vocational opportunities in the emerging desegregated culture, often seek to protect their own vested interests in segregation. Negro businessmen, professionals, and teachers, for example, largely owe their clientele, jobs, and incomes to the existence of segregated institutions; furthermore, in the segregated community they do not have to meet the more stringent competitive standards prvailing in the wider culture (42, 93, 120). An additional complication is the fact that even though they "cannot escape altogether the discrimination and contempt to which Negroes are generally subjected" (42, p. 299), they tend to identify with the values and ideology of the white middle-class and to dissociate themselves from other Negroes (42, 93, 107, 110, 114). Together with pride of race and grudging affirmation of their racial identity, members of intellectual Negro families "are led to assert their superiority over other Negroes, and look down on those who are 'no account,' shiftless, and 'mean' " (93, p. 240).

The degree to which Negro potential can be developed in America depends, according to Smuts (110),

. . . not only on the willingness of the white community to grant greater opportunity to Negroes in the struggle for integrated schools and equal access to jobs; but it also depends at least as much on what the Negro community does to help its own members prepare themselves for new opportunities.... In a democracy, how well the individual develops and utilizes his potential depends not only on the opportunities that come his way as a youth and a man, but equally on his own determination to seek and make the most of opportunity (p. 456).

In the past the real world that Negroes had to adjust to included segregation, discrimination, absence of opportunity. But the facts are changing and a new kind of adjustment is called for (p. 461).... The development of high ambition and firm self-confidence among Negro youth is one prerequisite for the fuller development of Negro potential (p. 462).... In a competitive society

integration means competition, and successful competition requires at least
equal preparation (p. 458) .... Negroes will not be able to take full advantage
of [new] opportunities unless they improve their preparation for work (p.
458) .... Negro children cannot develop an image of themselves as free and
equal members of American society unless they see their elders actually living
that role (p. 463).

Educational aspirations and achievement of Negro children. Partly as
a result of unequal educational opportunities, Negro children show serious
academic retardation. They attend school for fewer years and, on the
average, learn much less than white children do (5, 17, 21, 82, 110, 113).
One of the chief reasons for this discrepancy is the inferior education and
training of Negro teachers who themselves are usually products of segregated education. The inequality of educational facilities exists not only in
the South (5, 17, 127), but also in the urban North as well, where, for the
most part, de facto segregation prevails (110, 113). Eighty-four per cent
of the top 10 per cent of Negro graduates in one southern high school
scored below the national mean on the Scholastic Aptitude Test (17).
Thus the incentive of reaching the average level of proficiency in the group
is not very stimulating for Negro children, since the mean and even the
somewhat superior child in this group are still below grade level. Teachers
in segregated schools also tend to be overly permissive and to emphasize
play skills over academic achievement; they are perceived by their pupils
as evaluating them negatively, and as more concerned with behavior than
with schoolwork (34).

Even more important perhaps as a cause of Negro educational retardation is the situation prevailing in the Negro home. Many Negro parents
have had little schooling themselves and hence are unable to appreciate its
value. Thus they do not provide active, wholehearted support for high-
level academic performance by demanding conscientious study and regular attendance from their children. Furthermore, because of their large
families and their own meager schooling they are less able to provide help
with lessons. Keeping a large family of children in secondary school constitutes a heavy economic burden on Negro parents in view of their low
per capita income and the substantial hidden costs of "free" education.
The greater frequency of broken homes, unemployment, and negative
family atmosphere, as well as the high rate of pupil turnover (25,104), are
also not conducive to academic achievement.

Negro pupils are undoubtedly handicapped in academic attainment by
a lower average level of intellectual functioning than is characteristic of
comparable white pupils. In both northern and southern areas, particularly the latter, Negro pupils have significantly lower IQs (19, 39, 80, 82),
and are retarded in arithmetic, reading, language usage, and ability to

handle abstract concepts (17, 82). The extreme intellectual impoverishment of the Negro home *over and above* its lower social-class status reflects the poor standard of English spoken in the home and the general lack of books, magazines, and stimulating conversation. In view of the educational and psychological inequality of segregated schools, the inferior intellectual status of Negro homes, and the negative motivational effects of membership in a socially stigmatized group, any inferences from the lower IQ's and educational retardation of Negro pupils regarding *innate* differences in intelligence are obviously unwarranted. Organic brain damage, however, is a more frequent occurrence in Negro children because of inadequate prenatal care and nutrition and because of the higher incidence of prematurity (85).

Similar kinds of family and community factors depress the vocational strivings and accomplishments of Negro youth. Practically all of the following description of the occupational aspirations of Maori adolescents in New Zealand applies to the Negro in America:

Maori parents are less sophisticated than their [European] counterparts about vocational matters and are accordingly less capable of assisting their children with appropriate information, advice, and guidance.... In view of their smaller incomes and larger families, Maori parents are also more reluctant to commit themselves to supporting plans requiring long-term vocational preparation (9, p. 623).

... Maori parents tend to adopt more permissive and laissez-faire attitudes than [European] parents toward their children's vocational careers. Despite occasional and inconsistent displays of authoritarianism in this regard, they are usually content to let them drift. They apply fewer coercive pressures and extend less support and encouragement in relation to the long-term occupational ambitions of their children. Their own values concerning vocational achievement and the example they set their children also tend to encourage the adoption of a short-term view. In practice they make few demands for the deferment of immediate hedonistic satisfactions and for the internalization of supportive traits consistent with high academic and occupational attainment (p. 623).

... [Still] another factor limiting the vocational achievement of Maori youth is the relatively low occupational status and morale of Maori adults. Young people lack the encouragement [of visible emulatory models], of a tradition and a high current standard of vocational accomplishment in the ethnic group. They are also denied the practical benefits of guidance and financial backing that would follow from the existence of such a standard and tradition. On the other hand, they are discouraged by the marginal economic position of their elders [and] by social demoralization (p. 624).

Maori pupils also receive less encouragement from their peers than [European] pupils do to strive for vocational achievement. Not only is occupational success less highly valued in the Maori than in the European peer culture, but the greater availability of *derived status*—based solely on membership in and intrinsic acceptance by the group—also removes much of the incentive for seeking *primary status* based on individual competence and performance. In districts where community morale is low and juvenile delinquency flourishes, vocational achievement tends to be negatively sanctioned (p. 624).

Low vocational aspirations, of course, are in large part a reflection of the distressingly high rate of unemployment among Negro youth in the urban slums. Conant reports that in one large city 48 per cent of male Negro high school graduates and 63 per cent of non-graduates were unemployed (25).

The tone is not one to encourage education or stimulate ambition. One often finds a vicious circle of lack of jobs and lack of ambition; one leads to the other. It is my contention that the circle must be broken both by upgrading the educational and vocational aspirations of slum youth and, even more important, by finding employment opportunity for them, particularly for high school graduates. It does no good whatever to prepare boys and girls for non-existent jobs (25, p. 36).

Finally, because of their precocious desatellization and emancipation from parents, Negro youths have greater needs for *immediate* financial independence. They therefore find psychologically more intolerable a prolonged period of psychological dependence on parents, such as would be required in preparing for a profession.

Personality adjustment. The destructive impact of prejudice, discrimination, segregation, an inferior caste status on self-esteem, in addition to the usual mental hygiene consequences of lower social class membership, result in a much higher incidence of behavior disorders in Negroes than in whites (51, 111, 128). Personality disturbance is also more highly correlated with intelligence test scores in Negroes than in whites (94). Quite understandably, both high anxiety level (83, 94) and suppressed feelings of aggression (61) are prominent symptoms of Negro maladjustment. Overt expression of these same aggressive impulses leads to a juvenile delinquency rate that is two to three times as high as among white teen-agers (37, 38). The occurrence of delinquent behavior is abetted by the high rate of unemployment (25) and by many characteristic features of lower-class Negro family life, such as illegitimate births, broken homes, desertion, neglect, employment of the mother, intra-familial violence, harsh punishment, and tolerance for minor dishonesties (20). Under these circumstances, aggressive antisocial behavior may be considered both a form of individual and social protest (38), as well as an effective means of obtaining and maintaining status in the peer group of the lower-class Negro subculture (22). Drug addiction, on the other hand, represents a particularly efficient type of "dead-end" adjustment for the hedonistic, motivationally immature adolescent who refuses to face up to the responsibilities of adult life (10, 41).

Sex Differences

One of the most striking features of ego development in the segregated Negro community is the relatively more favored position enjoyed by girls in comparison to the middle-class model. It is true that middle-class girls have certain advantages over boys in early ego development. Since girls perceive themselves as more highly accepted and intrinsically valued by parents (13) and have a more available emulatory model in the home (84), they tend to satellize more and longer. In addition to enjoying more derived status in the home, they can also acquire more primary status from household activities (84) and from school achievement. The opportunity for acquiring primary status in school is greater for girls than for boys because of their superior verbal fluency and greater conformity to adult authority, and because school success is less ambivalently prized by their peers. In general, girls are less negativistic (46), more amenable to social controls (66), and less alienated from adults.

Middle-class boys, however, are not excessively disadvantaged. Their mothers tend to prefer them to girls (100), and their fathers are responsible and respected status figures in the home and the principal source of economic security. Furthermore, although girls enjoy more current primary status during childhood, boys have higher ultimate aspirations for primary status; their aspirational level both for laboratory tasks (121) and for possessions and achievement (24) are higher. Unlike boys, girls do not *really* expect to prove their adequacy and maintain their self-esteem as adults by means of their vocational accomplishments. Their fathers are satisfied if they are "pretty, sweet, affectionate, and well-liked" (1). Finally, the superordinate position of men in our society, and the accompanying male chauvinism, is reflected in childhood sex roles. From an early age boys learn to be contemptuous of girls and their activities; and although girls retaliate in kind by finding reasons for deprecating the male sex, they tend to accept in part the prevailing view of their inferiority (65). Whereas boys seldom if ever desire to change sex, girls not infrequently wish they were boys (124). The male counterpart of a "tomboy" who relishes sewing and reads girls' books is indeed a rarity.

In contrast to this picture, we find girls in the *segregated* Negro community showing much greater relative superiority in academic, personal, and social adjustment (34). They not only outperform boys academically by a greater margin, but do so in all subjects rather than only in language skills (34). These girls have higher achievement needs (44, 52) and a greater span of attention; they are more popular with classmates; they show more mature and realistic aspirations; they assume more responsible roles; and they feel less depressed in comparing themselves with other children (3). Substantially more Negro girls than Negro boys complete every level of education in the United States (110). Adequate reasons for these differences are not difficult to find. Negro children in this subculture live in a matriarchal family atmosphere where girls are openly preferred by mothers and grandmothers, and where the male sex role is generally deprecated. The father frequently deserts the family and in any case tends to be an unreliable source of economic and emotional security (28, 34). Hence the mother, assisted perhaps by her mother or by a daughter, shoulders most of the burdens and responsibilities of child rearing and is the only dependable adult with whom the child can identify. In this environment male chauvinism can obtain little foothold. The preferential treatment accorded girls is even extended to opportunities for acquiring ultimate primary status. If the family pins all of its hopes on one child and makes desperate sacrifices for that child, it will often be a daughter in preference to a son.[2] Over and above his handicaps at home, the Negro boy also faces more obstacles in the wider culture in realizing his vocational ambitions, whatever they may be, than the Negro girl in fulfilling her adult role expectations of housewife, mother, nurse, teacher, or clerical worker (34).

It seems, therefore, that Negro girls in racially incapsulated areas are less traumatized than boys by the impact of racial discrimination. This is precisely the opposite of what is found in studies of Negro children from less economically depressed and less segregated environments (45, 117). The discrepancy can be attributed perhaps to two factors: (1) the preferential treatment accorded girls in the incapsulated community is more pervasive, unqualified, and continuous, and (2) the fact that, unlike Negro girls in mixed neighborhoods, these girls are less exposed to slights and humiliation from white persons. However, because of less tendency to internalize their feelings and greater openness in their social organization, Negro boys are able to adjust more easily than girls to the initial impact of desegregation (18).

Individual Differences in Reactions to the Segregated Negro Environment

Only extreme cultural determinists would argue that all children in the incapsulated Negro community necessarily respond in substantially identical ways to the impact of their social environment. Although com-

[2] In lower-class Puerto Rican and Mexican families, just the opposite situation is to be found; that is, male dominance and superiority prevail (40, 49, 75).

mon factors in cultural conditioning obviously make for many uniformities in personality development, genically determined differences in temperamental and cognitive traits, as well as differential experience in the home and wider culture, account for much idiosyncratic variation. Would it be unreasonable, for example, to anticipate that an intellectually gifted Negro child in this environment might have a different fate than an intellectually dull or average youngster; that an active, assertive, outgoing, and tough-skinned child might react differently to discriminatory treatment than one who is phlegmatic, submissive, sensitive, and introverted?

Differences in early socializing experience with parents are probably even more important, especially since they tend to generalize to interpersonal behavior outside the home. At this point it is worth noting that, generally speaking, racial discrimination affects children indirectly through their parents before it affects them directly through their own contacts with the wider culture. This indirect influence is mediated in two ways. (1) General parental attitudes toward the child are undoubtedly determined in part by the parent's own experience as a victim of discrimination. Some racially victimized parents, seeking retribution through their children, may fail to value them intrinsically and may place exaggerated emphasis on ego aggrandizement. Others may be so preoccupied with their own frustrations as to reject their children. Still others may accept and intrinsically value their children, and through their own example and strength of character encourage the development of realistic aspirations and mature, self-disciplined behavior. (2) Parents transmit to their children some of their own ways of responding to discrimination, such as counter-aggression, passive sabotage, obsequious submission, or strident counter-chauvinism. Individual differences such as these undoubtedly explain in part why some Negroes move into unsegregated neighborhoods and transfer to unsegregated schools when these opportunities arise, whereas other members of the race choose to remain in the segregated environment. The decision to transfer or not to transfer to an unsegregated school, for example, was found to be unrelated to both social class status and academic ability (27).

Much inter-individual variability therefore prevails in the reactions of children to minority group membership. Fortunately, sufficient time is available for establishing some stable feelings of intrinsic adequacy within the home before the impact of segregation on ego development becomes catastrophically destructive. It was found, for example, that Negro children who are most self-accepting also tend to exhibit more positive attitudes toward other Negro and white children (117), and that Negro college students who identify most with their own race tend to be least prejudiced against other minority groups (64). Hence, while appreciating the generally unfavorable effects of a segregated environment on all Negro children, we may conclude on the more hopeful note that the consequences of membership in a stigmatized racial group can be cushioned in part by a foundation of intrinsic self-esteem established in the home (7, 76).

Implications for Education

Before Negroes can assume their rightful place in a desegregated American culture, important changes in the ego structure of Negro children must first take place. They must shed feelings of inferiority and self-derogation, acquire feelings of self-confidence and racial pride, develop realistic aspirations for occupations requiring greater education and training, and develop the personality traits necessary for implementing these aspirations. Such changes in ego structure can be accomplished in two different but complementary ways. First, all manifestations of the Negro's inferior and segregated caste status must be swept away—in education, housing, employment, religion, travel, and exercise of civil rights. This in itself will enhance the Negro's self-esteem and open new opportunities for self-fulfillment. Second, through various measures instituted in the family, school and community, character structure, levels of aspiration, and actual standards of achievement can be altered in ways that will further enhance his self-esteem and make it possible for him to take advantage of new opportunities.

Desegregation. Desegregation, of course, is no panacea for the Negro child's personality difficulties. In the first place, it tends to create new problems of adjustment, particularly when it follows in the wake of serious community conflict. Second, it cannot quickly overcome various long-standing handicaps which Negro children bring with them to school "such as their cultural impoverishment, their helplessness or apathy toward learning, and their distrust of the majority group and their middle-class teachers" (14, p. 158); nor can it compensate for "oversized classes, inappropriate curriculums, inadequate counseling services, or poorly trained or demoralized teachers" (14, p. 158). Yet it is an important and indispensable first step in the reconstitution of Negro personality, since the school is the most strategically placed social institution for effecting rapid change both in ego structure and in social status. A desegregated school offers the Negro child his first taste of social equality and his first experience of first-class citizenship. He can enjoy the stimulating effect of competition with white children and can use them as realistic yardsticks in measuring his own worth and chances for academic and vocational success. Under these circumstances, educational achievement no longer seems so pointless, and aspirations for higher occupational status in the wider culture acquire more substance.

It is also reasonable to anticipate that white children will be prejudiced and continue to discriminate against their Negro classmates long after desegregation accords them equal legal status in the educational system. Attitudes toward Negroes in the South, for example, are remarkably stable, even in periods of rapid social change involving desegregation (130), and are not highly correlated with anti-Semitic or other ethnocentric trends (50, 62, 90, 91). Prejudice against Negroes is deeply rooted in the American culture (92) and is continually reinforced both by the socio-economic gain and by the vicarious ego enhancement it brings to those who manifest it (14, 55, 95). It is hardly surprising, therefore, that racial prejudice is most pronounced in lower social-class groups (125) and that these groups constitute the hard core of resistance to desegregation (63, 118); anti-white prejudice is similarly most pronounced among lower-class Negroes (26, 126). Increased physical contact per se between white and Negro children does little to reduce prejudice (78, 122), but more intimate personal interaction under favorable circumstances significantly reduces social distance between the two groups (62, 73, 129).

Artificial attempts to end de facto school segregation, caused by neighborhood segregation of Negroes in particular urban slums, are socially and psychologically unsound (25). It is not only impractical to transport white children to schools in distant, predominantly Negro neighborhoods just for the purpose of maintaining the principle of racially mixed classes, but it also victimizes individual white children and thereby increases racial tensions. Unless de facto segregation is accomplished by the gerrymandering of school districts, and unless schools in Negro districts are *actually* inferior, it seems more reasonable to work for the elimination of this type of school segregation by directly attacking its underlying cause, that is, neighborhood segregation (25).

Community action. The support of parents and of the Negro community at large must be enlisted if we hope to make permanent progress in the education of Negro children.

One needs only to visit . . . a [slum] school to be convinced that the nature of the community largely determines what goes on in the school. Therefore to attempt to divorce the school from the community is to engage in unrealistic thinking, which might lead to policies that could wreak havoc with the school and the lives of children (25, p. 20).

Whatever can be done to strengthen family life and to give the fathers a more important role in it will make a significant contribution to the development of Negro potential (110, p. 462).

Working with mothers and getting them to adopt a more positive attitude toward school is an important first step in improving the educational achievement of urban Negro children (25). Typically only 10 per cent of Negro parents are high-school graduates and only 33 per cent complete elementary school (25). Thus enrollment of parents in adult-education programs would significantly raise the cultural level of the Negro home and "stimulate an interest in newspapers, magazines and possibly even books. One of the troubles . . . is that when the children leave the school they never see anyone read anything—not even newspapers" (25, p. 25). The "Higher Horizons" project in New York City is a good example of a recent attempt to discover academically talented children in slum areas and encourage them to aspire to college education. This program embodies cultural enrichment, improved counseling and instruction, and the sympathetic involvement of parents.

Counseling. Because of current grave inadequacies in the structure of the lower-class urban Negro family, the school must be prepared to compensate, at least in part, for the deficiencies of the home, that is, to act, so to speak, *in loco parentis*. Teachers in predominantly Negro schools actually perform much of this role at the present time. As one Negro teacher said to Conant:

We do quite well with these children in the lower grades. Each of us is, for the few hours of the school day, an acceptable substitute for the mother. But when they reach about 10, 11, or 12 years of age, we lose them. At that time the "street" takes over. In terms of schoolwork, progress ceases; indeed many pupils begin to go backward in their studies (25, p. 21).

It is apparent, therefore, that trained counselors must assume the role of parent substitute during pre-adolescence and adolescence. They are needed to offer appropriate educational and vocational guidance, to encourage worthwhile and realistic aspirations, and to stimulate the development of mature personality traits. In view of the serious unemployment situation among Negro youth, they should also assist in job placement and in cushioning the transition between school and work. This will naturally require much expansion of existing guidance services in the school.

Research has shown that Negro children's distrust of white counselors and authority figures in general makes it

. . . difficult for a white counselor to create an atmosphere wherein a Negro could gain insight. . . . The fundamental principle of counseling—to view the social or personal field as the counselor does—is difficult to attain in such a situation. The white person can only imagine, but never know, how a Negro thinks and feels, or how he views a social or personal situation. The cultural lenses which are formulated from unique milieus are not as freely transferable as it is assumed, or as we are led to believe (87, p. 188).

Educational measures. Specially trained teachers and smaller classes are obviously required to cope with the difficulties of educating culturally disadvantaged minority group children. Emphasis must be placed on acquiring such basic intellectual skills as reading, writing, and arithmetic before any attempt is made to teach algebra, literature, science, or foreign languages. In many urban high schools today, pupils who cannot read at a fifth grade level, and who cannot speak or write grammatically or do simple arithmetical calculations, are subject to irregular French verbs, Shakespearean drama, and geometrical theorems. Nothing more educationally futile or better calculated to destroy educational morale could be imagined! Slow readers and pupils with other educational disabilities should be identified early and given intensive remedial work (25). Going even one step further, Professor Strodtbeck of the University of Chicago is attempting to teach underprivileged children to read at the age of 4, combining instruction with personal attention and affection, in order to forestall later reading difficulties (79).

If Negro youth is to be adequately prepared for the changing job market, more realistic pre-vocational courses, integrated in some instances with work experience programs, should be established in the "general" urban high schools (25). In connection with vocational education, Conant makes these important four points:

First and foremost, vocational courses should not replace courses which are essential parts of the required academic program for graduation. Second, vocational courses should be provided in grades 11 and 12 and not require more than half the student's time in those years; however, for slow learners and prospective dropouts these courses ought to begin earlier. Third, the significance of the vocational courses is that those enrolled are keenly interested in the work; they realize the relevance of what they are learning to their future careers, and this sense of purpose is carried over to the academic courses which they are studying at the same time. Fourth, the type of vocational training programs should be related to the employment opportunities in the general locality (25, p. 44).

Opportunities should also be made available for part-time high school study in conjunction with trade apprenticeships, as well as for more advanced vocational training in community colleges and technical institutes. For underprivileged urban students capable and desirous of pursuing a regular course of university studies, programs such as the previously described "Higher Horizons" project, supplemented by liberal scholarship aid, are necessary. Finally, a special public works and job training program is currently needed to alleviate the calamitous problem of unemployment among urban youth (25).

Summary and Conclusions

The ego development of segregated Negro children in the United States manifests various distinctive properties, both because Negroes generally occupy the lowest stratum of the lower-class subculture, and because they possess an inferior caste status in American society. Their inferior caste position is marked by an unstable and matriarchal type of family structure, by restricted opportunities for acquiring educational, vocational, and social status, by varying degrees of segregation from the dominant white majority, and by a culturally fixed devaluation of their dignity as human beings. The consequences of this regrettable state of affairs for Negro children's self-esteem and self-confidence, for their educational and vocational aspirations, and for their character structure, interpersonal relations, and personality adjustment, constitute the characteristic features of their ego development.

Beginning in the pre-school period, the Negro child gradually learns to appreciate the negative implications of dark skin color for social status and personal worth. Hence he resists identifying with his own racial group and shows definite preference for white dolls and playmates. This reluctance to acknowledge his racial membership not only results in ego deflation, but also makes it difficult for him to identify with his parents and to obtain from such identification the derived status that universally constitutes the principal basis of self-esteem during childhood. Much of the derived status that white children obtain from their parents is made available to the Negro child by virtue of his membership in an unsupervised peer group, which accordingly performs many of the socializing functions of the white-middle-class home. This is especially true for the Negro boy who often has no adult male with whom to identify in the frequently fatherless Negro family, and who finds maleness deprecated in his matriarchal and authoritarian home. Early experience in fending for himself results in precocious social maturity, independence, and emancipation from the home.

During pre-adolescence and adolescence, segregated Negro children characteristically develop low aspirations for academic and vocational achievement. These low aspirations reflect existing social class and ethnic values, the absence of suitable emulatory models, marked educational retardation, restricted vocational opportunities, lack of parental and peer group support, and the cultural impoverishment of the Negro home. Because of loyalty to parents and rejection by the dominant white group,

Negro adolescents develop ambivalent feelings toward middle-class achievement values and the personality traits necessary for their implementation. In many instances they use the objective facts of racial prejudice and discrimination as a rationalization for personal inadequacies, apathy, lack of striving, and anti-social behavior. The seeming hopelessness of attaining adequate vocational and social status in the wider American culture induces many Negro youths to withdraw from contact and competition with whites, and to seek the psychological shelter of their own segregated subculture. Girls tend to develop a more mature ego structure than boys because of their favored position in the home, but face greater adjustment problems during desegregation. The detrimental effects of segregation and inferior caste status on Negro ego development naturally vary from one child to another depending on ability, temperament, and the degree of intrinsic self-esteem and ego maturity that can be acquired within the home environment.

The problem of raising aspirational and achievement levels among Negro youth is presently acute because Negroes can no longer adjust comfortably to their segregated caste status, and because automation has eliminated many of the unskilled jobs which formerly made some type of stable economic adjustment possible. Two different but complementary approaches are available in dealing with this problem. The more general approach, which primarily applies to educators in their role as citizens, involves the elimination of existing racial barriers in housing, education, employment, religion, and civil rights. The more specific educational approach is to attempt, through various family, school and community measures, an upgrading of the Negro child's aspirational level, standards of achievement, and character structure that will both enhance his self-esteem and enable him to take advantage of new opportunities.

In the educational sphere, school desegregation is an indispensable prerequisite for raising aspiration and achievement levels, but obviously cannot compensate, in and of itself, for the long-standing educational handicaps of the Negro child or for existing inadequacies in schools, teachers, curriculums, and counseling services. Before we can expect any permanent improvement in the educational performance of Negro children, we must strengthen Negro family life, combat the cultural impoverishment of the Negro home, and enlist the support and cooperation of Negro parents in accomplishing this objective. More intensive guidance services, utilizing Negro personnel, are required to provide the socializing and supportive functions that are currently lacking in many Negro homes. Other important needs are smaller classes, specially trained teachers, abundant remedial facilities, the provision of expanded and more realistic vocational education, and a public works program to alleviate the explosively dangerous problem of unemployment among urban Negro youth.

REFERENCES

1. Aberle, D. F., and Naegele, K. D., "Middle-Class Fathers' Occupational Roles and Attitudes Toward Children," *Amer. J. Orthopsychiat.*, 1952, 22:366-378.
2. Anastasi, Anne, and Cordova, F. A., "Some Effects of Bilingualism upon the Intelligence Test Performance of Puerto Rican Children in New York City," *J. educ. Psychol.*, 1953, 44:1-19.
3. Anastasi, Anne, and DeJesus, C., "Language Development and Non-verbal IQ of Puerto Rican Preschool Children in New York City." *J. abnorm. soc. Psychol.*, 1953, 48:357-366.
4. Angelino, H., Dollins, J., and Mech, E. V., "Trends in the 'Fears and Worries' of School Children as Related to Socioeconomic Status and Age," *J. genet. Psychol.*, 1956, 89:263-276.
5. Ashmore, H. S., *The Negro and the Schools*, Chapel Hill, N. C.: University of North Carolina Press, 1954.
6. Auld, B. F., "Influence of Social Class on Personality Test Response," *Psychol. Bull.*, 1952, 49:318-332.
7. Ausubel, D. P., *Ego Development and the Personality Disorders*, New York: Grune and Stratton, 1952.
8. _____, "Ego Development Among Segregated Negro Children," *Ment. Hyg.*, 1958, 42:362-369.
9. _____, "Acculturative Stress in Modern Maori Adolescence," *Child Develpm.*, 1960, 31:617-631.
10. _____, "Causes and Types of Drug Addiction: a Psychosocial View," *Psychiat. Quart.*, 1961, 35:523-531.
11. _____, "The Maori: A Study in Resistive Acculturation," *Soc. Forces*, 1961, 39:218-227.
12. _____, *Maori Youth*, Wellington, New Zealand: Price, Milburn, 1961.
13. _____, et al. "Perceived Parent Attitudes as Determinants of Children's Ego Structure," *Child Develpm.*, 1954, 25:173-183.
14. Bernard, Viola W., "School Desegregation: Some Psychiatric Implications," *Psychiatry*, 1958, 21:149-158.
15. Bernstein, B., "Some Sociological Determinants of Perception: an Enquiry into Sub-cultural Differences," *Brit. J. Sociol.*, 1958, 9, 159-174.
16. Boyd, G. F., "The Levels of Aspiration of White and Negro Children in a Non-segregated Elementary School," *J. soc. Psychol.*, 1952, 36:191-196.
17. Bullock, H. A., "A Comparison of the Academic Achievements of White and Negro High School Graduates," *J. educ. Res.*, 1950, 44:179-192.
18. Campbell, J. D., and Yarrow, Marian R., "Personal and Situational Variables in Adaptation to Change," *J. soc. Issues*, 1958, 14:29-46.
19. Carson, A. S., and Rabin, A. I., "Verbal Comprehension and Communication in Negro and White Children," *J. educ. Psychol.*, 1960, 51:47-51.
20. Cavan, Ruth S., "Negro Family Disorganization and Juvenile Delinquency," *J. Negro Educ.*, 1959, 28:230-239.
21. Clark, K. B., "The Most Valuable Hidden Resource," *Coll. Bd. Rev.*, 1956, No. 29, 23-26.

22. _____, "Color, Class Personality, and Juvenile Delinquency," *J. Negro Educ.*, 1959, 28:240-251.

23. _____, and Clark, M. P., "Racial Identification and Preference in Negro Children," *in* T. M. Newcomb and E. L. Hartley (Eds.), *Readings in Social Psychology*, New York: Holt, 1947, pp. 169-178.

24. Cobb, H. V., "Role-Wishes and General Wishes of Children and Adolescents," *Child Develpm.*, 1954, 25:161-171.

25. Conant, James B., *Slums and Suburbs: A Commentary on Schools in Metropolitan Areas*, New York: McGraw-Hill, 1961.

26. Cothran, T. C., "Negro Conceptions of White People," *Amer. J. Social.*, 1951, 56:458-467.

27. Crockett, Harry J., "A Study of Some Factors Affecting the Decision of Negro High School Students to Enroll in Previously All-White High Schools, St. Louis, 1955," *Soc. Forces*, 1957, 35:351-356.

28. Dai, B., "Some Problems of Personality Development in Negro Children," *in* C. Kluckhohn and H. A. Murray (Eds.), *Personality in Nature, Society and Culture*, New York: Knopf, 1949, pp. 437-458.

29. Davis, A., *Deep South: a Social Anthropological Study of Caste and Class*, Chicago: University of Chicago Press, 1941.

30. _____, "Child Training and Social Class," *in* R. G. Barker, J. S. Kounin, and H. F. Wright (Eds.), *Child Behavior and Development*. New York: McGraw-Hill, 1943, pp. 607-620.

31. _____, and Dollard, J., *Children of Bondage*, Washington, D. C.: American Council on Education, 1940.

32. Davis, A., and Havighurst, R. J., Social class and color differences in child rearing. *Amer. sociol. Rev.*, 1946, 11:698-710.

33. Deutsch, Martin, Minority group and class status as related to social and personality factors in scholastic achievement. *Soc. appl. Anthropol. Monogr.*, 1960, No. 2.

34. _____, et al. "Some Considerations as to the Contributions of Social, Personality, and Racial Factors to School Retardation in Minority Group Children," paper read at American Psychology Association, Chicago, September 1956.

35. De Vos, G., and Miner, H. "Algerian Culture and Personality in Changes," *Sociometry*, 1958, 21:255-268.

36. Dickens, Sara L., and Hobart, C., "Parental Dominance and Offspring Ethnocentrism," *J. soc. Psychol.*, 1959, 49:297-303.

37. Dinitz, S., Kay, Barbara A., and Reckless, W. C., "Group Gradients in Delinquency Potential and Achievement Score of Sixth Graders," *Amer. J. Orthopsychiat.*, 1958, 28:598-605.

38. Douglass, J. H., "The Extent and Characteristics of Juvenile Delinquency Among Negroes in the United States," *J. Negro Educ.*, 1959, 28:214-229.

39. Dreger, R. M., and Miller, K. S., "Comparative Psychological Studies of Negroes and Whites in the United States," *Psychol. Bull.*, 1960, 57:361-402.

40. Fernandez-Marina, R., Maldonado-Sierra, E. D., and Trent, R. D., "Three Basic Themes in Mexican and Puerto Rican Family Values," *J. soc. Psychol.*, 48:167-81, 1958.

41. Finestone, H., "Cats, Kicks, and Color," *Soc. Probl.*, 1957, 5:3-13.

42. Frazier, E. F., "The Negro Middle Class and Desegregation," *Soc. Probl.*, 1957, 4:291-301.

43. Frumkin, R. M., "Race, Occupation, and Social Class in New York," *J. Negro Educ.*, 1958, 27:62-65.

44. Gaier, E. L., and Wambach, Helen S., "Self-evaluation of Personality Assets and Liabilities of Southern White and Negro Students," *J. soc. Psychol.*, 1960, 51:135-143.

45. Goff, R. M., *Problems and Emotional Difficulties of Negro Children*, New York: Bureau of Publications, Teachers College, Columbia University, 1949.

46. Goodenough, F. L., "Anger in Young Children," *Inst. Child Welf. Monogr.*, 1931, No. 9.

47. Goodman, M. E., *Race Awareness in Young Children*. Cambridge, Mass.: Addison-Wesley, 1952.

48. Gould, R., "Some Sociological Determinants of Goal Strivings," *J. soc. Psychol.* 1941, 13:461-473.

49. Green, Helen B., "Comparison of Nurturance and Independence Training in Jamaica and Puerto Rico with Consideration of the Resulting Personality Structure and Transplanted Social Patterns," *J. soc. Psychol.* 1960, 50:27-63.

50. Greenberg, H., Chase, A. L., and Cannon, T. M., "Attitudes of White and Negro High School Students in a West Texas Town Toward School Integration," *J. appl. Psychol.*, 1957, 41:27-31.

51. Greenberg, H., and Fane, D., "An Investigation of Several Variables as Determinants of Authoritarianism," *J. soc. Psychol.*, 1959, 49:105-111.

52. Grossack, M. M., "Some Personality Characteristics of Southern Negro Students," *J. soc. Psychol.*, 1957, 46:125-131.

53. Hart, I., "Maternal Child-Rearing Practices and Authoritarian Ideology," *J. abnorm. soc. Psychol.*, 1957, 55:232-237.

54. Havighurst, R. J., and Taba, H., *Adolescent Character and Personality*, New York: Wiley, 1949.

55. Herr, D. M., "The Sentiment of White Supremacy: an Ecological Study," *Amer. J. Sociol.*, 1959, 64:592-598.

56. Hill, M. C., "Research on the Negro Family," *Marriage fam., Living,* 1957, 19:25-31.

57. Hollingshead, A. B., and Redlich, F. C., *Social Class and Mental Illness,* New York: Wiley, 1958.

58. Jefferson, Ruth B., "Some Obstacles to Racial Integration," *J. Negro Educ.* 1957, 26:145-154.

59. Jenkins, W. A., "An Experimental Study of the Relationship of Legitimate and and Illegitimate Birth Status to School and Personal Adjustment of Negro Children," *Amer. J. Sociol.*, 1958, 64:169-173.

60. Kahn, M. L., "Social Class and Parental Values," *Amer. J. Sociol.*, 1959, 64:337-351.

61. Karon, B. P., *The Negro Personality*, New York: Springer, 1958.

62. Kelly, J. G., Ferson, J. E., and Holtzman, W. H., "The Measurement of Attitudes Toward the Negro in the South," *J. soc. Psychol.*, 1958, 48:305-317.

63. Killian, L. M., and Haer, J. L., "Variables Related to Attitudes Regarding School Desegregation Among White Southerners," *Sociometry*, 1958, 21:159-164.

64. Kirkhart, R. O., "Psychological and Socio-psychological Correlates of Marginality in Negroes," *Dissert. Abstr.*, 1960, 20:4173.

65. Kitay, P. M., "A Comparison of the Sexes in Their Attitudes and Beliefs About Women: a Study of Prestige Groups," *Sociometry*, 1940, 3:399-407.
66. Koch, H. L., Some Personality Correlates of Sex, Sibling Position, and Sex of Siblings Among Five- and Six-Year-Old Children," *Genet. Psychol. Monogr.*, 1955, 52:3-51.
67. Kvaraceus, W. C., "Culture and the Delinquent," *NEA J.*, 1959, 48:14-16.
68. Landreth, C., and Johnson, B. C., "Young Children's Responses to a Picture and Inset Test Designed to Reveal Reactions to Persons of Different Skin Color," *Child Develpm.*, 1953, 24:63-79.
69. Lipset, S. M., "Democracy and Working-Class Authoritarianism," *Amer sociol. Rev.*, 1959, 24:482-501.
70. Maas, H., "Some Social Class Differences in the Family Systems and Group Relations of Pre- and Early Adolescents," *Child Develpm.*, 1951, 22:145-152.
71. Maccoby, Eleanor, Gibbs, P. K., et al., "Methods of Child Rearing in Two Social Classes," *in* W. E. Martin and C. B. Stendler (Eds.), *Readings in Child Development*. New York: Harcourt, Brace, 1954, pp. 380-396.
72. McLure, W. P., "Challenge of Vocational and Technical Education," *Phi Delta Kappan*, 1962, 44:212-217.
73. Mann, J. H., "The Effect of Interracial Contact on Sociometric Choices and Perceptions," *J. soc. Psychol.*, 1959, 50:143-152.
74. Markley, Elaine R., "Social Class Differences in Mothers' Attitudes Toward Child Rearing," *Dissert. Abst.*, 1958, 19:355-356.
75. Maslow, A. H., and Diaz-Guerrero, R., "Delinquency as Value Disturbance," *in* J. G. Peatman and E. L. Hartley, (Eds.), *Festschrift for Gardner Murphy*, New York: Harper, 1960, pp. 228-240.
76. Milner, Esther, "Some Hypotheses Concerning the Influence of Segregation on Negro Personality Development," *Psychiatry*, 1953, 16:291-297.
77. Morland, J. K., "Racial Recognition by Nursery School Children in Lynchburg, Virginia," *Soc. Forces*, 1958, 37:132-137.
78. Neprash, J. A., "Minority Group Contacts and Social Distance," *Phylon*, 1953, 14:207-212.
79. *The New York Times*, Sunday, March 11, 1962.
80. North, R. D., *The Intelligence of American Negroes*, New York: Anti-Defamation League of B'nai B'rith, 1954.
81. Omari, T. P., "Changing Attitudes of Students in West African Society Toward Marriage and Family Relationships," *Brit. J. Sociol.*, 1960, 11:197-210.
82. Osborne, R. T., "Racial Differences in Mental Growth and School Achievement: a Longitudinal Study," *Psychol Reps.*, 1960, 7:233-239.
83. Palermo, D. S., "Racial Comparisons and Additional Normative Data on the Children's Manifest Anxiety Scale," *Child Develpm.*, 1959, 30:53-57.
84. Parsons, T., "Age and Sex in the Social Structure of the United States," *Amer. sociol. Rev.*, 1942, 7:604-616.
85. Pasamanick, B., and Knobloch, Hilda, "The Contribution of Some Organic Factors to School Retardation in Negro Children," *J. Negro Educ.*, 1958, 27:4-9.
86. Pawl, J. L. H., "Some Ego Skills and Their Relation to the Differences in Intelligence Between the Middle and Lower Classes," *Dissert. Abstr.*, 1960, 21:368.
87. Phillips, W. B., "Counseling Negro Students: an Educational Dilemma," *Calif. J. educ. Res.*, 1959, 10:185-188.

88. Pierce-Jones, J., "Socio-economic Status and Adolescents' Interests," *Psychol. Reps, 1959, 5:683.*

89. ————, "Vocational Interest Correlates of Socio-economic Status in Adolescence," *Educ. psychol. Measmt, 1959, 19:65-71.*

90. Pompilo, P. T., "The Relationship Between Projection and Prejudice with a Factor Analysis of Anti-Semitic and Anti-Negro Attitudes," unpublished doctoral dissertation, Catholic University, Washington, D. C., 1957.

91. Prothro, E. T., "Ethnocentrism and Anti-Negro Attitudes in the Deep South," *J. abnorm. soc. Psychol., 1952, 47:105-108.*

92. Raab, E., and Lipset, S. M., *Prejudice and Society,* New York: Anti-Defamation League of B'nai B'rith, 1959.

93. Record, W., "Social Stratification and Intellectual Roles in the Negro Community," *Brit. J. Sociol., 1957, 8:235-255.*

94. Roen, S. R., "Personality and Negro-White Intelligence," *J. abnorm. soc. Psychol., 1960, 61:148-150.*

95. Rosen, B. C., "Race, Ethnicity, and the Achievement Syndrome," *Amer. sociol. Rev., 1959, 24:47-60.*

96. Rosner, J., "When White Children Are in the Minority," *J. educ. Sociol., 1954, 28:69-72.*

97. Schneider, L., and Lysgaard, S., "The Deferred Gratification Pattern: a Preliminary Study," *Amer. sociol. Rev., 1953, 18:142-149.*

98. Schpoont, S., "Some Relationships Between Task Attractiveness, Self-evaluated Motivation, and Success or Failure," unpublished doctoral dissertation, University of Illinois, Urbana, Ill., 1955.

99. Sears, P. S., "Levels of Aspiration in Academically Successful and Unsuccessful Children," *J. abnorm. soc. Psychol., 1940, 35:498-536.*

100. Sears, R. R., et al., "Some Child-Rearing Antecedents of Aggression and Dependency in Young Children," *Genet. Psychol. Monogr., 1953, 47:135-234.*

101. Sewell, W., and Haller, A. O., "Social Status and the Personality Status of the Child," *Sociometry, 1956, 19:113-125.*

102. ————, "Factors in the Relationships Between Social Status and the Personality Adjustment of the Child," *Amer. sociol, Rev., 1959, 24:511-520.*

103. ————, and Strauss, M. A., "Social Status and Educational and Occupational Aspiration," *Amer. sociol. Rev., 1957, 22:67-73.*

104. Sexton, Patricia C., "Social Class and Pupil Turn-over Rates," *J. educ. Sociol., 1959, 33:131-134.*

105. Siegel, A. I., and Federman, P., *Employment Experiences of Negro Philadelphians: A Descriptive Study of the Employment Experiences, Perceptions, and Aspirations of Selected Philadelphia Whites and Non-Whites.* Wayne, Pa.: Applied Psychological Services, 1959.

106. Singer, S. L., and Stafflre, B., "A Note on Racial Differences in Job Values and Desires," *J. soc. Psychol., 1956, 43:333-337.*

107. Smith, B. F., "Wishes of High School Seniors and Social Status," *J. educ. Sociol., 1952, 25:466-475.*

108. Smith, C. U., and Prothro, J. W., "Ethnic Differences in Authoritarian Personality," *Soc. Forces, 1957, 35:334-338.*

109. Smith, M. G., "Education and Occupational Choice in Rural Jamaica," *Soc. econ. Stud., 1960, 9:332-354.*

110. Smuts, R. W., "The Negro Community and the Development of Negro Potential," *J. Negro Educ.*, 1957, 26:456-465.

111. Srole, L., Langner, T. S., Michael, S. T., Opler, M. K., and Rennie, T. A. C., *Mental Health in the Metropolis: the Midtown Manhattan Study*, New York: McGraw-Hill, 1962.

112. Stafflre, B., "Concurrent Validity of the Vocational Values Inventory," *J. educ. Res.*, 1959, 52:339-341.

113. *The Status of the Public School Education of Negro and Puerto Rican Children in New York City*, New York: Public Education Association, 1955.

114. Steckler, G. A., "Authoritarian Ideology in Negro College Students," *J. abnorm. soc. Psychol.*, 1957, 54:396-399.

115. Stevenson, H. W., and Stevenson, N. G., "Social Interaction in an Interracial Nursery-School," *Genet. Psychol., Monogr.*, 1960, 61:37-75.

116. Stevenson, H. W., and Stewart, E. C., A developmental study of racial awareness in young children. *Child Develpm.*, 1958, 29:399-409.

117. Trent, R. D., "An Analysis of Expressed Self-Acceptance Among Negro Children," unpublished doctoral dissertation, Teachers College, Columbia University, New York, 1954.

118. Tumin, M. M., "Readiness and Resistance to Desegregation: a Social Portrait of the Hard Core," *Soc. Forces*, 1958, 36:256-263.

119. Turner, R. H., "Negro Job Status and Education," *Soc. Forces*, 1953, 32:45-52.

120. _____. "Occupational Patterns of Inequality," *Amer. J. Sociol.*, 1954, 59:437-447.

121. Walter, L. M., and Marzolf, S. S., "The Relation of Sex, Age, and School Achievement to Levels of Aspiration," *J. educ. Psychol.*, 1951, 42:285-292.

122. Webster, S. W., "The Influence of Interracial Contact on Social Acceptance in a Newly Integrated School," *J. educ. Psychol.*, 1961, 52:292-296.

123. Wertham, F., "Psychological Effects of School Segregation," *Amer. J. Psychother.*, 1952, 6:94-103.

124. West, J., *Plainville, U. S. A.*, New York: Columbia University Press, 1945.

125. Westie, F. R., "Negro-White Status Differentials and Social Distance," *Amer. Sociol. Rev.*, 1952, 17:550-558.

126. _____, and Howard, D., "Social Status Differentials and the Race Attitudes of Negroes," *Amer. sociol. Rev.*, 1954, 19:584-591.

127. Wilkerson, D. A., "Conscious and Impersonal Forces in Recent Trends Toward Negro-White School Equality in Virginia," *J. educ. Sociol.*, 1959, 32:402-408.

128. Wilson, D. C., and Lantz, E. M., "The Effect of Culture Change on the Negro Race in Virginia as Indicated by a Study of State Hospital Admissions," *Amer. J. Psychiat.*, 1957, 114:25-32.

129. Yarrows, Marian R., Campbell, J. O., and Yarrow, L. J., "Acquisition of New Norms: a Study of Racial Desegregation," *J. soc. Issues*, 1958, 14:8-28.

130. Young, R. K., Benson, W. M., and Holtzman, W. H., "Change in Attitudes Toward the Negro in a Southern University," *J. abnorm. soc. Psychol.*, 1960, 60:131-133.

Kenneth B. Clark | Educational Stimulation of Racially Disadvantaged Children

Within the past ten years, there has been increasing concern with the problem of providing the maximum educational stimulation for children from socially and racially disadvantaged groups. Probably the most dramatic single stimulus which aroused widespread discussion of this problem, as related to the education of Negroes, was the May 17, 1954, decision of the United States Supreme Court which ruled that state laws requiring or permitting racially segregated schools violated the equal protection clause of the Fourteenth Amendment of the United States Constitution. The decision discussed in rather simple direct language the general social significance of public education in American democracy. It stated: [1]

Today, education is perhaps the most important function of state and local governments. Compulsory school attendance laws and the great expenditures for education both demonstrate our recognition of the importance of education to our democratic society. It is required in the performance of our most basic public responsibilities, even service in the armed forces. It is the very foundation of good citizenship. Today it is a principal instrument in awakening the child to cultural values, in preparing him for later professional training, and in helping him to adjust normally to his environment. In these days, it is doubtful that any child may reasonably be expected to succeed in life if he is denied the opportunity of an education. Such an opportunity, where the state has undertaken to provide it, is a right which must be made available to all on equal terms.

Widespread public discussion of problems of education for any group of children in America necessarily involves discussions of general problems of education affecting all children. Once the emotional reaction to the Supreme Court's desegregation decisions and the various patterns of resistance to the demanded changes have decreased, it will be seen that an effective transition from segregated to non-segregated schools tends to raise the general level of democratic public education for all children.

[1] *Brown versus Board of Education,* 347 U.S. 483 (1954).

The interim reports which have been published by the Superintendent of Schools of Washington, D.C. indicates that since the desegregation of these schools, there has been a measurable improvement in the average academic achievement level of both Negro and white children (6, 7).

More recently—since the launching of the first Sputnik—some observers have expressed concern about the comparative effectiveness of the American and Soviet systems of public education. These discussions generally resulted in demands for re-examination of standards, methods, curriculum, effectiveness of teaching, and an insistence that the general level of achievement of the students in American schools be raised. It would be expected that discussions of the quality of education in terms of problems of international competition and demands for military superiority would result in the tendency to equate general educational excellence with the specifics of high achievement in mathematics, science, and technology.

An article published in 1956 in the College Board Review (1) presented evidence which pointed to the grave shortage in scientific, technical and other college trained individuals in America. This evidence indicated that during that year the Soviet Union would graduate 138,000 students in various scientific fields while the United States, at best, would graduate only 78,000 similarly trained students. It was also clear that while the number of individuals receiving Ph.D. degrees in all fields had remained constant during the preceding five years in the United States, it had increased dramatically in the Soviet Union. At that time, that nation awarded nearly twice as many Ph.D. degrees annually as were awarded in the United States. This evidence which suggested at least a quantitative inferiority of American education in stimulating and training individuals of superior intellect was being discussed before the Russians launched their first Sputnik. In the six years since the publication of that article, there has been no evidence to suggest that there has been any significant changes in the trends observed at that time. There is still no evidence that America has developed the procedures and facilities necessary to increase the number of trained intellects or that the effectiveness of Russian education has declined.[2]

In spite of this seeming difference in educational effectiveness, it is questionable whether competition with the Russians and the factor of national prestige are the significant reasons for being concerned with ob-

[2] There was a newspaper report to the effect that Premier Khrushchev was publicly dissatisfied with the overwhelming success of the Russian educational system which produced a disproportionate number of "intellectuals." It was reported that he was concerned that an overeducated population would develop a contempt for manual labor. He, therefore, suggested, or demanded that henceforth the curriculum in Russian schools must include vocational education and manual training.

taining for each child in America the most effective education without regard to such educationally irrelevant barriers as race, nationality, religion or low social and economic background. The goals of assuring equality of educational opportunity and providing the most effective education for every child are inherent imperatives of American education in this latter half of the twentieth century.

Any society which is to remain viable and dynamic must raise the educational standards for all of its people and must exploit and use constructively high intellectual potential wherever it is to be found. The argument in support of this is no longer sentimental.

The dangers inherent in not developing an effective approach to the discovery, stimulation and training of superior intellectual potential in all groups of American children seem to be greater than the dangers inherent in an inefficient and wasteful exploitation of our natural material resources. It is now axiomatic that trained human intelligence is the most valuable resource of a civilized nation. Like other natural resources, it must be discovered and transformed creatively into its most effective and usable form. At this period in world history, no nation can afford to waste any of its potential intelligence through indifference, inefficiency, ignorance or the anachronistic luxury of racial and social class prejudices. The economic, social, political, international, and, of course, primary, humanitarian reasons for this are becoming increasingly clear.

Another factor which must be taken into account in understanding these demands for more effective use of the intellectual potentials in previously disadvantaged groups is to be found in the pressure and demands which are coming from these groups themselves. One of the significant changes which characterizes the modern world is the fact that increasing automation in business and industry is relentlessly leading to an increase in leisure for the masses of working people. With this increasing automation and leisure, there will be a smaller proportion of the population required for unskilled or manual work. The educational implications of this social and economic change may be further complicated by the probably irreversible trend toward higher and higher wages and higher and higher living standards for the masses of people who earn their living through wages. If this trend continues, one may expect that there will be a raising of the social-class aspirations of these previously working class groups and that this will eventually result in an increasing desire for higher education for their children.

Education has been one of the most effective means for social mobility in the American society. This problem in the future may be different from the similar problem in the past only in that it will involve different and larger groups of previously disadvantaged individuals. The rising pressure for higher education which can be expected to come from the presently disadvantaged groups in our society must be met by appropriate and effective adjustments on the part of our educational institutions. If these pressures are not met effectively, then one could anticipate major consequences of frustration among the members of these groups. Some of the social manifestations of these personal frustrations which could be anticipated are: an increase in delinquency and criminality; intensification of bigotry, provincialism, intergroup tensions and hostility; increase in the chances of successful manipulation of the primitive passions of the masses by political cynics, fanatics or demagogues; an increase in the incidence of emotional instability among those upwardly mobile groups whose aspirations are being blocked; and other symptoms of personal and social disorganization.

Creative educators can help to prevent these personal and social disturbances by making the necessary modifications in curriculum and methods and by providing the educational leadership, guidance and stimulation which will make it possible for American society to strengthen and improve our system of democratic public education. When this is done, our schools will continue to function as the chief vehicles of upward class mobility and as a major source of social and economic vitality. If it is not done, our schools will contribute to social stagnation and more insidious forms of social-class cleavages and distinctions.

The most compelling argument for providing the maximum educational stimulation for all American children without regard to the social, economic, national, or racial backgrounds of their parents is the fact that the effective functioning of a dynamic democracy demands this. It is one of the cardinal assumptions of our American democracy that significant social changes may be brought about through education—through providing that type of intellectual training and information which will make it possible for the citizen to make the types of decisions which he must make in a democracy—rather than through tyranny or violence. The substance, rather than the verbalization, of democracy depends upon our ability to extend and deepen the insights of the people. Only an educated people can be expected to make the type of choices which assert their freedoms and reinforce their sense of social responsibility.

Some Research Problems and Findings Relevant to the Education of Deprived Children

During the past year a number of books dealing directly or indirectly with the problem of the education of children in depressed urban areas have been published. Among the more significant of these books are James B. Conant's *Slums and Suburbs* (4), Frank Riessman's *The Culturally Deprived Child* (9), and Patricia Sexton's *Education and Income* (10).

Dr. Sexton's analysis of the relationship between social and economic status and the quality of education provided for children in the public schools of a northern urban community is a model of objective social science and educational research. The data presented by her demonstrate conclusively that curricula, educational standards, quality of teaching, educational facilities and materials, and academic achievement of the children are directly related to the socio-economic status of the majority of children attending a particular school. Her findings add another significant dimension to the well known and often repeated fact that academic achievement varies directly with socio-economic status. Usually this fact is interpreted as reflecting some type of selective factor wherein individuals of high intelligence attain high socio-economic status and produce more intelligent children and that higher status families provide their children with more stimulation for academic achievement. The data presented by Dr. Sexton, however, make clear, at least to this observer, the crucial role of the school in determining the level of academic achievement of the children. The traditional interpretation would continue to argue that the standards and quality of the school reflect the limitations of the home and the immediate community from which the child comes and that the school must gear its level to these limitations. This interpretation has so far not been verified through objective research although it is widely accepted as if it were.

Attempts to determine the specific role of a particular school on the average level of academic performance of the children in that school must obtain data on the general attitudes of teachers in that school towards their children—particularly if there is a marked class discrepancy between teachers and students; the expectations of these teachers and the effect of these expectations on the actual performance of their children; and the children's perspective of themselves, their teachers, and their school. It is now imperative that social scientists study with rigorous objectivity and precision the complex and interrelated problems which seem relevant to an understanding of how children from depressed backgrounds can be motivated for maximum academic achievement.

At present, the work of Allison Davis and his colleagues, which demonstrates the educationally depressing effects of the gap between working-class children and middle-class teachers, is an important starting point for future more detailed research. It is important to know, for example, not only the particular attitudinal patterns which the teacher communicates to these children but also the particular ways in which she communicates her attitudes and how these block or facilitate the academic motivation of lower-class children. The empirical data on these specific problems are sparse, and one is required to speculate on the nature of the manner in which these blockages operate. Probably a core factor in the complex inhibiting dynamics involved in the interplay between middle-class and higher-status teachers and working-class and lower-status children is the pervasive and archiac belief that children from culturally deprived back-grounds are by virtue of their deprivation of lower status position inherently uneducable.

Professor Goodwin Watson, in his introduction to Frank Reissman's book (9), has defined this problem and suggested a general solution as follows:

In recent decades a spate of anthropological, sociological, and social-psychological studies, many of them mentioned by Professor Riessman, has revealed the appalling gap between our pretensions and our practices. We do not give the same kind of food, clothing, housing, medical care, recreation, or justice to the deprived children that we give to those in comfortably-well-off homes. We don't like to think of class distinctions in American life, so we tend to shy away from these unacceptable facts. Opportunities are far from equal.

The American public school is a curious hybrid: it is managed by a school board drawn largely from upper-class circles; it is taught by teachers who come largely from middle-class backgrounds; and it is attended mainly by children from working-class homes. These three groups do not talk the same language. They differ in their manners, power, and hierarchies of values... .

Under-cultured children have much to learn from education, but educators could well take some lessons from some of these youngsters. Their language may not be grammatical, but it is often more vivid and expressive than is the turgid prose of textbooks. These children face some of the "facts of life" more realistically than many of their teachers do. Even their pugnacity might be worth attention by some long-suffering, overworked, underpaid teachers. When it comes to making friends and standing by their pals, some children from under-privileged neighborhoods far outshine their priggish teachers.

The starting point is respect. Nothing else that we have to give will help very much if it is offered with a resentful, contemptuous, or patronizing attitude. We don't understand these neighborhoods, these homes, these children, because we haven't respected them enough to think them worthy of study and attention. Professor Riessman's book is likely to be the pioneer in a series of investigations that will reveal to America that we have neglected a major source of manpower and of creative talent. The stone which the builders rejected may even become the head of the corner.

One may assume that if a child is not treated with the respect which is due him as a human being, and if those who are charged with the responsibility of teaching him believe that he cannot learn, then his motivation and ability to learn may become impaired. If a teacher believes that a child is incapable of being educated, it is likely that this belief will in some way be communicated to the child in one or more of the many forms of contacts inherent in the teacher-pupil relationship.

Because of the importance of the role of teachers in the developing self-image, academic aspirations and achievements of their students, it was thought desirable to conduct a preliminary study of the attitudes of teachers in ten public schools located in depressed areas of a large northern city. The children in these schools came generally from homes and communities which were so lacking in educational stimulation and other determinants of self-respect that they seemed even more dependnt upon their teachers for self-esteem, encouragement, and stimulation. These children, like most deprived human beings, were hypersensitive and desperate in their desire for acceptance.

The findings of this preliminary study revealed that while there were some outstanding exceptions—individual principals and teachers who respected the human dignity and potentialities of their students—the overwhelming majority of these teachers and their supervisors rejected these children and looked upon them as inherently inferior.

For the most, the teachers indicated that they considered these children to be incapable of profiting from a normal curriculum. The children were seen as intellectually inferior and therefore not capable of learning. The qualitative flavor of this complex pattern of negative attitudes can best be communicated by the verbatim reports written by our observers:

> As soon as I entered the classroom, Mrs. X told me in front of the class, that the parents of these children are not professionals and therefore they do not have much background or interest in going ahead to college.... She discussed each child openly in front of the entire class and myself.... She spoke about the children in a belittling manner. She tried to give each child encouragement, but her over-all attitude was negative in that she did not think much of the abilities of her students. She told me in private that "heredity is what really counts," and since they didn't have a high culture in Africa and have not as yet built one in New York, they are intellectually inferior from birth.

Another teacher was described as follows:

> The teacher was a lady of about 50 who had no understanding of these children. She kept pointing to them when talking about them so that even I was slightly embarrassed. She kept repeating "You see what I mean?", which I didn't at all.... She took it for granted that these children were stupid and that there was little that she could do with them.

A third description illustrates some of the subtleties of the problem:

Mr. G. is a rather tense and nervous man. He continually played with his finger or with a pencil or tapped his fingers on the desk. What disturbed him most was the cultural deprivation that most of the students in his school suffered from. He said that often the teacher will refer to everyday facts which the children will be completely ignorant of. He says that it is most difficult if not impossible to teach them.

These and other examples clearly suggest that among many of the teachers who are required to teach children from culturally deprived backgrounds there exists a pervasive negative attitude toward these children. These teachers say repeatedly, and appear to believe, that it is not possible to teach these children. They offer, in support of their conclusion, the belief that these children cannot learn because of "poor heredity," "poor home background," "cultural deprivation," and "low IQ."

The Problem of the IQ

Probably as disturbing as these examples of rejection of these children on the part of those who are required to teach them, are the many examples of well-intentioned teachers who point to the low intelligence- and achievement-test scores of these children as the basis for their belief that these children cannot be educated. These teachers generally do not base their judgment on conscious racial bias or rejection of these children as human beings or necessarily on their "poor heredity." They point to the realities of a poor environment, cultural deprivation and lack of educational stimulation in the home as the determinants of low academic achievement of these children. They maintain that these children should not be expected to function up to the academic level of other children because the test scores clearly indicate that they cannot. Further, they state that to pressure these children for an academic achievement that they are incapable of reaching only creates frustrations and anxieties which will make even more difficult the possibility of adequate functioning on their own level. These individuals, therefore, argue that a special curriculum and a special form of education should be devised for these children from culturally deprived backgrounds who have consistently low IQs and achievement-test scores.

A disturbing aspect of this type of argument is that it does come under the guise of humanitarianism, psychology, and modern educational theory. It becomes necessary, therefore, to look with thorough objectivity at the basis of this argument; namely, the validity of test scores as an index of the intellectual potential of children from culturally deprived backgrounds. Do these test scores indicate some immutable level of intelligence, or do they reflect primarily the obvious cultural and educational deprivations and discriminations suffered by these children?

Modern psychology findings and interpretations would seem to leave no further room for argument that test scores must be interpreted in the light of the general social and cultural milieu of a child and the specific educational opportunities to which he has been exposed. It is generally known that children from deprived educational backgrounds will score lower on available standardized tests. The pioneer work of Otto Klineberg in the 1930's clearly established the fact that intelligence test score will increase on the average as children are moved from a deprived, inferior educational situation to a more positive and stimulating one (8).

We now know that children who are not stimulated at home or in the community or in school will have low scores. Their scores and, what is even more important, their day-to-day academic performance can be improved if they are provided with adequate stimulation in one or more of these areas. When a child from a deprived background is treated as if he is uneducable because he has a low test score, he becomes uneducable and the low test score is thereby reinforced. If a child scores low on an intelligence test because he cannot read and then is not taught to read because he has a low score, then such a child is being imprisoned in an iron circle and becomes the victim of an educational self-fulfilling prophecy.

Another aspect of the problem of the meaning of the IQ, which is not generally discussed and which seems to have been lost sight of by educators and the general public, is the simple fact that the IQ is merely a score that is offered as an index of a given individual's rate of learning compared with the learning rate of others with whom he can be reasonably compared. This interpretation of the IQ is consistent with the fact that a child with a lower IQ can be expected to take longer to learn that which a child with a higher IQ will learn more rapidly. The IQ itself—at least in the normal ranges and above—does not necessarily determine how much a child will learn or for that matter even the ceiling of what he can learn. Rather it reflects the rate of his learning or the amount of effort which will be required for him to learn. In other words, it is quite conceivable that children with lower IQs, even those low IQs which more nearly reflect inherent intellectual limitations, can and do learn substantively what other children can learn. But it will take a longer time, will require more care and skill on the part of the teachers and probably more encouragement and acceptance of the child.

IQ, Snobbery, and Humiliation

Unfortunately, an objective discussion of the problem of the meaning of the IQ is made even more difficult by the fact that this problem has been contaminated by non-educational considerations such as social class status factors. This point can be illustrated by an examination of the arguments in favor of homogeneous groupings. The most persistent arguments for grouping children in homogeneous classes according to IQs are largely assertions of the convenience of such groupings for overworked teachers. The proponents of the procedure of segregating children according to intelligence for educational purposes seem to base their argument on some assumptions of special privilege, special status, special educational advantages and conspicuous recognition which are to be given to an intellectual elite. It is implied and sometimes stated that these conditions will facilitate the maximum use of the already high intelligence of the gifted children and will reduce the frustrations of those children who are not gifted. It is further suggested that if the gifted child is not given special treatment in special classes, he will somehow not fulfill his intellectual potentials—"he will be brought down to the level of the average or the dull child." So far there seems to be little empirical evidence in support of these assertions in spite of their wide acceptance by the public and by many educators.

Those who argue against this form of educational intellectual segregation must nonetheless, eventually demonstrate by empirical research that it is not the most effective educational procedure. Are children who are segregated according to IQ in the classrooms of our schools being educated in a socially realistic and democratic atmosphere? The world consists of individuals of varying levels of intellectual potential and power. Those individuals of high intelligence must be prepared to function effectively with individuals of average or below average intelligence. One important function of the schools is to train children in a socially responsible use of human intelligence. A manifestation of this social responsibility would be the ability of children of high intelligence to use their superior intelligence creatively in working with and helping children of lower intelligence to function more effectively. Children of lower intelligence could be stimulated and encouraged, in a realistic school atmosphere, by the accomplishments of other children. This would be true only if the over-all school atmosphere is one consistent with the self-respect of all children. Children who are stigmatized by being placed in classes designated as "slow" or "dull" or for "children of retarded mental ability" cannot be expected to be stimulated and motivated to improve their academic performance. Such children understandably will become burdened with resentment and humiliation and will seek to escape the humiliating school situation as quickly as possible.

Probably the chief argument against homogeneous groupings is the fact that children who are so segregated lose their individuality in the educational situation. It would seem that the development of a creative individuality would be among the high priority goals of education. Homogeneous groupings tend to require that children be seen in terms of group characteristics rather than in terms of their own individual characteristics. This would seem to be true equally for the bright children as it is for average or dull children. Furthermore, it is questionable whether it is possible to establish a homogeneous group of children on any grounds other than the arbitrary selection of some single aspect of the total complexity that is the human being.

It may be argued on the basis of evidence that even the selection of children in terms of similarity in IQ is arbitrary in that the same range of IQs may mask significant differences in intellectual abilities, patterns, interests, and propensities among children who seem similar in level of general intelligence. Any oversimplification of this fact, concretized into an educational procedure, may not be worth the human and social cost.

It is conceivable that the detrimental effects of segregation based upon intellect is similar to the known detrimental effects of schools segregated on the basis of class, nationality, or race (2). This similarity, if it is found to exist, may reflect the fact that, in general, the average intellectual level of groups of children is related to the social and racial status of their parents. The educational level and achievement of lower-status children are depressed in segregated lower-status schools for those reasons already stated, plus the fact that the morale of their teachers tend to be depressed when they are identified with low prestige schools. Furthermore, some of these teachers may accept assignments in these schools because they may be aware of the fact that the staff in these schools is generally not held to the same high professional standards which prevail in schools where it is believed that the children can learn. Teachers in more privileged schools are probably held to more strict standards of professional evaluation and supervision.

Whatever the determining factors responsible for the low educational achievement of children from lower status groups, the fact remains that up to the present, the overwhelming majority of these children attend schools that do not have a systematic educational program designed to provide the extra stimulation and encouragement which they need if they are to develop their intellectual potential. Some school officials may question whether it is the proper function of the schools to attempt to compensate for the cultural deprivations which burden these children in their homes and in the larger community. As long as this is not done by the schools or some other appropriate social institutions, the motivation and academic achievement of these deprived children will remain depressed, inferior, and socially wasteful. What is more, the schools will have failed to provide them with an effective education and thereby failed to meet a pressing contemporary need.

Mr. Conant and the Education of Culturally Disadvantaged Children

Probably the most widely discussed, if not uncritically accepted, of the recent books dealing with the problem of the education of deprived and privileged children in American cities is James B. Conant's *Slums and Suburbs* (4). In spite of the fact that Mr. Conant is by training, background and experience a chemist, college president, and statesman—and not a professional educator or social scientist—he has assumed with the aid of the Carnegie Corporation of New York, the role of educational expert and spokesman to the nation. His book was reviewed extensively—and for the most part praised—by the important education editors of newspapers throughout the nation. In discussing the complexity of educational problems found in the schools in "slum neighborhoods," Mr. Conant coined the phrase "social dynamite" which has become part of the jargon of these discussions.

Before one engages in a critical analysis of Mr. Conant's assumptions and recommendations for the improvement of the education of deprived and privileged children, it should be stated that this book presents vividly some facts which help to clarify some of the issues related to the basic problem of the inferiority of educational opportunities provided for children of the lower socio-economic classes in the public schools of the ten largest cities in our nation. For example, the book states that half of the children in deprived neighborhoods drop out of school in grades 9, 10, and 11; that the per pupil expenditure in deprived schools is less than half the per pupil expenditure in a privileged school; and that there are seventy professionals per thousand pupils in privileged schools and forty or fewer professionals per thousand pupils in deprived schools. Mr. Conant appeals to the conscience of the American public and asserts that this consistent discrepancy "jolts one's notions of the meaning of equality of opportunity."

Critical reading and analysis of this book, however, reveal that Mr. Conant's prescription for this educational disease will not cure the patient, but, on the contrary, will intensify the illness. The implicit assumptions and explicit suggestions, if accepted by American education would concretize the very discrepancies which Mr. Conant calls "social dynamite" and would lead, if not to an educational explosion to educational dry rot and social stagnation.

The basic assumptions of this book are appalling, anachronistic, and reflect the social science naiveté of its author. The unmodified theme that runs throughout the book is that there are two types of human beings— those who can be educated and those who cannot be educated. Those who can be educated live in suburbs and those who cannot be educated live in slums. And for the most part, those who live in slums are Negroes and those who live in suburbs are white. Children who live in the slums should be provided with practical, vocational—job oriented—education and children in the suburbs should be provided with that level of academic education which is appropriate to their level of intelligence.

Mr. Conant's own words are quite explicit: "The lesson is that to a considerable degree what a school should do and can do is determined by the status and ambitions of the families being served." What changes the status and ambitions of the families?

One needs only to visit such a school (slum school) to be convinced that the nature of the community largely determines what goes on in the school.... . The community and the school are inseparable.

Why then have schools?

Foreign languages in Grade 7 or algebra in Grade 8 (recommendations in my Junior High School report) have little place in a school in which half the pupils in that grade read at the fourth grade level or below.

Why are these children reading at the fourth grade level or below?

Mr. Conant is most explicit in his defense of *de facto* segregated schools and in his support of the outmoded and impossible doctrine of "separate but equal" education for Negroes, and his aversion to the open enrollment program.

In some cities, political leaders have attempted to put pressure on the school authorities to have Negro children attend essentially white schools. In my judgment the cities in which the authorities have yielded to this pressure are on the wrong track. Those which have not done so, like Chicago, are more likely to make progress in improving Negro education. It is my belief that satisfactory education can be provided in an all-Negro school through the expenditure of more money for needed staff and facilities.

It would seem as if this opinion is contradicted by the very facts which Mr. Conant presents in his book and describes as "social dynamite." Mr. Conant's lack of social science training and insights probably accounts for his belief that mere money will make a "Negro" school equal—if indeed, he does mean "equal" when he uses the word "satisfactory" in describing education in an all-Negro school. Mr. Conant obviously does not understand the role of such psychological subtleties as the depressed morale, lowered aspirations, inadequate standards of performance which seem inherent in a stigmatized, rejected, segregated situation.

The following gratuitious advice must therefore be rejected:

... I think it would be far better for these who are agitating for the deliberate mixing of children to accept *de facto* segregated schools as a consequence of a present housing situation and to work for the improvement of slum schools whether Negro or white.

It seems incredible that a distinguished American statesman could continue to taik about American schools in terms of the designations "Negro" and "white" as if such racial designations were compatible with the American educational imperatives in this latter part of the twentieth century. This fact merely highlights a general deficiency of this book; namely, that it discusses problems of contemporary education in terms of the static assumptions and procedures of the past rather than in terms of the dynamic imperatives of the future. This book and its recommendations might have been acceptable in the first two decades of the twentieth century. It cannot be taken seriously now when it advocates without adequate supporting evidence:

An elementary syllabus varied according to socio-economic status of the children; ability groupings and tracks for students in grades 7 through 12; matching neighborhood needs and school services; and generally determining the nature of academic standards and expectations in terms of the "kinds of schools one is considering."

Aside from the archaic educational snobbery which permeates this book—its matter-of-fact assertion of the idea that American education should gear itself to train more efficiently the "hewers of wood and the drawers of water" and provide effective academic education to an "intellectual elite" to be drawn from the socially and economically privileged groups—its author does not seem to understand the crucial role that an imaginative, creative education must play in the contemporary world. He does not understand that it is the function of contemporary American education to discover and implement techniques for uncovering every ounce of the intellectual potential in all our children without regard to their racial, national, or economic background. Creative human intelligence is an all-too-rare resource and must be trained and conserved wherever it is found. It should now be clear that it is not likely to be found in sufficient abundance in the privileged minority. The best of educational stimulation of this group will still produce an inadequate yield. It is now the obligation of our public schools to adopt those procedures, whether open enrollment, higher horizon or other forms of special stimulation and techniques for raising the aspiration of previously deprived children which are necessary to increase the yield of trained intelligence from children whose potential would be lost to a society desperately in need of their future contributions.

Equally important is the fact that Mr. Conant seems unaware of the fact that segregated schools for the privileged suburban white child provide non-adaptive and unrealistic education. He does not seem to grasp that:

Segregated education is inferior and nonadaptive for whites as well as Negroes. Put simply, no child can receive a democratic education in a nondemocratic school. A white youngster in a homogeneous, isolated, "hot house" type of school situation is not being prepared for the realities of the contemporary and future world. Such a child may have brilliant college entrance scores, be extraordinary in his mathematical ability, or read and speak a foreign language with skill and precision, but he is likely to be blocked in many circumstances in his ability to use these intellectual abilities with the poise and effectiveness essential to personal and social creativity. A racially segregated school imposes upon white children the inevitable stultifying burdens of petty provincialism, irrational fears and hatreds of people who are different, and a distorted image of themselves. Psychologically, the racial segregated school at this period of American and world history is an anachronism which our nation cannot afford. This point must be made over and over again until it is understood by those who have the power to make the decisions which control our destiny (3).

Conclusion

What recommendations for curriculum and materials for culturally disadvantaged children can now be made on the basis of social psychological research, theory, and the imperatives of the contemporary world?

The available and most relevant research data on the effects of minority status—culturally disadvantaged, rejected, and stigmatized children—on personality development may be summarized as follows:

As minority-group children learn the inferior status to which they are assigned and observe that they are usually segregated and isolated from the more privileged members of their society, they react with deep feelings of inferiority and with a sense of personal humiliation. Many of them become confused about their own personal worth. Like all other human beings, they require a sense of personal dignity and social support for positive self-esteem. Almost nowhere in the larger society, however, do they find their own dignity as human beings respected or protected. Under these conditions, minority-group children develop conflicts with regard to their feelings about themselves and about the values of the group with which they are identified.... These conflicts, confusions, and doubts give rise under certain circumstances to self-hatred and rejection of their own group....

Minority-group children of all social and economic classes often react to their group conflicts by the adoption of a generally defeatist attitude and a lowering of personal ambition (2).

Upon the basis of these findings it is clear that a fundamental task of the schools in stimulating academic achievement in disadvantaged children is to provide the conditions necessary for building in them positive images of themselves—building in these children a positive self-esteem to supplant the feelings of inferiority and sense of hopelessness which are supported by an all-too-pervasive pattern of social realities. A non-segregated school situation seems basic (necessary if not a sufficient condition) to all other attempts to raise the self-esteem of these children. A child cannot be expected to respect himself if he perceives himself as rejected and set apart in a compound for those of inferior status or caste.

An important determinant of a reality-based, positive self-esteem for children is the opportunity to have successful experiences in meeting challenges. A minority-group child who is expected to fail will almost always fail. His failure will reinforce his sence of inferiority and the related resentments and hostility. A normal child who is expected to learn, who is taught, and who is required to learn will learn. His experiences of success will generally increase his self-respect, enhance his sense of his own worth. He might not need to engage in compensitory forms of anti-social behavior as attention-getting devices. Nor would he need to escape from the school situation which is a constant reminder of failure and personal inferiority. A single standard of academic expectations, a demanding syllabus, and skillful and understanding teaching are essential to the raising of the self-esteem of disadvantaged children, increasing their motivation for academic achievement and providing our society with the benefits of their intellectual potential.

Some attention should be given to the textbooks and materials which are used in our classrooms in order to be sure that they do not directly or indirectly add to the burdens of already psychologically overburdened disadvantaged minority-group children. Indeed it might be necessary to select or devise materials which would raise the self-esteem of these children at the same time that it broadens the perspectives and deepens the social and ethnical insights of more privileged children. Some students of this problem have been rather specific in their criticisms of available materials.

Frank Riessman (9) quotes Dr. Eleanor Leacock's observation:

A critical look at basic readers from the viewpoint of their discordance with "lower-class culture," reveals at a second look a discordance also with what is real experience for most middle class children. One might ask how typical are Dick and Jane, or more important, how meaningful are they and their neat white house in the suburbs to children whose world includes all the blood and thunder, as well as the sophisticated reportage, of television. In what sense do Dick and Jane even reflect middle class ideal patterns in the contemporary world? That such textbook characters help form ideal patterns in the early years is true, but does this not only create a problem for children, when the norms for behavior Dick and Jane express are so far removed from reality? One can even play with the idea of cultural deprivation for middle class children, since home and school join in building a protective barrier between them and so much of the modern world; and one can wonder what the implications of this protection are for their mental health. Certainly such readers do not arouse interest in reading, which develops in spite of, not because of, their content.

It would be an exciting idea to have primers which deal more directly with people and events which arouse the emotions of sympathy, curiosity and wonder in children, texts which recognize whimsy as important in the building of values, which accept the adventurous hero as a valid character for children to respond to, which deal with the "child's world" as reaching from home and family to the moon. What contrast to the vapid amiability of Dick and Jane! And how important to have basic readers in which some children live in white houses in suburbs, but many more, equally important as human beings, live in tenements, or apartments, or on farms, in the west, the north, the south, so that all children can read about all others, and, as Americans, get to know their world as it is. Nor, it should be added, is the same purpose served by a mechanical translation of Dicks and Janes to other places and periods in upper-grade readers.

The complex problem of increasing the effectiveness of education for culturally disadvantaged children cannot be resolved effectively by fragmentary approaches. Rather the gravity of the problem requires the development of bold, imaginative and comprehensive approaches. The Junior High School 43 Project, the forerunner of the Higher Horizons Program of the New York City Public Schools, is an example of the possible success of such a comprehensive approach to this problem. This project was designed to test whether it was possible to raise significantly the academic performance of disadvantaged children through the activities of the school itself in spite of the fact that the conditions of home and community deprivations remained constant.

An important aspect of the 43 Project was the fact that in its methodology it did not rely exclusively on test scores as the basis for selecting those students who were believed to have academic potential. Teacher's estimates, the judgment of guidance counselors, and any evidence of the capacity for superior intellectual interests or functioning were some of the criteria, in addition to tests results, which were used in selecting those children who were to be involved in the special program of the project. Once these children were selected they were subjected to a special program of educational stimulation. The ingredients of this program were systematic guidance and counseling; clinical services when indicated; a cultural enrichment program which consisted of trips to the theatre, museums, opera, college campuses; a parent education program; and a systematic supplementary remedial program in reading, mathematics and languages.

The results of this project as reported in the Third Annual Progress Report published by the Board of Education of the City of New York have justified the most optimistic expectations of those who planned and proposed this demonstration of the positive modifiability of human beings. These results may be summarized by the following quotation taken from this report:

> Although it is too early to assess completely the project academically, we have been heartened by some of the progress we have noted. In comparing the achievement of the pupils who entered the George Washington High School from Junior High School 43 in 1953 with that of the project classes that entered in 1957 and 1958, we find a tremendous difference. In the 1953 group, 5 out of 105 pupils (5%) passed all their academic subjects at the end of the first year; and 2 had averages of 80% or better. In the 1957 project group, 38 out of 148 pupils (25%) passed all their subjects at the end of the first year, and 18 had averages of 80% or better. In the 1958 project group, 43 out of 111 pupils (38%) passed all their subjects at the end of the first year, and 16 had averages of 80% or better.
>
> The evidence is conclusive that the scholastic accomplishment of the project students is far better than that of previous classes from Junior High School 43.

Those who are still concerned with the ubiquitous IQ, might be interested to note that, of the 105 children who were tested at the beginning of the project and three years later, 78 of them showed an increase in IQ. Forty of these students gained more than 10 points; 13 gained more than 20 points. One child gained as much as *40* points in his tested IQ.

While these measurable demonstrations of the success of this project are impressive, probably of even greater social significance are the positive qualitative and by product results which were observed. For example, while the drop-out rate from high school for these children prior to the project was around 40 per cent; the drop out rate for the project children was less than 20 per cent.

The principal of George Washington High School made the following observation:

> In the past, students from 43 were our worst behaved. More teacher and administrative time was spent on them than on any other group. Since we had the project group, this has changed. Not a single student in the project group has been reported to the Dean's office for discipline. Today, they are our best behaved.

The following quotation from the report may serve as summary evaluation of the profound positive effects of this approach to the special education of children from deprived backgrounds:

Judging by the reactions of the students themselves and our observations of them from day to day, it is our belief that all of them, whether they go to college or end their formal education with graduation from high school, will have higher horizons and a greater sense of commitment and purpose in their lives. In our opinion, it is these expected outcomes that make this project so significant, and so far-reaching in its influence.

Probably the fundamental dynamics for the success of this project is the fact that the project itself raised the self-esteem of these children, increased the aspirations of their parents and bolstered the morale of their teachers. The project and its ingredients of special stimulation, encouragement, and remedial help indicated to these children that someone—the principal, the guidance counsellor, the teacher—believed that they could learn. Someone believed in them—believed in their educability and respected them as human beings. The cumulative effects of these changes in the psychological atmosphere and the changes in the self-image of these children were found in the higher academic achievements and the marked improvement in self-respect and general social behavior.

The special stimulation, the creative approach to the education of these deprived children, can be and should be provided for all children. These positive results can be duplicated in every school of this type. The Superintendent of Schools of the City of New York has extended some aspects of the 43 project to nearly forty other schools. This expanded program is now known as the Higher Horizons Program.

The Challenge of the Future

There are aspects of the problem of raising the level of educational achievement among deprived children which cannot be solved by the public schools and teachers without the help and understanding of the total community and our teacher training institutions. Certainly the community and its leaders must come to understand the importance of providing adequate education for all children and must through this understanding be prepared to pay the cost of socially effective and democratic education. It can be demonstrated that this would be more economical than the cost of delinquency, crime, bigotry, and other symptoms of personal and social disorganization.

The curricula of our teacher training institutions must be re-examined to determine whether they make adequate and systematic use of that fund of modern psychological knowledge which deals with such problems as:

the meaning of intelligence and problems related to the IQ and its interpretation; the contemporary interpretation of racial and nationality differences in intelligence and academic achievement; the role of motivation, self-confidence and the self-image in the level of academic achievement; and general problems of the modifiability and resilience of the human being.

The evidence is now overwhelming that high intellectual potential exists in a larger percentage of individuals from lower status groups than was previously discovered, stimulated and trained for socially beneficial purposes. In order to increase the yield of desperately needed trained intellects from these previously deprived groups, it will be necessary to develop systematic educational programs designed to attain this specific goal. These programs must raise the aspirational levels of these children and their parents. They must change the attitudes of teachers and school officials from one of rejection and fatalistic negation to one of acceptance and a belief in the educability and human dignity of these children. And, of course, the programs must provide appropriate guidance and remedial services designed to compensate for the past educational inferiorities and the deprivations in their homes and communities. It would seem that the chances of success for such an imperative educational program would be minimal in a non-democratic school atmosphere characterized by intellectual, social, national or racial segregation.

In providing the necessary conditions for a more effective education of children from lower status groups, the education of the more privileged children at the same time will be made more realistic, more meaningful, and more consistent with the demands of the contemporary and future world. One of the realities of the contemporary world is the fact that the destiny of one group of children is tied to the destiny of all other groups of children. Our schools can no longer afford the luxury of a snobbish, status-dominated approach to the hard problems of increasing educational effectiveness for all children. The democratic pressures on our educational institutions are no longer merely verbal or sentimental. They now seem to have the imperative realities of survival.

REFERENCES

1. Clark, Kenneth B., "The Most Valuable Hidden Resources," *College Board Review*, No. 29, pp. 23-26, Spring, 1956.
2. ————, *Prejudice and Your Child*, Boston: Beacon, 1955.
3. ————, "Desegregation: The Role of the Social Sciences," *Teachers College Record*, 62 (1) 1-17, October 1960.
4. Conant, James B., *Slums and Suburbs*, New York: McGraw-Hill, 1961.

5. Davis A., "American Status Systems and the Socialization of the Child," *Amer. sociol. Rev.*, 6:345-354, 1941.

6. Hansen, C. F., *Addendum: A Five Year Report on Desegregation in the Washington, D. C. Schools*, New York: Anti-Defamation League of B'nai B'rith, 1960.

7. ————, *Miracle of Social Adjustment*, New York: Anti-Defamation League of B'nai B'rith, 1957.

8. Klineberg, Otto, *Negro Intelligence and Selective Migration*, New York: Columbia University Press. 1955.

9. Riessman, Frank, *The Culturally Deprived Child*, New York: Harper, 1962.

10. Sexton, Patricia C., *Education and Income*, New York: Viking, 1961.

Martin Deutsch | The Disadvantaged Child and the Learning Process

This paper will discuss the interaction of social and developmental factors and their impact on the intellectual growth and school performance of the child. It will make particular reference to the large number of urban children who come from marginal social circumstances. While much of the discussion will be speculative, where appropriate it will draw on data from the field, and will suggest particular relationships and avenues for future investigation or demonstration.

Among children who come from lower-class socially impoverished circumstances, there is a high proportion of school failure, school drop-outs, reading and learning disabilities, as well as life adjustment problems. This means not only that these children grow up poorly equipped academically, but also that the effectiveness of the school as a major institution for socialization is diminished. The effect of this process is underlined by the fact that this same segment of the population contributes disproportionately to the delinquency and other social deviancy statistics.

The thesis here is that the lower-class child enters the school situation so poorly prepared to produce what the school demands that initial failures are almost inevitable, and the school experience becomes negatively rather than positively reinforced. Thus the child's experience in school does nothing to counteract the invidious influences to which he is exposed in his slum, and sometimes segregated, neighborhood.

We know that children from underprivileged environments tend to come to school with a qualitatively different preparation for the demands of both the learning process and the behavioral requirements of the classroom. These are various differences in the kinds of socializing experiences these children have had, as contrasted with the middle-class child. The culture of their environment is a different one from the culture that has molded the school and its educational techniques and theory.

We know that it is difficult for all peoples to span cultural discontinuities, and yet we make little if any effort to prepare administrative person-

163

nel or teachers and guidance staff to assist the child in this transition from one cultural context to another. This transition must have serious psychological consequences for the child, and probably plays a major role in influencing his later perceptions of other social institutions as he is introduced to them.

It must be pointed out that the relationship between social background and school performance is not a simple one. Rather, evidence which is accumulating points more and more to the influence of background variables on the patterns of perceptual, language, and cognitive development of the child and the subsequent diffusion of the effects of such patterns into all areas of the child's academic and psychological performance. To understand these effects requires delineating the underlying skills in which these children are not sufficiently proficient. A related problem is that of defining what aspects of the background are most influential in producing what kinds of deficits in skills.

Environmental Factors

Let us begin with the most macroscopic background factors. While it is likely that slum life might have delimited areas that allow for positive growth and that the middle-class community has attributes which might retard healthy development, generally the combination of circumstances in middle-class life is considerably more likely to furnish opportunities for normal growth of the child. At the same time, slum conditions are more likely to have deleterious effects on physical and mental development. This is not to say that middle-class life furnishes a really adequate milieu for the maximum development of individual potential: it doesn't. The fact that we often speak as though it does is a function of viewing the middle-class environment in comparison to the slum. Middle-class people who work and teach across social-class lines often are unable to be aware of the negative aspects of the middle-class background because of its apparent superiority over the less advantageous background provided by lower-class life. We really have no external criterion for evaluating the characteristics of a milieu in terms of how well it is designed to foster development; as a result we might actually be measuring one area of social failure with the yardstick of social catastrophe.

It is true that many leading personalities in twentieth-century American life have come from the slums, and this is a fact often pointed out by nativistic pragmatists in an effort to prove that if the individual "has it in him" he can overcome—and even be challenged by—his humble surroundings. This argument, though fundamentally fallacious, might have had more to recommend it in the past. At the turn of the century we were a massively vertical mobile society—that is, with the exception of certain large minority groups such as the Negroes, the Indians, and the Mexican-Americans who were rarely allowed on the social elevator. In the mid-twentieth century, it is now increasingly possible for all groups to get on, but social and economic conditions have changed, and the same elevator more frequently moves in two directions or stands still altogether. When it does move, it goes more slowly, and, most discouragingly, it also provides an observation window on what, at least superficially, appears to be a most affluent society. Television, movies, and other media continually expose the individual from the slum to the explicit assumption that the products of a consumer society are available to all—or, rather, as he sees it, to all but him. In effect, this means that the child from the disadvantaged environment is an outsider and an observer—through his own eyes and those of his parents or neighbors—of the mainstream of American life. At the same time, when the child enters school he is exposing himself directly to the values and anticipations of a participant in that mainstream—his teacher. It is not sufficiently recognized that there is quite a gap between the training of a teacher and the needs limitations, and unique strengths of the child from a marginal situation. This gap is, of course, maximized when the child belongs to a minority group that until quite recently was not only excluded from the mainstream, but was not even allowed to bathe in the tributaries.

What are some of the special characteristics of these children, and why do they apparently need exceptional social and educational planning? So often, administrators and teachers say, they are children who are "curious," "cute," "affectionate," "warm," and independently dependent in the kindergarten and the first grade, but who so often become "alienated," "withdrawn," "angry," "passive," "apathetic," or just "trouble-makers" by the fifth and sixth grade. In our research at the Institute for Developmental Studies, it is in the first grade that we usually see the smallest differences between socio-economic or racial groups in intellectual, language, and some conceptual measures, and in the later grades that we find the greatest differences in favor of the more socially privileged groups. From both teacher's observations and the finding of this increasing gap, it appears that there is a failure on some level of society and, more specifically, the educational system. Was the school scientifically prepared to receive these children in the first place? And, in addition, were the children perhaps introduced to the individual demands of the larger culture at too late an age—that is, in first grade?

Before discussing these psychological products of social deprivation, it is appropriate to look more closely at the special circumstances of Negro slum residents. In the core city of most of our large metropolitan areas, 40 to 70 per cent of the elementary school population is likely to be Negro. In my observations, through workshops in many of these cities, I have often been surprised to find how little real comprehension of the particular problems of these youngsters exists as part of the consciousness of the Negro or white middle-class teachers. While in middle-class schools there is great sensitivity to emotional climates and pressures and tensions that might be operating on the child in either the home or the school, in lower-class schools the problems of social adaptation are so massive that sensitivity tends to become blunted.

In the lower-class Negro group there still exist the sequelae of the conditions of slavery. While a hundred years have passed, this is a short time in the life of a people. And the extension of tendrils of the effects of slavery into modern life has been effectively discouraged only in the last few decades, when there have been some real attempts to integrate the Negro fully into American life. It is often difficult for teachers and the personnel of other community agencies to understand the Negro lower-class child—particularly the child who has come, or whose parents have come, from the rural South. There is a whole set of implicit and explicit value systems which determine our educational philosophies, and the institutional expectation is that all children participate in these systems. And yet for these expectations to be met, the child must experience some continuity of socio-cultural participation in and sharing of these value systems before he comes to school. This is often just not the case for the child who comes from an encapsulated community, particularly when the walls have been built by the dominant social and cultural forces that have also determined the value systems relating to learning.

A recent article in *Fortune* magazine asked why the Negro failed to take full advantage of opportunities open to him in American life. At least part of the answer is that the Negro has not been fully integrated into American life, and that even knowledge about particular occupations and their requirements is not available outside the cultural mainstream. Implications of this for the aspirations and motivations of children will be discussed later.

Another source of misunderstanding on the part of school and social agency people is the difficulty of putting in historical perspective the casual conditions responsible for the high percentage of broken homes in the Negro community. Implications of this for the child's emotional stability are very frequently recognized, but the effects on the child's motivation, self-concept, and achievement orientation are not often understood.

The Negro family was first broken deliberately by the slave traders and the plantation owners for their own purposes. As was pointed out earlier, the hundred years since slavery is not a very long time for a total social metamorphosis even under fostering conditions—and during that period the Negro community has been for the most part economically marginal and isolated from the contacts which would have accelerated change. The thirteen depressions and recessions we have had since Emancipation have been devastating to this community. These marginal economic and encapsulated social circumstances have been particularly harsh on the Negro male. The chronic instability has greatly influenced the Negro man's concept of himself and his general motivation to succeed in competitive areas of society where the rewards are greatest. All these circumstances have contributed to the instability of the Negro family, and particularly to the fact that it is most often broken by the absence of the father. As a result, the lower-class Negro child entering school often has had no experience with a "successful" male model or thereby with a psychological framework in which effort can result in at least the possibility of achievement. Yet the value system of the school and of the learning process is predicated on the assumption that effort will result in achievement.

To a large extent, much of this is true not only for the Negro child but for all children who come from impoverished and marginal social and economic conditions. These living conditions are characterized by great overcrowding in substandard housing, often lacking adequate sanitary and other facilities. While we don't know the actual importance, for example, of moments of privacy, we do know that the opportunity frequently does not exist. In addition, there are likely to be large numbers of siblings and half-siblings, again with there being little opportunity for individuation. At the same time, the child tends to be restricted to his immediate environment, with conducted explorations of the "outside" world being infrequent and sometimes non-existent. In the slums, and to an unfortunately large extent in many other areas of our largest cities, there is little opportunity to observe natural beauty, clean landscapes or other pleasant and aesthetically pleasing surroundings.

In the child's home, there is a scarcity of objects of all types, but especially of books, toys, puzzles, pencils, and scribbling paper. It is not that the mere presence of such materials would necessarily result in their productive use, but it would increase the child's familiarity with the tools he'll be confronted with in school. Actually, for the most effective utilization of these tools, guidance and explanations are necessary from the earliest time of exposure. Such guidance requires not only the presence of aware and educated adults, but also time—a rare commodity in these marginal circumstances. Though many parents will share in the larger value system of having high aspirations for their children, they are unaware of the operational steps required for the preparation of the child to use optimally the learning opportunities in the school. Individual potential is one of the most unmarketable properties if the child acquires no means for its development, or if no means exist for measuring it objectively. It is here that we must understand the consequences of all these aspects of the slum matrix for the psychological and cognitive development of the child.

Psychological Factors

A child from any circumstance who has been deprived of a substantial portion of the variety of stimuli which he is maturationally capable of responding to is likely to be deficient in the equipment required for learning.

Support for this is found in Hunt who, in discussing Piaget's developmental theories, points out that, according to Piaget, ". . . the rate of development is in substantial part, but certainly not wholly, a function of environmental circumstances. Change in circumstances is required to force the accommodative modifications of schemata that constitute development. Thus, the greater the variety of situations to which the child must accommodate his behavioral structures, the more differentiated and mobile they become. Thus, the more new things a child has seen and the more he has heard, the more things he is interested in seeing and hearing. Moreover, the more variation in reality with which he has coped, the greater is his capacity for coping." (2, pp. 258-259).

This emphasis on the importance of variety in the environment implies the detrimental effects of lack of variety. This in turn leads to a concept of "stimulus deprivation." But it is important that it be correctly understood. By this is not necessarily meant any restriction of the quantity of stimulation, but, rather, a restriction to a segment of the spectrum of stimulation potentially available. In addition to the restriction in variety, from what is known of the slum environment, it might be postulated that the segments made available to these children tend to have poorer and less systematic ordering of stimulation sequences, and would thereby be less useful to the growth and activation of cognitive potential.

This deprivation has effects on both the formal and the contentual aspects of cognition. By "formal" is meant the operations—the behavior —by which stimuli are perceived, encouraged, and responded to. By "contentual" is meant the actual content of the child's knowledge and comprehension. "Formal equipment" would include perceptual discrimination skills, the ability to sustain attention, and the ability to use adults as sources of information and for satisfying curiosity. Also included would be the establishment of expectations of reward from accumulation of knowledge, from task completion, and from adult reinforcement, and the ability to delay gratification. Examples of "contentual equipment" would be the language-symbolic system, environmental information, general and environmental orientation, and concepts of comparability and relativity appropriate to the child's age level. The growth of a differentiated additudinal set toward learning is probably a resultant of the interaction between formal and contentual levels.

Hypothesizing that stimulus deprivation will result in deficiencies in either of these equipments, let us examine the particular stimuli which are available and those which are absent from the environment of the child who comes from the conditions discussed above. This reasoning suggests also certain hypotheses regarding the role of environment in the evolving of the formal and contentual systems.

As was pointed out in the previous section, the disadvantaged environment as well as certain aspects of the middle-class circumstance offers the child, over-all, a restricted range of experience. While one does see great individual variability in these children, social conditions reduce the range of this variation; with less variety in input, it would be reasonable to assume a concomitant restriction in the variety of output. This is an important respect in which social poverty may have a leveling effect on the achievement of individual skills and abilities. Concomitantly, in the current problem of extensive under-achievement in suburban lower-middle-class areas, the over-routinization of activity with the consequent reduction in variety may well be the major factor.

In individual terms, a child is probably farther away from his maturational ceiling as a result of this experiential poverty. This might well be a crucial factor in the poorer performance of the lower socio-economic children on standardized tests of intelligence. On such tests, the child is compared with others of his own age. But if his point of development in relation to the maturational ceiling for his age group is influenced by his experience, then the child with restricted experience may actually be developed to a proportionately lower level of his own actual ceiling. If a certain quantum of fostering experience is necessary to activate the achievement of particular maturational levels, then perhaps the child who is deficient in this experience will take longer to achieve these levels, even though his potential may be the same as the more advantaged child. It might be that in order to achieve a realistic appraisal of the ability levels of children, an "experience" age rather than the chronological age should be used to arrive at norms.

This suggests a limitation on the frequent studies comparing Negro and white children. Even when it is possible to control for the formal attributes of social class membership, the uniqueness of the Negro child's experience would make comparability impossible when limited to these class factors. Perhaps too, if such an interaction exists between experiential and biological determinants of development, it would account for the failure of the culture-free tests, as they too are standardized on an age basis without allowing for the experimental interaction (as distinguished from specific experimental *influence*).

Let us now consider some of the specifics in the child's environment, and their effects on the development of the formal, contentual, and attitudinal systems.

Visually, the urban slum and its overcrowded apartments offer the child a minimal range of stimuli. There are usually few if any pictures on the wall, and the objects in the household, be they toys, furniture, or utensils, tend to be sparse, repetitious, and lacking in form and color variations. The sparsity of objects and lack of diversity of home artifacts which are available and meaningful to the child, in addition to the unavailability of individualized training, gives the child few opportunities to manipulate and organize the visual properties of his environment and thus perceptually to organize and discriminate the nuances of that environment. These would include figure-ground relationships and the spatial organization of the visual field. The sparsity of manipulable objects probably also hampers the development of these functions in the tactile area. For example, while these children have broomsticks and usually a ball, possibly a doll or a discarded kitchen pot to play with, they don't have the different shapes and colors and sizes to manipulate which the middle-class child has in the form of blocks which are bought just for him, or even in the variety of sizes and shapes of cooking utensils which might be available to him as playthings.

It is true, as has been pointed out frequently, that the pioneer child didn't have many playthings either. But he had a more active responsibility toward the environment and a great variety of growing plants and other natural resources as well as a stable family that assumed a primary role for the education and training of the child. In addition, the intellectually normal or superior frontier child could and usually did grow up to be a farmer. Today's child will grow up into a world of automation requiring highly differentiated skills if he and society are to use his intellect.

The effect of sparsity of manipulable objects on visual perception is, of course, quite speculative, as few data now exist. However, it is an important area, as among skills necessary for reading are form discriminat

tion and visual spatial organization. Children from depressed areas, because of inadequate training and stimulation, may not have developed the requisite skills by the time they enter first grade, and the assumption that they do possess these skills may thus add to the frustration these children experience on entering school.

The lower-class home is not a verbally oriented environment. The implications of this for language development will be considered below in the discussion of the contentual systems. Here let us consider its implication for the development of auditory discrimination skills. While the environment is a noisy one, the noise is not, for the most part, meaningful in relation to the child, and for him most of it is background. In the crowded apartments with all the daily living stresses, is a minimum of non-instructional conversation directed toward the child. In actuality, the situation is ideal for the child to learn inattention. Furthermore, he does not get practice in auditory discrimination or feedback from adults correcting his enunciation, pronunciation, and grammar. In studies at the Institute for Developmental Studies at New York Medical College, as yet unreported in the literature, we have found significant differences in auditory discrimination between lower-class and middle-class children in the first grade. These differences seem to diminish markedly as the children get older, though the effects of their early existence on other functioning remain to be investigated. Here again, we are dealing with a skill very important to reading. Our data indicate too that poor readers within social-class groups have significantly more difficulty in auditory discrimination than do good readers. Further, this difference between good and poor readers is greater for the lower-class group.

If the child learns to be inattentive in the pre-school environment, as has been postulated, this further diminishes incoming stimulation. Further, if this trained inattention comes about as a result of his being insufficiently called upon to respond to particular stimuli, then his general level of responsiveness will also be diminished. The nature of the total environment and the child-adult interaction is such that reinforcement is too infrequent, and, as a result, the quantity of response is diminished. The implications of this for the structured learning situation in the school are quite obvious.

Related to attentivity is memory. Here also we would postulate the dependence of the child, particularly in the pre-school period, on interaction with the parent. It is adults who link the past and the present by calling to mind prior shared experiences. The combination of the constriction in the use of language and in shared activity results, for the lower-class child, in much less stimulation of the early memory function.

Although I don't know of any data supporting this thesis, from my observations it would seem that there is a tendency for these children to be proportionately more present-oriented and less aware of past-present sequences than the middle-class child. This is consistent with anthropological research and thinking. While this could be a function of the poorer time orientation of these children or of their difficulty in verbal expression, both of which will be discussed below, it could also relate to a greater difficulty in seeing themselves in the past or in a different context. Another area which points up the home-school discontinuity is that of time. Anthropologists have pointed out that from culture to culture time concepts differ and that time as life's governor is a relatively modern phenomenon and one which finds most of its slaves in the lower-middle, middle-middle, and upper-middle classes. It might not even be an important factor in learning, but it is an essential feature in the measurement of children's performance by testing and in the adjustment of children to the organizational demands of the school. The middle-class teacher organizes the day by allowing a certain amount of time for each activity. Psychologists have long noticed that American Indian children, mountain children, and children from other non-industrial groups have great difficulty organizing their response tempo to meet time limitations. In the Orientation Scale developed at the Institute, we have found that lower-class children in the first grade had significantly greater difficulty than did middle-class children in handling items related to time judgments.

Another area in which the lower-class child lacks pre-school orientation is the well-inculcated expectation of reward for performance, especially for successful task completion. The lack of such expectation, of course, reduces motivation for beginning a task and, therefore, also makes less likely the self-reinforcement of activity through the gaining of feelings of competence. In these impoverished, broken homes there is very little of the type of interaction seen so commonly in middle-class homes, in which the parent sets a task for the child, observes its performance, and in some way rewards its completion. Neither, for most tasks, is there the disapproval which the middle-class child incurs when he does not perform properly or when he leaves something unfinished. Again, much of the organization of the classroom is based on the assumption that children anticipate rewards for performance and that they will respond in these terms to tasks which are set for them. This is not to imply that the young lower-class child is not given assignments in his home, nor that he is never given approval or punishment. Rather, the assignments tend to be motoric in character, have a short time-span, and are more likely to relate to very concrete objects or services for people. The tasks given to pre-school

children in the middle-class are more likely to involve language and conceptual processes, and are thereby more attuned to the later school setting.

Related to the whole issue of the adult-child dynamic in establishing a
basis for the later learning process is the ability of the child to use the
adult as a source for information, correction and the reality testing involved in problem solving and the absorption of new knowledge. When
free adult time is greatly limited, homes vastly overcrowded, economic
stress chronic, and the general educational level very low—and, in addition, when adults in our media culture are aware of the inadequacy of
their education—questions from children are not encouraged, as the adults
might be embarrassed by their own limitations and anyway are too preoccupied with the business of just living and surviving. In the child's
formulation of concepts of the world, the ability to formulate questions
is an essential step in data gathering. If questions are not encouraged or
if they are not responded to, this is a function which does not mature.

At the Institute, in our observations of children at the kindergarten
level and in our discussions with parents, we find that many lower-class
children have difficulty here. It follows that this problem, if it is not com-
pensated for by special school efforts, becomes more serious later in the
learning process, as more complex subject matter is introduced. It is here
that questioning is not only desirable but essential, for if the child is not
prepared to demand clarification he again falls farther behind, the process
of alienation from school is facilitated, and his inattentiveness becomes
further reinforced as he just does not understand what is being presented.

It is generally agreed that the language-symbolic process plays an important role at all levels of learning. It is included here under the "contentual" rubric because language development evolves through the correct labeling of the environment, and through the use of appropriate words
for the relating and combining and recombining of the concrete and abstract components in describing, interpreting, and communicating perceptions, experiences, and ideational matter. One can postulate on considerable evidence that language is one of the areas which is most sensitive to
the impact of the multiplicity of problems associated with the stimulus
deprivation found in the marginal circumstances of lower-class life. There
are various dimensions of language, and for each of these it is possible
to evaluate the influence of the verbal environment of the home and its
immediate neighborhood.

In order for a child to handle multiple attributes of words and to associate words with their proper referents, a great deal of exposure to language is presupposed. Such exposure involves training, experimenting
with identifying objects and having corrective feedback, listening to a

variety of verbal material, and just observing adult language usage. Exposure of children to this type of experience is one of the great strengths of the middle-class home, and concomitantly represents a weakness in the lower-class home. In a middle-class home also, the availability of a great range of objects to be labeled and verbally related to each other strengthens the over-all language fluency of the child and gives him a basis for both understanding the teacher and for being able to communicate with her on various levels. An implicit hypothesis in a recent Institute survey of verbal skills is that verbal fluency is strongly related to reading skills and to other highly organized integrative and conceptual verbal activity.

The acquisition of language facility and fluency and experience with the multiple attributes of words is particularly important in view of the estimate that only 60 to 80 per cent of any sustained communication is usually heard. Knowledge of context and of the syntactical regularities of a language make correct completion and comprehension of the speech sequence possible. This completion occurs as a result of the correct anticipation of the sequence of language and thought. The child who has not achieved these anticipatory language skills is greatly handicapped in school. Thus for the child who already is deficient in auditory discrimination and in ability to sustain attention, it becomes increasingly important that he have the very skills he lacks most.

The problem in developing preventive and early remedial programs for these children is in determining the emphasis on the various areas that need remediation. For example, would it be more effective to place the greatest emphasis on the training of auditory discrimination, or on attentional mechanisms, or on anticipatory receptive language functions in order to achieve the primary goal of enabling the child to understand his teacher? In programming special remedial procedures, we do not know how much variation we will find from child to child, or if social-class experiences create a sufficiently homogeneous pattern of deficit so that the fact of any intervention and systematic training may be more important than its sequences. If this is so, the intervention would probably be most valid in the language area, because the large group of lower-class children with the kinds of deficits mentioned are probably maturationally ready for more complex language functioning than they have achieved. Language knowledge, once acquired, can be self-reinforcing in just communicating with peers or talking to oneself.

In observations of lower-class homes, it appears that speech sequences seem to be temporally very limited and poorly structured syntactically. It is thus not surprising to find that a major focus of deficit in the children's language development is syntactical organization and subject continuity. In preliminary analysis of expressive and receptive language data on samples of middle- and lower-class children at the first- and fifth-grade levels, there are indications that the lower-class child has more expressive language ability than is generally recognized or than emerges in the classroom. The main differences between the social classes seem to lie in the level of syntactical organization. If, as is indicated in this research, with proper stimulation a surprisingly high level of expressive language functioning is available to the same children who show syntactical deficits, then we might conclude that the language variables we are dealing with here are by-products of social experience rather than indices of basic ability or intellectual level. This again suggests another possibly vital area to be included in an enrichment or a remedial program: training in the use of word sequences to relate and unify cognitions.

Also on the basis of preliminary analysis of data, it appears that retarded readers have the most difficulty with the organization of expressive language.

In another type of social-class-related language analysis, Bernstein (1960), an English sociologist, has pointed out that the lower-class tends to use informal language and mainly to convey concrete needs and immediate consequences, while the middle-class usage tends to be more formal and to emphasize the relating of concepts. This difference between these two milieus, then, might explain the finding in some of our recent research that the middle-class fifth-grade child has an advantage over the lower-class fifth grader in tasks where precise and somewhat abstract language is required for solution. Further, Bernstein's reasoning would again emphasize the communication gap which exists between the middle-class teacher and the lower-class child.

Though it might belong more in the formal than in the contentual area, one can postulate that the absence of well-structured routine and activity in the home is reflected in the difficulty that the lower-class child has in structuring language. The implication of this for curriculum in the kindergarten and nursery school would be that these children should be offered a great deal of verbalized routine and regulation so that expectation can be built up in the child and then met.

According to Piaget's theories, later problem-solving and logical abilities are built on the earlier and orderly progression through a series of developmental stages involving the active interaction between the child and his environment. This is considered a maturational process, though highly related to experience and practice. Language development does not occupy a super-ordinate position. However, Whorf, Vygotsky, and some contemporary theorists have made language the essential ingredient in concept formation, problem-solving, and in the relating to an interpretation of the environment. Current data at the Institute tend to indicate that class differences in perceptual abilities and in general environmental orientation decrease with chronological age, whereas language differences tend to increase. These might tentatively be interpreted to mean that perceptual development occurs first and that language growth and its importance in problem solving comes later. If later data and further analysis support this interpretation, then the implication would be that the lower-class child comes to school with major deficits in the perceptual rather than the language area. Perhaps the poverty of his experience has slowed his rate of maturation. Then by requiring, without the antecedent verbal preparation, a relatively high level of language skill, the school may contribute to an increase in the child's deficit in this area, relative to middle-class children. Meanwhile, his increased experience and normal maturational processes stimulate perceptual development, and that deficit is overcome. But the child is left with a language handicap. The remedy for such a situation would be emphasis on perceptual training for these children in the early school, or, better, pre-school, years, combined with a more gradual introduction of language training and requirements.

This theory and interpretation are somewhat, but by no means wholly, in conflict with the previous discussion of language. In an area where there is as yet much uncertainty, it is important to consider as many alternatives as possible, in order not to restrict experimentation.

In any event, whether or not we consider language skills as primary mediators in concept formation and problem solving, the lower-class child seems to be at a disadvantage at the point of entry into the formal learning process.

The other contentual factors that so often result in a poorly prepared child being brought to the school situation are closely interrelated with language. Briefly, they revolve around the child's understanding and knowledge of the physical, geographic, and geometric characteristics of the world around him, as well as information about his self-identity and some of the more macroscopic items of general information. It could be reasonably expected, for example, that a kindergarten or first-grade child who is not mentally defective would know both his first and last names, his address or the city he lives in, would have a rudimentary concept of number relationships, and would know something about the differences between near and far, high and low, and similar relational concepts. Much of what happens in school is predicated on the prior availability of this basic information. We know that educational procedures frequently proceed without establishing the actual existence of such a baseline. Again, in the lower-class child it cannot be taken for granted that the home experience has supplied this information or that it has tested the child for this knowledge. In facilitating the learning process in these children, the school must expect frequently to do a portion of the job traditionally assigned to the home, and curriculum must be reorganized to provide for establishing a good base. This type of basic information is essential so that the child can relate the input of new information to some stable core.

From all of the foregoing, it is obvious that the lower-class child when he enters school has as many problems in understanding what it is all about and why he is there as school personnel have in relating traditional curriculum and learning procedures to this child. Some reorientation is really necessary, as discussion of these problems almost always focuses on the problems the school has, rather than on the enormous confusion, hesitations, and frustrations the child experiences and does not have the language to articulate when he meets an essentially rigid set of academic expectations. Again, from all the foregoing, the child, from the time he enters school and is exposed to assumptions about him derived from experience with the middle-class child, has few success experiences and much failure and generalized frustration, and thus begins the alienating process in the direction of the apathetic and disgruntled fifth grader described earlier.

The frustration inherent in not understanding, not succeeding, and not being stimulated in the school—although being regulated by it, creates a basis for the further development of negative self-images and low evaluations of individual competencies. This would be especially true for the Negro child who, as we know from doll-play and other studies, starts reflecting the social bias in his own self-image at very early ages. No matter how the parents might aspire to a higher achievement level for their child, their lack of knowledge as to the operational implementation, combined with the child's early failure experiences in school, can so effectively attenuate confidence in his ability ever to handle competently challenge in the academic area, that the child loses all motivation.

It is important to state that not all the negative factors and deficits discussed here are present in every or even in any one child. Rather, there is a patterning of socially determined school-achievement-related disabilities which tends initially to set artificially low ceilings for these children: initially artificial, because as age increases it becomes more and more difficult for these children to develop compensatory mechanisms, to respond to special programs, or to make the psychological readjustments required to overcome the cumulative effects of their early deficits.

It is also important to state that there are strengths and positive features associated with lower-class life. Unfortunately, they generally tend not to be, at least immediately, congruent with the demands of the school. For example, lack of close supervision or protection fosters the growth of independence in lower-class children. However, this independence—and probably confidence—in regard to the handling of younger siblings, the crossing of streets, self-care, and creating of their own amusements, does not necessarily meaningfully transfer to the unfamiliar world of books, language, and abstract thought.

School Conditions

Educational factors have of course been interlaced throughout this discussion, but there are some special features that need separate delineation.

The lower-class child probably enters school with a nebulous and essentially neutral attitude. His home rarely, if ever, negatively predisposes him toward the school situation, though it might not offer positive motivation and correct interpretation of the school experience. It is in the school situation that the highly charged negative attitudes toward learning evolve, and the responsibility for such large groups of normal children showing great scholastic retardation, the high drop-out rate, and to some extent the delinquency problem, must rest with the failure of the school to promote the proper acculturation of these children. Through some of the responsibility may be shared by the larger society, the school, as the institution of that society, offers the only mechanism by which the job can be done.

It is unfair to imply that the school has all the appropriate methods at its disposal and has somehow chosen not to apply them. On the contrary, what is called for is flexible experimentation in the development of new methods, the clear delineation of the problem, and the training and retraining of administrative and teaching personnel in the educational philosophy and the learning procedures that this problem requires.

In addition, the school should assume responsibility for a systematic plan for the education of the child in the areas that have been delineated here by the time the child reaches kindergarten or first grade. This does not mean that the school will abrogate the family's role with regard to the child, but rather that the school will insure both the intellectual and the attitudinal receptivity of each child to its requirements. Part of a hypothesis now being tested in a new pre-school program is based on the assumption that early intervention by well-structured programs will significantly reduce the attenuating influence of the socially marginal environment.

What might be necessary to establish the required base to assure the eventual full padticipation of these children in the opportunity structure offered by the educational system is an ungraded sequence from age 3 or 4 through 8, with a low teacher-pupil ratio. Perhaps, also, the school system should make full use of anthropologists, sociologists, and social psychologists for description and interpretation of the cultural discontinuities which face the individual child when he enters school. In addition, the previously discussed patterning of deficits and strengths should be evaluated for each child and placed in a format which the teacher can use as a guide. In the early years this would enable diagnostic reviews of the intellectual functioning of each child, so that learning procedures, to whatever extent possible, could be appropriate to a particular child's needs. New evaluation techniques must be developed for this purpose, as the standardized procedures generally cannot produce accurate evaluation of the functioning level or achievement potential of these children.

Possibly most important would be the greater utilization by educators in both curriculum development and teacher training of the new and enormous knowledge, techniques, and researches in the social and behavioral sciences. Similarly, social and behavioral scientists have in the school a wonderful laboratory to study the interpenetration and interaction of fundamental social, cognitive, psychological, and developmental processes. Close and continuing collaboration, thus, should be mutually productive and satisfying, and is strongly indicated.

REFERENCES

1. Bernstein, B., "Language and Social Class," *Brit. J. Psychol.*, 11:271-276, September 1960.
2. Hunt, J. McV., *Intelligence and experience.* New York: Ronald Press, 1961.

PART III

Sociological Aspects of Education in Depressed Areas

Research evidence documents the relationship between the social status of a family and the academic achievement and aspirations of its children. As Alan B. Wilson points out, "the utilization of educational opportunities, to a large degree, follows the lines of the stratification system of the society." Differences in the length of schooling, in scholastic performance, in educational aspirations, and in orientation to higher education follow, in general outline, social class differentials. Ethnic, racial, and religious affiliations—often related to social class as well—influence and qualify socio-economic stratification and the individual's life chances as well. Educational opportunity is not equally accessible to all socio-economic classes, nor is occupational mobility. The more education, the higher the occupational attainment; but not all social classes have or use educational opportunities to the same extent.

Studies have indicated a generally direct relationship between social class and scholastic attainment. Bernard Barber has observed that the fact of average difference in IQ scores *among* the social classes and the considerable dispersion of IQ scores *within* any given social class, suggests that "we must look into the social, cultural, economic, and political spheres to discover the sources of social-class differences in IQ score and their effects on differentials in educational life-chances."[1] Differences in "valuing education" are class-oriented; further, the emphasis or value placed on acquiring an education influences scholastic achievement. Hyman reports survey data which indicate "reduced striving for success among the lower classes, an awareness of lack of opportunity, and a lack of valuation of

---

[1] Bernard Barber, "Social-Class Differences in Educational Life-Chances," *Teachers College Record*, 63: 102-113, November 1961.

education, normally the major avenue to achievement of high status."[2] In essence, these lowered aspirations, this weak motivation may represent a factual appraisal by low-income persons of the existence of barriers to occupational and social mobility based on their race, ethnic and social class origins. As Cloward has said, academic performance may be devalued because youth from depressed areas see no relationship between high levels of educational achievement and the realities of their future. These perceptions travel from parents and other adults to children.

Increasingly, there is evidence that the ethos of the school contributes to social class differentials in educational achievement as well. Rogoff's data from a national sample indicate clearly that the higher the student's family's social class, the more likely he is to attend a larger and better high school. The data also suggest that the social composition of the school, as well as the size and resources of the school and its community, affect aptitude scores, college aspirations, and general educational achievement.[3] The patterns of social-class differentials in educational life-chances may be altered by the structural forces of the school itself.

Predilection towards school and academic achievements is determined fairly early in the child's development. Kahl has pointed out that early success in school raises the hopes of both child and parent for future achievements. Basic patterns of school behavior, affinity or distaste for educational achievement, are established in the early grades.[4] Talcott Parsons has argued that it is "not stretching the evidence too far to say broadly that the primary selective process occurs through differential school performance in the elementary school and that the 'seal' is put on it in the junior high school."[5] Thus, academic achievement or its lack in the primary grades is crucial to the separation of youngsters into achievers and non-achievers, into college goers and non-college-goers, and, eventually into the various trades, occupations, and professions.

Differing school milieux, variations in the structure and cohesion of peer groups, the predominant values systems among students, all color the relationship between familial background and academic aspirations and achievement. The social-class composition of the school, Edwards and Wilson found, clearly modifies the ambitions, norms, and achievement of

[2] Herbert H. Hyman, "The Value Systems of Different Classes: A Social Psychological Contribution to the Analysis of Stratification," *in* R. Bendix and S. M. Lipset (Eds.), *Class, Status, and Power,* New York: Free Press, 1953, pp. 426-442.

[3] Barber, *op. cit.,* pp. 110-11.

[4] Joseph A. Kahl, "Educational and Occupational Aspirations of 'Common Man' Boys," *Harvard Educational Review,* 23:186-203, Summer 1953.

[5] Talcott Parsons, "The School Class as a Social System: Some of Its Functions in American Society," *Harvard Educational Review,* 29: 297-318, Fall 1959.

students in that school.[6] Variations in teachers' expectations and standdards contribute to differences in pupil attainment and aspirations. Edwards and Wilson found that peer groups of elementary school children from lower-class families were more tightly knit than those from middleclass families. They recognized that "students are influenced by their perceptions of the values, interests, and actions prevalent among their peers; and that this influence contributes to the homogenization of behavior within strata and the differences between strata." Sociometric data indicate that boys in the lower-class schools who were not interested in extending their education were well-integrated and accepted into their peer groups. On the other hand, more boys in the "better schools" who were non-college aspirants were seen as isolates. In the lower-class schools, the terminal students are viewed as the social leaders by their peers and set the pace without "adopting the standards of success prevalent in the wider community of adults." These findings suggest that deviation from the accepted middle-class educational goals is socially supported and buttressed by the school environment.

Academic prowess in a setting unfriendly to such performance may, in fact, alienate the child from his peers and even from his family. In a study of the relationship between education and social change in an English city, Mays reports the problems that arise when social structure responds to modifications in the school system. For example, extending secondary schools to age 15 and increasing the number of places in grammar school (academic, university-oriented curriculum) opened educational opportunities to a group in which the prevailing attitude has been one of inertia and disinterest. This experiment, in which the schools are being called to promote social change, presents a major challenge to educators to find the means by which "new ideas and values may be grafted upon an established cultural pattern without totally disrupting the existing way of life and without succumbing to the pressures, or indeed, to the social inertia, of the neighborhood."[7] The task, as Mays sees it, is one of leveling up and leveling out social differences without *"sacrificing the individual child as the ultimate objective of the whole educational process."*

Professor Richard A. Cloward and Mr. James A. Jones discuss the relationship between academic achievement and socio-economic position. While the correlation is generally direct for large populations, there are

[6] T. Bentley Edwards and Alan B. Wilson, "A Study of Some Social and Psychological Factors Influencing Educational Achievement" (mimeographed), Berkeley: University of California, Department of Education, June 1961, 116 pp. plus appendixes.

[7] John B. Mays, *Education and the Urban Child,* Liverpool, England: Liverpool University Press, 1962, p. 12.

significant variations in academic performance for certain subgroups. Cloward and Jones point out that differences in attitudes toward education do not by themselves explain the low-level academic performance of lower-class children but that other forces and factors combine to depress scholastic attainment. They discuss three such forces: (a) less actual instruction time, (b) perceived obstacles to occupational rewards—a major inducement to educational achievement, and (c) schools' failure to consider alternative values influencing lower-class youth. Other factors were explored, such as regular employment opportunities for males, enabling them to support a monogamous, stable family structure. The same factors tend to reduce illegitimacy and female-dominated households, which may be two reactions of some men to unemployment. Schools in depressed areas are depicted as having inferior facilities, high teacher turnover, inexperienced staffs, shortages of materials. Individual differences in learning patterns are minimized, as are differentials in socializa-patterns. Socio-economic groupings usually consign lower-class students to a vocational or general track. The school does control certain conditions—notably, provision of equal educational opportunity. When it fails to practice equality, Cloward and Jones maintain, the school may "contribute to the very problem which it otherwise deplores."

They go on to examine attitudes toward education among various social classes and the impact on such attitudes resulting from involvement in school activities. Data are drawn from a sampling of adult residents in New York City's lower east side, the traditional gateway for immigrants and, not accidentally, a slum area for generations. The Lower East Side is presently the focus for a large scale demonstration-research project for the prevention and control of delinquency through a systematic effort to expand opportunities for the area's children, youth and adults, most of whom live in tenements and low-income public housing projects.[8] The data on attitudes toward education and the schools were culled from detailed interviews with 988 adult residents, representing a proportionate, random sample, geographically stratified.

The tentative conclusion drawn by Cloward and Jones is that attitudes toward the importance of education relate to occupational aspirations: lower occupational goals mean lower educational aspirations. Contrary to the general view that lower-class individuals fail to see education as a means of social mobility, such individuals strive for different social targets and therefore, show comparably lower educational aspirations. In addition, the data suggest that participation in school activities does affect the

[8] For further information concerning this project, write to Mobilization for Youth, Juc., 214 East Second Street, New York 9, New York.

individual's judgment of the importance of education and of the school as an institution. Both of these findings have implications for educational programs, Cloward and Jones point out; greater efforts to involve lower-class people in educational matters can deepen their interest in the academic achievement of their children.

Cloward and Jones suggest that a major problem in depressed areas is greater community integration; they chide the school for contributing little toward this end, compared with what it could. Community disintegration, the keynote of recent years, grew out of a number of factors. Political machinery is no longer neighborhood-centered and productive of close bonds. Some of the functions of the political machine have been taken over by the modern social welfare enterprise which tends to be impersonal, not integrative. Massive demolition of slum areas and their replacement with high-rise low-income housing has broken up neighborhood areas and the stability of social organizations. Progressive bureaucratization of cities has increased the number of impersonal agencies and restricted local participation and influence, especially among the lower-class residents—agencies have replaced neighborhood organizations, project directors have replaced landlords, city-wide school systems have replaced neighborhood-controlled schools. While bureaucracy itself may not be bad (it may, for example, provide a wider range of services), there must be sensitive channels for reflecting the attitudes, concerns, and interests of diverse groups—including the lower classes. In addition, unorganized aggregates of people lose the function of a community as transmitter of values to the young—norms, values, consensus, and social controls are not readily visible to children and youth. Community agencies—public and private—in depressed areas are typically middle-class dominated, insofar as policy and decision-making are concerned. Agencies that work in depressed areas too often impose their middle-class values and standards, appearing to residents as paternalistic and patronizing.

Cloward proposes that agencies involve local people in efforts to raise levels of living by sharing power with them—forming indigenous groups representative of varying points of view and spearheaded by local leadership. Although such indigenous leadership may be hidden, it does exist. Bringing in new points of view, fostering political competition between groups, organizing within rather than across ethnic, racial, and interest groups, may seem disruptive at first. However, involvement in policy-making and sharing of power with lower-class groups can be a healthy propellant towards middle-class orientation. The role of the school in fostering community integration and participation is not yet clear. Besides involving lower-class parents in the educational enterprise, the school's function may be to work with other social and community institutions on appropriate joint projects.

Professor Alan B. Wilson reports his findings on the effects of social stratification and of segregation on the academic attainment of elementary school children. While gross differences in scholastic achievement can be accounted for in part by family backgrounds, subcultural factors and other environmental factors, these are not the whole story. Wilson suggests that we look at the school itself as a contributing factor in achievement. Specifically, he points to the tendency of schools to homogenize standards, particularly through the influence of teacher expectations and peer-group pressures.

Reporting on an earlier study at the high school level, Wilson noted that school climate affected pupils' educational and vocational aspirations. For example, the proportion of students from similar family background who aspired to college varied with their high schools and the prevailing modes. In their median grades as well, boys from comparable backgrounds tended towards the mode of the school.

Wilson's study of sixth-grade pupils yields similar findings. The effects on achievement of socio-economic status and race, as well as sex difference, are confirmed again. However, the data indicate a "homogenizing effect of the school milieu" as well. Two mechanisms of uniformity are the lateral transmission of values and attitudes among students and the normalization of differing achievement standards by teachers. As the students progress through junior and senior high school, those from the middle-class schools tend to be assigned to the academic stream while pupils from the lower-class schools are placed in general or vocational programs. This tracking, Wilson states, "comes to many of them as an unanticipated and discriminatory jolt."

In the sociometric data, Wilson found that the social leaders in the lower-class schools are the terminal students: "they gain social support from their peers, and, in turn, set the pace for them, without adopting the standards of success prevalent in the wider community of adults." In the middle-class schools, both parents and teachers have higher expectations for the children and exercised greater supervisory control. The consequence seemed to be a greater congruence with adult values as well as a more fragmented peer-group structure. In the lower-class schools, Wilson found a more flexible program, especially centered around social studies projects. However, teachers did not set as high standards nor did they concern themselves as much as teachers in the middle-class schools with "bringing the children up to grade level."

These two papers and parts of some others, as well, evoke a thorn tree of questions about the nature of cultural deprivation and the ways to thaw frozen opportunities. That social-class differentials affect life chances is a principle generally accepted and substantiated. However, we remain baffled at how the many forces—economic, political, social, cultural, and racial—interact and why such wide variance marks the responses of individuals and groups to apparently similar stimuli.

Several speakers suggested that schools should draft programs to inform low-income families about the rapidly changing occupational structure, the creation of new opportunities in education and employment, the availability of training resources. The problem is to design programs which can crash through these families' incomprehension, ignorance, resistance. What is the school's role in marshaling labor, industry, business, and political forces to broaden opportunities for mobility? If education is valued in terms of occupational aspirations, what means will upgrade such aspirations? What are the significant similarities and differences in the various subcultures—low-income and poverty-ridden, ethnic and racial minority, rural in-migrant, and immigrant—which influence the responses to deprivation? How shall the schools study and understand these subcultural differences in response? Are there positive aspects in the life of lower-income groups—such as cohesiveness or mode of expression—which offer leads to school and community program development.

To what extent can and should the school, social agencies, religious institutions, voluntary organizations, and political units reach into the home and neighborhood to rearrange living patterns? Public housing, slum clearance, and urban renewal all have a direct impact on life in depressed areas, alleviating some problems, producing new ones. What kinds of planning will reduce some of the social perplexities which are by-products of urban redevelopment? How does the school fit in? As Havighurst points out, many urban renewal and slum clearance programs actually have created new patterns of segregation and aggravated social and political divisiveness and discontent. Can curriculum and instructional modifications (such as enrichment programs, smaller classes, and more personnel) compensate for the consequences of economic, ethnic, and racial segregation? Are more drastic steps required, such as location of buildings so as to create mixed-class schools; open enrollment and mass student transfers from depressed area schools; rezoning or elimination of district lines? What are the effects of such programs on middle-class families? How can they be reassured that innovations will not shortchange their children educationally? How can the exodus to suburban schools of the aspiring middle-class student population be curbed?

Should school and community agencies attempt to alter family life and child-rearing patterns? The initiation of programs which remove the depressed area child from the family at a much younger age than his middle-class peer—programs such as day care centers, pre-school nurseries, and pre-kindergarten programs—constitute attempts at early intervention in the child's readiness for school tasks. Can such programs be broadened? With whose money? Should they be made mandatory? Are they or would they then be perceived as discriminatory? Can enough skilled staff with positive attitudes toward culturally disadvantaged children be recruited and trained?

What is significant about the climate of a school whose student population is of differing social classes? Segregated housing, politics and economic conditions result in socially stratified schools. What program modifications are needed to alter teacher expectations, create higher standards, increase pupil motivation in the depressed area schools? Can the ethos of a school be changed without major transfer of pupils? Can a "leveling up" proceed without a corresponding "leveling down"? What steps will prevent the "disintegration" of a good school program? Is de facto segregation in cities (segregation caused by residential concentrations of minority groups) less of a problem for the schools than de jure segregation?

What is the impact of high student mobility in a depressed urban area? How can curriculum stability, program articulation and continuity be maintained in schools with a revolving-door student body? How about the non-transient child in such a school? What kinds of special programs are necessary to balance the negative effects of transiency? Some school districts are permitting children to remain in a school even though they have moved, unless the distance from the new home is prohibitive; transfer is required only at the end of a year or a semester. Is this an effective tactic? Should a highly transient school receive additional resources to satisfy the special educational and vocational guidance, remedial and health needs of the student population.

What major changes are required in the policy making and planning structures of cities to facilitate the kind of citizen participation and local leadership for which Cloward and Jones plead? Should local (that is, neighborhood or borough, in giant cities) educational authorities be created with power to levy supplementary taxes to support local programs? To what extent should educational planning be local, area, regional? The power structure of most community agencies—both private and public— tends to be dominated by middle-class individuals with little representation from low-income and minority groups? How can policy makers effectively involve indigenous leaders? Are middle-class leaders willing to take the risks accompanying decentralization of authority? Does the school have a legitimate role to play in fostering community integration? How can the depressed area resident change his perception of the "outsider, or do-gooder," to that of cooperating fellow-citizen? To what extent should the school aim at becoming the center for social integration of the community? How do the goals of the school differ from that of other social agencies in the depressed area?

The two papers that follow examine some sociological aspects of education in depressed areas. The first sets apart educational attitudes and the meshing of educational activities with other phases of community life. The second analyzes the thesis that schools with differing social compositions and traditions may limit the range of achievement and aspirations of their students. Both underline the importance of looking at the problems of education in depressed areas from the broader perspective of urbanization.

Richard A. Cloward and James A. Jones | Social Class: Educational Attitudes and Participation

What we do about a persisting social problem, such as poor academic achievement, depends in large part on our assumptions about the forces that produce it. Every approach to this problem is based on certain assumptions, explicit or implicit, about why the problem it is seeking to solve exists in the first place. In this paper, we shall set forth some ideas which we hope are helpful in dealing with the problem of poor academic performance among certain categories of children.[1]

The problem we have been asked to focus upon is that of the generally direct correlation between socio-economic position and academic achievement. There are, of course, important qualifications which should be noted when this correlation is discussed. Although the correlation holds generally when the various strata of our society as a whole are compared, it may not necessarily hold for certain important subgroupings; some ethnic groups may tend to perform well despite their low socio-economic position; some groups may tend to perform poorly despite very high socio-economic position. The point is not that the correlation is unvarying, whatever the specialized status categories which one compares, but rather that it tends to hold for very large aggregates of the population despite these internal variations.

If we ask whether this general correlation can partly be explained by class differences in emphasis on education, the answer is probably yes. However, the problem of under-achievement in low-income groups cannot be explained simply by differences in emphasis on education, although the representatives of educational institutions may find it convenient to do so. It must also be recognized that other forces combine to produce

[1] The data upon which this paper is based were drawn from surveys conducted by the New York School of Social Work, Columbia University, in conjunction with Mobilization for Youth, Inc.

lower levels of achievement in low-income groups, several of which might be noted.

One force making for lower levels of academic achievement among impoverished youth is the fact that they receive less instructional time. A number of factors combine to diminish instructional time, not the least of which is teacher turnover. For a variety of reasons, many teachers are reluctant to teach in the slum school. A study of the career patterns of Chicago public-school teachers documents the fact that teachers normally begin their careers in lower-class neighborhoods, where there are more vacancies, and transfer out as soon as they can (2). In addition to high turnover, this also means that teachers in slum schools are generally less experienced. The effect of this situation is especially unfortunate when one considers the characteristic instability of many slum communities, not to mention the economic uncertainties of slum youngsters' lives and the frequent changes in the composition of their family. It is important that the school, as represented by its teachers, be a constant, stable, omnipresent force in the community.

Because of the greater turnover of teachers in slum schools, their relative inexperience, and the geographic mobility of low-income families, slum youth receive less actual instructional time than do school children in middle-class neighborhoods. Indeed, one study of a deprived-area school indicated that as much as 80 per cent of the school day was devoted to discipline or organizational detail; even with the best teachers this figure never fell below 50 per cent (6).

A second force making for under-achievement stems from the strong tendency in our society to motivate academic achievement by holding out the promise of future occupational rewards. It should be pointed out, however, that educational attainment does not necessarily enable the lower-class person to overcome the disadvantages of his low social origins.

Thus workers' sons with "some college" education are about as well off [financially] as a group as the sons of non-manual fathers who have graduated from high school but not attended college. Similarly, high school graduation for the sons of workers results in their being only slightly better off than the sons of non-manual workers who have not completed high school (10).

To the extent that one's social origins, despite education, still constitute a restraining influence on upward movement, we may assume that other objective consequences of social position intervene, such as the ability of one's family to give one a start in a business or profession by supplying funds or influential contacts.

The influence of social class as a deterrent to social mobility, despite the possession of education, becomes all the more important when coupled with influences stemming from race and nationality. It hardly needs to be said that race usually acts as a major barrier to occupational mobility no matter what the educational achievement of the person involved. This situation is easing, to be sure, as progress in fair employment practices for all racial groups is slowly achieved. Nevertheless, it would be grossly inaccurate to say that a Negro youth in our society has the same chance as a white youth to become upwardly mobile given an equivalent level of education. It is not in the least uncommon to find Negro youth with college training forced to take employment in semi-skilled and lower white-collar positions. Among the professions, only teaching and social work have been readily available to them.

The point is, of course, that the major inducement to educational achievement in our society is the promise of future occupational rewards. If, however, it is known in advance that these rewards will be largely withheld from certain socio-economic and racial groups, then it is unlikely that high levels of educational achievement can be sustained in such groups. Thus, academic performance may be devalued because the young in such groups see no relationship between it and the realities of their future.

What we have been saying about the relationship between educational performance and occupational rewards assumes, of course, that discrepancies between the two tend to be perceived by low-income and minority groups in our society. Generally speaking, the evidence available does suggest that perceptions of opportunity do accord with the reality. In this connection, Hyman summarizes data which show that there are distinct differentials by socio-economic status in judgments regarding the accessibility of occupational rewards. Thus, 63 per cent of one sample of persons in professional and managerial positions felt that the "years ahead held good chances for advancement," while only 48 per cent of a sample of factory workers gave this response. Furthermore, the factory workers were more likely to think that "getting along well with the boss" and being a "friend or relative of the boss" were important determinants of mobility; professional and executive personnel were more likely to stress "quality of work" and "energy and willingness" (7). Such findings suggest that low-income persons do indeed perceive the impact of social origins upon their life changes. If these are the perceptions of occupational mobility held by parents in such groups, it is hardly likely that children in such families would hold contrary views on a wide scale. Under such circumstances, the perception of the role of education as a channel of mobility may fail to assume the importance which we might otherwise wish.

Third, it should be noted that the distinctive socialization of slum youth poses a barrier to academic achievement if the school is organized essentially in terms of middle-class values, as is typically the case. In the development of curricula and the structuring of teacher roles, this culture conflict (as distinct from the time-worn emphasis on cultural deprivation) has never been fully recognized—a fact that puts the lower-class child at a distinct disadvantage in competition with the middle-class child.

The problem of differential socialization vis-à-vis educational achievement can best be seen by looking at certain ethnic and nationality values. By and large, immigrant groups historically have entered our social structure at the bottom, and thus it is in the lower class that these values have had the greatest impact. In many of the groups which have come to this country, distinctive systems of values were already well established and thus tended to persist here for a number of generations. Although the more superficial aspects of the American middle-class value system may have been acquired rapidly, the more subtle and deeply embedded aspects of the Old World values were abandoned less readily. Indeed, there is good reason to think that many of these values continue to exert a profound influence upon the behavior of many persons in the second and third generations.

The point to be made about these persisting value orientations is that they do not always facilitate success in the school. Our system of education places a strong stress upon doing rather than being, upon a future orientation rather than an orientation toward the present or the past, upon the notion that man is superordinate to nature rather in harmony with it or subjugated by it, upon the notion that man is flexible and plastic and capable of change rather than that he is essentially, and perhaps immutably, evil. A child who has not acquired these particular value orientations in his home and community is not so likely to compete successfully with youngsters among whom these values are implicitly taken for granted.[2] Part of the problem of under-achievement among some lower-class persons may therefore be attributed to the existence of these alternative value orientations to which the young are different socially.

The failure of the school to take these differing value patterns into account constitutes a striking form of inequality. In this connection, there are at least three respects in which equality can be understood. First, equality means that equivalent educational facilities shall be available, whatever the socio-economic position of the child. Second, equality

[2] For one account of these value orientations, see Florence Kluckhohn (9) and the recent book by Frank Riessman (13) which goes directly to the relationship between value differences and educational achievement.

means that individual differences in learning patterns shall be taken into account. Finally, equality means that the educational system shall not be organized in such a way as to favor children who are socialized in one rather than another part of the social structure. Differentials in socialization, arising from socio-economic position and ethnic origins, must, like individual differences in learning, also be adjusted to by the school system. If the educational enterprise is simply an extension of the middle-class home, then it follows that only middle-class children will tend to do well in it. If the school fails to practice equality in these several respects, then it can be understood as contributing to the very problem which it otherwise deplores.

Keeping such factors as these in mind, we propose to examine the limited problem of differences in attitudes toward education by social class. In addition, we shall ask whether involvement in educational activities —such as visiting the school or participating in parent-teacher associations—appreciably influences these attitudes and, if so, in which socio-economic strata.

Data and Indices

The data upon which this paper is based were gathered in the course of a survey of attitudes of adult residents living in the Lower East Side of Manhattan. For generations the Lower East Side has been labeled a slum. Traditionally, it has been the first residential area for immigrants to this country. At present, about half of the 100,000 residents of the community were born outside of the United States. Ethnic groups in the area include Italians, Jews, Negroes, East Europeans, Chinese, and a large segment of Puerto Ricans. The last represent the most recent wave of immigrants to the city. Except for a smattering of middle-income cooperatives, about half of the population lives in tenements, and the other half in low-income public housing.

The Survey Sample. A sample of residents was drawn by listing every known dwelling unit in the area, stratifying this list into 250 equal intervals of 133 housing units, and randomly selecting five households within each interval. Since the listing of households corresponded to the geographical arrangement of housing units, the sample is a proportionate random sample, geographically stratified.[3] In this way, 1,250 households were selected. Within each of these households, an effort was made to interview one person twenty years old or older The person to be interviewed was also randomly selected.

[3] That is, a stratified random sample in which the sampling proportion is the same within all strata (4).

Interviews were actually conducted with 988 of the 1,250 potential respondents, for a completion rate of 79 per cent. About half of the persons with whom interviews were not conducted refused to be interviewed. Preliminary probes of the data, and comparisons with census materials indicate that the obtained 988 interviews can be taken reasonably representative of the community under study. Interview losses were greatest among the older residents of the community, and in households with no adolescent members. Completion rates were quite high among Puerto Ricans and residents of low-income public housing. Interviews were conducted entirely or partly in thirteen languages,[4] thus reducing any bias in the sample towards those residents who were more culturally assimilated.

The measure of social class. Since the topic of this paper deals with the impact of involvement in educational matters upon attitudes towards education by social class, let us turn now to a brief discussion of the indices of social class and of involvement in education which will be used.

The notion of social class generally refers to an individual's general standing in a hierarchy of positions. Since we can always locate some individuals whose general standing in the society is higher or lower than others, every society is stratified into social classes. Social class seems to have two dimensions: a productive dimension and a consumptive dimension. The former involves the degree to which an individual possesses wealth, knowledge, and power. It is most commonly represented by an individual's income, education, and occupation. The consumptive dimension of social class involves expressions of a particular style of life, and is measured by how a person spends his money, where his children are educated, and what values he espouses (1, 8, 12). The index of social class which is employed in this study is a measure of a person's general position with respect to the *productive* aspects of class. It is, therefore, a measure of a person's general educational, occupational, and economic position.

In the course of the survey interview, the respondent was asked his occupation, how many years of school he had completed, and the total family income. Information on the education and occupation of the respondent's spouse, if any, was also obtained. The measure of social class is based upon the education and occupation of the head of the household, and the total family income, adjusted for the number of persons living on that income. The head of the household was classified into one of four occupational groupings: (1) professionals, semi-professionals, managers, and officials; (2) clerks and salesmen; (3) craftsmen, foremen, and

[4] The languages were: English, Spanish, Yiddish, German, Polish, Italian, Russian, Ukrainian, French, Hungarian, Japanese, Chinese, and Greek.

self-employed white- and blue-collar workers; and (4) operatives, service workers, laborers, and permanently unemployed persons. The head of the household was also classified into one of four educational groups: (1) completed some college or more; (2) finished high school; (3) completed some high school; and (4) finished grade school or less. Finally, the adjusted family income was classified into one of four categories: (1) less than the minimum wage of $1.25 per hour; (2) more than the minimum wage, but less than the Lower East Side median income; (3) more than the Lower East Side median income, but less than the national median income; and (4) more than the national median income. These classifications were then combined into three groups which roughly correspond to the lower class, the working class, and the lower-middle class and above. On the basis of this index of social class, 44 per cent of the residents were classified as lower class, 36 per cent as working class and the remainder, 20 per cent, as lower-middle class or above. The typical lower-class person in our index has had less than an eighth-grade education, is employed as an unskilled or service worker, and lives in a family whose income per person is less than the minimum wage. The typical lower-middle-class person, on the other hand, is a professional or semi-professional, has had some college education, and lives in a family whose income per person is above the national median. The working-class member falls between these two extremes. He is usually a skilled worker, clerk, or salesman having at least some high school education, whose family income per person is about average for residents of the Lower East Side.

Measuring involvement in educational activities. One of the most striking things about our educational system is that there are virtually no formal channels through which persons without children in the public schools can make known their feelings about educational matters. Those without children in school are restricted to participation in the educational system through budget hearings or ad hoc "citizens for better schools" committees. Thus, involvement in educational matters is virtually restricted to persons with children in the public schools. For such persons there are two ways to become involved in education. One, the most preferred way, is through active participation in the local Parent-Teacher Association. The second is through informal visits to the school and discussions with educational personnel. Persons involved in the first way are likely to focus upon problems of the educational system, such as obtaining funds to conduct special programs, motivating more participation by parents, and attempting to grasp the reasons for certain school procedures and problems. Parents who confine their participation to visiting the school are much more likely to focus upon the educational problems or success of their particular children. It is generally conceded that involvement in education through the Parent-Teacher Association is preferable to involvement through visiting the schools. By participating in the meetings and activities of the organization, the parent, it is felt, gains a better perspective of the problems of the school, and that he finds himself in a better position to make his desires known and acted upon.

Our measure of involvement attempts to take these matters into account by: (1) being restricted to persons with children in the public schools; and (2) by weighing more heavily active participation in the Parent-Teacher Association. Persons who are past or present officers of the PTA, therefore, are considered most involved in educational matters. Slightly less involved are those who, although not officers of the Association, attend most of its meetings. Persons who are nominal members of the PTA are considered more involved than those who just visit the schools, while parents who do not even visit the school are deemed to be least involved. Excluded from the index are respondents in households where no one is attending school (61 per cent of the sample), and respondents in the households where all of the children attend private or parochial schools (2 per cent of the sample). The distribution of respondents according to the five categories of the involvement index is as follows:

Past or present officers of the PTA	4%
Attend most or all of the meetings of the PTA	7
Belongs to PTA but attends few meetings	15
Does not belong to PTA, but visits the school	45
No contact with the schools	29
Total number of cases (with children in public schools)	360

As shown by the above figures, nearly half of the residents of the community who become involved in educational matters do so at the lowest level—visiting the school, presumably to discuss their own children's educational progress. Over one-fourth of the persons in the community to whom avenues of participation in educational matters are open fail to avail themselves of these opportunities.

Because of the small number of persons who are highly involved in education, only three divisions of the index will be used. We shall distinguish between those who have no contact with the schools, those who visit the school but do not belong to the Parent-Teacher Association, and those who do belong.

Attitudes Toward Education and Schools

In this section, we shall seek to discover whether there are significant differences by social class in attitudes toward education and toward schools as institutions. Although our findings generally confirm the re-

sults of earlier studies, it will also be shown that the relationship between
social class and attitudes toward education is more complicated than previously assumed.

The importance of education. There is a great deal of evidence which
suggests that although education is widely valued in our society, it is not
equally valued among the several social classes. For example, Hyman
summarized à national survey in which a sample of youths was asked:
"About how much schooling do you think most young men need these
days to get along well in the world?" The results are shown in Table 1.

Table I. Class differentials in emphasis on the need for college education
(201 males aged 14 to 20)[a]

Socio-Economic Position of Family	Per Cent Recommending a College Education	Number of Respondents
Wealthy and prosperous	74	39
Middle class	63	100
Lower class	42	62

[a] Reference 7, p. 432.

These data, like others that Hyman presents, show that a sizable proportion of persons at each point in the social structure consider a college
education desirable. Even in the lowest level of society, the proportion
who emphasize the need for education is not small. But it is also true that
there are strong differences from one stratum to another. In general, the
proportion recommending higher education increases with each upward
step in the socio-economic hierarchy.[5]

When in our community survey, we asked the same question reported
by Hyman, the results obtained showed the same general relationship
between social class and attitudes toward education. Table 2(A) shows
the results for all respondents in each class grouping, while (B) shows
the results for respondents in households where children are attending
school. In both instances the proportion of respondents saying that a
young man needs more than a high school education (that is, at least
some college, or high school graduation plus technical training) increases
as position in the class hierarchy increases. Thus, although three-fourths
of the middle-class respondents stated that it was desirable for a young
man to have more than a high school education, only 59 per cent of the

[5] At least one study in a foreign country (Sweden) indicates that this differential
evaluation of education is not restricted to the American class structure (3).

Table 2. Percentage of respondents in each class who think that a young
man needs more than a high-school education in order
to "get along well in the world."[a]

| | (A) All Respondents | | |
	Lower Class	Working Class	Middle Class
Per cent saying more than high-school education	41%	59%	76%
Number of cases	(434)	(354)	(200)

| | (B) Respondents with Children in School Only | | |
	Lower Class	Working Class	Middle Class
Per cent saying more than high-school education	43%	68%	81%
Number of cases	(187)	(142)	(55)

[a] The specific question asked was: "About how much schooling do you think most young men need these days to get along well in the world?"

working-class respondents, and 41 per cent of the lower-class respondents stated that a young man needs this much education. If just those respondents from households where children are attending school are compared (B), the same relationship is observed, except that the proportion of respondents saying more than a high school education is larger for each class grouping. That is, those respondents with children in the household attending school place a higher valuation on education than those in households with no children.

Table 3 shows the proportion of respondents in each class grouping who mentioned education when asked what "getting ahead" meant to them. Again there is a direct relationship between position in the class hierarchy and the importance placed on education. The relationship, however, is not especially strong. For all respondents, about one-fourth of the middle-class and less than one-fifth of the lower- and working-class respondents said that obtaining or providing a good education came to mind when talking about getting ahead. If parts (A) and (B) of Table 3 are compared, the same relationship holds, except that working-class respondents are much more like middle-class respondents than lower-class respondents.

Results such as these have often been taken to mean that low-income

Table 3. Percentage of respondents in each class who say that "getting ahead" means obtaining or providing a good education.[a]

(A)
Total Number of Respondents

	Lower Class	Working Class	Middle Class
Per cent saying good education	17%	19%	24%
Number of cases	(434)	(354)	(200)

(B)
Respondents with Children in School Only

	Lower Class	Working Class	Middle Class
Per cent saying good education	19%	26%	25%
Number of cases	(187)	(142)	(55)

[a] The specific question asked was: "When we talk about getting ahead, or rising in the world, what sorts of things come to mind? (What does getting ahead mean to you?) Anything else?"

people fail to understand the basic relationship between educational achievement and occupational mobility. While this may in part be true, such an interpretation may also be oversimplified. In this connection, we asked people whether or not they thought that "a good education is essential to getting ahead." At least 95 per cent of all respondents in *all* social classes replied in the affirmative. It is true, of course, that questions of such a general and abstract order often elicit rather stereotyped responses, and this may account for the uniformity of responses to this question by social class. On the other hand, there is also the responsibility that other forces operate to produce class differences in the importance of education.

One possibility, of course, is that educational attitudes are influenced by the occupational levels which people define as meeting the criterion of "getting ahead." The answer to the question of how much education a person needs to get ahead in the world may be influenced considerably by the respondents definition of an appropriate occupational level. Thus low-income people may perceive the relationship between education and mobility, but nevertheless give lower estimates of the amount of education required to get ahead simply because they are oriented toward correspondingly lower positions in the social structure than their middle- and upper-income counterparts.

A partial test of this possibility is available with data from the survey. Residents of the Lower East Side were asked: "Suppose some outstanding young man asked your advice on what would be one of the best occupa tions to aim toward. What *one* occupation do you think you would advise him toward?" Most of the respondents said that they would advise him to take up one of the professions or semi-professions. Many of the respondents, however, did not. They said that they either could not advise the young man, or would advise him toward a non-professional career. If differences in the occupational level toward which persons are oriented account for class differences in the amount of education deemed necessary, then there will be no differences between the classes when occupational level is controlled. The data are presented in Tables 4 and 5.

Table 4. Percentage of respondents in each class who think that a young man needs more than a high-school education in order to "get along well in the world" by level of occupational aspiration.[a]

	Lower Class		Working Class		Middle Class	
	Professional and Semi-Professional	Other	Professional and Semi-Professional	Other	Professional and Semi-Professional	Other
Per cent saying more than H. S. education	50%	29%	62%	54%	75%	77%
Number of cases	(248)	(186)	(243)	(111)	(131)	(69)

[a] The specific question asked to determine level of occupational aspiration was: "Suppose some outstanding young man asked your advice on what would be one of the best occupations to aim toward. What *one* occupation do you think you would advise him toward?"

When members of the three classes are subdivided into those who would and those who would not advise the young man to take up a professional or semi-professional career, and the responses about how much education a young man should have are then examined (Table 4), the differences between the classes observed previously still remain. It can be seen, however, that respondents' definitions of an appropriate career for a talented young man have a much greater impact among lower-class persons than working- or middle-class persons. Among lower class respondents who would advise a young man to take up a professional or semi-professional career, half state that a young man needs more than a high school education to get along well in the world, whereas among those who would not advise a young man towards such a career, only about 30 per cent feel that more than a high school education is needed. As we move up the class ladder, this difference gradually decreases, and, in fact, among middle-class respondents, the definition of an appropriate career for a young man makes no difference at all. It would seem, therefore, that lower-class persons place less of an emphasis upon education for education's sake, since their estimates to the amount of education a young man needs are most affected by the level of occupational aspiration.

When occupational aspiration is controlled and the responses of the several social classes to questions regarding the meaning of "getting ahead" are compared, the results, as shown in Table 5, are generally similar.

Table 5. Percentage of respondents in each class who say that "getting ahead" means obtaining or providing a good education by level of occupational aspiration.

	Lower Class		Working Class		Middle Class	
	Professional and Semi- Professional	Other	Professional and Semi- Professional	Other	Professional and Semi- Professional	Other
Per cent saying good education	22%	11%	24%	9%	25%	22%
Number of Cases	(248)	(186)	(243)	(111)	(131)	(69)

The impact of the definition of an appropriate career for a talented young man is greater in the lower and working classes than in the middle class. Members of the middle class who do not feel that the profession or semi-professions are an appropriate career for a talented young man are just as likely to mention education as a meaning of getting ahead as are those who do feel this way. One may conclude from this that middle-class persons are more likely than lower- and working-class persons to think of education as good in and of itself, regardless of the occupation they have in mind when advising a young person about careers.

Yet, the matter is not this simple, for adding to the complications of the picture of the relationship between class attitudes towards education are perceptions of the place of education in a person's conception of "the good life." One question asked was "What kind of things come to mind when you think of a good life for (the children in this household?") The results are shown in Tables 6 and 7. Both of these tables—the first for boys and the second for girls—show the percentage of respondents in each class grouping who mentioned education as an aspect of a "good life" for the children in the household. Both tables *fail* to show that the importance placed on education increases as position in the class hierarchy increases. If anything, each shows that the working-class respondents are slightly more likely to mention education than are their middle- and lower-class counterparts. This is especially true for respondents in households where children are attending school.

The results of Tables 6 and 7, which indicate that education is slightly more salient for working-class parents, are difficult to interpret. One possibility is that education is more problematic for working-class parents than for either lower- or middle-class parents. It has already been shown that members of all classes perceive the connection between education and social mobility. Tables 6 and 7 may reflect reality considerations. Middle-class parents with a more secure economic position probably are less concerned about providing adequate education for their children, take such education for granted, and hence are less likely to report it when thinking of a good life for their children. Lower-class parents, on the other hand, probably perceive education as a bit beyond their financial capacity and react by de-emphasizing education when thinking of a good life for their children. For working-class parents, however, an adequate education is neither assured nor beyond the realm of possibility. This would make education more problematic for working-class parents, and heighten its saliency. Bolstering this would be the tendency of middle-class parents to perceive education as an end in and of itself, and the tendency of lower-class persons to perceive it as a means toward an end. Both may operate to reduce the saliency of education as an element of parents' conception of a good life for their children. In comparisons of class conceptions of a

Table 6. Percentage of respondents in each class who say that education comes to mind when they think of a good life for the boys in the household.[a]

	(A) All Respondents		
	Lower Class	Working Class	Middle Class
Per cent mentioning education	56%	62%	57%
Number of cases	(208)	(155)	(60)

	(B) Respondents with Children in School Only		
	Lower Class	Working Class	Middle Class
Per cent mentioning education	59%	67%	59%
Number of cases	(157)	(123)	(41)

[a] The specific question asked was: "Most people would like to see children have a good life. Could you tell me what comes to mind when you think of a good life for (name boys in house)? Anything else?"

Table 7. Percentage of respondents in each class who say that education comes to mind when they think of a good life for the girls in the household.[a]

(A)
All Respondents

	Lower Class	Working Class	Middle Class
Per cent mentioning education	56%	61%	62%
Number of cases	(196)	(134)	(53)

(B)
Respondents with Children in School Only

	Lower Class	Working Class	Middle Class
Per cent mentioning education	56%	65%	59%
Number of cases	(148)	(105)	(37)

[a] The specific question asked was: "Most people would like to see children have a good life. Could you tell me what comes to mind when you think of a good life for (name girls in house)? Anything else?"

good life for children, therefore, education would be more salient for working-class parents.

The school as an institution. Residents' evaluations of the local public schools undoubtedly have a profound affect on the ability of the school to mobilize public support for its programs. School authorities often complain of public apathy toward school problems and the difficulty of generating support for new ventures in education. At the same time, it has been charged that the schools are in, but not of the community—that, especially in low-income areas, school authorities are uninterested in, if not antagonistic towards, the local residents and their offspring. The school, it is said, fails to adapt its educational techniques and routines to the values and learning habits of the population it serves. This, in turn, is supposed to create a barrier between the school and its community, resulting in mutual misunderstanding and hostility. For these reasons, and because the school is deemed a middle-class institution (5, 11), our expectation was that lower-class residents would evaluate the schools more negatively than middle-class residents. Yet, as Tables 8 through 12 show, the reverse turned out to be true in the community which we studied.

The data presented in Table 8 were constructed from respondents' selections of community problems from a list of five.[6] In general, schools

[6] The five problems were: the transportation, the public schools, the city police protection, the way teenagers behave around here, and the way certain racial groups behave.

Table 8. Percentage of respondents in each class who consider the public schools to be the first or second biggest problem in the community.[a]

	(A) All Respondents		
	Lower Class	Working Class	Middle Class
Per cent mentioning school first or second	13%	15%	25%
Number of cases	(434)	(354)	(200)

	(B) Respondents with Children in School Only		
	Lower Class	Working Class	Middle Class
Per cent mentioning school first or second	19%	22%	31%
Number of cases	(187)	(142)	(55)

[a] The specific question asked was: "Here is a list of problems that some communities have. What in your opinion is the *biggest* problem around here? What is the *next biggest* problem around here?

were not considered much of a problem, ranking fourth in the list of five. It can be seen from Table 8 that designation of the public schools as the first or second biggest problem in the area increases with position in the class hierarchy. Although about one-fourth of the middle-class respondents selected it as the number one or two problem of the community, only about one-half that proportion of the working and lower-class respondents did so. The same relationship exists when only respondents in households with school children are compared. It should be noted, however, that the proportion of such residents in each social class designating the schools as one of the major problems of the community is higher than for residents without children in the public schools.

Table 9 presents data on residents' evaluation of the job being done by the public schools. As in the previous table, middle-class residents are more negative. For all respondents, about one-fifth of the middle-class respondents compared to nearly two-fifths of the lower- and working-class respondents feel that the schools are doing an "excellent" or a "good" job. When respondents in households with children actually in school are compared, the negative relationship between class position and positive evaluation of the schools increases. About half of the lower- and working-class respondents give a positive evaluation, while only three out of every ten middle-class respondents do so.

Table 9. Percentage of respondents in each class who think that the public schools are doing an "excellent" or a "good" job.[a]

(A)

| | All Respondents | | |
	Lower Class	Working Class	Middle Class
Per cent saying excellent or good	37%	37%	21%
Number of cases	(434)	(354)	(200)

(B)

| | Respondents with Children in School Only | | |
	Lower Class	Working Class	Middle Class
Per cent saying excellent or good	50%	45%	31%
Number of cases	(187)	(142)	(55)

[a] The specific question asked was: "In general, do you feel the public schools around here are doing an excellent, good, fair, poor, or very poor job?"

In Table 10, it is possible to discern a possible reason for class differences in evaluation of the schools. When evaluating the schools, middle-class respondents are more likely to think of conditions in the schools: overcrowding, rundown buildings, and the like. Lower-class residents, on the other hand, are more likely to think of the teachers when evaluating the public schools. Members of the working-class stand between these two groups, stressing conditions in the school more than teachers, but not to the same degree as do members of the middle-class These general tendencies also exist when comparisons are made just for respondents in households with children in school.

Tables 11 and 12 are drawn from a battery of agree-disagree items. The results of Table 11 conform to those of previous tables. Middle-class respondents evaluate teachers more negatively than do lower- and working-class respondents. Whereas almost three out of ten middle-class respondents disagree that teachers are really interested in their pupils, less than two out of ten lower-class respondents feel this way. When respondents from households with children actually in school are compared, this relationship becomes even stronger. In addition, it should be noted that negative appraisal of teachers' interest is slightly higher for all class groups.

Table 12 is the only table that fails to conform to the general pattern. The item involved in this table is also the only one which contains an ex-

Table 10. Criteria for the evaluation of the public schools by class.[a]

(A)		
	All Respondents	
Lower Class	Working Class	Middle Class

Per cent stressing:			
conditions	27%	32%	40%
teachers	27	21	19
discipline	16	23	20
learning	21	19	16
other	9	5	5
Number of responses	(409)	(354)	(197)

(B)		
	Respondents with Children in School Only	
Lower Class	Working Class	Middle Class

Per cent stressing:			
conditions	26%	32%	41%
teachers	28	23	13
discipline	14	20	23
learning	22	21	17
other	10	4	6
Number of responses	(256)	(183)	(64)

[a] The specific question asked following the respondents rating of the job being done by the public schools was: "Why do you say that?"

Table 11. Percentage of respondents in each class disagreeing that "the teachers here are really interested in the kids."

(A)		
	All Respondents	
Lower Class	Working Class	Middle Class

Per cent disagreeing	19%	25%	28%
Number of cases	(434)	(354)	(200)

(B)		
	Respondents with Children in School Only	
Lower Class	Working Class	Middle Class

Per cent disagreeing	22%	27%	35%
Number of cases	(187)	(142)	(55)

Table 12. Percentage of respondents in each class agreeing that "the schools don't pay much attention to kids who come from poor families."

(A)

	All Respondents		
	Lower Class	Working Class	Middle Class
Per cent agreeing	31%	19%	18%
Number of cases	(434)	(354)	(200)

(B)
Respondents with Children in School Only

	Lower Class	Working Class	Middle Class
Per cent agreeing	34%	16%	18%
Number of cases	(187)	(142)	(55)

plicit reference to economic position. Lower-class respondents are more likely than those from the middle-class and the working-class to feel that the schools do not pay enough attention to kids from poor families. Nearly one out of every three lower-class respondents gives this response, compared to less than one in five of the middle- and lower-class respondents. The relationship holds when respondents in households with children in school are examined separately. Thus, when the school's attitude towards pupils from the lowest economic stratum is explicitly asked about, respondents in that class are more negative than those in the classes above them.

In general, then, middle-class respondents have the more negative opinion of the public schools. They are more likey to consider the public schools one of the major problems of the community, are less likely to feel that it is doing a good job, and are more likely to disagree with the assertion that the teachers are really interested in their students. Only when the reaction of the schools towards pupils from the lowest economic stratum is mentioned, do middle-class respondents exhibit a less negative attitude than persons at the bottom of the class ladder.[7]

It is not yet clear what these findings mean. Several interpretations are

[7] It is worthwhile pointing out that a negative attitude towards the schools is not automatically a cause for despair. It is not at all uncommon for positive consequences to flow from negative attitudes. It seems certain, in fact, that if improvements in school plant and curricula are to be effectuated, there must be discontent and negativism to provide the motivation for such change.

possible. It may be that lower-class respondents, faced with the certainty of sending their children to public school, develop a more positive attitude towards the schools as a means of feeling better about what has to be done. Middle-class persons, with the alternative of sending their children to private schools, can afford to be more negative about the state of the schools. A second interpretation is that the middle-class person imagines the school unable to cope with a discipline problem presented by lower-class pupils and concludes that public education cannot be very good. Finally, it is possible that members of the middle-class have higher expectations of what the schools are supposed to accomplish, thus making their evaluation of the performance of the school more negative than that of members of the working and lower classes.

Spurious relationships. The persons who occupy the various strata of the class hierarchy differ in many ways other than those used to define class position. Puerto Ricans, Negroes, the foreign-born, and short-term residents in the community are more likely to be in the lowest stratum. Correlatively, Jews and other whites, those who were born in the United States, and long-term residents of the community are more likely to be in the upper strata. It may be that *these* characteristics, rather than class position, produced the results just presented. In addition, the results may be solely a product of the amount of schooling a respondent has had, rather than his general class standing. The findings relating to class reported above were, therefore, examined for various racial, religious, and immigrant groupings. They were also examined for persons with varying amounts of education, and years of residence in the community. Although the class trends were more pronounced in some groups than in others, the findings, with one exception, appear to be a consequence of class position. The single exception is the relationship between class position and appraisal of teachers' interest in their pupils (Table 11). This was found to be a consequence of amount of education alone. The more years of school a respondent had completed, the more likely he was to disagree with the assertion that teachers were really interested in their pupils. Thus, in the exploration of the impact of involvement in educational matters upon class attitudes towards education, which follows, this item will not be examined.

The Impact of Educational Involvement

We turn now to the question of whether involvement in educational activities influences attitudes toward education generally and toward the school particularly. As noted earlier, our measure of involvement yields three general categories of people, those with children in the school who:

(1) have no other contact with the school, or (2) visit the school, or (3) participate in Parent-Teacher Association activities.

In the pages which follow, we shall be discussing the changes in attitudes towards education and evaluation of the public schools which are brought about as a result of participation in PTA activities or contact with school personnel. It is quite possible that rather than attitude changes being the result of participation that attitudes determine participation. What is even more probable is that attitudes and participation are mutually intertwined, that each is both a cause and effect of the other. We have chosen, for the present, to ignore the possibility of mutual effects, and the possibility that the relationships run directly opposite to the way we will discuss them, because our preliminary examination of the data indicates that attitudes towards education and the schools are greatly affected by the presence of children in the household, and whether or not those children are in school. Comparisons between parts (A) and (B) of Tables 2, 3, and 6 through 12 indicate that the attitudes of respondents with children in school are quite different from those without children in school. As will be subsequently shown, the direction of these differences are the same as differences between respondents participating in the educational system and those not. This, however, is minimal evidence for taking the position that we have. It is expected that subsequent analyses of our data will permit a precise detailing of cause and effect relationships, thus highlighting the mutual effects, if any, between attitudes towards education and participation in educational matters.

The importance of education. Generally speaking, our data show that the value of education is heightened for parents who visit the school or who participate in Parent-Teacher Associations. Furthermore, the impact of involvement in the school upon definitions of the importance of education tends to be greater in the lower and working-classes than in the middle-class. These findings may be demonstrated by examining Tables 13 through 18.

One question asked was: "How much education do you think that a young man needs to get along well in the world?" As noted earlier, the responses to this question show a direct relationship to class; the higher the social class, the more likely that the respondent would indicate that more than a high school education was necessary.

The critical point to be made about Table 13, however, is that participation in educational activities through visits or membership in Parent-Teacher Association affects estimates of the importance of education in the various social classes differently. The greatest impact is shown to be upon the working-class group: 63 per cent of the working-class persons

Table 13. Percentage of respondents in each class who think that a young man needs more than a high-school education in order to "get along well in the world" by extent of involvement in education.

	Lower Class			Working Class			Middle Class		
	NC[a]	VO[b]	FP[c]	NC	VO	FP	NC	VO	FP
Per cent saying more than high-school education	43%	43%	46%	63%	69%	78%	76%	78%	87%
Number of cases	(63)	(86)	(28)	(33)	(53)	(45)	(8)	(22)	(22)

[a] "No contact."
[b] "Visits only."
[c] "Formal participation."
These abbreviations are used throughout the remaining tables.

who have no contact with the school feel that more than a high school education is essential; 69 per cent of those who report having visited the school in the past year give this response; and 78 per cent who report participating in parent associations are so minded. With respect to this one measure, however, the lower-class shows the least change in definitions of the importance of education as a result of participation. But, as we shall presently see, on all other measures of the importance of education which we used, the impact of education turns out to be greatest for the lower class.

Elsewhere in our interview we asked respondents to define what "getting ahead" meant to them. Although persons in the lower class were least likely to mention getting an education (Table 14), they were the most likely to be influenced in this respect by participation: 16 per cent of the lower-class persons who had no contact with the school mentioned getting an education, but 25 per cent of those connected to PTA's gave this answer. The impact of participation upon working-class persons is almost as great as in the lower class. In the middle class, however, participation appears to have no appreciable influence.

Table 14. Percentage of respondents in each class who say that "getting ahead" means obtaining or providing a good education by extent of involvement in education.

	Lower Class			Working Class			Middle Class		
	NC	VO	FP	NC	VO	FP	NC	VO	FP
Per cent saying education	16%	22%	25%	21%	26%	29%	25%	27%	23%
Number of cases	(63)	(86)	(28)	(33)	(53)	(45)	(8)	(22)	(22)

Table 15. Percentage of respondents in each class who say that education comes to mind when they think of a good life for boys and for girls in the household by extent of involvement in education.

	Lower Class			Working Class			Middle Class		
	NC	VO	FP	NC	VO	FP	NC	VO	FP
Boys:									
Per cent of education	54%	61%	76%	69%	64%	65%	50%	53%	65%
Number of cases	(54)	(74)	(21)	(29)	(47)	(37)	(4)	(17)	(17)
Girls:									
Per cent of education	47%	56%	78%	70%	64%	61%	83%	40%	71%
Number of cases	(47)	(70)	(23)	(23)	(39)	(36)	(6)	(15)	(14)

The extent to which people name education as an element in "What comes to mind when you think of a good life for your children?" also provides a way of measuring the impact of educational involvement upon attitudes toward education (Table 15). The attitudes of people in the lower class are especially influenced by educational participation: among those who are involved in formal educational activities, three out of four suggest that the good life for both boys and girls is equated with getting an education; however, only half of those who have no contact with the school give this response. The middle class also shows an increasing tendency to equate education with the good life as the degree of participation increases (although there is an exception in one cell, it should be noted that the number of cases is very small). In the working-class group, however, there is a slight and inexplicable tendency for participation to lessen the emphasis on education.

The school as an institution. Evaluations and appraisals of the school as an institution were also influenced by involvement in school activities. Generally, the greater the exposure to the school and its personnel, the less favorable the views tended to become.

Table 16 shows, for example, that with greater exposure to the school there is a definite tendency for more respondents to define the public schools as the first or second biggest problem in the community. It should also be noted that the influence of exposure upon appraisals is greatest in the middle class, where the percentage difference between low and high participators is 28 per cent; the difference in the working class is 12 per cent, and in the lower class only 10 per cent. At the same moment, how-

Table 16. Percentage of respondents in each class who consider the public schools to be the first or second biggest problem in the community by extent of involvement in education.

	Lower Class			Working Class			Middle Class		
	NC	VO	FP	NC	VO	FP	NC	VO	FP
Per cent of schools	19%	18%	29%	15%	23%	27%	13%	32%	41%
Number of cases	(63)	(86)	(28)	(33)	(53)	(45)	(8)	(22)	(22)

ever, the proportion of people who appraise the school as a major problem in the community never exceeds 41 per cent (middle-class high participators). Even with greater exposure to the schools, most people continue to feel that other problems in the community are of greater importance.

With respect to whether people think that the schools are doing a good or poor job, exposure has little impact or negative impact (Table 17). In the working class there is a tendency for more negative appraisals to result from exposure; in the lower and middle classes, appraisals remain relatively constant whatever the degree of participation.

These results would tend to suggest that school administrators must be prepared to deal with more negative attitudes toward the school if greater efforts are made to involve people in school activities. Such involvement, as we noted earlier, is functional for attitudes toward the importance of education generally; but as attitudes toward education improve the school as an institution is more likely to come under attack. Skillfully managed, however, these negative attitudes can become a source of pressure for better educational facilities and programs.

In Table 18, we find some reason to qualify our earlier remarks about

Table 17. Percentage of respondents in each class who think that the public schools are doing an "excellent" or "good" job by extent of involvement in education.

	Lower Class			Working Class			Middle Class		
	NC	VO	FP	NC	VO	FP	NC	VO	FP
Per cent saying excellent or good	54%	48%	54%	57%	41%	42%	38%	23%	41%
Number of cases	(63)	(86)	(28)	(33)	(53)	(45)	(8)	(22)	(22)

Table 18. Criteria for evaluation of public schools by class and extent of involvement in education.

Per cent stressing:	Lower Class			Working Class			Middle Class		
	NC	VO	FP	NC	VO	FP	NC	VO	FP
conditions	18%	31%	27%	19%	32%	42%	42%	44%	40%
teachers	25	31	24	22	19	27	8	19	10
discipline	14	12	16	27	22	13	25	22	20
learning	24	22	24	27	26	12	17	11	15
other	19	4	8	5	1	7	8	4	5
Number of responses	(93)	(117)	(37)	(37)	(74)	(60)	(12)	(27)	(20)

the positive impact of participation in educational activities toward the school. If we look at changes in the aspects of the school as an institution to which people refer when making appraisals, it turns out that the lower and working classes shift in the direction of exhibiting greater concern about facilities. The tendency to evaluate the school from the standpoint of the adequacy of its facilities—as distinct from such other characteristics as the quality of its teachers—is, as noted earlier, more typical of middle-class people than of those in either the lower or the working class. Participation in educational activities, however, appears to produce significent changes. As a result of formal participation, the working-class respondent refers to conditions as much as his middle class counterpart, and the lower-class participant shows a smaller but neverthesess dramatic shift in the same direction. This change could be produced by a number of factors. Sheer exposure to schools through visits and the like may make the respondent more aware than previously of the state of school facilities. Another possibility is that Parent-Teacher Associations are dominated by a concern with physical plant because they are controlled by middle-class persons who express this concern more than others in the class structure. Through association with middle-class PTA members, the lower- and working-class persons may thus be made more aware of physical plant and may identify with middle-class definitions of it.

This particular effect of participation would not otherwise cause concern except that in the working class it is accompanied by a sharp decline in emphasis upon matters such as discipline and learning. The effect, in short, may be one of heightening concern about education in the sense of focusing attention upon physical plant at the expense of interest in matters of program and curriculum. In the lower and working classes, this would not appear to be a desirable consequence, all of which suggests that the content of educational involvement is as important as the fact of involvement itself.[8]

In conclusion, two general findings—however tentative—emerge from this research. The first is that evaluations of the importance of education in the lower and working classes appear to be influenced by occupational aspirations. The point is not, as has been so often suggested, that low income people fail to perceive the importance of education as a channel of mobility, but rather that their level of occupational aspiration influences their evaluation of education much more than is characteristic of the middle-class person. From a programmatic standpoint, this suggests that public information programs designed to acquaint low income people with the rapid changes taking place in our occupational structure, especially the restricted number of unskilled and semi-skilled positions, may have the effect of heightening occupational aspirations and thus the importance of education.

Second, our data suggest that participation in educational activities does influence evaluations of the importance of education, and attitudes toward the school as an institution. The tendency of participation to heighten the emphasis on education is especially pronounced in the lower class. This suggests that efforts to involve lower-class people in educational matters are quite likely to be rewarded by increased interest in the academic

---

[8] It will be recalled that in Table XII lower class people were most likely to feel that the schools "do not pay much attention to kids from poor families." The impact that involvement in education has upon this attitude is difficult to interpret. It is clear from the table presented below that involvement in education tends to produce a more negative attitude among middle class persons, a less negative one among lower class persons, and apparently has no impact among working class persons. As yet, we do not know what to make of this result. A tentative interpretation is that middle and lower class persons are tending toward a more realistic assessment. Upon becoming involved, middle class persons discover that the children of poorer families are not as well treated as had been initially supposed, while lower class persons who become involved discover that children of poorer families are treated better than had been supposed. Essentially, however, the results of this table remain puzzling to us, and call for further analysis.

Percentages of Respondents in each Class Agreeing that "The Schools Don't Pay Much Attention to Kids Who Come from Poor Families" by Extent of Involvement in Education

	Lower Class			Working Class			Middle Class		
	NC	VO	FP	NC	VO	FP	NC	VO	FP
Per cent agreeing	41%	31%	32%	18%	13%	18%	—	14%	27%
Number of cases	(63)	(86)	(28)	(33)	(53)	(45)	(8)	(22)	(22)

achievement of their children. Participation also tends to result in more critical attitudes toward the school as an institution. These generally more negative attitudes, we noted, can be employed by school administrators as a basis for bringing about needed improvements in school facilities and programs.

REFERENCES

1. Barber, Bernard, *Social Stratification*, New York: Harcourt, Brace, 1957.
2. Becker, Howard. "The Career of the Chicago Public School Teacher," *Amer. sociol. Rev.*, July 1952, 17 (7):470-476.
3. Cantril, Hadley, *Public Opinion, 1935-1946*, Princeton, N.J.: Princeton University Press, 1951, pp. 180-181.
4. Cochran, William G., *Sampling Techniques*, New York: Wiley, 1953, p. 67.
5. Cohen, Albert K., "Schools and Settlement House," *in* Herman D. Stein and Richard A. Cloward (Eds.), *Social Perspectives on Behavior*, New York: The Free Press, 1958, pp. 341-344.
6. Deutsch, Martin, *Minority Group and Class Status as Related to Social and Personality Factors in Scholastic Achievement*, New York: Society for Applied Anthropology, Monograph No. 2, 1960, p. 23.
7. Hyman, Herbert H., "The Value Systems of Different Classes: A Social-Psychological Contribution to the Analysis of Stratification," *in* Reinhard Bendix and S. M. Lipset (Eds.), *Class Status and Power*, New York: The Free Press, 1953.
8. Kahl, Joseph A., *The American Class Structure*, New York, Rinehart, 1957.
9. Kluckhohn, Florence, "Variations in the Basic Values of Family Systems," *in* Norman W. Bell and Ezra F. Vogel (Eds.), *A Modern Introduction to the Family*, New York: The Free Press, 1960, pp. 304-316.
10. Lipset, S. M., and Bendix Reinhard, *Social Mobility in Industrial Society*, Berkeley and Los Angeles, University of California Press, 1959, p. 99.
11. Mayer, Martin, *The Schools*, New York: Harper, 1961, pp. 114-135.
12. Pfautz, Harold W., "The Current Literature on Social Stratification," *Amer. J. Sociol.*, January 1953, 58:391-418.
13. Riessman, Frank, *The Culturally Deprived Child*, New York: Harper, 1962.

Alan B. Wilson | Social Stratification and Academic Achievement

Free public education in the United States has had, and continues to have, the manifest function of widening opportunities for individual achievement regardless of adventitious circumstances of birth and origin.[1] While the perceived purposes for schooling have varied—from personal salvation to the enhancement of monetary reward or social position—the democratization of opportunity has remained a continuing rationale for publicly supported schools. "Education, then, beyond all other devices of human origin," is to be "the great equalizer of the conditions of men—the balance-wheel of the social machinery"(7).

A continuously accumulating body of research over the past few decades has made it clear, however, that the utilization of educational opportunities follows, to a large degree, the lines of the stratification system of the society. The largest portion of this past research has been devoted to documenting the association between a youth's plans for or entrance into college and his father's social class or status. It has been shown that students' academic achievements, and the division of students into sections, curricula, or streams within schools reflect the status distinctions of the community. In large city school systems the allocation of students to specialized high schools—"academic," "general," or "technical"—likewise reflects, in considerable measure, the socio-economic status of their parents.

In recent years, attention has increasingly turned to the investigation of mechanisms sustaining the intergenerational inheritance of position within an educational system which emphasizes reward for individual achievement. Some of the more salient modes of transmission which have been noted are differences in the willingness and ability of parents to bear the costs of continued education or forego the potential earnings of their son,

[1] The data which are discussed in this paper were originally collected pursuant to a contract with the United States Office of Education, Department of Health, Education, and Welfare.

regional differences in the occupational relevance and in the quality of available education, variations in knowledge of mobility skills, differences in familial socialization of their children's aspirations, their "need to achieve," their willingness to defer immediate gratifications, and variations in acquired linguistic and conceptual skills.

Gross differences between the educational achievements of students in different geographical regions, and in different schools in effectively segregated metropolitan areas, are popularly, and to a considerable degree properly, attributed to such differences in familial and sub-cultural backgrounds. However, schools with differing social compositions develop distinctive traditions and norms which perpetuate and sharpen the initial differences between their students. While the ethos of a school depends in part upon the dominant social character of its clientele, the school in turn is a socializing agent shaping the behavior and sentiments of the students. T. H. Marshall, for example, questioning the validity of the selective examinations for English grammar schools asks: "On the other hand may not a school have an assimilating influence and mould its members into a more homogeneous group than they were to start with, thus, producing in reality the category of children which until then existed only in the imagination of the selectors?" (8).

Some evidence supporting the contention that the attitudes of students within a school are laterally diffused among peers was reported in a study of the educational plans of students in several high schools in the San Francisco-Oakland Bay area (14). The proportion of students from roughly comparable family backgrounds who aspired to go to college was found to tend toward the mode of the school in which they were enrolled. For example, while 93 per cent of the sons of professionals in predominantly upper white-collar schools said they wanted to go to college, only 64 per cent of their compeers who were enrolled in schools where the majority of students were children of manual workers had comparable aspirations. Conversely, while only one-third of the sons of manual workers in these latter schools hoped to go to college, almost three-fifths of the manual workers' sons who attended the largely white-collar schools wanted to enter college.

In the study to be reported here, effects of social stratification and the homogenizing effect of segregation upon the academic achievement of elementary school children will be analyzed. Some of the social mechanisms within schools mediating these effects will be explored. In addition to the lateral diffusion of sentiments among peers, the normalization of differing standards by teachers is hypothesized as a contributory factor.

Sample

The data to be discussed derive from a study of high-sixth-grade students in Berkeley, California. While this is a limited, and in some ways distinctive, sample, the broad patterns which emerge are congruent with national data, and many of the details are supported by findings from other studies. The distinctiveness of Berkeley makes it particularly apt for this study. The presence of the University of California results in an unusually high proportion of professional persons in the community who send their children to the public schools, while at the same time Berkeley has a very high proportion of Negro working-class residents.

The fourteen elementary schools in the unified school district can be divided into three clearly distinct strata—following the lines of residential segregation in the community. In the schools in the Berkeley Hills, surrounding the university, the fathers of some three-fifths of the students are professionals or executives. Very few manual workers are to be found in the Hills. In the "Flats," on the other hand, where most of the Negro population of Berkeley is concentrated, the proportions are reversed. About four-fifths of the students in the Flats come from working-class homes. Between these extremes (both geographically and in terms of social composition) is a group of schools which are more heterogeneous—dubbed the "Foothills." Details of the occupational, educational, and racial distributions in the three school strata are presented in Table 1, on page 220.

Inasmuch as education, occupation, and race are highly intercorrelated, the several variables presented in Table 1 show a similar pattern of segregation—the Hills being composed predominantly of white, college educated professionals, executives, and other white-collar employees and the Flats heavily populated by Negro manual workers with less than a college education.[2]

Academic Achievement by School Strata

Several evidences of achievement were gathered during the course of this survey. Among them were reading and arithmetic scores from tests which had been administered that year by the schools (10, 11), IQ scores from tests administered the year before when these students were in the fifth grade (9), the level of the reader to which they were assigned by

---

[2] Data on fathers' occupations were confirmed by school records and also by a questionnaire sent to parents which received an 87 per cent response. The information on parents' educations, however, derives solely from students' responses.

Table I. Percentage distributions of selected "background" variables of high-sixth-grade students in Berkeley, by school strata.

Variable Category	School Strata			
	Hills	Foothills	Flats	Total
Father's occupation				
Professional	45%	13%	1%	21%
Executive	15	3	0	6
Merchant	12	6	2	7
White-collar	20	23	12	18
Skilled manual	4	27	26	18
Semi-skilled and unskilled manual	0	18	40	18
Not available	4	11	19	11
Father's education				
16 years and over	74%	28%	19%	42%
13 to 15 years	9	13	10	10
12 years	10	24	21	18
9 to 11 years	1	7	12	6
8 years	0	3	3	2
0 to 7 years	0	3	6	3
Not available	7	23	28	18
Mother's education				
16 years and over	65%	27%	23%	40%
13 to 15 years	15	14	9	13
12 years	12	33	28	23
9 to 11 years	2	7	9	6
8 years	0	3	3	1
0 to 7 years	0	3	7	3
Not available	6	13	20	13
Race				
White	97%	71%	22%	65%
Oriental	3	12	10	8
Negro	1	14	62	24
Not available	0	3	6	3
Number of cases	317	236	263	816

their teachers, and marks assigned by their teachers in several subject areas.[3]

Inspecting these indices of achievement in the three school strata (see Table 2) it is evident that the students in the Hills are far superior, on the average, to those in the Foothills, and the students in the Foothills, in turn are superior in achievement to those in the Flats. Virtually all of the students in the Hills, for example, were reading at grade level—in a high-

Table 2. Mean test scores, percentages reading at grade level, and percentages receiving A or B marks in reading and arithmetic, by sex and school strata.

Variable	Boys			Girls		
	Hills	Foothills	Flats	Hills	Foothills	Flats
Reading test	106	92	73	105	96	82
	(148)	(121)	(118)	(167)	(108)	(128)
Arithmetic test	83	67	54	79	71	60
	(146)	(117)	(114)	(163)	(95)	(119)
IQ test	126	112	101	123	115	103
	(130)	(104)	(93)	(145)	(89)	(98)
Per cent reading	97%	50%	40%	98%	69%	62%
at grade level	(150)	(125)	(121)	(167)	(106)	(127)
Per cent receiving	61%	41%	21%	63%	60%	35%
A or B in reading	(150)	(126)	(129)	(167)	(110)	(134)
Per cent receiving	56%	50%	19%	51%	65%	34%
A or B in arithmetic	(150)	(126)	(129)	(167)	(110)	(134)

sixth-grade text or some additional enrichment text at the time of the survey in April. But only half of the boys in the Foothills, and two-fifths of those in the Flats were at grade level. A similar pattern of achievement exists for the girls—the only exception to the rank order being the fact that the teachers in the Hills only indicated one-half of the girls as warranting A or B grades as contrasted with 65 per cent in the Foothills. This exception does not reflect the actual achievement of these girls, however, but rather the more stringent standards and expectations of the teachers in the Hills. (The diverging norms of the teachers, of which we have our first indication here, will be shown much more strikingly later in the analysis.)

[3] While teachers do not assign formal grades in the Berkeley elementary schools, they were asked, for the purpose of this survey, to check those students in their classes to whom they would assign A or B grades were they called upon to assign traditional letter grades.

Before leaving our consideration of Table 2, we should note another facet of the relationships. Educators are well aware of the fact that girls, in general, achieve more highly than boys in school. While this is clearly true in the schools of the Berkeley Foothills and Flats, it is not true in in the Hills schools. What slight differences there are between boys and girls in the Hills schools more often favor the boys than the girls. This, too, foreshadows a specification which will emerge more sharply with further analysis. The superiority of the girls to the boys in academic performance is particularly pronounced among the most underprivileged groups.

The main differences in academic achievement are due, at least to a large extent as was initially suggested, to the differences in the backgrounds of the children assigned to the three strata. Since most of the students in the Hills come from professional home backgrounds, while in the Flats students come from working-class homes, we might anticipate that the aver-

Table 3. Indices of academic achievement of high-sixth-grade boys, by fathers' occupations.

Father's Occupation	Achievement Variables[a]					
	(1)	(2)	(3)	(4)	(5)	(6)
Executive	106	81	125	73%	65%	92%
	(25)	(25)	(23)	(26)	(26)	(26)
Professional	105	82	126	67	56	91
	(92)	(88)	(74)	(93)	(93)	(93)
Merchant: self-employed	105	83	125	63	67	90
	(29)	(29)	(26)	(30)	(30)	(30)
Upper white-collar	101	79	122	54	46	84
	(37)	(34)	(32)	(37)	(37)	(37)
Lower white-collar	84	63	107	32	29	65
	(29)	(29)	(27)	(31)	(31)	(31)
Artisan: self-employed	88	66	114	39	61	39
	(17)	(18)	(16)	(18)	(18)	(18)
Skilled manual	84	59	103	27	31	42
	(43)	(42)	(35)	(48)	(48)	(45)
Semi-skilled and unskilled manual	75	55	101	11	20	33
	(70)	(66)	(55)	(75)	(75)	(72)

[a] The achievement variables are as follows: (1) mean *California Reading Achievement Test* scores; (2) mean *California Arithmetic Achievement Test* scores; (3) mean *California Mental Maturity Test* (IQ) scores; (4) percentages assigned A or B grades in reading; (5) percentages assigned A or B grades in arithmetic; (6) percentages reading at grade level.

age differences between strata would be "explained" by these occupational differences.

The achievement of the boys from different occupational groups illustrates an association which has been often reported in the literature—the children of professionals and executives doing far better in their school work than working-class children. Over 90 per cent of the sons of professionals and executives are reading at grade level, whereas only a third of the sons of semi-skilled and unskilled manual workers are at grade level, as shown in Table 3.

The initial question arises, then, as to whether there are differences in the achievement of children from comparable occupational strata who are attending different schools. This question is examined in Table 4, using reading achievement test scores as a criterion.

Reading down the columns in Table 4, we can see that in each school stratum, among boys as well as girls, the socio-economic background of the child has a substantial impact upon his achievement. This impact is less in the Hills schools than in the Foothills and Flats, however. As we saw earlier, in Table 2, virtually all of the children in the Hills (97 per cent of the boys and 98 per cent of the girls) are reading at grade level. In fact, all the children of manual workers in the Hills (eleven girls and three boys) are at grade level.

In Table 4, we can also see more clearly that the largest discrepancy between the achievement of boys and girls, which was pointed out earlier in connection with Table 2, appears in the Flats schools—and especially among the children of manual workers in those schools.

The comparison of particular concern in Table 4 is between the children from comparable backgrounds who are attending schools in the different strata. Reading across the rows we can see that, within occupational

Table 4. Mean reading achievement-test scores of high-sixth-grade students, classified by sex, school strata, and fathers' occupations.

Father's Occupation	Boys			Girls		
	Hills	Foothills	Flats	Hills	Foothills	Flats
Professional and	107	100	—[a]	107	108	—[a]
executive	(94)	(21)	(2)	(93)	(15)	(1)
White-collar and	106	93	81	102	99	81
merchant	(46)	(31)	(18)	(55)	(38)	(16)
Manual and artisan	—[a]	91	71	103	93	84
	(3)	(55)	(72)	(11)	(46)	(87)

[a] Means are not reported for cells containing fewer than ten cases.

groups, there are substantial discrepancies in the average levels of achieve-ment of children attending different schools. The mean reading-achieve-ment-test scores of the sons of white-collar workers in the Hills, for ex-ample, was 106; in the Foothills, 93; and in the Flats, 81. This discrepancy is congruent with the hypothesis that the schools have the homogenizing effect suggested by T. H. Marshall for English grammar schools.

Gross occupational classifications, of course, by no means assure com-parable familial influence. It is doubtless true that one of the reasons manual workers choose to live in the Hills is to obtain greater educational and social advantages for their children. Very likely they place an em-phasis upon the value of school success which is more comparable to other residents of the Hills than to their occupational compeers in the Foothills and Flats.

Thus far, moreover, we have taken no account of the unequal distribu-tion of racial groups in the schools. Since Negroes are concentrated in the Flats, and most of them are manual workers, the question arises as to whether differences between occupational groups and between schools "hold up" within racial groups. Is the average in the Flats, for example, lower than in the Foothills because of the large number of Negroes in the Flats? Or is the achievement of the white children in the Flats lower than that of white children in the Foothills?

However, further cross-classification by race—white, oriental, and Negro—would lead to an unmanageable fifty-four cell table. If we con-tinue to ignore cells containing fewer than ten cases, a large proportion of the already limited data would be wasted. At this point it seems de-sirable to introduce a method of estimating the independent effects of each variable which will more efficiently utilize the available data.

Let us adopt the model that each reading test score is a function of the over-all sample mean, plus additive effects of the student's sex, race, school, and father's occupation, plus some idiosyncratic residual due to variables which have not been included in the model.

$$Y_{ijklp} = m + a_i + b_j + c_k + d_l + e_{ijklp}$$

Data are available for all of the variables which are under consideration for 555 of the 816 students in the original population. Of these, 263 are boys, 292 are girls, 99 are Negroes, 48 are oriental, ... On the basis of the assumed model, minimizing the sum of squares of the residuals, we may generate a set of "normal equations" (1, 15, 16) which take the form, for the total sum of scores, for example:

$$54247 = 555_m + 263a_1 + 292a_2 + 99b_1 + 48b_2 + \ldots$$

Table 5. Matrix formulation of a set of simultaneous linear "normal equations."

																x		=
555	263	292	99	48	408	263	158	134	193	161	201	0	0	0	0	m		54247
263	263	0	48	26	189	125	80	58	95	77	91	263	0	0	0	a_1		25301
292	0	292	51	22	219	138	78	76	98	84	110	292	0	0	0	a_2		28946
99	48	51	99	0	0	1	19	79	1	14	84	0	99	0	0	b_1		7728
48	26	22	0	48	0	7	23	18	5	18	25	0	48	0	0	b_2		4588
408	189	219	0	0	408	255	116	37	187	129	92	0	408	0	0	b_3		41931
263	125	138	1	7	255	263	0	0	164	85	14	0	0	263	0	c_1		27686
158	80	78	19	23	116	0	158	0	29	50	79	0	0	158	0	c_2		15344
134	58	76	79	18	37	0	0	134	0	26	108	0	0	134	0	c_3		11217
193	95	98	1	5	187	164	29	0	193	0	0	0	0	0	193	d_1		20478
161	77	84	14	18	129	85	50	26	0	161	0	0	0	0	161	d_2		16209
201	91	110	84	25	92	14	79	108	0	0	201	0	0	0	201	d_3		17560
0	263	292	0	0	0	0	0	0	0	0	0	0	0	0	0	λ_1		0
0	0	0	99	48	408	0	0	0	0	0	0	0	0	0	0	λ_2		0
0	0	0	0	0	0	263	158	134	0	0	0	0	0	0	0	λ_3		0
0	0	0	0	0	0	0	0	0	193	161	201	0	0	0	0	λ_4		0

This set of simultaneous equations is presented in matrix form as Table 5 (cf., 12).

Solving this matrix equation for the unknowns—the independent effects of the several categories of each variable—we obtain the estimates which are tallied in Table 6.

Table 6. Estimates of the main orthogonal effects of sex, race, school strata, and fathers' occupations upon reading-test scores.

Source of Variation	Main Effect
Sex	
Male	− 1.7
Female	+ 1.5
Race	
White	+ 3.0
Oriental	+ 0.9
Negro	−12.7
School stratum	
Hills	+ 2.3
Foothills	− 0.1
Flats	− 4.3
Father's occupation	
Professional and executive	+ 3.7
White-collar and merchant	+ 1.1
Manual and artisan	− 4.4
Mean	97.7

While the achievement of the Negro children is much poorer than the achievement of either the oriental or white children—allowing for the fact that they are concentrated in the Flats, and come from working-class homes—nevertheless each of the variables under consideration continues to have an independent and cumulative effect.

The model which has been imposed upon these data in order to make these estimates presumed the effects to be additive rather than interactive. When the actual cell means in the complete cross-tabulation are compared with the values which would be "expected" on the basis of the linear model, a substantial discrepancy is found in the cell of the Negro working-class boys in the Flats. Assuming the cumulative effect of each variable, we should expect the mean achievement of this group of twenty-eight boys to be:

$$97.7 - 1.7 - 4.3 - 4.4 = 74.7$$

whereas the mean achievement of this group is actually only 65.8.

The combined effect of these circumstances operates to depress achievement to a greater extent than they do operating separately. Earlier, in Table 2, it was seen that the superiority of girls to boys was greatest in the Flats; and in Table 4 it was further specified to be especially true among the children of manual workers. Now this discrepancy can be further narrowed down to apply most strongly to the children of Negro manual workers in the Flats. (The mean achievement of the forty-one Negro girls in the Flats whose fathers are manual workers is 81.7.) (cf., 5)

While the differences between sexes, and the effects of socio-economic status and race, which have been described above, are, in general outline, well-known, the homogenizing effect of the school milieu is less well established. Two of the mechanisms of this process have been intimated above—the lateral transmission of values and attitudes among students, and the normalization of differing standards of achievement by teachers.

Diffusion of Attitudes Among Peers

In order to investigate the social contacts of the students with their peers, a simple sociometric inventory was administered. Each student was given a mimeographed list of the names of his classmates. He was asked to check the names of his friends—those with whom he talked and played during recesses, lunch period, or after school.

The students were also asked, in a questionnaire, about their future plans, including a forced choice question as to whether or not they hoped eventually to go to college.

Taking the percentage of classmates choosing him as a crude indication of each boy's integration in his peer group, and contrasting the average "popularity" of the boys aspiring to go to college with those who do not in each school stratum, an interesting pattern emerges. (See Table 7.)

In the Flats boys are mentioned, on the average, by almost half of their

Table 7. Mean "popularity" of high-sixth-grade boys, according to school strata and educational aspirations.

Sociometric Location	School Strata		
	Hills	Foothills	Flats
College	35%	42%	48%
	(132)	(87)	(91)
Non-college	25	39	46
	(18)	(39)	(38)
All aspirations	34%	41%	47%
	(150)	(126)	(129)

classmates, while in the Hills the boys are mentioned as friends by only a third of their peers. The more fragmented social structure in the Hills reflects—in addition to the more formal classroom climate and tighter parental supervision—more stringent discrimination in the selection of friends. It can be seen from the difference in popularity between the college and non-college aspirants in the Hills, that this value constitutes one line of discrimination, whereas in the Flats it makes virtually no difference whether or not a student hopes to go to college.

When the sociometric structure of each class is analyzed more intensively,[4] and students are classified according to their positions within the structure of their own classes, the differing status of the non-college aspirants in the three strata is more apparent. (See Table 8.)

Table 8. Sociometric locations of the non-college aspirants among high-sixth-grade boys according to school strata.

Sociometric Location	School Strata		
	Hills	Foothills	Flats
"Stars"	39%	38%	55%
"Isolates"	11%	5%	0%
Number of cases	18	39	38

In the Flats the boys who are disinterested in extending their education are well-integrated in their classes. None of them are "isolates," and they are, in fact, far over-represented among the leaders of their peers. In the Foothills, the most heterogeneous schools, college aspirations are irrelevant to social location. Those who do not want to go to college are "stars" and "isolates" in about the same proportion as those who do. In the Hills, more of the non-college aspirants are isolated than in either Foothills or Flats. Relatively, then, terminal students are the social leaders in the lower economic strata. They gain social support from their peers, and, in turn, set the pace for them, without adopting the standards of success prevalent in the wider community of adults.

Teacher Standards

The other factor which was mentioned as tending to homogenize student achievement within schools was the differences between teachers' expectations. While the elementary teachers in Berkeley do not actually

[4] The methodology for this sociometric analysis may be found in the author's unpublished Ph.D. dissertation (13). The discussion in this section is, with slight modification, based upon the dissertation.

dispense grades to their students, their indication of those students to whom they would assign A's or B's if they were to give grades—those students whom they consider to be outstanding in reading—does indicate which students, and the proportion of students, they are satisfied with academically.

Inasmuch as the average achievement in the Hills is considerably higher than in the Foothills, and achievement in the Foothills higher than in the Flats, we should expect the proportion of high grades assigned, if they are realistic, to follow the same rank order. We find, in fact, the percentages of high grades assigned in the three school strata to be 62, 50, and 28 per cent, respectively.

When the variation in teacher marks is analyzed by the same set of independent variables which we have considered in relation to measured achievement,[5] however, it is found that while sex, race,[6] and fathers' oc-

Table 9. Estimated orthogonal effects of sex, race, school strata, and fathers' occupations upon the percentages of A and B grades assigned by teachers in reading.

Source of Variation	Main Effect
Sex	
Male	− 7.6%
Female	+ 6.9
Race	
White	+ 3.5
Oriental	+ 9.5
Negro	−18.9
School stratum	
Hills	− 3.9
Foothills	+ 4.6
Flats	+ 2.2
Father's occupation	
Professional and executive	+14.1
White-collar and merchant	+ 4.0
Manual and artisan	−16.7
Mean	53.2%

[5] The number of high grades allotted in each category is substituted for the sum of reading test scores as the dependent variable vector in the matrix equation presented in Table 5.

[6] Notice, however, that the oriental students are awarded more high grades than white students, when sex, fathers' occupations, and school differences are held constant.

cupations have pronounced effects in the same direction as before, that within groups actually fewer high grades are dispensed in the Hills than in either the Foothills or the Flats. The average effects of each of these variables upon the percentages of high grades assigned are listed in Table 9.

In order to make these results more vivid a portion of the fifty-four cell cross-tabulation reflecting these same data are presented in conventional form in Table 10.

Table 10. Percentages of white high-sixth-grade girls receiving A or B marks in reading, by school strata and fathers' occupations.

| Father's Occupation | School Strata | | |
	Hills	Foothills	Flats
Professional and	69%	77%	—
executive	(83)	(13)	(8)
White-collar and	62	77	—
merchant	(42)	(22)	(3)
Manual and artisan	36	54	50
	(11)	(26)	(16)

Looking at the bottom row of Table 10—the grades of the daughters of white manual workers in the three school strata—we see that only a third of them are awarded high marks in the Hills, as opposed to half their compeers in the Foothills and Flats. Yet the mean reading-achievement-test scores of these three groups are 103, 96, and 99, respectively, and we may recall that all of these girls in the Hills are reading at grade level whereas only 65 and 75 per cent of the girls in the Foothills and Flats are at grade level. Although fewer high grades, altogether, are allocated in the lower-stratum schools, when considering the achievement of the students, the proportion is relatively too high as contrasted with the Hills schools.

This raises a question as to the extent to which the differences in teachers' evaluations of boys and girls, of children from different occupational backgrounds, and of different racial groups, reflect differences in measured achievement. We had noted that the effects of these variables upon marks, shown in Table 9, with the exception of the oriental children who were given a disproportionate number of high grades, were in the same direction as the effects of the same variables upon test scores, shown in

Table 6, earlier. But, since the units of measurement are different, one cannot directly compare the magnitude of the effects.

Considering the combination of reading-test scores and mental maturity test scores, which are closely correlated with one another,[7] as joint indications of reading proficiency, an analysis of covariance was performed allowing for the average regression of marks upon test scores.[8] The results estimate the effects of each of the independent variables upon teach-

Table II. Estimates of the main orthogonal effects of sex, race, school strata, and fathers' occupations upon the percentages of A and B marks assigned in reading, adjusted for the regression of marks on IQ and reading-test scores.

Source of Variation	Main Effect
Sex	
Male	− 6.0%
Female	+ 5.4
Race	
White	− 0.7
Oriental	+ 5.0
Negro	+ 0.4
School stratum	
Hills	− 9.9
Foothills	+ 5.5
Flats	+12.9
Father's occupation	
Professional and executive	+ 6.7
White-collar and merchant	+ 0.5
Manual and artisan	− 6.9
Average percentage increase in A and B grades per unit increase in IQ test scores	+ 1.2%
Average percentage increase in A and B grades per unit increase in reading-test scores	+ 0.8
Mean	53.2%

[7] The zero-order product-moment correlation between the two tests in this sample is .750.

[8] For a paradigm of this analysis see L. N. Hazel (6).

ers' marks after adjusting those marks for differences in measured achievement. The solutions are listed in Table 11.

The IQ-test scores are actually slightly more highly correlated with teachers' marks in reading than are the reading-test scores.[9] After allowing for proficiency, as jointly indicated by these two tests, we can see that there is very little difference between teachers' evaluations of Negro and white children (the slight difference which remains favoring the Negro children), but, as we saw before, the oriental children receive higher marks than their measured achievement would account for. Girls, also, and children from professional or executive home backgrounds are perceived as better students than their test performances would warrant.

Considering the constellation of attributes of the students who are seen as good students, it would appear that the teachers add extra weight to industry, effort, and cooperation, above and beyond its reflection in the quality of performance. (The better motivated students do, of course, do their work more regularly and cooperate in daily lessons. This behavior doubtless contributes to the teachers' over-all impression of their competence.)

This analysis brings out more sharply, at the same time, the fact that the students in the Flats are relatively overevaluated, and those in the Hills relatively underevaluated, when due allowance is made for differences in tested performance.

Discussion

Because of the segregation of social classes school societies tend to develop differing norms, values, and social structures. In the middle-class schools parents and teachers supervise children more closely and have high academic expectations for them. A result of this strong intergenerational control is a more fragmented peer-group structure and a greater saliency of adult values for the children. In the working-class schools values are more readily communicated laterally among peers. Attitudes towards schooling are largely irrelevant to the students assessments of one another, and teachers, although concerned about academic achievement, tend to normalize a lower level of achievement.[10]

As the children progress through the grades, merge in the junior high schools, high schools, and junior colleges, and compete for positions in

[9] The point-biserial correlation between teachers' marks and IQ test scores is .570, and with reading test scores it is .552.

[10] Despite the obvious circularity, considering the accumulated research evidence on the environmental antecedents of test performance, the correlation between IQ test scores and school performance continues to be a rationale for this normalization. "Well, what can you expect?"

the colleges and universities, uniform achievement criteria are applied for which they are inadequately prepared. Students coming from the Hills schools are assigned to the academic stream in high school, and those from the Flats are almost automatically and necessarily assigned to general or vocational curricula. As adolescents this comes to many of them as an unanticipated and discriminatory jolt.

Table 12. Percentages of high-sixth-grade boys reading at grade level, and aspiring to go to college, by fathers' occupations.

Father's Occupation	Per Cent Reading at Grade Level	Per Cent Aspiring to Go to College
Executive	92%	92%
	(26)	(26)
Professional	91	83
	(93)	(93)
Merchant: self-employed	90	80
	(30)	(30)
Upper white-collar	84	81
	(37)	(37)
Lower white-collar	65	71
	(31)	(31)
Artisan: self-employed	39	72
	(18)	(18)
Skilled manual	42	71
	(45)	(48)
Semi-skilled and unskilled manual	33	65
	(72)	(75)

A high proportion of working-class, and especially Negro, students aspire to go to college. In large numbers they enter the "open-door" junior colleges (4) in the Bay Area in hopes of becoming transfer students to the state colleges or university. At this late point they are counseled or "cooled" out into terminal vocational training. The discrepancies between the current placement and the aspirations of the sons of manual workers listed in Table 12 clearly foreshadows this eventual set-back.[11]

The seeds of this anomic situation—the maintenance of culturally shared goals without concommitant command of the means—are sown in the early elementary-school years. School systems serve a social function of screening and sorting the oncoming generation into different streams of

[11] That the greatest disparity between aspiration and achievement is to be found among depressed groups has been noted many times (e.g., 2, 3).

life according to impartial criteria of achievement. At the same time one of the assumed goals of public education is to foster social mobility, and minimize the ascription of position according to the circumstances of birth. In the absence of clear and accurate evaluations of their achievement, however, students are deprived of the opportunity for rational choice. Whatever pedagogical adaptations may be desirable for the education of underprivileged children, misguidance and obscurantism are surely not among them.

Summary and Implications

An analysis of the achievement records of elementary school students in a district characterized by residential segregation reveals gross retardation in depressed areas. In addition to the anticipated differences between children from varying socio-economic strata and ethnic groups which contribute to the disparity in achievement, social processes within schools are found to reinforce and sustain different levels of achievement. Two mechanisms are the diffusion of educational attitudes among students and the normalization of diverging standards by teachers. It is suggested that the latter must bear some responsibility for the divergence between aspirations and achievement among underprivileged youth.

REFERENCES

1. Anderson, R. L., and Bancroft, T. A., *Statistical Theory in Research,* New York: McGraw-Hill, 1952, pp. 278-284.
2. Beckham, A. S., "A Study of the Intelligence of Colored Adolescents of Different Social-Economic Status in Typical Metropolitan Areas," *J. soc. Psychol.,* 1933, 4:70-91.
3. Boyd, G. F., "The Levels of Aspiration of White and Negro Children in a Non-segregated Elementary School," *J. soc. Psychol.,* 1952, 36:191-196.
4. Clark, Burton R., "The 'Cooling-Out' Function in Higher Education, *Amer. J. Sociol.,* May 1960, 65:569-576.
5. Deutsch, Martin, *Minority Group and Class Status as Related to Social and Personality Factors in School Achievement* (Monograph No. 2), Ithaca, N. Y.: The Society for Applied Anthropology, 1960.
6. Hazel, N. L., "The Covariance Analysis of Multiple Classification Tables With Unequal Subclass Numbers," *Biometr. Bull.,* 1946, 2:21-25.
7. Mann, Horace, "Report for 1849," in *Life and Works of Horace Mann,* vol. IV: *Annual Reports of the Secretary of the Board of Education of Massachusetts for the Years 1845-1848; and Oration Delivered Before the Authorities of the City of Boston, July 4, 1842,* Boston: Lee and Shepard, 1891, p. 251.
8. Marshall, T. H. "Social Selection in the Welfare State," *Eugen. Rev.,* July 1953, 45:90.
9. Sullivan, Elizabeth T., Clark, Willis W., and Tiegs, Ernest W., *California Short-Form Test of Mental Maturity: Elementary: Grades 4-5-6-7-8, S-Form,* Los Angeles: California Test Bureau, 1950.

10. Tiegs, Ernest W., and Clark, Willis W., *California Arithmetic Test: Elementary: Grades 4-5-6,* Los Angeles: California Test Bureau, 1950.

11. _____, *California Reading Test: Elementary: Grades 4-5-6,* Los Angeles: California Test Bureau, 1950.

12. Wilks, S. S., *Mathematical Studies,* Princeton, N. J.: Princeton University Press, 1950.

13. Wilson, Alan B., "The Effect of Residential Segregation upon Educational Achievement and Aspirations," unpublished doctoral dissertation, University of California, Berkeley, California, 1960, pp. 85-99.

14. _____, "Residential Segregation of Social Classes and Aspirations of High School Boys," *Amer. sociol. Rev.,* December 1959, 24:836-845.

15. Yates, Frank, *Sampling Methods for Censuses and Surveys* (2nd ed. rev.), New York: Hafner, 1953, pp. 137-141.

16. _____, "The Analysis of Multiple Classifications With Unequal Numbers in the Different Classes," *J. Amer. statist. Assn.,* March 1934, 29: 51-55.

PART IV

Teachers for Depressed Areas

The central role of the classroom teacher in the education of disadvantaged children has been a recurring theme in these papers. Whatever other modifications are made in programs, practices, materials, and services, the most significant improvements in schools in depressed areas depend on the recruitment and retention of staffs of competent, committed teachers. To staff such schools is perplexing, for they are not the first choices of most teachers. Many of the new recruits are young teachers who must accept placement in schools where there are openings. Thus, the "difficult," the "special services," the "project" schools reveal the highest turnover rates, the greatest number of vacancies, and the least experienced teachers.

The two papers which follow focus primarily on the pre-service preparation of teachers for depressed urban schools. However, the questions and discussions ranged far beyond the recruitment and training of prospective teachers to their assignment, supervision, in-service education, and retention. How to get the competent, skillful teachers with feeling for working with children from disadvantaged homes is a key problem for the public schools and for the teacher-preparing institutions. As Dean Harry Rivlin said: "It is clear . . . that even the most imaginative superintendent and the most cooperative board of education cannot solve the problems of urban education until the schools get an adequate supply of skilled and understanding teachers, and then make optimum use of these teachers' abilities."[1]

How can college students be attracted to enter training programs for positions in the depressed urban schools? Such schools are publicized as "difficult" where maintaining classroom discipline is perceived as the most time-consuming task; where little, if any, creative teaching is pos-

[1] Harry N. Rivlin, "Teachers for the Schools in Our Big Cities," a paper prepared for the University of Pennsylvania Schoolmen's Week Program, October 12, 1962, p. 5.

sible; where teacher mobility is matched only by student transiency; where a probationary teacher "serves his time" before moving to a better situation. What constitutes a positive challenge to young people to enter such teaching posts voluntarily and to stay in these positions because they recognize their inherent rewards? Are special teacher-preparation programs required at the pre-service level?

As Professor Vernon F. Haubrich points out, the creative performance of teachers who do stay in depressed-areas schools needs to be recognized and supported by all concerned; the many factors which cause teachers to reject appointments to schools in depressed areas, or to leave as soon as they have an option to do so, must be understood and taken into account in the selection and preparation of teachers. The new teacher rejects the situation, he suggests, because of "an inability to comprehend, understand, and cope with the multiple problems of language development, varying social norms, habits not accepted by the teacher, behavior which is often not success oriented, lack of student 'cooperation' and achievement levels well below expectancies of teachers." There are other factors, as well, including a large gap in orientation and education which leave new teachers ignorant of appropriate methods, curriculum, and approaches to discipline and classroom control.

Some serious questions are raised by Haubrich about the adequacy of traditional teacher-preparation as a source for the insights, understandings, and attitudes needed for working with children from culturally disadvantaged homes and neighborhoods. He suggests that such programs carry no message to student teachers to practice-teach in so-called "difficult schools" nor to seek appointments there.

Haubrich describes some details of the Hunter College program for preparing teachers for service in depressed-area schools. The underlying philosophy is that "prospective teachers should be specifically prepared in schools where they will eventually teach." Some notions being tested by the program are: student teaching can be both challenging and rewarding in a personal and professional sense; the apprehensions of prospective teachers are best alleviated and their perceptions modified by direct, wide contact with education and community workers and leaders; a team of professionals from the depressed-area school itself—such as subject-matter specialists, curriculum experts, and social psychologists—is required for introducing the student teacher to the particular demands of these schools and for helping orient him to working with children in this special context; participation in a program for teaching in a depressed-area school should be voluntary on the student's part and must begin early in his college career.

The Hunter College program adds five supplemental experiences to the regular pre-service activities: the prospective teacher in the special program spends a greater number of hours directly responsible for a class—planning, teaching, and evaluating pupil progress under supervision. He has wider contact and direct involvement with community agencies and institutions so that he can understand better the problems faced by children and adults in the depressed area. He participates in weekly conferences with college and school personnel to run the gamut of teaching problems—curriculum content, classroom management, remedial techniques, instructional resources. He observes the work in various school offices to appreciate how administrative, service and other personnel can facilitate his classroom job. And finally, he receives considerably more supervisory help from both college and school personnel than the usual cadet teacher. The special program bases undergraduate instruction on the realities of the teaching situation. Beyond that, with luck, it helps the prospective teacher experience some of the actual rewards which come from working with culturally disadvantaged children.

On the basis of the assessment of the program to date, Haubrich suggests that preparation of teachers for urban schools will require more interchange of personnel and environments. College students and their instructors should move to the school and its environs. School personnel need to visit the college classroom to share their insights and experiences with prospective teachers. He suggests that the liberal arts faculty be involved to a far greater extent in reconstructing courses and experiences for prospective teachers. Finally, Haubrich proposes a drastic reappraisal of the policies for staffing schools in depressed urban areas, notably reduced teaching loads in the early years, plus greater orientation and supervision.

Professor Leonard Kornberg reviews briefly the current efforts of educators to cater to students in depressed urban schools—"the flurry of new testing, guidance, remedial reading, extra-curricular enrichment programs"—and suggests that such programs do not really alter the essential conditions of classroom experience. Kornberg takes a skeptical glance at the premise which underlies many of these efforts, that something can be done outside the classroom which will help disadvantaged children adjust to the usual experiences and normal demands inside the classroom. He suggests that the proper question is, what kind of classroom can reach these children: what kinds of curriculum activities, teaching materials, and teaching strategies will spur their learning? A great deal of innovation and experimentation is currently under way in schools, most of it dealing with the education of gifted pupils in educationally privileged schools.

Kornberg urges that we capitalize on this "new mood for school experimentation" to build a new kind of school for disadvantaged children—new in the sense of a different kind of classroom life and services.

Kornberg describes a program at Queens College, a project called BRIDGE (Building Resources of Instruction for Disadvantaged Groups in Education). The program, like that Haubrich describes, aims to upgrade the teacher-education program. A school-within-a-school arrangement, consisting of three seventh-grade classes, has been set up for instruction in the academic subjects. Teachers of these demonstration classes will remain with the students for the three-year junior high period, during which they will have time to study the children and learn how to work most effectively with them. A coordinating teacher—experienced, successful in the classroom—provides the type of cheek-by-jowl assistance Kornberg feels is essential for new teachers working with disadvantaged classes. The teachers are experimenting with new course sequences, content organization, and instructional materials and at the same time, helping children with their individual problems.

An important aspect of the BRIDGE is the observation and case conference procedures involving the Queens College team and the school's staff. Students at Queens College are working with and observing adolescents in various kinds of club and recreational situations. "BRIDGE groups" consisting of college undergraduates are being placed in junior high schools to work with small groups of pupils who come voluntarily for one afternoon a week for special help. The BRIDGE program is based on the idea that experience in working with disadvantaged children is most effective at the pre-service level, when young student-teachers are pliable and susceptible to changing insights. Kornberg believes that the teacher's professional growth is the key to vigorous staffing schools in depressed areas. He proposes salary and status differentials, internships, and greater continuity between teacher-preparation and school programs. He suggests increased attention to the kind of teachers being recruited and trained for service in disadvantaged schools. The issue, as he sees it, "is whether the classroom life creates alienation or relationships." Youngsters who come to school with impoverished or discrepant cultural interests and skills sorely need teachers who understand these deficiencies and the conditions from which they stem. Only such experiences, Kornberg argues, can develop the teacher's professional commitment to the special demands of work in depressed urban schools.

Many observations have been made about the notion of teaching as a middle-class profession, with teacher behavior guided by middle-class values and virtues alien to or in conflict with the lower-class values systems of underprivileged children. Granting this condition as an accepted fact, what is its real significance for both recruitment and preparation of teachers? Will seeing more of children help prospective teachers view the youngsters as individuals rather than as stereotyped members of a minority group? What kinds of direct contacts will foster a clear picture of each child as a special personality?

To take another tack, what means will increase the supply of teachers from the various minority groups and lower-income classes? Although there was considerable agreement on tapping this reservoir of undeveloped manpower through special recruitment efforts, the problem of how to do it remained. Participant consensus that college admission standards should not be lowered led to the principle that secondary school programs should be enriched to stimulate able youngsters from lower classes and minority groups to seek higher education. The teaching profession has been one of the means of upward mobility for many immigrant groups in the past; can it provide the same opportunities for the present in-migrant groups? One promising approach called "The Homework Helper Program" is being tested by Mobilization for Youth, Inc. High school sophomores and juniors from low-income families are being trained and employed as tutors for elementary-school pupils. Basically set up to encourage and aid the younger children, the tutoring scheme also provides the high school students with a small weekly income and a positive exposure to teaching— it is hoped—that may suggest education as a career.

Dean Harry Rivlin points to the need of all children for good teachers but feels that the "in-migrant children need good teachers desperately, for most of these youngsters do not have access to the kind of family and community resources which can compensate for many inadequacies in the educational opportunities offered by schools."[2] What special qualities are required for the "good teacher" in a depressed area school as distinct from those in the suburban or privileged school? Are these qualities indentifiable in the college years of the prospective teacher? Should administrative and supervisory personnel "come up through the ranks" or do they require some kind of custommade training for leadership?

Parents anywhere may be apathetic, hostile, uninformed about school but this is especially true for parents in depressed areas. How can these particular parents, with varied attitudes about education and the school program, be reached? Should teachers relate to low-income parents differently from the rapport of their colleagues and parents in suburbia? What modifications are needed in school organization to enable teachers to work more closely with home and family?

[2] *Ibid.*, p. 5.

Finally, there seemed to be consensus that there should be extra compensation for teaching in depressed urban areas, but that this should not come in the form of extra pay. Instead, compensation should be made in extras such as smaller classes, additional teaching materials, supervisory assistance, specialist personnel, and lighter loads to permit better planning and preparation. The two papers in this section describe two pre-service projects for preparing teachers for service in depressed urban areas. Each aims at modifying the total college program for the students—academic as well as professional—and to extend college experiences into the disadvantaged neighborhood. Both programs attempt to blend the philosophical and behavioral sciences with practical insights into the culture and needs of the individuals and groups in depressed areas.

Similar explorations are needed with respect to the other members of the professional staff. What qualities in an administrator lead to the kind of climate that encourages good teaching; that enables reticent or hostile families to enter freely into school programs; that draws teachers to the faculty because they know they can secure the kinds of assistance needed to do an effective job; and that will make the school the center for community efforts to upgrade living conditions? What particular kinds of supervisory activities are needed for schools in depressed areas? How do counselors modify their roles in working with disadvantaged children? How do they operate most effectively in such schools? What is needed in the way of group workers, social workers, school-home liaison persons, visiting teachers? What is the relation of these special service personnel to other members of the professional staff and to other agencies and institutions in the community? Is special preparation a must? Selection, training, and utilization of staffs for depressed-area schools are topics which deserve more rigorous study than in the past. Service in such schools must be made a positive challenge with potential for high personal and professional rewards, not a punishment or a frustration.

Vernon F. Haubrich | Teachers for Big-City Schools

The Circle

Eileen Morse received her appointment as a regular teacher from the Board of Education. One look at the address was enough—she and thirty-four out of one hundred appointed to this Borough decided they weren't having any. The influence of the press, "always looking for a good story"; of parents— "you'll type before you teach in that neighborhood"; of a fiancé—"you nuts or something?"; of friends—"one *could* do it, I suppose"; all these and more had effectively done the job of turning Eileen to other schools in other places. Addresses tell a story as Aesop never could.

Eileen Morse has problems with addresses, and the people who try to keep the schools open and going have problems with all the Eileens in the city. Eileens, who have built in the short span of 20 years plus, a mode of perception and attitude that school and college did not touch. As one principal put it, "Who will we get to cover the classes?" Each year the same question; each year the same Eileens. The circle is tough to break.[1]

The Social Situation

About one in three children who attend school in New York City come from "culturally deprived" homes.[2] The children so classified tend to attend school together, and, consequently there tend to be areas of New York City where 80 per cent and more of the children in a school can be so classified. The results of segregated housing and ghetto living lead to schools serving children coming from neighborhoods which are vastly different from one another.

---

[1] I am indebted to the *Journal of Teacher Education* for allowing me to use in this paper much of my article (3) to be published by the *Journal*.

[2] The terms "culturally deprived," "culturally different," "culturally depressed," and "culturally disadvantaged" all tell the same story. They tend to be lower-class people with special problems. The Federal Bureau of Labor Statistics estimates that a worker with two children in New York City needs $5970 to maintain a "modest but adequate" standard of living. Using this figure as a base, a recent study by the Teamsters Union indicates that 49 per cent of the families in New York City should be classified as "deprived." The study also indicates that 70.8 per cent of Negro and Puerto Rican families were under that level (8).

The culturally deprived child in New York City tends to be the son or daughter of a recently arrived family from the South or from Puerto Rico, and he faces problems that have been well documented (2). The newcomers, the in-migrants, come for a wide variety of reasons not the least of which may be hope for their children as to social mobility, better jobs and a decent place to live.

A word must be said about the in-migrants to New York City. Oscar Handlin (2) points out that the newcomers have much in common with former immigrant groups but that basic differences exist. The story that is told is fundamentally this: the newcomers, the in-migrants, come from a society called United States, but not from a culture called "big city." The in-migrants have close ties with former places of residence, and there is some movement back and forth between the former and the present residence; the break is not final.

A recent study (6) indicates that 20 per cent of the third-grade and 25 per cent of the sixth-grade youngsters are in-migrants to New York City. The in-migrants of Puerto Rican and Negro background have concentrated in the boroughs of Brooklyn and Manhattan, and in particular sections of these two boroughs. It rapidly becomes apparent that, in New York City (as in other large cities), large numbers of in-migrants live in sections where there is a heavy concentration of other in-migrants.

When many of the in-migrants face a series of problems, such as poor educational background, deficiency in reading skills, non-English-speaking background, poverty, and other attendant problems, the schools will be one of several institutions to face this situation. The entire social situation in which these in-migrant families find themselves has an impact on the schools. The manner in which the schools face these problems and the rapidity with which these problems are solved by the in-migrant are crucial issues for educators and, indeed, for the entire society.

The School Situation

The social problems of neighborhood, educational background, and family circumstance find a roost in many schools in New York City. Other publications (1, 7) have ably assessed these problems and, to some extent, have translated their meaning in terms of the school context. It is important to take note of these unique school problems, for they make up the gist of the situation facing teachers and administrators in schools serving culturally deprived youngsters.

The reading problem pervades the context of many other school problems. The non-English-speaking child, typically Puerto Rican, faces a language, cultural, and social barrier in coming to the schools of New

York (7). Other in-migrant children, who come from areas where schools are poor or where compulsory education laws are not strictly enforced, face similar problems in attempting to adjust to the pace and tempo of the city's schools. When one adds to these factors a home which is at subsistence level and which is economically at the bottom of the income scale, educators face gigantic problems in teaching children to read.[3] One discovers very quickly just how interrelated is the social and educational context when the unique relationship between money, occupation, home, and school comes home to the teacher's classroom. Children, who have not been beyond a ten-block area after arriving in New York, who have great problems raising the necessary money[4] for school "extras," and who live in desperately overcrowded apartments, will have difficulty in learning the key skill in school—reading.

The world of the teacher (middle-class or middle-class striving) and the world of the child (lower-class) represents a problem with several dimensions. Much has been said of lower-class children faced with the middle-class teacher and school. Most of what is said is reliable and valid. Children who have meager educational backgrounds, who, for a wide variety of reasons, are ambivalent (9) towards the work of the school, who see little to aim for in a society which discriminates against them, who use language which is more "colorful" and who may rebel more often than other children in other areas, are in somewhat of a conflict with the teacher who has achieved a measure of success and wishes to convey the skills and ambitions she "knows" and has learned. And, of course, there's the rub.

Taking examinations, filling out forms, going to libraries, valuing the competitive life, striving to get ahead, and wanting what success the middle class wants are part of the outlook of most of our teachers. In a realistic sense many teachers and students in this kind of a situation are talking past one another. They live in different worlds.

Additional factors, which grow out of the social situation and compound the difficulties that teachers and administrators face, include the following: high truancy rates, high rates of pupil turnover resulting from families who move frequently, "low" IQ scores resulting from tests which are not culture free, high rates of turnover, and large numbers of families on the

---

[3] A series has been published on this problem by the Board of Education, New York City, 110 Livingston Street, New York City, New York.

[4] In the Hunter project described below we did a survey of one eighth-grade class for a three-month period as to "extra money" children were asked to bring to school. It amounted to $26.50. In this class 70 per cent of the children were in families on the welfare rolls of New York City. A family on welfare with a child in junior high school receives $0.25 a month extra for the child's extra expenses!

welfare rolls. What does it add up to for the teacher? Marya Mannes, writing for *The Reporter,* was able to obtain this most perceptive statement from a teacher in a "culturally deprived" neighborhood: "Rightly or wrongly, justified or not, teachers prefer to teach in an integrated school which is predominantly white, than in a segregated or difficult school" (5). The story of the middle-class teacher and the lower-class child boils down to something resembling this statement.

One factor, mentioned by prospective teachers, which contributes to the schools' inability to recruit for schools serving depressed areas, is the transportation problem. Most teachers live outside the area served by these schools, and they prefer to teach in neighborhoods closer to their homes. Another point mentioned by many prospective teachers, especially female, is an expressed fear of walking through the neighborhood to the school. One cannot judge at this point if these expressed reasons are primary; but they do tend to highlight the resistance of many prospective teachers to teaching in these schools.

It must be noted that many teachers do choose to remain in schools serving depressed areas, and their work and contribution must be recognized and supported by all concerned. But many choose not to stay or do not accept appointments to these schools. The entire situational context, which includes many educational and social problems beyond the skill of many teachers, is just too much for some.[5] To conclude, many factors tend to cause the teacher to reject appointment in depressed areas, and among these are:

1. Large numbers of in-migrant children, who have special needs, will face the incoming teacher, and, for a wide variety of reasons, the teacher tends to reject this kind of situation.

2. The incoming teacher probably rejects the situation because of an inability to comprehend, understand, *and cope with* the multiple problems of language development, varying social norms, habits not accepted by the teacher, behavior which is often not success-oriented, lack of student "cooperation," and achievement levels well below expectancies of teachers.

3. The distance one lives from the culturally deprived neighborhood and a fear of going through the neighborhood surely have been contributing factors in the schools' inability to recruit teachers.

4. There seem to be gaps in the orientation and preparation of teachers

---

[5] As noted previously, thirty-four out of a hundred teachers appointed to the borough of Manhattan do not accept appointment to the schools to which they have been assigned. Some selected schools have much higher rates.

for urban schools, which leaves the new teacher "at sea" with respect to methods, curriculum, and approaches to the "discipline" problem.

Teacher Preparation—One View

When a principal of a special service school[6] recently asked, "Where will the new teachers come from? Who will do the job?" he was echoing the desperate situation many administrators face in the day-by-day struggle to maintain a semblance of order, productivity, and morale. The urban schools serving depressed areas need, literally, thousands of teachers and administrators who can do the job.

One view of teacher preparation includes the usual sequence of courses —social and philosophical foundations, psychological foundations, methods, and student teaching—with a strong background in one or more content areas. The professional sequence, in most cases, views the content of teacher preparation as a universal, and applicable in all normal school situations. Teacher preparation in college classrooms and student teaching in school X has point and substance in schools Y, Z, etc. Student teaching is probably the culmination of the sequence, and a license is issued to the graduate. He is "prepared." Kids are kids.

Several issues arise when this conception of teacher preparation is applied to schools serving culturally depressed areas. First, these children and these neighborhoods have unique problems that one does not usually encounter in Psychological Foundations I or in student teaching which is done in a "good" neighborhood.

Second, the curriculum of the college or university may or may not inform and influence the prospective teacher about the problems and relevant issues of depressed urban areas. This information and influence depends on the pattern of experiences in college, both in the professional sequence and in the liberal arts curriculum. Recently, a student teacher was attempting to show the pattern of immigration to the United States. She listed the Irish, the Germans, the Italians, the English, and the Scandinavians; she also indicated through class discussion the contributions these groups had made. Even though the class was entirely made up of Negro and Puerto Rican children, she made *no mention* of Negro or Puerto Rican immigration, in-migration, or contributions. When asked why this was so, she indicated she did not know about these things, for they were not part of her college work or her own reading!

Third, the traditional view of teacher preparation has an appeal to cer-

---

[6] "Special service" schools are schools having a series of problems related to the condition and background of the students. The school is eligible for special services from the Board of Education.

tain kinds of students with certain kinds of goals and ambitions. The student who is looking for a type of security, who wishes a relatively easy road to professional status, who has family and home pressures to get "something practical" from college, and the student who may feel that teaching is a second or subsidiary choice among occupational goals—all of these may enter teaching (4). It should be noted that these obverse motives are neither good nor bad taken alone. But when one views the upward mobility patterns of prospective teachers (10), the great concern with the gifted student, which has been part of our entire contemporary scene, and the exposure of students in college to these concerns, then the reluctance of prospective teachers to enter teaching via schools in culturally depressed areas is understandable.

One never lives in a cultural vacuum. The cultural milieu which surrounds the prospective teacher includes the views, ideas and notions of his fellow students, his parents, his professors, and his own experience. His appointment to a "good" school, where parents and neighbors are proud of his work, where there are ambitions and goals among the student body similar to his own, and where one finds the student adjusted to the work of the school and the norms of the teacher, is the goal of most prospective teachers.

In interviewing students for the special project which Hunter College has undertaken we encountered time and time again the expressions: "I just wouldn't be good for that type of school," or "I feel that my contributions to education can best be made at the Bronx High School of Science" (a selective school for gifted students), or "My parents wouldn't allow me to go into that school or neighborhood." The situation is such that the prospect of teaching in culturally depressed areas is just not in the cards for many of these prospective teachers. They do not view teaching in culturally depressed areas as a distinction, and the biting issue is that our society does not usually view it as a distinction.

Teacher Preparation—Another View

Before launching into a description of the Hunter College project in teacher preparation for schools in depressed areas, let us take a moment to look at the purposes which undergird the program. The thesis of this report is simple: the problems and challenges of the culturally depressed areas will not be solved unless there is a basic change in the education, housing, and employment patterns which pervade the entire life of the people in these areas. Of the three factors, education, housing, and employment, we view education as crucially important; for until the school provides these children with the necessary skills and understandings needed to compete successfully in our interdependent, industrial society, the fundamental situation will not change.

However, to speak of the "school" in this academic fashion is to miss the point, for it is the quality of the administrative and teaching personnel, their professionalism and the leadership they provide which will make a difference. One immediately recognizes that many other factors, such as housing, family, community agencies, and church, are important; but at the heart of the matter one still asks, who will do the teaching? The kind of slow, arduous, and sometimes completely frustrating effort is what is most often required, and this can only be handled by teachers who understand the problems and issues at stake. And these issues revolve about the future of our democratic society, for one cannot speak of a democratic society in which *all* participate unless one is willing to face up to the kinds of dilemmas which immediately make themselves known in depressed areas. The educational question is, shall there be educational disenfranchisement for some people in some areas?

Specifically, there are only two ways big cities can recruit for this task. First, devices may be employed to encourage experienced teachers to enter these schools. In New York City a teacher must serve a number of years in "special-service" schools before he is eligible for promotion to administrative posts. Recently the Board of Education had under consideration the idea of paying teachers in "special-service" schools a bonus or extra salary. (This proposal was not put into effect.) Other ways exist to bring teachers, voluntarily or involuntarily, into these schools, and the simplest way is to send all newly appointed teachers into those areas which have the greatest need. The problem one encounters here is the high refusal or "turn-down" rate. Many teachers just will not accept appointment to these schools.

Another manner of obtaining the qualified teachers is to afford beginning teachers the opportunity to begin their professional careers in schools serving depressed areas, *after doing their student teaching in these same schools.* Student teaching becomes the introductory phase to a full-time teaching position in the self-same school where the student teaching was done. The central view of the special program at Hunter has been, and will continue to be, that *prospective teachers should be specifically prepared in schools where they will eventually teach.* Some basic formulations grew out of our planning for the program. Among these were:

1. Student teaching in schools serving depressed areas can be rewarding and challenging, both in a personal and professional sense.
2. The demands on the teacher in these schools will require more in-

tensive experience and preparation than the ordinary student teaching situation.

3. The chief manner in which the fears and perceptions of prospective teachers can be modified is by wide, direct contact with school officials, teachers, and neighborhood leaders.

4. The kinds of tasks the student teacher will face requires a team of professional workers to introduce and prepare students in the demands of schools in these areas. Among these professionals would be various personnel from the school itself, subject-matter specialists, curriculum experts, and social psychologists.

5. The school principal and the entire teaching staff should welcome this program, for while it would mean burdens and extra work, it would also aid, if successful, in providing well trained, competently prepared, able and willing teachers in the semester following student teaching.

6. No student should be forced to participate in the program. We called for, and will continue to call for, volunteers to undertake this program. These prospective student teachers are contacted in the various pre-service courses at the college.

7. If the student teacher wished to remain in the school after student teaching and after passing the necessary license examinations, he could do so. The Associate Superintendent and the Bureau of Appointment of New York City guarantee placement in these schools for those student teachers who wish to remain.

8. If the student teacher decided not to stay on in the school after student teaching, he would be free to leave without prejudice.

The program which developed during the past five semesters has been thoroughly reconstructive. A central proposition of the program has been continuous self-evaluation and self-criticism by all concerned.[7] We began and have remained in the junior high school,[8] for it is this segment of the New York City 12-year program which suffers the greatest teacher shortage. The program has grown from one school in Harlem to four schools in Harlem and one in the East Bronx. We began with six volunteers during the first semester, and the number of volunteers has grown to nineteen during the fifth semester. All schools are "special service" and all serve culturally depressed areas. All the schools have the classic prob-

[7] This may seem easier said than done. However, the teachers and administrators in these schools are remarkably honest. Student teachers were also critical of aspects of the program, for they perceived the program as relating directly to their immediate occupational status.

[8] There is a strong possibility that we will expand the program to the elementary and senior high schools in the near future.

lems of truancy, behavior difficulties, high teacher turnover, problems in language proficiency, low measured scores on verbal IQ tests, and a high percentage of families on welfare.

All student teachers, in the special or regular program, spend the entire morning in a school for one full semester. Briefly, the program resembles the normal student teaching situation but with significant variations.

Part one: During the first three weeks of the semester the student teacher devotes his time to observation, orientation and adjustment. He spends time getting to know the class, familiarizes himself with school regulations, and observes his cooperating teacher. Cooperating teachers, selected by the school, work closely with personnel from the college.

Part two: The next two weeks of the semester (total time elapsed is now five weeks) is spent inducting the student teacher into the actual classroom teaching situation. Planning lessons, constructing units, learning procedures of evaluation, and first experiences in actual teaching are the highlights of this phase of the program. Normally, at least one and probably two classes come under the direction of the student teacher towards the end of the period.

Part three: During the final ten or eleven weeks of the semester the student teacher assumes control of and responsibility for "his" classes. The cooperating teacher, supervisors from the school, and college personnel are always ready and willing to help. Daily observations and critiques are part of the regular order of business. The student teacher is also familiarized with the official-class (homeroom) procedures and handles much of this work as well.

In many respects this three-part program resembles the ordinary student-teaching program, with the exception that the schools are "special service" and are in areas which would be understood as culturally depressed. However, in this program, five additional features are employed to bring the prospective teacher to a point of greater competence in these schools. These additional experiences supplement, rather than replace, the student teaching program of the college.

The first of these experiences is a greater number of actual hours taught by the student teacher. The student teacher is not "along for the ride," nor is he looked on as an errand boy or additional clerical help. He becomes responsible for "his" classes after five weeks of induction. He plans the work, executes the lessons, and evaluates the progress of the class. He makes mistakes—lots of them. We feel it is better to make the mistakes while student teaching and while supervision is readily available, than to make the mistakes with a full program of five or six classes during the first year of teaching. The student teacher punches a time clock, has a mail box, meets a homeroom class, and participates as fully as possible in the on-going life of the school.[9]

The second of these supplementary experiences consists of wide contact with community agencies, institutions, and leaders. A welfare receiving center, public housing developments and private tenements, a local newspaper and its editor, the local youth board, a mental hygiene clinic, and a childrens' shelter make up some of the visits of the student teachers during the course of the semester. These visits are about two hours in length and extended discussions regarding the institution or agency and its relationship to children and youth follow each visit. Through these experiences student teachers come to partially understand the problems faced by the people in the community. The community becomes something more than charts and statistics. A degree of perception begins to come through to the prospective teacher, and the school's task, as affected by these problems, becomes a bit clearer through these experiences.

The third supplementary experience employed in this program is a weekly conference, in the school, among school and college personnel and the student teachers. The problems of teaching in the school, managing a classroom, curriculum problems, discipline, special methods, remedial procedures, and specific aids make up some of the topics discussed. A key feature of this aspect of the program is the utilization of school personnel who can help in the resolution of specific points at issue. Guidance counselors, attendance officers (truant officers), assistant principals, and remedial reading specialists are called on to contribute whatever insights they may have in relationship to the problem at hand. Since the student teacher will soon be working with these same personnel on a full-time basis, and since he should realize what resources are available in the school, these contacts with specialized staff personnel serve to better equip the student for the next semester.

The foregoing leads to the fourth set of supplementary experiences designed to aid the student in this school setting. He spends some time, usually three or four hours, in the various offices of the school to gain some insight into the daily work of these personnel, and to see how they may facilitate his work as a regular teacher. These administrative and service personnel are essential to the functioning of the teacher and are on hand to aid in specific ways.

Unless the prospective teacher understands the function of these offices and the outlook and procedures of the staff, he may be severely handicapped as a beginning teacher. It is one thing to tell a beginning teacher

---

[9] Sometimes so much so that one student teacher kept "cutting" a one-o'clock class at the college to stay on an extra hour.

about these things, it is another to let him see, understand, experience, and utilize these services. The student teacher, by spending some time in the guidance office, the attendance office, the supervisor's office, and the office of the assistant principal gains a view of the school which encompasses the entire picture of a school's operation. He learns that many people are in the school to aid him in the classroom, to facilitate teaching and learning, and that teachers can use these services in various ways.

The fifth supplement to the "normal" program is the high degree of cooperation that obtains between the personnel in the school and the personnel from the college. The student teacher is the intended beneficiary of this cooperative effort, but all of those concerned have learned a great deal from one another. It is a difficult task to teach in these schools, and the kind of cooperative venture that has characterized this program is absolutely essential if the student teacher is to be adequately prepared. Diagrammatically, the three-part program with the five supplementary areas would appear more or less as shown in Table 1 (see page 254).

A comparison of Table 1 with a more normal student-teaching situation would yield the following points of difference:

Regular Program	*Special Program*
1. Limited number of hours spent in actual teaching.	1. Early in the semester the student teacher handles one and, in most cases, two classes daily.
2. Supervision by school personnel is limited.	2. School personnel and college personnel work closely in supervision.
3. Biweekly conferences at the college; students grouped according to subject-matter areas.	3. Weekly conferences in the school; all areas meet together.
4. Few, if any, community visits.	4. Regular program of community visits and discussion of same.
5. Little, if any, contact with the offices of the school and the personnel of these specialized areas.	5. Regular program for contact and observation of these offices.
6. School provides a means for entering teaching in general.	6. School provides a direct means to enter teaching.

An Assessment

Any assessment of this program would have to be done by all those concerned with its prime objective—the preparation of teachers for profes-

Table I.

Experiences	Part One: Orientation (3 weeks)	Part Two: Induction (2 weeks)	Part Three: Student teacher begins to handle classes independently, but with supervision (10 to 11 weeks)
1. Much more actual teaching		X	X
2. Community visits and discussion with community leaders	X	X	X
3. Weekly problems conference	X	X	X
4. Participation and orientation to the work of school offices and personnel		X	X
5. Cooperative venture and effort	X	X	X

sional service in schools serving culturally depressed areas. A principal of one of the schools has remarked on more than one occasion, "These young people just don't have the problems that other first year teachers seem to have." One of the former student teachers, now a regular teacher in the school remarked, "This is the place I want to be, doing the job that's needed."

The staying power of these teachers is most heartening. Among the staff of the junior high school where we first began the program two and a half years ago, there are twenty-two teachers prepared through the program. The school has a teaching staff of about ninety. Teachers and administrators in the school indicate that the esprit and morale of the school have vastly improved during the past five semesters.

In five semesters, there have been fifty-one volunteers who entered the program and there are now thirty-seven teaching in the five project schools. The fourteen who did not remain had, in most cases, entirely legitimate reasons for leaving. Some did not pass the license examinations. Several moved from the New York City area. Several went on to graduate work on a full-time basis. Only two felt they could not continue in the school because of inability or lack of desire to stay.

In retrospect, one would have to credit several factors for the success of the program thus far. The volunteer aspect of the program cannot be overemphasized. These young people, for a wide variety of reasons, deliberately chose to enter the program after they were apprised of the problems, what would be afforded them, and what they would have to contribute. They were frankly told of the problems in the school and that this program would take more time and effort than the normal program. We tried, in a cursory fashion, to find out the "reasons" for their interest in the program. Among the more typical answers were:

If the college thinks I can help, I'll volunteer.

With all the help that one gets, I'll be a better teacher for it.

The satisfaction must be great.

This seemed like a chance to do something worthwhile.

If I can teach here in these schools, I can teach anywhere.

We did not have the time to go any further than this in assessing the reasons why these student teachers volunteered. It is possible that the direct appeal for volunteers tapped a reservoir of good will, strong idealism or practical sense—practical sense, because many realized that, with teacher shortages being what they are, and with schools serving depressed areas having the greatest shortages, they would probably be assigned to the same type of school when they became regular teachers without the aid and assistance that were available through this program. It may have struck some that this program was something like preparing for the inevitable; however, we feel that these negative reasons disappeared with the semester of student teaching. Also, given the situation, some volunteers may have been influenced by the link between the program and entrance into teaching. In the sense that this program leads directly to the position they will have in teaching, some may well have looked upon the program as a direct aid to their teaching career. I have a hunch that because it was a volunteer program and because the job would not be easy, it had an appeal for many who wanted to help in the giant task that faces the big city schools. In a society that is so often dominated by the material reward or the attitude of "what's in it for me," the attitude and outlook of these young people has been refreshing and uplifting.

Whatever the reasons, a self-selective factor was introduced by the volunteer aspect of the program. This factor loaded the dice, so to speak, because the student had actively enlisted in the project.

On the other hand, there is a basic disadvantage to the volunteer aspect of the program, and this concerns the number woo volunteer. The fifty-one volunteers over a five-semester period represent about 10 per cent of the total number of students who undertook student teaching during this time. The first semesters we had fewer, proportionately, than the later semesters. We are hopeful of a continuing rise in interest and a continuing rise in the number and proportion who volunteer, and we anticipate that eventually about 20 per cent of the total number eligible will enter the program. In view of the critical need for teachers for these schools and also in view of the fact that many of the non-volunteers will be placed in special service schools, this percentage is low. Perhaps it is high, given the kinds of blocks that one has to overcome in entering the program, but to increase the number of volunteers, more than an appeal will be necessary.

This relatively low number of volunteers represents a classic picture of prospective teachers choosing professional goals, and the means to achieve these goals (one of which is student teaching) which are compatible with their aspirations. Most prospective teachers do not see themselves operating in "difficult" schools, and because of this, all the talk about their eventually being placed in these schools is meaningless. The prospective teacher clings until the last moment to the thought that someone or something will rescue him from the "difficult" school. Of course, the real problem comes when these students enter teaching, are assigned to a "difficult" school and then, because of inadequate preparation, dislike the entire business. In addition to previously noted responses we received these typical replies from those who did not volunteer:

> My mother (or father) wouldn't let me go into that neighborhood.
>
> It is too far to travel.
>
> I just can't see operating in that situation.
>
> I feel that I can better teach in a high school.
>
> I would be afraid of the problems that might come up.

In effect, prospective teachers tend to request schools for student teaching which best coincide with their perception of what a "good" educational situation should be.[10] Professional goals are translated in terms of the backgrounds, the perceptions, and the understandable aspirations of young prospective teachers.

If student teaching represents one of the means for entry into the profession, then it may be that the prospective teacher wishes this means to conform as closely as possible to his long-term goals in teaching. If we are right on this score, a general hypothesis may be offered: as long as

---

[10] Quite unlike medicine, for instance, where the placement of the prospective physician is most often in hospitals serving the "underprivileged." Consider what would happen if physicians were asked to "volunteer" for the city hospital. Prospective physicians intern in these hospitals as a matter of course. It's probably better experience.

the outlook of prospective teachers and the content of pre-service preparation remain as is, colleges of education and all agencies interested in preparing young people for teaching will experience difficulty in recruiting teachers for "difficult" schools. Our major task will be to find some way to indicate the professional rewards in the culturally different situation and to base instruction and experience in the undergraduate years on the realties of these situations. *Unless this is done, we can look forward to a limited number of teachers, both prospective and regular, who will actively seek the kinds of challenges in these schools.*[11]

The second major area that must be indicated in the assessment of the program includes the degree of responsibility, effort and professional outlook shown by all involved. The staffs of the school and college worked constantly on the problems that came up. The issue of reading was thorny, but was resolved satisfactorily when discussed in conferences, and when the students were able to see a demonstration of a developmental lesson in an English class. The question of the non-English-speaking child was (and is) extraordinarily difficult because of the kinds of problems which grow from this basic situation. This too was resolved when the school indicated that certain kinds of skills, such as word attack and vocabulary, are taught by all teachers in the school during each period of the day. In meeting and speaking with the "new-entrants teacher," a teacher who knows Spanish and teaches English as a second language, the student teachers gained a new insight into the kinds of skills necessary to teach the child who has a non-English-speaking and -reading background.

The student teacher learns quickly that many children have a need for an orderly structure in the classroom situation, and that the teacher must plan each minute of the day's work. These kinds of appreciations and skills came about only because of the close cooperation between the staff of the school and the staff of the college. And now, the situation has reached the point where much of the staff of at least one school consists of our former student teachers, and we consequently have a running start on the preparation of recent volunteers.

A third area of assessment would be the deep appreciation of the community and its problems. When students meet community leaders and see first-hand the kinds of situations they must face, it docs produce differences in their outlooks and attitudes. To realize that many of the students they teach face unbelievably difficult situations at home and have, in spite of the problems, achieved what they have, helps them appreciate the school-

---

[11] It may well be that the necessity for *all* teachers to understand the problems of the school which is "difficult," may require those responsible for the preparation of teachers to *require* experience in these schools.

community relationship. Statements like: "I never realized the kinds of problems these kids face," or "Harlem is more than a street corner meeting or a subway ride," indicate that these student teachers have at least begun to see the deprived neighborhood in its community and school setting. This aspect of the program has, we trust, helped prospective teachers understand the background and gain some insights into the lives of children from depressed areas.

Lastly one would have to note the active involvement of the student teacher in the work of the classroom. Nothing can substitute for this experience. We are most fortunate in having worked with principals and teachers who understand what we were attempting to do and who have given over much of their classroom time to these prospective teachers. Without this large block of actual teaching experience we would surely have had a much more difficult time, for it is in the process of teaching, with guidance and help, that the beginning teacher learns much of what must be learned. He learns the value of planning, and he learns to carry forward the day to day task of the teacher, which is sometimes difficult, but always rewarding.

Implications

Most often, implications are guesses. The guesses to be made about this program have point and substance for future investigations concerning teacher education in urban schools. The following should be considered:

1. Could it be that the preparation of teachers for urban schools will have to move from the college classroom to the public school? As one looks at teacher-preparation programs and then turns his attention to the demands of many schools in the urban context, he is struck by the disproportionate amount of time the student spends sitting and listening. The usual pattern of courses, both in and out of the professional sequence, need revision, and part of the necessary revision may be a greater allocation of time spent in "internships" under the guidance and supervision of a team of skilled professionals. The pattern of courses culminating in one semester programs of student teaching for one half day is not realistic if the student is going to teach in urban schools.

It may be that all teachers in urban areas, whether they are in "difficult" schools or not, must have a greater degree of understanding in dealing with the unique kinds of problems which will surely be with the big cities for decades to come. Included in this kind of rethinking must be a long, hard look at the content of courses and the kinds of experiences which will precede a more intensive internship. For whom are textbooks in educational psychology written? What role shall philosophy of education play in this new situation? How shall we look at the methods of teaching this or that in relationship to a whole new set of concepts about urban schools? What shall the role for evaluation and measurement be in a context where children do not fit the traditional molds? These and other kinds of questions need looking at by those who wish to have teacher-preparation programs meet certain kinds of basic social needs. I would venture the point that we either do this rethinking and retooling or we will have to accept the proposition that we will find ourselves more and more in a vacuum—a vacuum in which the social realities of our time play little role in the preparation of teachers.

2. While on the subject of reconstruction in the pre-service area, let us not forget the entire college and university program which should play a role in this new venture. It is impossible for me to conceive of a teacher-education program that would ignore the giant contribution that the entire liberal arts faculty could make in this cooperative endeavor. The various disciplines may well wish to undertake, in conjunction with those specifically charged with teacher preparation, a reconstruction of the courses and experiences deemed necessary for the enlightened, able, and skilled teacher. The new challenges of the urban schools require that the best minds from all fields come together for a parley on what needs to be done and how to go about doing it.[12]

3. It is apparent that when someone has a direct stake in a problem he is more likely to pay attention to what the problem is about. When a school has a more direct interest and stake in the preparation of teachers it seems that an entirely different atmosphere is born. We may have to rethink the different ways in which the public school can afford guidance and aid to the teacher preparation program. While many of us in the colleges have seen incompetence in the schools, it is time that we admit that many highly skilled, well trained and very able professionals in the schools can and will help us in the preparation of teachers. They can and they will, and we must find ways to involve, more directly, the able personnel in the schools. This cooperative venture need not be a one way street where we utilize only their talents in the schools. Indeed, it is time that we enable the most able in the schools to come to our bailiwick, to our classrooms in the college, and give us a few lessons. Nothing could be more refreshing than to have a person who is a *teacher* in the public schools come to an educational-psychology classroom and discuss with

---

[12] In our program, the gaps in cultural anthropology, urban sociology, Negro and Puerto Rican history, and social psychology proved to be severe handicaps for the teachers.

prospective teachers the problems and issues of learning in the "difficult" school.

4. If what we have found is valid and reliable, then school systems must look at the policy they are following in staffing schools in depressed areas. The "forced transfer" has little to recommend it, and the appointment of new teachers without advance preparation for the situation they will face seems to be asking for trouble. It seems that schools in big cities will have to explore new ways to induct the newly appointed teacher into the skills, understandings and abilities necessary to get on with the job of teaching. Possibilities include: (a) a two-week workshop for all newly appointed teachers who have received their appointment in "difficult" schools; (b) a reduced teaching load for a semester or a year to give experienced personnel the opportunity to work, in a systematic fashion, with newly appointed teachers. If our program indicates anything, it does tell the story that a lot of time and effort must go into the preparation of teachers for these special situations.

Summing Up

All of us engaged in the preparation of teachers must review every so often just what it is we are trying to do and what we have available to do the job. From the experience of the past two and one half years we have learned that some things may need to be changed and that we will have to continue reassessing what we are doing in terms of the objectives we seek. At base, this program has been an experiment in seeking those ways in which the democratic ethic can be extended to groups of people who seem to be educationally disenfranchised. It has been, and will continue to be, exciting work.

A final note. Nothing, absolutely nothing, can substitute for the determination, drive, skill, motivation, and understanding shown by the students—now teachers—in their work. It has been my privilege to be part of the work they are doing; it is my conviction that much more needs to be done.

REFERENCES

1. Conant, James B., *Slums and Suburbs,* New York: McGraw-Hill, 1961.
2. Handlin, Oscar, *The Newcomers,* Cambridge, Mass.: Harvard University Press, 1960.
3. Haubrich, Vernon F., "The Culturally Different: New Context for Teacher Education," *Journal of Teacher Education* (in press).
4. —————, "The Motives of Prospective Teachers," *Journal of Teacher Education,* Fall, 1961.
5. Mannes, Marya, "School Trouble in Harlem," *The Reporter,* February 5, 1959.

6. Moriber, Leonard, "In-Migration into the New York City Schools," *Strengthening Democracy*, New York: Board of Education, 1961.

7. Morrison Report, The, *The Puerto Rican Study; 1953-1957*, New York: Board of Education, 1958.

8. *New York Times*, Monday, June 11, 1962.

9. Reissman, Frank, *The Culturally Deprived Child*, New York: Harper, 1962.

10. Stiles, Lindley J. (Ed.), *The Teacher's Role in American Society*, Fourteenth Yearbook of the John Dewey Society, New York: Harper, 1957.

Leonard Kornberg | Meaningful Teachers for Alienated Children

In all the planning for an improved education of children who live in slum ghettos and have been denied the experiences of the American middle-class culture, it seems to me that the classroom life in a school has always been the key to any progress and the area of most neglect. The thinking has been—what can we do with these children outside the classroom to help them adjust to the usual experiences and demands of a classroom? But how often have we reversed the question and asked—what kind of classroom can reach these children? It has been asked rarely—if at all.

Focus on the New Classroom

The talents and energies of educators, in recent years, have gone into other concerns. There has been the important work with less-biased and more-comprehensive intelligence testing. The reading problem has been recognized, and facilities for remedial help have grown. There has been greater awareness of the need for guidance and psychological services in the slum-area schools. With lower-class groups in the big cities, there are increasing efforts to change parental indifference or despair about the value of school. Their children are being counseled individually about future goals and are being exposed to new "horizons" on trips after the school day. There has been a flurry of new testing, guidance, remedial reading, and extra-curricular enrichment programs. And all of this has been outside the classroom life, providing the latter with indirect effects but not really altering the essential conditions of classroom experience.

It is true that now a change seems to be in the wind. All the specialists and activities outside the classroom, it becomes clear, do not provide the panaceas for which bewildered and harassed educators had hoped. And the new supply cannot meet the demand: the problem children involved in the new services are but a handful of the many children whose needs put the teacher in despair. Where can we get all the specialists that these children require, whose individual problems are so diverse and many—and upon whom fall all the depriving, crippling effects of poverty, racial restrictions, and family breakup? There may not ever be a sufficient number of non-classroom specialists to help so many children. The classroom alone is capable of handling the mere problem of logistics, of providing the techniques and tools that can help so many children to learn.

But how to reach all the bored, defiant, confused, sullen children who have had so much failure that they will scarcely try again to pay attention in school and do the work there? It was once easy to dismiss this problem as being the responsibility of the classroom. The outside specialists would treat the most difficult children and this would sufficiently relieve the teacher to do her work. But in our schools we have seen that the "very difficult children" are almost a norm among the culturally disadvantaged youngsters, and those who are given the special help often return to the classroom as difficult as ever. There is no overnight cure for the attitudes, fears, defenses, deficiencies in children that grew so early, over so many years. Neither the teacher nor the school, therefore, have their panacea, and we are all learning to be more patient and to look again at what we can do *in* the classroom.

There are new questions about the curriculum activities that must be developed for these children, and about the teaching materials and strategies that will spur their learning in a classroom. These are subjects that are now especially open for exploration. This seems to be a time when educators are again daring to overturn the traditional classroom and to develop school designs for various class sizes, for new kinds of teacher-pupil and teacher-teacher interaction, for new mechanical and electronic tools of instruction, and for new ways of structuring the different fields of knowledge. Everywhere in the professional literature now one reads about these developments. But we who work with culturally disadvantaged youngsters are well aware that this ferment of new ideas did not arise from any concern with educating slum children more effectively. We know it originates in the long debate over standards and hopes for the educationally privileged and capable children who do not live in the depressed areas of the city.

Though the new mood for school experimentation arose out of such one-sided concern, we can still welcome it as a support for our own efforts to change the status quo, and we may hope that it becomes contagious. We seem to be similarly struggling with new insights about intelligence and about a school's role in society. Just as the suburban communities may require a new kind of school, so too may our tenement communities of people disinherited from the main-line culture and its opportunities require one. We may see that our efforts so far have been piecemeal, or that they have been leading all along to a new kind of school for disadvantaged children.

The question is—do we know the kind of school we want, the services and classroom life it ought to have? Will we be led by the need to copy the educational changes elsewhere, or by a set of goals that relate to our children's potentials and problems. It is no secret that there are strong pressures to merely seek equal school facilities and curricula, or to see that slum children have aspirations equal to those in the more privileged youngsters. The trouble is, what we want may not be equal to what our children need.

There may be irony too, in that the schools we emulate on the other side of the tracks may not be meeting their own children's needs. After all, an education guided by the demand for more scientists and linguists may be as narrow as the one we are often urged to give to our children— an education based on preventing juvenile delinquency. Both objectives have their importance, no doubt, and both may legitimately influence the planning of a school; but surely they do not begin to consider the values that a child can realize for himself and his society.

What is of value for our children to learn, in a society that limits the opportunities of dark people and of uneducated people? In determining what to teach, shall we guide ourselves by the fact that many of our Negro, Puerto Rican, Mexican children will remain in lower-class worlds, employed in temporary or menial jobs—where the literature they have read in school, the languages and history studied, perhaps even the reading and writing skills will be irrelevant or of little value? Or should we simply "bet on the best" and gear our teaching to that stubborn, talented minority of children who can break through to the middle-class jobs and style of living? Since we hold to the principles of a democratic society, these alternatives will make us ill at ease. We will ask whether a way can exist between such choices. But there is none, we will discover eventually. The choices are unreal and do not exist in a classroom where there is freedom to learn. The children see to that—not just slum youngsters but any children for whom a special future is projected. They will not be claimed by our visions—even if we resolve to break their will and rigorously train them in a certain outlook or set of skills.

This, too, is a choice. Many teachers are making it, though it is again a choice without reality or consideration of the values gained and lost. Some teachers feel they must protect themselves by the repression of children's impulses and interests. Some think these underprivileged youngsters are too limited for any other classroom approach. In any case they choose the way of rigorous training, unbending structure and discipline, careful avoidance of any stimulation. Perhaps the idea of a blackboard jungle in a slum school is now archaic, for in spite of occasional disorder the norm may be something else: apathy, listlessness, quietly tuning out the teacher's drone and the classroom irrelevancy.

The "training" choice does not work, no matter how quiet and malleable the children become in a classroom. Whatever useful knowledge is gained can never cancel the loss in self-confidence, and in intelligence too. We have learned from clinical and educational research that being dominated means the denial of feelings. And this not only insults one's integrity—with the consequence rage one must control; it constricts the abilities that help one to perceive and to think effectively. This insight is not new, as anyone who has taken education courses in the last two decades knows. But many teachers in the slum schools will deny it. They are bewildered and desperate, they feel they cannot reach these children, they clutch at the teaching choices mentioned (which their own experience and education contradict), they bitterly submit to a "trainer's" role or misguidedly try a clinician's role, and they no longer have faith that they can be teachers any more—in these classrooms.

In how many schools is this true? I feel that the loss of teacher morale is widespread, though my experience with it has been mostly in New York. Why is it occurring? I have already sketched some of the mislaid hopes for improvement and some of the confusion about educational values and goals. But there are many other reasons for this, too complex and far afield from the scope of the present remarks. I have tried, so far, to present the broad scope of a problem in which many educators are deeply involved, and in which most of my professional life has been involved—as a teacher having to learn his own lessons about teacher disadvantaged youngsters, and as a teacher-educator currently trying to prepare young, middle-class persons to teach in the underprivileged neighborhoods. Now I want to put this over-all problem of providing a good education for slum children, on the scale of one small effort to seek solutions.

BRIDGE—A Teacher-Education Study

The original focus in this paper was on the classroom's importance. I have asked questions about a new kind of classroom and school for deprived lower-class children, and about the values to guide us in such innovation. It may be these are questions that we cannot answer yet, because we do not have enough experimentation and experience to be able to do so. But in the area of developing teacher competency and morale for the "difficult" city schools, we can clarify, perhaps, some issues that are central to these questions.

This is the area of concern for a research study on which several colleagues and I at Queens College are presently collaborating.[1] The project is called BRIDGE, and the name is a code for the following phrase: Building Resources of Instruction for Disadvantaged Groups in Education. Our main objective has to do with our teacher-education program and how we can better prepare teachers to help slum children to learn. In a way, our project is meant to be a bridge for ourselves, to close a gap between our perspectives on a quiet campus remote from a slum— and the realities in teaching children whose attention is limited, whose language is meager or different, and whose concerns are with failure and loss rather than the good future that a middle-class child believes in and is motivated to reach. We knew we had a lot to learn. In the one year that our project has been in operation we think we have gained something valuable for ourselves, and perhaps for educators in a larger field.

The design that has been developed in BRIDGE encompasses an inquiry along several lines. One phase of this design is a three-year "demonstration," in a junior high school in a lower-class Negro neighborhood. To have a teaching and curriculum laboratory, we have set up a small school in an existing large school. We have been able to take at random ninety youngsters from an incoming seventh grade and put them into three classes, whose group sizes are average in such a school. We have selected three teachers who are recent graduates of our teacher-education program, to instruct these youngsters in the major academic areas of English, social studies, math and science. For all other subjects or activities, our youngsters will participate with the rest of the school population and teachers. It is our plan to have our three teachers stay with this demonstration for the entire time of the junior high school period. Thus they will have a three-year opportunity to learn about these children and how to teach them effectively.

Another key factor in our demonstration is the role of someone we call the "coordinating teacher," who represents a supervisory experiment in meeting teachers' needs in such a school. We have hired an experienced teacher to fill this role. Her reports and frequent consultations with us have done much to clarify our own shortcomings in preparing these teachers and the in-service help that the young, new teachers need. We feel that our coordinating teacher, if not involved in the BRIDGE research activities, could supervise an additional three or four teachers. She is,

[1] Professors Helen Storen, Albert J. Harris, Robert Edgar, and Leonard Kornberg are conducting this study, which is partly supported by funds from the United States Office of Education (Project #935) and from the following private agencies: New York Foundation, New York Fund for Children, Taconic Foundation, Hofheimer Foundation, and the New York *Times* Foundation. Public Education Association of New York is sponsoring this project.

therefore, partially modeling a supervisory arrangement that we think could be economically feasible and of special value to the "difficult" schools. Our year's experience, so far, has strengthened our belief that teacher supervision must be radically different from the usual advice and ratings, or the in-service courses. We feel that it must be an on-going guidance of teacher-child familiarization and relationship. For this personal interaction seems to be basic to whatever helps disadvantaged children to learn—or to work at learning.

We are attempting to cover the prescribed three-year syllabus in our subject-matter areas, though trying out sequences, content organizations, and material that are new and not ordinarily in use. We are exploring various techniques, especially ways of individualizing in large classroom groups. The reading deficiencies plague us (only fifteen children read at grade level, and the average retardation is two years). The lack of attention skills among these children continually harasses our teachers. The peer group jealousies and conflicts are volatile forces in the classroom, unpredictably erupting—especially as the youngsters grow to like and depend on our teachers. It is a day-to-day struggle of structuring and clarifying the reality of group procedures and of verbal concepts and of the teacher's feelings for me: me the Negro child, almost always preached at in school by people who cared only for a better, different "me"—not for what I really am.

We do not have measurable results so far, that would show we have had significant impact on the youngsters of our demonstration classes. We have initiated a plan involving two control groups, with which to compare our classes' performance on intelligence and achievement testing. (The *Wechsler Intelligence Test for Children* and the *Metropolitan Achievement Tests* are being used.) But in the event that our experimental group at the end of three years shows significant progress, we will not be able to point to any one teaching strategy as the causative factor. This may distress the very research-minded person who disdains any but the tightest experimental design. We had a choice to lower our sights and control a very narrow scope of teaching experiences, or to observe the vast flow of events that make up teaching and learning in a classroom. One of the reasons we chose the latter approach was because in a slum school the classroom was simply so unfamiliar and new to us. We called this part of BRIDGE, therefore, a demonstration study, rather than experiment. We also agreed that what was at stake was a design for the growth of a teacher—rather than any one pattern for instruction.

If our youngsters show important gains, we will be able to say that many things worked: within our supervisory design, our young teachers learned to reach these children and to make school work meaningful for them. If the testing results show no gains, at least we will have evidence of class material and activities that stirred interest, of potentials in these children we had not expected, and of the varied behavior and learning difficulties to anticipate in teaching such youngsters. In addition, perhaps, we will have found ways to help the teacher remain a professional person in a school whose pressures often are demoralizing. Regardless of the test results, at the end of our study we should be better able to prepare our future teachers for the "difficult" schools and disadvantaged children.

One finding is already on hand, even though we can offer no statistical proof for it. It represents a one-year tryout of a supervisory technique which our teachers feel has been especially helpful. The technique is to have a weekly case study conference on one child, with all teachers present and with each one having independently prepared a report before the meeting. In this way the conference participants are able to read about the child's behavior in three classrooms, as well as to study the summary of pertinent information from school records and psychological testing. The conference focus is educational: what do and should the classroom teachers know about the child's ability and interests, about the reasons for his misconduct or withdrawal, about ways of building his trust and self-confidence, about classroom activities that could be adapted to his needs?

We do not claim that every case study conference produces revealing insights and absolute solutions, but we do believe this framework for regular inquiries about individual children has a cumulative effect. It is a weekly struggle to understand child behavior, to explore new teaching approaches, and inevitably to become aware of one's own feelings and distorted views about these children. We feel that it could be instituted in most schools like the one in which we are working. Wherever a school population has so many skill deficiencies and emotional handicaps, requiring classroom individualization and sensitive relationships with the teacher, the case study process might be of great value. It has one other possibility, not yet mentioned, in that it offers a concrete way for the guidance and psychological staff in the school to both help and learn from the classroom teachers.

I have gone into extensive detail describing the demonstration phase of our study. It might be necessary to recall, therefore, that there are other aspects of the BRIDGE Project. One of these involves the work of our full-time psychologist, who has been testing our experimental and control groups and who will be using a variety of psychological instruments to probe the learning potentials of these youngsters. We also hope to get sufficient sociological data on our children's backgrounds and present circumstances, so that we might further clarify the patterns of school readiness that we find in our classrooms.

Enriching the College Program

Another phase of the project involves the effort to share with our colleagues in Queens College what we are learning about the education of underprivileged children. One form this has taken is in arranging conferences on topics like "the reading problem" or "the new teacher's adjustment" in secondary schools. But the most meaningful contribution is simply to use project funds so that faculty members can visit the slum schools. We are doing this on a rotation basis, making part of a semester schedule available to those who want to see the different classrooms in difficult schools and in our demonstration.

One other phase of the BRIDGE Project also affects our colleagues and college classes. I would like to speak about it in some detail. It involves the development of a new field-experience program for our students in the adolescent- and educational-psychology courses. In the Queens College program for secondary-school teacher preparation, these courses provide a foundation in theories of adolescent behavior, group leadership, educational measurement, and classroom learning. They are similar to courses in other undergraduate programs of teacher education, in that they precede the "methods" courses and in that they frequently require field experiences with children. This is done either through the use of child studies or, as in our case, through cooperation with community recreation and group-work agencies. In this way, our students work with and observe adolescents in lounges, clubs, or mass recreational activities. We have been placing them in such settings for a number of years, with varying success. Many of our students have gained confidence in leadership skills with adolescents, and in relationships with lower-class youngsters. Many others have had less productive experiences, without opportunities for leadership, being put in passive roles, and often working with middle-class youngsters with whom they just overidentify.

In judging the value of this program for our teacher-education goals, we have had the dilemma that hounds teacher educators everywhere. What early experiences promote a teacher's "professional self?" Does this participation in an agency spur or limit these students' interest in teaching adolescents? Does it help the college student to sharpen his identity as a young adult and to combine this new feeling about himself with greater patience for the immaturity and growing pains of adolescents? Does it create false impressions about working with adolescents in a classroom, or about group leadership in a classroom? (Regardless of our ideals and wishes, the realities of a classroom in a typical, city school are different from the realities of an evening youth program in a community agency.)

These are still unresolved questions for us, and they have led to experimentation with a new field experience for our psychology courses. We call it a program of "Bridge Groups," and it works in the following manner: ten students are placed in a junior high school in an underprivileged neighborhood, for the same afternoon a week over a period of twenty-four weeks, each student to work with a small group of youngsters who will come voluntarily for help with school problems. Our project funds enable us to hire an experienced teacher in each school to supervise the Queens College students. The cooperation of the school principal and guidance counselors is necessary to support and publicize the work. Our Queens students meet with five or six youngsters, and gradually there evolve "bridges" to reading—or to science, algebra, history, arithmetic, French. All of these are areas in which particular "Bridge Groups" have built a program of activities.

We try to be realistic about the abilities of our Queens students, and remind them as well as the junior high school supervisors that they are not trained teachers or remedial experts. We do not want them to lecture and drill these youngsters, or extend in other ways the 9 to 3 o'clock school experiences. They can answer questions, help with homework, make up instructional games, feel free to go on tangents about personal experiences, or encourage group projects like tape-recording a play or writing to "pen pals." The important thing is to get to know these youngsters and to become meaningfully related to them—and not to expect that they individually in this short time can make up all the skills these children lack in school. This is hard for our college students to accept as first, but they learn—and their struggle to have school material make sense to these youngsters becomes part of learning to build personal relationships with them. It is good preparation, we believe, for some of the future dilemmas and opportunities in teaching.

In the past year this program of "Bridge Groups" was tried out in five junior high schools, all located in depressed areas of the city. There were some fifty college students involved for a year, with some three hundred to four hundred youngsters, at an expense that came to about $1500. The point is that for a little money a lot of disadvantaged youngsters had experiences of school enrichment, and many future teachers had opportunities to understand and work with such children. Again, we feel we are trying out a model that is economically feasible and that can be duplicated in other programs of teacher-education.

Next year we will repeat this project with new students, in a framework of more systematic evaluation. We will use controls and attempt to see the impact that the "Bridge Groups" and other types of field-experience will have on our students. We will get data on student backgrounds, on their attitudes and perceptions, on drop-outs from our program, and on the preferences for the types of youngsters our students want to teach. This may deepen our understanding of the predominantly white, middle-class young people whom we teach—and in whom we try to instill a professional commitment that often goes counter to their late-adolescent values. With the "Bridge Groups" we are playing hunches that may be difficult to prove: (*a*) that our 20-year olds will be significantly affected by this experience of really being needed and being able to offer help; and (*b*) that some kind of teacher experience is needed at the beginning of a teacher-education program rather than (as is frequent now) only at its end. We assume that such early experience with disadvantaged children will jar the stereotypes about teaching and learning that our college students have—who are typically so grade conscious, so bent on taking notes and memorizing, and so oblivious to the fact that learning is a personal enrichment. These slum youngsters will enlighten them about this fact—and may also encourage more of them to want to teach such children.

New Demands on Teachers and Professionals

This is the scope of and some of the rationale for what we are doing in the BRIDGE Project. The comprehensive focus is on preparing teachers for the "difficult" schools, in which staff recruitment barely matches the staff turnover. We do not have a special recruitment goal, though we hope to attract our students to such schools. We are interested more in the long-term question of how our graduates can be competent and confident teachers in such schools. In its first year, the BRIDGE experiences have had an effect on us that seems unshakable. We are convinced that a better professional education must be found, on the pre-service and in-service levels, to make meaningful teachers for these alienated children. This is not a new or remarkable insight, but it has hit us with the special urgency of an idea that personal experience confirms and widespread indifference abuses. We have seen what the pressures demand in teaching disadvantaged youngsters: the professional's ability to know where his needs end and the children's begin, to use himself as a real person who is not the punitive stereotype of "teacher" in these children's eyes, to be able to free the bars to communication and to caring, and to be devoted to values that make the current dilemmas understandable, if not yet solved.

We have also seen so many instances where this need for professional development is ignored. Do we not all see this indifference in the recruitment programs now under way in many cities, where untrained people are being encouraged to teach? The excuse is always reasonable. If there are not enough qualified people, somebody has to be brought into the classroom. So provisional licenses are granted, and later permanent ones, too, to people who never wanted to teach and do not care to teach now except that they liked other jobs less. Surely this is not the way and these are not the persons to staff the schools we have been talking about. Where the greatest needs exist we cannot rely on those who are least capable. And yet we do, in so many of these slum schools.

The point in question is not the need for, but the rule of such expediency, that ends in having staff recruitment undermine the long-term staff competency. I believe that the teacher's professional growth is the key to the staff problems in the "difficult" schools. In the long run it has the most bearing on recruitment, as well as the most effect in educating the children. Is it not time to change our recruitment techniques by stressing the professional nature of the work to be done: by offering salary and other status differentials to the trained teachers, by supporting internships and other forms of teacher education for newcomers to the job, and by creating continuity between the schools and the programs of professional education? This latter point is central to what we are seeing in BRIDGE. Professional development is a continuous learning process; it occurs in the pre-service and in-service evaluation of a continuing practice to teach children. If we end this process prematurely or deny it altogether, are we not giving up on teaching as professional work? Or have some school officials simply concluded that teaching disadvantaged children is not "teaching," not in the scope of the professional's work?

What I have been stressing is that we had better become preoccupied with the kinds of teachers we are getting. The real issue in educating slum children, as we see in visiting their schools, is whether the classroom life creates alienation or relationships. Whatever it is will depend on the kind of professional person the teacher is. It will depend on insights about these children and on competencies for teaching them. Let me review what some of this understanding and skill might involve.

One thing I have learned about these children's needs is that they cannot be "relativized," or attributed to a specific lower-class culture. The idea of some educators that anthropologists are required in each school to inform teachers of lower-class experience and behavior, has only a limited value to me. For the individual child's needs revolve around specific families and people rather than this aggregate pattern of a lower-class culture. I am not denying the insights that come by knowing about the larger social world in which the child and his family live. But I think we are in danger of mis-using this sociological view, to the neglect of seeing the child's struggle simply to grow up, to cope with more than a particular culture or culture conflict.

In spite of my own recourse to abbreviations, we are not educating a particular-class child or a "culturally deprived" child (which is a phrase I have avoided studiously). The reason is that there is no such child. It is obvious, once it is pointed out, that to be deprived of a culture means not to exist in any human terms. In other words, every child grows up with a culture. But he grows up with something more, which is not so obvious. He moves from the magical self-centeredness of early childhood to the reality of separation, of being alone with a body and feelings that are his, that he must protect in a world that goes its own way regardless of his wishes. This is the human state, not a particular culture's condition, and every child everywhere learns—or does not learn—to cope with this reality. The point I am getting to is that there is an aspect of intelligence that should develop very early in life—we can call it "ego ability" —that makes it possible to learn about a culture, about its expectations and symbols and heritage. Ego ability enables us to keep our balance with reality, to learn how to meet its changing demands: to develop attention skills, to recognize and care for tools, to wait for and earn one's pleasure, to tolerate pleasant surprise as well as disappointment, to withstand the contagion of group moods, to differentiate the painful past from the present, to share with others—particularly to share with others the people who are important to oneself. This list is obviously incomplete, but perhaps it indicates some of the ego deficiencies (rather than cultural lacks) that can severely handicap children in a classroom.

Do most children from slum ghettoes lack adequate ego abilities? I do not know. Here is where research is desperately wanting. We do know something about the conditions in which ego development occurs. And we wonder how these conditions can exist with the pressures of inferior caste and poverty: with parental absence or neglect, with too many indifferent or briefly caring people around the child, with unpredictable times and places for the child's eating and even sleeping. For this child there are few "anchoring" relationships—by which to find one's place in a world one trusts, by which to learn because one wants to please someone whose care one has grown to need.

There is no doubt that many slum children have deficiencies of ego development and must be helped to learn how to learn. But it must not be thought that this is a unique responsibility in schools of depressed neighborhoods. Every kindergarten or early grade teacher, wittingly or not, must help her children to mature in ego abilities. And sensitive teachers of adolescents know that their students are having trouble coping with the reality-balance of inner feelings and outer demands. I am convinced that education as a theoretical discipline must include ego development as a dimension of intelligence and an objective in teaching. The practical problem of promoting ego ability in a classroom, however, brings us to the question about teacher competencies which I would like to defer for a while. I have a few more remarks about the problems that slum children have when they try to learn in our schools.

To me the salient characteristic about these children in a classroom is their alienation. To use their jargon, they are not "with it." They go through the motions of class activity or remain indifferent to it, finding their own distractions—a few simply putting their heads on the desk and sleeping. With the teacher they are sullenly distant or sometimes shrewdly defiant—and always suspicious. One wonders what has brought this "armed truce" to so many classrooms. (There are occasional relapses into "war.") Part of the answer has to do with the weak ego abilities and controls. Some of these children have to use so much energy to stay out of trouble, to check their impulses and feelings, that they become very tired and very anxious. But even where ego development is adequate, there is in the classroom a burden that these children can scarcely bear. They have had so much past failure in school, that now there is rarely hope for something else. Why try? And besides, the classroom work rarely has to do with what they have experienced or find real. Why listen?

In this situation, a basic factor involves what has been most obvious about disadvantaged children: that they have impoverished or discrepant culture interests and skills. Their language deficiency, for example, comes out in the well-known reading retardation and, more subtly, in their confusion about what teachers are saying—a confusion that begins in the earliest grades and that hardly ever gets relieved. It is not the result of bilingualism, as some assert. These children simply have not had models of such speech, of the intricate combinations of words and phrases. And since many teachers mistakenly judge their language readiness or believe only that "good English" can affect this readiness, the children remain bewildered in school. In this way and others they give up the frustrating efforts to learn in school.

I need not elaborate on this matter of culture abilities. From the most basic type involving language and study skills, to the more differentiated kind involving the culture's knowledge, these slum children are obviously and sadly wanting. What is ignored, however, are the culture abilities they do have. Perhaps they have special interest in and information about jobs—or about sports, machines, food, policemen, the fight for racial equality, the feelings other people have. The list could go on indefinitely, and what it would reflect would be forms of intelligence shaped by culture—that is, curiosity, imagination, ways of thinking, patterns of knowledge. Do these attributes seem euphemistic when applied to the slum children we see in our schools?

It may be that we have created what we are seeing. We have worked with a narrow view of a general ability of intelligence—one these children always seemed to lack, one that sometimes seemed to be a middle-class invention. But we are beginning to find that not only were our intelligence tests lacking; so was our very concept of a general ability. It is becoming clear that many forms and capacities of intelligence exist, and that teachers must learn to respect them in all children. For youngsters from ghetto homes, whose feeling of being intellectually adequate has often been crushed in school, this new view of intelligence may bring a new self-esteem. For their teachers, it may support the old adage about good teaching: that you value and build on what the child knows.

This brings me to the question about teacher competencies for a depressed-area school. In previous remarks, I have already implied or alluded to some of the requirements, as I have seen them in the BRIDGE study and elsewhere. The teacher should respect these children's feelings, even when he does not condone their actions; he must be able to individualize his instruction; he has to stimulate many kinds of reading and oral language experiences and guide the listening and comprehension; he will have strategies of reasonable, consistent structure and stimulation in his classroom; he can use and enlarge on what the child has already mastered; and he should be warm, dependable, the kind of person a youngster will want to please. These are the skills and qualities of any good teacher, it is true, and disadvantaged children need good teachers.

But in the schools of depressed urban areas, these skills alone are incomplete and do not suffice for the job required. There are important competencies to be added, and I would like to briefly describe what I think they are. The first one I would mention, however, is hard to see as a competency. It is rather a quality of feeling about one's work—a professional's intense commitment to his role and objectives. Unless the teacher has this commitment, I do not think he will survive the pressures in such a school. The difficulties with his children will be severe enough. But he will face, too, the ridicule and cynicism of many colleagues. How can he be so brash as to really try to teach these children, and do what these other teachers have given up trying to do! Many of us have seen this withering, self-defensive abuse of the new teacher, and my graduates always give me new details.

Another important quality for the teacher in such a school is that he can be himself—that he is an adult and not "one of the boys," that he respects his own adult difference. There are, at present, a number of notions that contradict the value of this, that say in effect: the teacher should adopt the peer group's values, or he should act as "lower-class" as he can —to reach his resistive children. They are misguided notions. The fact is that these children always know the "phonies," and they deeply resent such patronizing and deceit. I think it is a myth that they shy off from the middle-class qualities of a teacher. They respond rather to his personal qualities—to his directness, his self-assurance, his respect for them, his enthusiasms, his consistency. The point is these children need somebody who can be straight with them and straight with himself—which is not easy in the trials of a classroom with such children. It will take some maturity to be this kind of person, and it will require the most careful consideration of the teacher's professional growth.

This brings me to the final point about teacher competencies for the slum schools. What I have already said is necessarily incomplete, and whatever generalizations I add must still leave much unsaid. I am now more conscious than ever of the limitations of such a discussion about teaching ability. It might have been better had I simply advised: find the rare classrooms in such schools where good teaching goes on, and see the competencies. To generalize about them leaves out the rich, fine details which are the heart of the matter. But I am stuck, and I am left to cringe at the platitudes I have probably "committed" by my generalizing. If I persist a little longer, it is only because my final remarks relate to some of the intangibles and details so far unmentioned.

What makes a teacher meaningful to slum children? I have talked about this meeting their needs and about his "reaching" them through his caring for them. One other pattern of teacher competency has to do with caring about something besides the children. I am not referring to a passion for subject matter, although it is an aspect of what I mean. I am thinking of a passion for ordering, knowing, and creating reality.

There are teachers who live in a verbal world primarily, but they do not order or create what I conceive as reality. Slum children are lost with them, and other children too are lost in their verbalism—though less dramatically so. There are other teachers, however, who can use the classroom to discover and make a world. They delight in doing things, in mastering real problems, in transforming what is already known. It is not beneath these teachers to reiterate what the rules are for sitting, for passing papers, for taking turns with the classroom jobs. They do not see it as trivial for children to have responsibilities in the classroom, to be teacher's "assistants," to care for the walls and the windows and the closets.

By doing and encouraging this, some of the important needs of disadvantaged children are met—to have clear boundaries and expectations, to feel "big," to have a world which in part they "own." But there is something more in this than the children's needs. The teacher of whom I am thinking does this to satisfy himself as well. *He* must live in a structure that is clearly defined; *he* must master a world by knowing and shaping it. By this necessity in him to make things clear (from a simple routine to a complex rule in grammar) and by his faith that all aspects of reality are essentially good to know (the children's interests as well as his own), he provides (and completes, as far as I can describe it here) a model of teaching which alienated children need desperately.

PART V

School Programs in Depressed Areas

From a number of descriptions of large city efforts to provide for children from depressed urban areas, one observer suggested that the programs could be categorized into three different approaches as follows:

1. *The enrichment or "middle-class surrogate" approach.* Since children from depressed areas either have been deprived of the early readiness experiences of their middle-class peers or have had different experiences, it is necessary to compensate for these deficiencies and differences by program enrichment. In effect, this involves taking the child from his family—at least psychologically—and raising him as a middle-class child. This, of course, takes a great deal of money.

2. *The "we're not-going-to-let-them-do-better-than-we-are-we?" approach.* This calls for a creative, outstanding individual who is able to meld the familial, school, religious, civic, community and political forces into a massive effort to upgrade achievement and attain higher standards to show the outsiders this can be done. Basically a bootstrap effort to reach higher standards, this requires unusually forceful, magnetic leadership.

3. *The "Shavian" or "these-problems-are-rooted-deeply-in-society" approach.* Since the problems of education in depressed areas are essentially those of the broader society, efforts must be made to change community power structures, stratification, familial structures, and school procedures. This approach requires idealism, courage, imagination and cooperation.

Such a categorization is descriptive rather than analytic. The underlying assumptions, either explicit or implicit, are seldom examined and a sound theoretical framework to guide program planning is yet to be developed. The elements of a curriculum design—goals, content, method and organization, materials and resources, evaluation—and the relationships among these elements have not been analyzed systematically in terms of the unique conditions of the urban setting, the realities of urban life, and the conditions of the depressed areas. This is not to say that program improvement efforts lack rationale; rather, the assumptions remain vague. They need to be spelled out and formulated, for they have meaning for the school's role, for its instructional program, for the methods and materials used, for the relationships with other agencies.

In general, there has been no major redesign of educational objectives for children residing in depressed areas. Instead, with a heavy Procrustean hand, programs have attempted to mold all pupils into traditional school products by seeking to alter the conditions in the classroom, the family, and the community. Traditional school achievement is verbally oriented and concerned, at least at the most idealistic level, with the cultivation of individual potential as well as acculturation to societal requirements. The Educational Policies Commission poses the challenge in educating the disadvantaged child as follows:

> The educated man, in the American ideal, possesses the motivation and the developed mind to dignify his life and to contribute to his society, and he views learning as a life-long process. Some children are so far from this ideal as to raise doubts about their ability to approach it. For several reasons these doubts arise most often in reference to children from deprived backgrounds.[1]

The underlying motives for improving school programs for children in depressed urban areas are many. They range from the conviction that the basic American ideal of fullest opportunity for individual development is intrinsic to national preservation; to the recognition that children from disadvantaged homes are poor scholastic performers and constitute a severe academic and behavioral problem; and, consequently, to the concern that the uneducated are responsible for a considerable portion of police, welfare and institutional costs. As the Educational Policies Commission put it, "the unrealized promise in the ignorant mind disturbs not only the idealist and the humanist; increasingly it haunts as well those concerned with the grim demands of national survival."[2]

Efforts to improve school programs in depressed areas vary considerably in scope and comprehensiveness. Almost all focus in some way on the improvement of reading and language skills, for academic success depends largely on ability to read. There are projects aimed at revising curriculum content, modifying teaching techniques, developing more appropriate instructional materials, adding professional services and providing remedial aid. Some are experimenting with increased use of new technological media—educational television, programmed instruction, individualized materials. A few school systems are testing the possibilities of different approaches to staff utilization and class organization such as team teaching, non-graded primary units, and special service staffs. Some

[1] Educational Policies Commission, *Education and the Disadvantaged American*, Washington, D.C.: The National Education Association, 1962, pp. 11-12.
[2] *Ibid.*, p. 10.

projects are primarily preventive—modifications of school or pre-school experiences that will reduce the possibilities of failure and consequent frustration with school tasks. More programs, however, are remedial and corrective of the academic deficiencies of non-achieving pupils. The prevention or alleviation of delinquency or deviant behavior is the focus of some school efforts. Increasingly, schools have begun to measure these special improvement projects against the outcomes of education in the whole system. Redistricting or rezoning schools, for instance, directly affects the climate and the social composition of the buildings involved. Designation of certain buildings for special services and additional staff can curtail the availability of personnel, funds, and programs in other, perhaps more favored schools. The need for whole-picture planning of education in metropolis has emphasized the urgency for reappraising the practical meaning of equal educational opportunity for all.

Dr. John H. Fischer analyzes the problems of schools in dealing with educational and racial problems while simultaneously helping each individual to make the most of himself for his own satisfaction and for his place in a modern, technological society. In the paper written for the Fourth Annual Conference of the United State Commission on Civil Rights, Fischer evaluates the psychological and cultural aspects of segregation in schools. He questions the effectiveness of administrative action in resolving educational problems, too many of which disguise the legal or political nature of their roots. He declares that the administrator's focus must be on securing the conditions for first rate teaching, learning, and building positive pupil-teacher relationships.

Fischer outlines four guidelines for educational policy and plans structured around these problems of growing up in depressed areas. First, since education is a highly personal affair, there is the need for adapting teaching to individual differences. Second, each individual deserves greater understanding—of his history and of his present environment—the better to ease curriculum adjustments and teaching techniques. Third, the concept of "compensatory educational opportunity" should replace the traditional concept of equal opportunity. It is possible that "to achieve equality of opportunity within the whole of our culture, it may be necessary to offer those who are handicapped by their history or their current situation not merely equal, but compensatory educational opportunity." Finally, Dr. Fischer argues that social engineering, the manipulation of pupils solely on the basis of race or cultural deprivation, is irrelevant and improper.

How Detroit Public Schools developed a multiple or total approach to the educational problems of the inner core of the city is described by Dr.

Carl Marburger. Detailing what he labels the "social pathology" underlying the problems of the depressed area, Marburger examines the effects
of the middle-class exodus to the suburbs and the city's periphery areas
and the in-migration of predominantly unskilled, low-income groups. The
plight of these groups, mainly racial and ethnic minorities, is described in
the recurring theme of "not enough"—not enough income, home life, information, skills, motivation—all of which are reflected in the child's preparation for school tasks and in his performance. The child from a limited
and disadvantaged background, says Marburger, is "indifferent and purposeless, a poor communicator who does not respond to normal teaching
methods and subject matter." Consequently, such children's capabilities
are largely unfulfilled. Marburger's position is that the school must provide more for the disadvantaged child than it normally would, and at the
same time, it must work with other agencies and services to rebuild the
family's influence in positive directions. The school, he believes, is the
single force available to counteract the negative environment which affects
the child.

The Detroit Great Cities School Improvement Program has a five-part
approach aimed at modifying the teaching-learning conditions as well as
influencing and upgrading the home and neighborhood. The five areas
include: (a) teacher orientation and training—attempting to modify the
teacher's perceptions of the culturally deprived child (his background and
scholastic potential) and to develop teaching competencies and insights
in working with such children; (b) improved use of available instructional
materials and equipment and the development of appropriate instructional
materials and teaching aids; (c) modification of organizational patterns
for greater flexibility and more efficient programming—by means of, for
example, experiments with team teaching, non-graded primary unit, pre-
school experiences, extensive use of urban facilities and resources;
(d) addition of such personnel as coaching and remedial teachers, visiting
social workers, and school-community agents, and (e) involvement of
public and private agencies in developing school-home-community activities. Detroit uses the area schools as the instrument for initiating,
leading, and coordinating efforts to upgrade community life. Where other
agencies are functioning effectively, the schools simply cooperate with
them.

Primary emphasis on improving instructional practices has been
through workshops and in-service experiences for teachers. These efforts
seek to change teachers' perceptions through involvement in curriculum
studies. Teachers are encouraged to innovate, to experiment, to adapt
and modify. The project's focus on teacher-expectation has pointed up

the impact such anticipations have on pupil achievements; teachers hopeful of their students' progress convey this through the nuances of their behavior in the classroom. The Detroit program is striving to create and test instructional materials and other resources to "combat the corrosive influences of emotional and physical poverty with which many . . . students live day in and day out." Other efforts are aimed at making the curriculum as meaningful and as rich as possible—tailoring, but not restricting, the school program to the experiential backgrounds of the children.

The schools have become, in effect, community educational centers, operating from early morning until late at night, year round. The after-school and evening programs are of both a remedial and an enrichment nature and serve adults, youth and children. The summer school program is especially important, not only as a source of educational and recreational opportunities but as a bridge from one school year to the next.

Marburger underscores the significance of the school principal's administrative style in determining how extensively teachers will test out new ideas and try imaginative approaches in the classroom. A school principal who is restrictive rather than non-restrictive, authoritarian instead of democratic and legalistic rather than expeditious can curtail enthusiasm and circumscribe invention to the point of nullifying experimental programs.

Henry Saltzman urges the development of community schools in depressed urban areas. Such schools would work for recognition as institutions dedicated to the neighborhood and its children, capable of action which appears significant to the community. Planning for community schools in depressed areas must precede the design and construction of the building itself and should allocate budget for the necessary administrative talent. Four agencies—the Board of Education, the Urban Renewal Agency, the publicly supported social agencies, and the health and welfare council—would each contribute to long-range planning for community-based programs. Thus, many agencies, both public and private, would plan together. Selecting principals and key staff members and assigning them to the depressed area long before school opens, enable these personnel to participate in school planning, to become involved in and recognized as part of the community. Inevitably, such personnel develop greater understanding of and identification with the community, its needs and its leaders.

Saltzman calls for more effective collection of data about each child, data which can be fed to the classroom teacher and to other professional staff members responsible for better planning. In addition, systematic feedback procedures should circulate information from after-school community activities to classroom teachers, as an aid in planning richer educational experiences.

The main thesis of Saltzman's paper is that school leaders must identify with the neighborhood in which they serve. On the quality of the principal's leadership turns the success or failure of the school program. Consequently, the principal should be appointed at least two years ahead of the opening of the building so that he can serve as a bridge between the school as in idea and the school as an operating fact. The principal must be skilled in helping individuals and groups to approach the school and to become immersed in it. Timidity about how to approach the school —not lack of interest or motivation—may be the main block to parent and citizen participation in depressed urban areas. Saltzman advocates the establishment of advisory committees consisting of parents, other lay persons, teachers and administrators to continue school-community program planning beyond the initial contacts. The school has a central role to play in promoting and coordinating inter-agency cooperation, at the levels of resources, information, ideas, plans, and even personnel.

The questions raised during the discussions of school programs and practices dealt generally with the nature and scope of curriculum modifications for disadvantaged children. What are appropriate educational goals for schools in depressed areas? How are these goals related to those of other social agencies and institutions? Are the priorities in either short- or longe-range objectives for culturally disadvantaged children different from those of middle-class children? How much time should be spent on non-academic goals, such as interpersonal relations, citizenship skills, enhanced self-image, raised aspirations? How is a balance in educational ends to be determined and maintained?

The contrast of the expressive styles of the lower-class and middle-class children—the former described earlier by Professor Goldberg as more often "motoric, concrete, 'thing-oriented' and non-verbal," and the latter as more frequently "conceptual, abstract-symbolic, idea-oriented, and verbal"—suggested the need for modifying teaching methods and materials. Several other researchers have also proposed classroom procedures which are more motor-oriented and which take into account the cognitive style of the disadvantaged child.

Frank Reissman has argued that, by placing almost complete emphasis on verbal ability—a quality muted in lower-class society, we may have curbed the potential creativity of the underprivileged child. Typically, Reissman indicates, the deprived child's style is:

1. Physical and visual rather than aural.
2. Content-centered rather than form-centered.
3. Externally oriented rather than introspective.

4. Problem-centered rather than abstract-centered.
5. Inductive rather than deductive.
6. Spatial rather than temporal.
7. Slow, careful, patient, persevering (in areas of importance) rather than quick, clever, facile, flexible.[3]

Should the significance of these differences in learning style be reinforced by further study, schools might lay greater emphasis on developing classroom procedures which utilize the concrete, the manipulative, and other means of non-verbal expression. Pointing to the colorful expressiveness of "inarticulate" children in informal situations, Deutsch proposes methods which stimulate verbal expression of many different kinds; teachers need to sacrifice quality and correctness of language, at least as a start, to stimulate the youngster's quantity and production. The "present" as opposed to the "future" orientation, the urge for "immediate" rather than "delayed" or "future" need-gratification, suggests a reconsideration of how tangible rewards help disadvantaged children identify positively with learning tasks.

What distinguishes the disadvantaged child who succeeds in school from the one who does not?[4] To what extent is success or failure the net yield of teacher characteristics and classroom atmosphere and procedures? The need for a structured classroom and deliberately organized instructional program has been suggested as especially appropriate for the disadvantaged child. How do these arrangements—inevitable reflections of various kinds of teacher styles—affect the child's self-image and his acquisition of the "readiness for learning" and the "learning how to learn" skills?

What kinds of program modifications will compensate for the lack of readiness for school tasks? At what stages of individual development are program modifications likely to be most effective: pre-school, early elementary, or even later? At what points are enrichment programs likely to work best in overcoming the handicaps of the culturally deprived child? How can schools broaden the experience base of these children, thus compensating for the earlier deficiencies? How can the various services and programs available in the school, recreational centers, and other nonschool agencies be effectively coordinated to reach total impact on individual children?

[3] Frank Reissman, *The Culturally Deprived Child,* New York: Harper and Brothers, 1962, p. 73.

[4] For some promising hypotheses concerning the personality differences between achievers and non-achievers, see Helen H. Davidson, Judith W. Greenberg and Joan M. Gerver, "Characteristics of Successful School Achievers from a Severely Deprived Environment" (mimeographed report), New York: The City University of New York, Division of Teacher Education, October 1962, pp. 43.

Much has been written about the inappropriateness of text and other instructional materials for disadvantaged children. Tannenbaum sees life in basal readers as bland and unexciting:

> To the lower-class child it looms as a "never-never world" that may excite in him vague dreams of attainment, but which will probably elude him forever. He finds it only less improbable than the fairyland he encounters in fable, except that the plots and characters in the latter type of literature are far more memorable.[5]

How life-like should materials be in depressed areas? Can materials be developed which are true to the spirit, the language and the backgrounds of lower-class children and, at the same time, which contribute to the development of middle-class values? It has been suggested that materials be produced which are more realistic, more meaningful, and more interesting—crystallizing the contributions to American life of Negroes, Puerto Ricans and other minority groups. These contributions must be presented interestingly in ways which will enhance the self-images of children from depressed areas without appearing to be patronizing or obvious. The Detroit experience points up the need for instructional materials which are acceptable to the pupils, the teachers, and the community at large.

Talcott Parsons has described the "achievement content" of the elementary school as consisting of two components: one cognitive and the other moral. The purely cognitive component is the acquisition of information, written language, primary arithmetic and other basic skills. The "moral" one consists of responsible school-community citizenship: respect for the teacher, considerateness for and cooperation with fellow pupils, good work habits, initiative and leadership. The achievement content tends to become blurred and confused when teachers judge pupils' behavior and equate it with accomplishment. Consequently, a "good" pupil is one who manages a fusion of the moral and cognitive components. The elementary school, Parsons points out, "differentiates the school class broadly along a single continuum of achievement, the content of which is relative excellence and living up to the expectations imposed by the teacher as an agent of the adult society."[6] The culturally deprived youngster's early experiences may put him at both a cognitive and emotional disadvantage in "achieving" in the school's terms.

Reading is the basic tool subject for school success, as is evident from

---

[5] Abraham J. Tannenbaum, "Family Life in Textbook Town," *Progressive Education,* 31:133-140, March 1954.

[6] Talcott Parsons, "The School as a Social System: Some of Its Functions in American Society," *Harvard Educational Review,* 29: 297-318, Fall, 1959.

the time devoted to instruction. Success in reading to a large extent determines the teacher's judgment of students as "good" or "poor"—with the consequential rewards and punishments. Limited success in reading and the other language arts can stunt educational growth and implant a sense of inability to cope with classroom learning tasks.

A study by Thomas for the Detroit GCSIP has pointed up the urgency of promoting oral language development of children from depressed areas as early as possible to stimulate reading growth. Thomas's findings also indicate that the standard primary-grade word lists may not be suitable for written materials for depressed area children. His comparison of oral vocabularies and word structures of lower- and upper-class children showed that the poorer children use a smaller number and variety of words to express themselves; they speak in shorter phrases, using a much higher proportion of incomplete sentences; their sentences have far fewer compound, complex and elaborate constructions; they tend not to elaborate their ideas verbally; they commit many more grammatical errors, such as disagreement of verb and subject; they use more slang and colloquialisms. Thomas also found that from 20 to 50 per cent of the words used by deprived children were different from the standard primary-grade word lists.[7] Investigations such as these underscore the need for developing reading materials with stories, vocabulary, interest level, and illustrations which recognize the limited background and experience of culturally disadvantaged children but which can raise levels for them. The earlier reading and language problems of disadvantaged children are controlled, the less will be the need for large-scale remediation.

For many youngsters, English is a second language, rarely used at home and seldom heard outside the school. Even for some English-speaking children, classroom English is practically a second language. Curriculum planners confront specific problems of modifying methods, content, and materials when teaching English as a second language to non-English speaking children or to in-migrant, mountain-white or rural-Negro children, whose speech patterns, colloquialisms, and modes of expression are so different from the prevailing urban pattern.

Programmed instructional materials have been suggested as having possibilities for education of disadvantaged youth. These self-instructional devices with their small increments of information, the provision of immediate feedback and reinforcement, and their tutor-like structures

[7] An unpublished Ed.D. Dissertation by Dominic R. Thomas summarized in Gertrude Whipple, "The Culturally and Socially Deprived Reader," *in* H. Alan Robinson (Ed.), *The Underachiever in Reading,* Chicago: The University of Chicago Press, 1962, pp. 132-135.

may be particularly helpful with children in depressed areas. However, programs must be properly selected and developed, intrinsically interesting enough to motivate youngsters to stay with them.

Several national curriculum projects have been revising the content and organization in specific subject areas such as mathematics, sciences, and foreign languages. One of the common beliefs of programs such as the Physical Sciences Study Committee, the Biological Curriculum Study Committee, and the School Mathematics Study Group, is that the "structure of the discipline" should be the basis for content selection and organization. In addition, these programs emphasize intuitive thinking abilities. Are these new academic programs appropriate for children from depressed areas? Do they widen still further the gap between socio-economic groupings in schools? Is there more value in curriculum designs built around broad fields or social process and life functions than in designs which select learning experiences from subject or academic disciplines?

What are the necessary modifications in curriculum provisions for so-called non-academic programs for depressed area youngsters—home economics, industrial arts, pre-vocational and vocational education? In what way do these areas need to be custom designed to the unique measurements of the students? Are changes in standards needed for assignment to various programs? What kinds of content will prevent non-academic programs from becoming "dumping grounds" for students from depressed areas? How can individual potential be assessed to minimize the limitations of the IQ tests in predicting performances? Which work-study and similar programs are effective for reducing drop-outs among depressed-area children? Can potential drop-outs—both those who physically leave school and those who remain in class but withdraw psychologically—be detected early enough and recaptured by program modifications? What are the particular vocational education needs of disadvantaged youngsters which, if met, will open up new career opportunities for them? How can schools organize vocational and general education programs to keep abreast of career opportunities and dead ends caused by automation, by development of new industries and services, and by the mushrooming needs for trained personnel?

The range of special personnel staff and services—guidance, psychological, social, recreational, remedial, parent education—all continue to grow in response to some of the learning problems faced in the depressed areas. Is there a valid rationale for determining how special staff will be deployed? Are certain kinds of personnel or services so central to a smoothly functioning school for depressed area children that their absence curtails the success of other program activities?

A number of programs, in effect, saturate depressed area children with special services, counseling, materials, and enrichment opportunities in an effort to raise their achievement levels and aspirations for higher education. How can these additional services and efforts serve to "wean" the child and help him acquire the self-direction and independence required for adequate performance at the secondary and higher education levels? If academic success and higher aspirations separate the child from his peers, his family, his social community, can and should the school help build the inner resources against regression? Are school-generated forces adequate to combat outside pressures for conformity which play upon the child's vulnerability?

A vital question had to do with the way job barriers dampen enthusiasm for learning, and thus, hamper the effectiveness of school programs. Can the school really gain its objectives if vocational and professional opportunities are not opened? Is it possible that educational programs are doomed to limited success unless labor and management join with educational, political, and other leaders to open opportunities in all areas—housing, vocational, religious, political, as well as educational?

In addition to curriculum considerations, other aspects of programs and practices need to be re-examined in terms of their effects on the educational picture as a whole. Is a special kind of administrative leadership necessary in a depressed area school? How should administrators be recruited and trained? Are particular kinds of supervisory activities needed? How should tax structures be modified and school financing procedures? What kinds of financing are needed beyond what the school district itself can provide? In what ways can non-professional staff be used most effectively? The four papers that follow look at some of these dimensions of school programs in depressed areas, philosophically and practically.

John H. Fischer | Educational Problems of Segregation and Desegregation

To say that the problems of race relations in the United States are complex hardly helps to clarify our situation, but, unless the complexity of this matter is seen and taken constantly into account, no single step is likely to be very useful.[1] The problems of American education are no less complex. In a nation as diversified as ours, universal education can never be simple, and it is universal education, with emphasis on both adjective and noun, that we must now achieve. As the issues of race relations permeate almost every aspect of our life, so events in our schools are interlaced with virtually everything we do or hope to do. The difficulties of operating schools which can cope successfully and, as they must, simultaneously with both racial and educational issues are therefore among the most puzzling of all the problems facing the American people.

The other side of the coin, however, is that the benefits that can flow from the solution of these two problems will be of a magnitude comparable to the difficulties themselves.

Virtually all the purposes for which our schools are maintained may be grouped under two major classifications. First, the school is expected to give every student the opportunity and the means to develop to the full whatever individual potential he may have. One purpose of the school, to say it more briefly, is to help each student make the most of himself.

The second purpose is related to the first but not entirely congruent with it. This is to induct the young person systematically into the culture and society to which he is an heir and in which he should be a partner. The school's success in respect to this purpose must be gauged not only by the competence of its graduates but by the quality of their sense of moral responsibility.

By viewing what we do with any child, of any race, against these considerations, one personal, the other social, we should be able to reach

[1] Prepared for delivery at the Fourth Annual Conference of the Commission on Civil Rights, Washington, D. C., May 3, 1962.

reasonably sound conclusions about the effectiveness of our schools and the extent to which their performance approaches the ideals we project in our statements of philosophy.

Limitations of time make it impossible to include in this paper more than passing reference to the fact that the educational problems of desegregation and integration have important political, legal, and social aspects. I shall concentrate upon the more purely educational dimensions of the matter, which is to say its cultural and psychological aspects.

The temptation is always strong to say that the Negro child should be seen merely as any other child, respected as an individual, and provided with an educational program that will best meet his particular combination of needs. Of course the Negro child, like every other child, is entitled to be treated as an individual. Such treatment is the only sound basis for projecting his or any other child's education, but the easy generalization does not always come to grips with the whole truth.

The American Negro youngster happens to be a member of a large and distinctive group that for a very long time has been the object of special political, legal, and social action. This, I remind you, is not a question of what should be true, or might have been, but an undeniable and inescapable fact. To act as though any child is suddenly separable from his history is indefensible. In terms of educational planning, it is also irresponsible.

Every Negro child is the victim of the history of his race in this country. On the day he enters kindergarten, he carries a burden no white child can ever know, no matter what other handicaps or disabilities he may suffer. We are dealing here with no ordinary question of intercultural understanding, although admittedly cultural difference is a part of the difficulty. Nor are we concerned with only the usual range of psycho-educational problems, for the psychological situation of the Negro child is affected by quite special social considerations.

I recognize the hazard in speaking of "the Negro child." It is equally unsatisfactory to speak of "the white child" or "the Puerto Rican child" or "the Spanish-American child" as though any child could be encompassed in a stereotype. Whatever a child's ethnic or racial background, he may be bright or slow, attractive or unpleasant; his parents may be rich or poor, well-educated or illiterate, responsible or shiftless. Every racial group distributes itself in some fashion over the whole social and economic scale. But when all the variability is conceded, it cannot be denied that every American Negro child must expect to encounter certain problems which none of our other children face in quite the same way.

Many of the recent efforts to integrate Negro pupils into the mainstream of American public education have been built on the assumption that the problems are essentially administrative, legal, or political. As a consequence, we have seen drives for what is called "open enrollment" and other schemes to bring about, usually through directive action, a desired combination of races in particular classrooms or schools. Having worked in school administration for some twenty-seven years, I claim some knowledge of at least its limitations. Although I hold that administrative procedures and actions can be useful in education, I grow steadily more certain that no major problem of education—by which I mean really effective teaching and learning—has ever been solved solely, or even primarily, by legal or administrative action. To be sure, such action often lays the necessary groundwork and provides the setting in which good teachers may carry on their work, but the critical point in any educational system is found ultimately in the relation between the teacher and the pupil.

What, then, can be done to produce the sort of pupil-teacher relationship that will contribute most to the tasks we are thinking of today?

For one thing, we must continue to recognize the element of cultural difference. As the Educational Policies Commission pointed out in a recent statement, a principal part of the difficulty of what the Commission calls the "disadvantaged American" is the fact that a substantial minority of Americans have grown up in cultures which are not compatible with much of modern life. This minority consists by no means only of Negroes, nor are all Negroes culturally disadvantaged. But vast numbers of them are, as a direct consequence of legal and social segregation.

The situation is not new. The mountain whites and rural Negroes, among others, have lived in cultural isolation for a long time. Now, however, the negative influence of poor economic conditions in their former homes combined with the positive illusory attraction of the city have caused a vast and growing migration. The congregation of tens of thousands of these people in places for which their customary living patterns are ill-adapted tragically dramatizes their cultural dislocation.

Many of the Negro children who now come to school are the victims of their parents' lack of knowledge and of schooling. The parents in turn are the victims of a situation over which they have had little or no control themselves. Parents and children alike elicit sympathy and attract charity, but praiseworthy as these responses may be, they form no adequate approach to the education of the disadvantaged urban child. The response of the community and the school must be based also on objective knowledge and mature understanding of the underlying difficulty and an inventive turn of mind among teachers and administrators. Teaching reading, for example, to a first-grade child who has never seen an adult read anything requires an approach quite different from one appropriate to a child in whose home books are as normal as food.

Similarly, a child who has never known sustained conversation with his parents must actually learn the skills of continuing discussion before he can learn much else in school.

Nor is it enough to say that the school should accept the child where it finds him and raise him as high and as fast as it can toward an adequate level of cultural attainment. To be sure, this is one of the school's functions; no teacher ever succeeds unless he first establishes rapport and communication with the pupil at the pupil's level. But the school's procedures and its success will necessarily differ between the child whose home background daily complements what the school does, and the one who is caught, so to speak, in a cultural downdraft the moment he steps outside the school.

In dealing with a population which is racially and culturally integrated, the school must begin by encouraging teachers to understand the special factors in the backgrounds of all their children, to take these differences imaginatively into account, and to build curricula and teaching techniques that reflect not only idealism but realism as well.

In addition to the cultural aspect, intellectual considerations are involved in meeting the problems of racial integration. A good school is responsibly concerned with all of the aspects of a child's development, but the central purpose that must run through all sound education is the development of intellectual strength. Unless the school is able to help every child to use his mind effectively, none of the other purposes of education can be satisfactorily achieved. We customarily cite physical health as a fundamental goal of education, but unless the child learns to apply his own intelligence to the problem of remaining healthy, he is not likely to do much either for his own well-being or for the public health of his community. The young person who does not become critically thoughtful about moral values, who behaves well only when someone is watching him or forcing him to conform, cannot be trusted to manage his own morality. But the school's success in pursuing this central purpose of education is subject, like so many of its other efforts, to what happens to the pupil outside the school.

In respect to the development of intellectual competence, many Negro children face special problems that should be better understood than they often are. Obviously many Americans of Negro ancestry have attained distinction in fields requiring intellectual eminence and millions of others daily apply their minds with excellent results in more humble ways. Yet the fact remains that during years of oppression, first under slavery and later under more subtle forms of discrimination, the opportunities for large numbers of Negroes to apply their own rational powers with initiative and freedom to important problems have been far more limited than the opportunities available to other racial groups. Many Negro children, therefore, carry the disabling scars of the culture in which they were nurtured, a culture which encouraged the use of muscles and not only discouraged but often penalized those who sought to use their minds creatively. The school must take all of this into account and build programs and provide opportunities which not only reflect these facts but move aggressively to compensate for them.

Every educational problem has its emotional side, and the special problems of educating Negro children in desegregated schools have theirs. Not being a psychologist, I do not intend to examine this complex question at any length. But there can be little doubt that the education of many Negro children is adversely affected by emotional considerations. The fact that it is often difficult to distinguish among the cultural, the intellectual, and the emotional aspects of education is one reason why teaching any child is so complex.

One of the most serious of the details is the problem of motivation. The Horatio Alger story is a well established part of our folklore, but few Americans would argue that the typical Alger hero would have made it had his skin been of a darker shade. The sense of frustration which any minority child may experience is heightened in the case of the Negro child, who discovers all too early that his minority has both a special history in the United States and quite unique problems. As a consequence, his attitude toward himself and toward his racial group complicates the effort to help him secure an adequate education. In some cases, he may rationalize his failures by attributing them to limitations which do not, in fact, exist for him. In others, he may develop an understandable aggressiveness which will neither compensate for external difficulties nor correct his own shortcomings. The wise and well-informed teacher is aware of these emotional complications and undertakes to deal with them in positive ways.

In the face of these facts, and in the light of our democratic values, what guidelines for policy and practice in the conduct of American public schools are implied?

In the first place, it is essential to emphasize on every possible occasion and in everything we do in schools that the rights of students, the assessment of their needs, and the release of their potentialities must be approached on an individual basis. What I have said about the identification of students as members of groups is important only insofar as it helps the teacher to understand a particular student. My point, you may remember, is that the individual cannot be understood unless he is seen against the history from which he has come and in terms of the situation in which he currently lives. But his education is peculiarly his own. The opportunities afforded any child may not properly be limited because he happens to be a member of one or another racial group. In this connection, again, we face the hazard of stereotyped treatment, a hazard which at all costs must be avoided.

This implication for policy and practice cuts more than one way, however, for just as certainly as no person should be subjected to discriminatory treatment which depresses him because of his race, so it follows that none should be given preferential treatment simply because his complexion or his ancestry is different from another's. A practical application of this principle may arise if a school organizes classes according to the academic ability of students. If, after the most reliable estimates of ability the school can make, it should develop that one classroom contains pupils largely of one racial group while a second classroom is composed mostly of another, the school should not be criticized for the result. If, on the other hand, the school authorities have used an ostensibly educational device simply to justify some predetermined racial arrangement, the action is totally indefensible. It should be attacked not only as a violation of the constitutional rights of children but as a flagrant instance of professional malpractice.

A second guideline for the development of policy and practice centers about the concept of equality of opportunity. "Equality of opportunity," as we customarily use the phrase, means much more than a schoolroom desk for every child. It connotes, rather, a condition in which every American may rightfully expect to find himself in fair competition with every other American. This condition is achieved and maintained by the operation of a host of agencies and forces, some political, some social, others economic or cultural. The public school has never been the only agency concerned with producing equality of opportunity, but its role is fundamental to the total effort.

In the cases of some Americans, and in that of the Negro American most dramatically, our traditional system has failed for a long time and in countless ways to provide that equality of opportunity that should be the condition of all our people. Recent improvements have helped correct the imbalance, but much more correction is required. Especially is this true of children whose parents and grandparents were deliberately, systematically, and by law denied what is now clearly recognized as fully equal treatment.

Is it not a reasonable contention—and a just one—that to compensate for past injustice, we should offer these children educational services beyond the level of what might be called standard equality?

Could it be that to achieve total equality of opportunity in America we may have to modify currently accepted ideas about equality of opportunity in education itself? Is it conceivable that some of our children are entitled to more and better educational opportunities than most of the others? In fact, of course, the question has already been answered. Thousands of mentally and physically handicapped children, regardless of race, regularly receive teaching service, physical facilities, and supporting services more extensive and more costly than those furnished children who are considered physically or mentally normal. In the cases of many Negro children—and the generalization would apply also to certain other minority groups—we may need to substitute for our traditional concept of equal educational opportunity a new concept of compensatory opportunity.

Such compensatory opportunity might take the form of lower student-teacher ratios in cerain schools, or additional guidance services, or better physical facilities. The idea might mean more scholarships for higher education, or, in some cases, custodial and boarding care for children whose welfare required their removal from a crippling environment.

I doubt that anyone is in a position now to say precisely what the concept of compensatory educational opportunity would mean in every case, but my purpose here is not so much to answer the question as to raise it for discussion. The concept of compensatory opportunity should certainly not be restricted to any one group, and, as I have suggested, it has already been applied to other types of disability. But, to the degree that a child's race or cultural background handicaps him—and especially where the handicap is attributable, at least in part, to earlier governmental action—they should be taken into account in adjusting his educational program.

A third guide to educational policy and practice seems relevant to this discussion. If we are to keep the focus of our educational effort on the welfare of the individual child, we shall do well to avoid what is sometimes called social engineering. The very term is inconsistent with the purposes and values of democracy. Even the most desirable end does not justify manipulating people to creat a structure pleasing to some master planner. To put it precisely, I am disturbed about the growing pressure to locate schools, draw district lines, and organize curricula in order to achieve a pre-determined racial pattern of enrollment. By no means am I opposing the desirability of having in the same school children of different racial backgrounds. Quite the contrary! But decisions about school organization based entirely or primarily on racial criteria seem to me to violate the principle of non-discrimination. All school districting arrangements should provide a maximum of free choice for all children, subject only to common sense protection against unnecessary overcrowding. Indeed, if

I had my way, I should have no school attendance districts at all. In a well conducted school system every school should be so good that those who live near it would never think of going elsewhere except for some extraordinary reason. In the case of secondary schools, or others where specialized curricula might be a factor, the importance of the neighborhood location would, of course, be somewhat less significant. But here again the greatest possible freedom of choice should be allowed all pupils, so long as they are qualified for the programs involved.

The concept of freedom of choice should be interpreted, however, only to allow positive choice and never to permit any group to restrict the opportunities of another. The basic principle is that all public schools of a community belong to all the people of the community, that none is the exclusive preserve of a single racial group.

The most offensive aspect of the engineered approach is the assumption that any group can be improved if members of another race are introduced into it. If all the races of mankind are equally to be valued and respected, a group composed of thirty members of Race A cannot be improved merely by substituting a few members of Race B. If, on the other hand, the group is to be improved with regard, let us say, to mathematical performance, the introduction of a couple of mathematical wizards will obviously raise the average. A musical group short of tenors can surely be improved by recruiting three good tenors, but the point of origin of their grandfathers or the color of their hair are scarcely relevant criteria. We cannot have it both ways: we cannot say that race *per se* makes no difference and then argue that important decisions should be based on this inconsequential factor.

To summarize then, briefly what I have tried to say about the educational problems of desegregating schools:

1. The focus of sound teaching is always on the individual, for education is an intensely personal matter, having its principal effect always within the person.

2. If we are to achieve good education, we must respect the individuality of each student, relating his instruction to his background, his needs, his possibilities.

3. To achieve equality of opportunity within the whole of our culture, it may be necessary to offer those who are handicapped by their history or their current situation not merely equal, but compensatory educational opportunity.

4. In the organization of education, many considerations are important, many characteristics are relevant, but racial differences in themselves are not. In the administration of schools, therefore, the manipulation of pupils on purely racial grounds is irrelevant and improper.

Carl L. Marburger | Considerations for Educational Planning

In Detroit and other large cities across the nation, are concentrated families whose children are severely hampered in their schooling by a complex of community, home, and school conditions. To engage the total problem faced by urban educators, we shall make a brief foray into the social pathology which produced it.

Introduction to the Problem [1]

Change in the population of the inner cores of most large cities has created areas where the majority of children have extraordinary needs which the public schools are not prepared to meet. Where once the inner city population was typically "all kinds," it has now become typically stratified. The majority of upper and middle income urbanites have moved to the suburbs or to the outer rings of the city. The population that remains is predominantly unskilled or semi-skilled, low-income, racial and ethnic minorities. When representatives of other strata moved out, the vacuum was filled by southern-Appalachian white and southern Negro in-migrants similar in many ways to the low-income minority groups that had remained in the inner city.

Numbers of the city's manufacturing and service industries have followed the upper- and middle-income exodus. What remains is the glowing downtown section, a great multi-story civic and merchandising complex, serviced by expressways and surrounded by miles of slums and "transitional" or "gray" areas, still containing a few pockets of more affluent residential areas and high-rent apartment districts.

From these slums and transitional areas come one-third of the more than 3,000,000 children now enrolled in America's fourteen largest school systems. Many of them have limited backgrounds, and most of them are concentrated in the inner city schools.

---

[1] Extracted and paraphrased from Charles Mitchell (3). Mr. Mitchell is the Project Writer for the Detroit Great Cities School Improvement Project.

The families of these children live for the most part in low-cost public housing, or in overcrowded, substandard, multiple-dwellings of every type —or in single- and two-family homes in neghborhoods which are, in reality, transitional. Some of these neighborhoods are not yet slums, but their people are often in difficult straits, and the children reflect this in school.

The families of these children may have resided in Detroit for many years; but most came during and immediately after the Second World War to fill industry's needs for unskilled labor, or are very recent in-migrants from rural areas, particularly rural areas of the southern states, who shifted from a land of no current or foreseeable opportunity to a land of possible—maybe—opportunity.

The in-migrant comes into a portion of the total community which is fragmented and uncohesive, which lacks trained leadership and organization, and which physically reflects the low, inconsistent income and the lack of information and skills of its inhabitants. Here, whatever booms or economic upturns may occur in other places, depression seldom ceases. A job is a will-o'-the-wisp affair.

The family of the child with limited background may have many meritable standards and values. Even when its material well-being is limited to basic necessities, the family may be close-knit with love and caring.

But always, there is a common denominator: not enough. Not enough income, information, and skills to get along successfully; no precedent for success; insufficiencies of many sorts. The child reflects this. He is poorly prepared and poorly motivated for school. School has never seemed important to his family or to him. Obviously there are some significant adjustments to be made.

With a sufficiency of income, information, motivation, and time—in short, in an ideal situation—urban life adjustment might evolve quite pleasantly. But the situation is poor, and many children have little to do except, as one teacher's report put it, "think about the hills of home, go to school each day unprepared and purposeless, and be 'sick to mah stomach from the gas stove' (quote from child) that heats a three-room flat."

The parents of these children are not against education. At worst they see no need for it, are indifferent. Many have hopes and ambitions for their children which involve obtaining a good education. They are glad if their child does well in school, but they often have little formal education themselves, know little about studies or how children learn. They feel that they cannot, in their lack of success, understand how to help the child succeed.

The child with limited background has normal intelligence. He is not different in this respect. He can grow up in school studies and in his life if reached and interested by what the school offers. And yet, the typical child with limited background in the typical classroom is indifferent and purposeless, a poor communicator who does not respond to normal teaching methods and subject matter. His capabilities remain unrealized.

Why?

The traditional responsibilities of school staff and objectives of school services are based upon a uniform "Successful American" social and economic pattern and do not obtain effectively to the non-uniform social and economic patterns which characterize the neighborhoods from which these children come.

The typical school cannot compensate for the various lacks in the lives of children with limited backgrounds. The typical school does not provide these reinforcements to school learning which, in a stable, middle-income area, are normally provided each child by his home and out-of-school life.

Many of these reinforcements are intangible. They include: an acceptable self-image; knowledge of essentials such as nutrition and health; an implicit sense of identification with a stable family in a stable neighborhood; security and freedom from want, both material and emotional; the self-confidence and motivation to achieve which rub off on the child who is surrounded by things and involved in experiences which are accepted both *at home* and *in school* either as symbols of success or significant achievements.

Such positive factors are essential in some form in the growing up of a child. If they are insufficient or lacking, and no compensation is made for them, then the child's ability to learn in school is impeded or lost.

It seems reasonable that the educator should be concerned with *all* that affects the child he is trying to educate, and in fact teachers and administrators often informally cross traditional lines and do "unorthodox" things to help children who are not doing well in school. But except through the attendance officer, the public schools, especially the urban public schools, seldom make official organized attempts to alter the "other lives" of children. If the family does little to help prepare the child for life, and the cultural environment of the child is limited and negative, then the one force left to do the necessary shaping is the school. It must provide more for the child than it normally would, at the same time attempting, with other community services, to revive the family's positive influence and to introduce portions of our culture and our society which tend to equalize the child's limited and negative environment.

In truth, we must say with Harold Taylor that,

The educator must go to the root of the matter, and he must deal with the whole child. The root is in the social and economic conditions in which the child exists. The educator must deal bluntly with those who support the residential segregation of the colored people and the poor. He must fight those who wish to profit in real estate at the expense of the children. He must think of education as a total process, in which the conditions of society deeply affect the child's mind, the level of his achievement, and the range of his possibilities. The curriculum, the classroom, the guidance office are instruments for dealing with one part of the child's life. But they do not and cannot function in a social vacuum.

Nor is it permissible any longer to say that the social environment of the child is not the problem of the educator, that it belongs to city planners, social workers, economists, housing experts, or society. It belongs to everyone, but most of all to the educator. The educator is not a personnel manager, an administrator, an organization man, although his work involves organizing, managing, and administering. He is a social and intellectual leader, and he begins to exercise his leadership when he recognizes the conditions of his society and brings to bear upon them the force of a humanitarian philosophy (5).

The Great Cities Projects

The superintendents and board-of-education members of the fourteen largest city school systems met in 1957 in Atlantic City, New Jersey, to share their concerns about the problems of education in large urban areas. Their first cooperative exploration took them into the World of Work and a careful study of current and prospective youth employment opportunities. A vocational education specialist was appointed to coordinate the efforts of the Great Cities in this area. The World of Work study continues, and findings are being implemented in programs seen as appropriate by each of the cities.

Another difficulty shared by large-city educators, that of limited fiscal resources, has led to a cooperative study of fiscal policy. If educators are to equalize and expand educational opportunity, or simply to hold ground against the press of increased enrollment, from where is the money to come? Again, a consultant was secured, and along with staff persons from each city, began to study possible resources and to formulate recommendations for revision of Great Cities fiscal policies.

The third problem shared by the large-city educators was that of educating the increasing numbers of children with limited backgrounds. After intensive analysis of the factors which indicate educational deprivation —low achievement levels, lack of kindergarten experience, poor attendance, high truancy, over-agedness in grade, high rate of failure, and the range of home and community deprivation—the Great Cities teams developed what they called "The Central Hypothesis." This hypothesis states that the problems of children with limited backgrounds can be effectively and economically solved by:

1. Development of a program of education adapted to the needs of these children,
2. Modifications in the organizational patterns within the school,
3. Proper selection and utilization of personnel,
4. Improved utilization of instructional equipment and materials,
5. Involvement of parents and of the community in the educational program.

Under the leadership of Dr. S. M. Brownell, superintendent of schools, and the direction of Dr. Carl Byerly, Detroit began testing this hypothesis in September, 1959. Detroit's pilot project, involving three schools in the central city, was the first demonstration project among the Great Cities. Further, the pilot demonstration project was financed entirely by the Detroit Board of Education. In July, 1960, the Ford Foundation provided financial support to the Detroit Project and to several other great cities as well. This initial one-year grant made it possible to "buy time," by intensifying project activities and expanding project coverage from three to seven schools. The Ford Foundation extended the initial Detroit grant for an additional three years in July, 1961. Grant extensions have also been made to other Great Cities Projects.

The Great Cities teams of superintendents and board-of-education members have recently formed the Research Council of the Great Cities Program for School Improvement to coordinate the various activities under their jurisdiction. The most current result of their concern is an investigation of pre- and in-service education of teachers. The Research Council intends to find and recommend more effective ways to prepare teachers for the demanding work of teaching not only the children with limited backgrounds, but all children.

Thus, the Great Cities are engaged in cooperative study and action programs designed to solve the many problems peculiar to large city school systems. They intend to develop, and to prove effective, a *total educational program* for large urban areas.

Although many of the difficulties encountered by urban schools ensue from "urban blight" and its effect on children and families, it is clearly recognized that educational planning needs to be for all children and all schools, and not only for the children and the schools in depressed urban areas. Certainly the central hypothesis, put forward by Great Cities educators as a viable solution for the problem of providing a good education for the child with limited background, can be used to provide a good education for all children.

The Detroit Project—Working Toward More Effective Education

The objective of the Detroit Great Cities School Improvement Project is to increase the competence of children with limited backgrounds. By competence, we mean not academic competence alone, but competence of the "whole child" in the Harold Taylor meaning of the phrase—social competence, urban living competence, and job, or work skill competence —including the ability to learn new job skills if needed. In addition to the five points of the great cities hypothesis, the Detroit Program has these special emphases:

1. A program of teacher-school-community improvement is more effective if all levels of a school system serving an area (kindergarten through grade 12) are involved. Therefore, the seven schools in the Detroit Project include three elementary schools (kindergarten through grade 6); one elementary school (kindergarten through grade 8); two junior high schools (grades 7 and 9); and one senior high school (grades 10 through 12).

2. The program should be one which can be financed within the resources of the school budget over a long period, if it can be shown (as we anticipate) that the results of the project warrant the programs's continuation and extension into other areas of the city whose school populations have similar problems and needs. Therefore, the yearly budget for the five years of the demonstration project represents an increase of less than 10 per cent above normal costs per pupil for the city. Thus, the budget, including the Ford Foundation grant (30 per cent of the total budget), is realistic in terms of the fiscal support expected for schools in the Detroit area.

3. Any program designed to solve the problem of educating the child with limited background must operate intensively for several years. Solution of the educational problem involves making long-term changes in family and community attitudes and behavior, as well as changes in a more-or-less immediate nature in the pupil-teacher relationships and services available to the pupil. Time is needed to assure that systems of change shall be functional and lasting in effect. Therefore, Detroit's is a six-year project in the three pilot project schools, and a five-year project in the remaining four. Further, there is a commitment to evaluate the working effect of the project far beyond the actual completion date of its program.

With regard to the Great Cities hypothesis, the Detroit projects makes use of several major approaches to the solution of the problems of educating children with limited backgrounds.

One major approach is our work with teachers. Improvement of schooling depends to a great extent upon more effective teaching. Therefore, we strive to modify the perceptions of the teachers of children with limited backgrounds as this perception relates to these children, their community, and their curriculum. Many teachers initially perceive these three negatively; that is, in the light of their own experiential backgrounds. Teachers may bring to their work a rigid value system different than that of the populace of depressed urban areas—a value system, for instance, which presupposes certain limits on the intelligence and ability of the child with limited background. Some teachers have been reared in a different socioeconomic situation, and have difficulty in objectively assessing the child with limited background. Other teachers have, through their profession, moved up the socio-economic ladder, and may possibly (and paradoxically) reject the all-too-familiar values of the children they teach. In any case, it is not unusual to find in the classroom a critical need for belief in the universal learning ability of humankind, regardless of socio-economic condition.

Our first attempt to bring about appropriate changes was through a series of workshop experiences. Competent consultants were secured in many disciplines: education, sociology, social work, and psychology. Our experience leads us to believe that very few significant changes in the behavior of teachers take place as a result of listening to experts. Those teachers who were tuned in to hear the expert believed and behaved in terms of what they had heard. Those teachers who were not tuned in to hear the experts did not change their behavior to any noticeable degree as a result of hearing them. The key to modification of behavior seems to be involvement.

Our workshops and in-service experiences have, therefore, been structured around local school curriculum problems and have usually involved only a single school staff. We have found that curricula vary from school to school, from community to community, and from school staff to school staff. To achieve the kind of involvement that brings positive change, *each* school staff must look seriously at its unique community, the unique problems of its youth, and its own unique strengths and weaknesses as a staff. Then the school staff may search for appropriate curricular and organizational modifications to strengthen its own school situation.

Our attempts to assist staffs to do this have taken several forms. We have provided workshop experiences through the local university. If teachers and administrators wish to have a course for credit toward an advanced degree or a number of hours beyond the Bachelor's or Master's, they may pay tuition to the university for the workshop experience. If they wish to take part in the workshop but do not wish the credit, the Detroit Great Cities Project pays their tuition so that they may audit the course.

Other local school-curriculum workshops have taken place on Saturdays, and also during the summer months. As a part of the Detroit school policy, teachers involved have been paid for their time on Saturdays and during the summer. Furthermore, some released time has been devoted to in-service education. Indications are that more released time is now an essential need.

As a result of these in-service experiences, some organizational and curriculum changes have been made. We have instituted the non-graded primary in two elementary schools. Block-time and core classes are being held in the junior high schools. Team teaching is being tried in two of the schools.

Curriculum modifications come more slowly. One significant curriculum change has taken place in our early elementary reading materials—but not without difficulty. It has long been felt that children might read with greater facility if the material with which they were dealing was more nearly related to their own real backgrounds. Negro youth, for example, rarely have an opportunity to see a Negro child illustrated in the little picture books with which they learn to read. Through a series of writing workshops we set out to build a series of pre-primers which would focus on the life of a working-class family, living in a typical, racially mixed, urban neighborhood. In spite of the sophistication of the writing committee members, we now know first hand the perils of revolutionary primer writing. The artist doing illustrations for the series depicted some typical housekeeping situations (brooms leaning in the corner, a kitchen sink with exposed pipes beneath it) and this—at least relative to other pre-primers, which do not treat the realties of housekeeping quite as fully—was taken simply as poor housekeeping, and thereby as a derogation of the Negro since this was the home of a Negro family.

The first pre-primer was only one-third the length of a normal pre-primer, because we wanted each child to have the satisfaction of completing a book in a short time. Thus, we inadvertently left the father out of the first pre-primer; indeed, we did not even refer to him. This was also interpreted as a derogation, not only of the Negro family depicted, but of Negro families in general. Finally, we called the little-boy hero of the series "Sammy." It was an unfortunate choice, since it was seen by middle-class Negro families as "stereotype by insinuation."

Having gleaned some important lessons from this experience, we expanded our primer writing committee with a number of consultants, both lay and professional, and revised the series. The first three pre-primers of this series were available in four-color reproduction in September of 1962, for experimental testing.

Other minor curriculum changes have taken place at different levels. We have produced some units for block-time classes at the secondary level, which have been found to be very useful throughout the entire school system for block-time classes.

Perhaps the only significant change in curriculum is what happens when the individual teacher closes the door of her classroom. Assuming the requisite skills in teaching the basic materials, the teacher's attitude is the most crucial factor.

At this point in our project, we conceive the formula that teacher-expectations have surprising impact on pupil-achievement. Indeed we might even say that teacher expectations have a similar impact on pupil intelligence scores. The teacher who expects achievement, who has hope for the educability of his pupils, indeed conveys this through every nuance and subtlety of his behavior. The teacher who conveys hopelessness for the educability of his children usually does so without ever really verbalizing such an attitude—at least, in front of his pupils.

With regard to expectations of pupil ability to learn, a significant experiment was done recently by Robert Rosenthal and Kermit L. Fode of the University of North Dakota. In a carefully controlled experiment, twelve senior division students in experimental psychology were assigned a group of five albino rats for running through a maze ten times a day for five days. Although the rats were randomly selected, each student was informed that the rats were either "maze-bright" or "maze-dull."

Results indicated that on three of the five days and for the experiment as a whole, E's [experimenters] believing their S's [subjects] to be bright obtained performance from them significantly superior to that obtained by E's believing their S's to be dull. The S's believed to be bright appeared to be learning the problem while those believed to be dull did not. These results occurred in spite of the fact that on the level of verbal report *both* groups of E's wanted their S's to perform well. In addition, a research assistant following the identical experimental procedure, was able to obtain, without "cheating," performance from her S's superior even to that obtained by E's believing their S's were bright. Comparing the degree of correlation between what each E specifically expected to obtain from his S's and what he actually did obtain from them for the "Bright" and "Dull" groups suggested that these groups were about equally biased although, of course, in opposite directions (4).

Thus, even when dealing with non-human subjects, the experimenter's expectations seem most significant in determining the performance of the subject. Certainly the expectations of the teacher for her pupils can determine, particularly in depressed-urban-area schools, the school survival or non-survival of the youth. If nothing else, teacher expectations affect the time spent in preparing to teach, the amount of real concern for individual students, and the degree of "soul" the teacher gives to his work.

The involvement of an almost total staff, including administration, would seem then to be essential for innovation in curriculum, and for modification of behavior to insure truly effective teaching. We obviously cannot expect anything approximating 100 per cent involvement of staff, but the nearer we come to this ideal, and to the contagion of enthusiasm which results from it, the greater the possibility of creating the milieu in which youth, particularly disadvantaged youth, can learn.

In order that teachers of children with limited backgrounds may maintain enthusiasm for teaching, and hope for the educability of their children, they must be continually reinforced. The teacher needs adequate resources to combat the corrosive influences of emotional and physical poverty with which many of his students live day in and day out. The teacher needs help to teach effectively in spite of the inadequate facilities which often seem typical of inner city schools. High transiency rates and the generally low achievement of pupils beset by out-of-school difficulties which carry over demonstrably into the classroom can overwhelm the most conscientious teacher.

The Detroit Project does provide some reinforcement to teachers. Additional personnel, whose duties are discussed at length later in this paper, provide some aid in working with children whose reading, speech and arithmetic disabilities are pronounced, in developing stronger ties and understanding between families and the school, and so forth. Referrals of children with physical or emotional difficulties can be made more readily by the classroom teacher in Great Cities Project schools. After school and evening programs, with clubs, remedial and enrichment classes, and recreational activities tend to provide a more beneficient climate for the child than street play might provide, and to orient the child more specifically to the school and the teacher than would otherwise be so. A full summer-school program involving a large percentage of the school population not only provides interesting learning and recreational experiences for the child, but helps him to carry over what he has learned, in behavior as well as in actual knowledge, from one school year into the next.

One more concrete means of reinforcement is the addition to the general fund of each school a sum ranging from $350 to $450 to be used by the staff for the purchase of small supplies and materials which are not available through normal requisition channels. Another is the provision of funds and transportation for an additional four to five hundred bus trips to farms, parks, museums, and the like for the seven schools in the project.

Significant though these additions may be, they are basically without purpose if the teacher does not have the opportunity in his classroom to be experimental, to be innovative, to be free to do those things which are important for the children. Such freedom to do what is needed is there, or is lamentably lacking, in accordance with the administrative style of the principal of the school. Is the school's administrative staff restrictive or non-restrictive, authoritarian or democratic, legalistic or expeditious? These are knotty questions to ask, difficult questions to answer, but they are important since they are germane to the nature of the teaching and learning processes which exist in each school. It has often been stated that the most important single individual in any community is the elementary school principal. I would extend this to all levels of school administration, elementary and secondary. To illustrate, the most obvious deterrent to enthusiastic and imaginative teaching is the authoritarian who sees his school as an armed camp which admits a school population in the morning, regiments them until early afternoon, and then sends them home, five days a week. More insidious and difficult is the legalist, who represses his staff, who processes each decision with perfect logic and imperfect premises, who operates exclusively through a tight chain of command, who so dampens enthusiasm and subverts innovation that any external assistance provides only short-term palliative results.

Documentation of the statements made above regarding teacher attitude and administrative behavior is very difficult. We have considerable evidence to support these statements. However, because of the experimental nature of the project there is need to preserve a modicum of security since release of research data could indeed contaminate the results of the experiment, particularly with our control schools. Some of the methodology used in our research will be discussed later in this paper.

Work with Parents and Community

The second primary focus of our attention is upon the parents and the community. Once again, this is a question of involvement. Parents who are not involved, who do not know what is taking place in the school, can certainly not reinforce what the school is doing with their children. We also see a need to involve parents and the community so that we may raise the aspirations of the parents and their children with regard to academic and social achievement. Parents in depressed urban areas typically stay away from schools. They stay away from school because their own experiences have been either unpleasant or short-lived or both. They are fearful of the institution of the school and they lack information about what is taking place in the school. They do not typically join organizations and therefore do not normally attend parent-group meetings, do not participate in adult-education classes—they generally avoid all school contacts.

We have tried to make our Great Cities Project schools true community schools. This means that the schools must necessarily be open from eight o'clock in the morning until late at night. One of our first approaches to parents was to ask them to tell us the kinds of experiences they would like to have in the afternoons and evenings for themselves and for their children. The parents so contacted were normally those who were more articulate and more solvent economically and who had higher aspirations for themselves and their youth. The so-called hard-to-reach parents were not particularly interested regardless of what the school might offer. Using those parents who could and would respond to our inquiries, we first provided free clubs and classes which were of the upgrading nature. These classes were designed to help parents gain more skills. Often parents had unrealistic expectations about these classes, believing that jobs would become available to them as a result of their classwork. A few have gained some skills through these classes and have been able to obtain, if not better employment, at least techniques which enhanced their leadership potential and communications skills. These first classes included shorthand, speech, typing, sewing, millinery, cake decorating, and the like. The parents then told us that such classes were fine, but asked if it might be possible to provide some classes in reading and arithmetic so that parents could refresh these skills and help their children in their studies. This we did.

Even more crucial than these skill classes were the informal groups, clubs, and classes which were organized around parents' newly expressed needs. Simply the opportunity to meet together, to plan for their youngsters, to take short-term enrichment classes, to learn how to budget, how to prepare food, how to repair furniture, to be more efficient and effective in household tasks and family relations—all of these provided the adults with opportunities to bolster self-esteem and to raise aspirations for themselves and their children.

These clubs and their classes have been taught by teachers on both a voluntary and paid basis and by lay persons from the local community and from the total metropolitan area. In addition, many youth from the community have been hired as baby-sitters, teacher's aides and assistants for afternoon and evening classes and clubs. Altogether there are more than two hundred after-school clubs and classes for youth and adults in the seven schools.

Each school has had to organize after-school and evening activities in terms of its own community and the needs of that community. Some of the schools have put a greater emphasis on the enrichment programs for youth in the afternoon, others on adult programs in the evening. The greatest difficulty in involvement of youth and adults has naturally come at the secondary level, where the ambivalence of youth toward their parents and the size of the school attendance area mitigate against parental participation in school functions.

We have reached not only the "parents who go to PTA meetings"; we have been able, through the skills of some of our additional personnel, to involve a great many of the so-called hard-to-reach parents. The number of people involved in these after-school and evening activities varies, because of the short-term duration of some of the classes and clubs, but it averages between fifteen hundred and two thousand youth and adults each week.

One of the dangers inherent in such involvement of parents is the over-involvement of certain parents. We found that many of our adults would attend as many as four and five evenings a week, with the result that our program tended to fragment rather than bind families closer together. We have gone a long way in solving this problem by scheduling family nights, when the entire family participates in the available activities. We further restrict the number of evenings any family may be involved. We have also experienced some difficulty as a result of the hiring of local people. The moment that one hires people from the local community, one gives them a status which then raises them above their peers and sometimes causes a degree of rejection and considerable resentment of their new leadership capacity.

A further difficulty is the tendency to develop "programs for program's sake" rather than in terms of the needs of the community. Competition often sets in between schools and results in the scheduling of classes without any inquiry into the needs, expressed and otherwise, of the local school community.

One additional hazard that is very real in this community-school sort of operation in urban depressed areas is the danger of making the parents too dependent on the school. Parents must become dependent on the school initially, if they are to be involved at all. They must see the school as a resource for helping them with their personal and community problems. This project will not succeed if it does not develop an indigenous leadership, which assumes responsibility on its own for the problems of individuals and the local community. We have no intention of relieving parents of their responsibilities as parents, but we want them to ask for help so that they can find ways of working out the solutions to their problems themselves. We attempt in this manner to revive the positive parent-child relationship which is so often lacking in the disadvantaged family.

In order to accomplish both the teacher and parent reinforcement, we must have additional help for the regular staff of each school. This we have provided by adding three additional personnel to each of the school staffs: a school-community agent, a full-time visiting teacher, and a full-time coaching teacher or language arts consultant.

The School-Community Agent

Theoretically, the school-community agent should be a trained social worker with experience in both community organization and group-work. We were not able to achieve this ideally, but have some persons with this background and others with professional training (usually in education) and considerable experience in community organization and group-work activities. The school-community agent is, simply enough, a liaison between the community and the school. This person interprets to the community the functions of the school and interprets to the staff of the school the realities of the community. One of the agent's most important functions is to work with organized block clubs, community councils, and parent groups, if these exist, and to help organize such groups if they do not exist. In addition, we have asked these agents to assume responsibility for the after-school and evening programs for youth and adults. Often these two roles are in serious conflict. The administrative and supervisory functions which are part of the after-school and evening programs do not allow the school-community agent the freedom he requires to become the detached worker; a role which we have found is essential to successful organization of a fragmented and uncohesive depressed-area neighborhood. Further, the administrative style of each school can limit the agent to a program director's capacity or free him to become a detached expert doing constructive work in the neighborhood.

The visiting teacher is the school social worker. This person has had specific training in the case-work methodology and operates primarily with children and the parents of children who have crucial school-adjustment problems. The visiting teacher is normally assigned in the Detroit schools; but she is usually assigned to six or more schools and spends perhaps a half a day a week in each school attempting to handle an unrealistic case load in this fragmented fashion. In the Great Cities Project, the visiting teacher is assigned full time and is thus able to establish roots in the neighborhood and to work closely with the specific problems of the school and the community, its youth and parents. She is able to deal more successfully with fewer cases, to know and understand the school staff and politics, and to become identified with her school and hence with parents. As we examine the role of the visiting teacher in the new five-day-a-week involvement in a single school, we are asking additional questions about the training and certification of these persons. A Michigan law requires that visiting teachers be certified as teachers and, in addition, have Master's degrees in social work with emphasis in case work. We are questioning the necessity for the teaching certificate and are examining the possibility of a combination case and group-work training because the needs of the clients often dictate group-work rather than case-work therapy.

The coaching teacher is actually a language-arts teacher who is performing special remedial functions with children who are retarded in reading. She often conducts small classes ranging from five to fifteen children working on the particular skill deficiencies of children. Once again, the coaching teacher's role is changing. She often finds it more effective to work less specifically with small groups of children and more with total staff in helping all teachers gain the necessary skills to work with the reading deficiencies of children regardless of the subject matter area.

We have seen some startling results show up in achievement in the relatively short period of a semester or a year as a result of this individualized attention given to students by the coaching teachers. We cannot make any claims about this progress in achievement until we have a look at it over a long period to see if there is a retention of the gain.

School-Agency Cooperation

In addition to the use of these specialized personnel we have also had intensive public and private agency involvement. The success of any community-school venture depends in large measure on the concentrated use of available public and private agency personnel and resources. The Detroit Great Cities School Improvement Project has therefore developed these programs:

1. In cooperation with the Neighborhood Service Organization and the Detroit Behavior Project, day camps were conducted at one of our schools during the summer of 1961 for fifty-five emotionally disturbed children from the project schools.

2. We have used the YMCA and YWCA programs and facilities. In addition to the use of their busses and physical facilities, we have many YMCA and YWCA groups meeting in our after-school program with agency, school, and lay personnel involved in leadership capacities.

3. We have shared facilities and personnel with the Detroit Parks and

Recreation Department. We use one of their large recreation centers, and they use the swimming pools in the school buildings. The Detroit Parks and Recreation Department, a municipal agency separate from the schools, has also provided new programs in project schools where no recreation program had existed before.

4. We have increased the school's use of public library facilities, by shuttle-bussing children in "library caravans" to inner-city libraries. Parents served as assistant librarians on these ventures.

5. We are conducting intensive research into the relationship between physical and nutritional needs of children and the learning process, in co-operation with the Detroit Department of Health, which is a separate city agency. The health examination clinic, which was established in one of our schools by the Pilot Club of Detroit, contains all of the equipment and facilities necessary to do a complete physical examination of the school population. The Detroit Department of Health is providing funds to reimburse the examining pediatricians.

6. We have had continuing contacts with local churches as an integral part of the school-community agents' function.

Often in urban depressed areas there is a tendency for churches and both public and private agencies to move their services from that area to other areas where progress is more easily identified. The agencies which remain in the depressed area often provide overlapping services to the hard-to-reach parents of the community. This leads to the duplication of financial aid and conflicting advice being given to families.

As a result, the Detroit Great Cities Program has developed a theoretical rationale clarifying the role of the school as it relates to the agencies and social work methodologies. This rationale is dynamic, in that it changes as new insights and role definitions develop.

We feel that the public schools, particularly the elementary schools, provide the structures in which social-work functions may best be performed. The encapsulated, or limited and defined, elementary-school *population* and the inclusion within elementary school *boundaries* of a relatively fixed population, offer one of the best field situations presently available. The school has other assets. It is established, it has access to the home, and its records for each child will automatically provide information on a large percentage of the population in the school's boundaries. Such boundaries do include the families of parochial and private students and citizens whose children have gone through school. In these cases, even though the social work contact is not as readily made, at least the boundaries are fixed and provide a localized area for social work operation. The elementary school, therefore, could provide the basis of operations for case-work, group-work and community-work functions. These functions could be operated by school personnel or by public, private, and agency personnel. Yet at the present time, exclusive of this project, Detroit's schools are involved only in limited casework through the Visiting Teacher Program.

The schools provide little in the way of group-work functions. The one best example of group-work therapy presently in the Detroit Schools is the School Behavior Project which uses "Action Teams" of school and agency personnel in work with disturbed children referred by the school. Otherwise, the only existent group-work functions are basically of a recreational and instructional nature and performed, after school, both by Detroit Public School personnel and by agency people from many organizations and institutions. In spite of the school's ideal locus, community organization functions are left almost entirely in the hands of non-school personnel, with the rare exception of the sophisticated administrator who operates in this area to a limited extent.

The Great Cities School Improvement Project is embarked upon activities in all three aspects of social-work functions. With regard to the community organization aspect, the community agent already serves as an organizer in each of the local communities. Thus the school-community agent, particularly the agent in the elementary school, can be a most effective instrument for the performance of the crucial community organization activities as the project develops from its demonstration stage into a program for all schools in depressed urban areas.

With regard to the aspect of group-work services of a recreational and instructional nature, the schools can fill many of the needs of a local community. Adult evening programs offering appropriate up-grading, training, and retraining courses might be conducted on a non-fee or "ability-to-pay" basis in the high schools and junior high schools. At all school levels, but with emphasis at the elementary, parent and youth groups and clubs, meeting informally, could partially fulfill the project's objectives by increasing parent reinforcement of the school program and raising the aspirations of the participants. In addition to organizing and operating these informal groups in the schools, the school-community agent can act as the catalyst in bringing to the schools those group-work services of a recreational, crafts, and character-building nature as already provided by agencies in the community. Further, the school could serve in a coordinating capacity with the agencies which have facilities within the school area, so that services would cover the school evenly without duplication and wasteful expenditure of time and energy.

With regard to the aspect of group work used in rehabilitation of disturbed children, it is obvious that competent, trained group workers and therapists would be more effective than school personnel. In addition, the school setting is one in which most disturbed youngsters have met defeat and failure, and often presents a block to the progress which might be made with group therapy. It may be appropriate, therefore, to use existing neighborhood facilities other than the school building. The school team needs to be involved in these kinds of activities, however, in much the same way as it is involved presently in the work of the School Behavior Project. The school team would continue to be a source of referrals to the therapy group.

The case-work methodology has already been mentioned in the discussion of the role of the visiting teacher. We feel that the full-time utilization of this school social worker in the Great Cities Project schools adds real strength to this dimension of each school's social work functions.

The implication might be drawn, from this emphasis upon a rationale for the school as a social-work agency, that we have a dream that the school should be all things to all people. The answer to this is emphatic: certainly not! The school must concern itself primarily with the academic enhancement of children. Yet, if the school is to prepare all youth for the world of work, and for independent social, economic, and political lives, the school needs to examine its traditional role in the light of past successes and failures. Who can say we have really succeeded with educationally disadvantaged youth in the past? It would seem that both school and society must face, and work to disarm, the "social dynamite" referred to by Dr. Conant in his *Slums and Suburbs*.

Here, the implication stands: it is very possible that the school must be more effective if it expects to produce competent, well-educated young adults. The rationale for incorporation of the social-work methodologies into the school's program is an attempt to enhance the school's effectiveness in an area of great importance, particularly in depressed urban communities, where the effects of a deprived out-of-school life impinge upon the child's in-school life, and limit his ability to learn.

We propose, along with renewed and creative efforts with staff and curriculum, the intensive use of the social work methodologies as a part of the school's daily operation. Acceptance of the concept of the school as a social work agency affords a new opportunity to do preventive rather than remedial work with problems of youth and adults in the local community; with the goal of reinforcing the academic competence of youth. There is no intent to suggest that the schools should or could do this alone. Indeed, cooperation between school and agency is the only feasible solution. The schools, however, are in a strategic position to be the case-finding agency, the referral agency, and the catalytic agency to those groups organized to render appropriate services. In addition, the school is a public facility which needs to be utilized—by individuals and agencies and by the community for the common good.

Evaluation

The Detroit Project is unique in that a full-time evaluator, Dr. William M. Rasschaert, has been assigned to its staff. In initiating the project in Detroit, it was recognized that programs with demonstrated effectiveness should be continued and extended to schools currently uninvolved in the project—with the stipulation that an expanded program could not exceed an annual 10 per cent per student cost increase. Not every part of the project program will remain in use. To meet cost limits, project staff must analyze statistics and data computed and filed during the five-year run, and use its findings to establish a priority list, top-rating the elements of the project program which had the most significant effect in increasing school success of the child with limited background. Recommendations from this priority list will become the program used in extended project activities (3, p. 419).

In the original evaluation design, two types of control schools were used:

Control Type A:

These four schools (two elementary, one junior high, and one senior high school) are in generally the same geographic area of the city as are the experimental schools. The achievement and ability levels of the pupils are quite similar to those of pupils in the experimental schools.

Control Type B:

In this group there are five schools (three elementary, one junior high, and one senior high school) and these are located in obviously different geographic parts of Detroit than the project schools. As measured by Detroit city-wide testing programs, the achievement and ability scores of the pupils in these schools consistently reflect higher levels of attainment.

As part of the total evaluation design, the project staff has prepared a document entitled *A Plan for Evaluating Major Activities in Great Cities School Improvement Programs*. Nine categories of teaching-learning, school-community, and pupil-parent-teacher activities have been considered in terms of the specific (1) nature of each activity, (2) suggested treatment of data accruing from such measurement. Among the broad categories into which all activities are ordered according to their function in the program are pupil achievement, attitude changes, behavioral changes, evaluation of teaching materials and techniques, school-community relations, and school health. Activities in each of these nine categories receive careful evaluation as we attempt to determine to what degree each activity is effective relative to the total program. For instance, in the category of behavioral change, which is most effective, the workshop at which experts speak or the workshop which involves school staff in planning curriculum change? And, relative to the total program, which has proved more effective in educating the child, modification of teacher perception or a more intensive school health program? In other words, where do we put our money to get results?

The Great Cities School Improvement Program has taken advantage of data made available by the various city-wide testing programs—the *Iowa Test of Basic Skills,* the *SCAT-STEP,* and the various intelligence testing programs at several grade levels. In addition, results of achievement and intelligence tests administered to project and control school pupils with tests other than those used city-wide will continue to supply us with more and different kinds of measurement data. Examples of such additional tests are the *California Achievement Tests* and the *Lorge-Thorndike Tests of Intelligence, Verbal and Non-Verbal.*

In addition to comparing pupils in project schools to pupils in Control Types A and B schools, we also intend to "follow" project-school children and measure their individual growth in ability and achievement areas over the next three years. Similarly, we are evaluating the children who attend our summer schools to attempt to determine if this type of enrichment effects improvement over a full school year of pupil-work. In terms of evaluation, the over-all pattern of this project will include two methods of looking at results with children:

1. Measurement of pupil growth in project schools as interpreted relative to two different control groups; one group in a depressed area very similar to that in which the project schools are located, and one group in an area which is very substantial and middle-class.

2. Examination of growth in selected characteristics from one period to another; this could mean using subpopulations and doing individual and group measurements or using the case study method with selected individuals.

In addition to the above, school and sociological base-line data have been collected regarding attendance, failure, lack of kindergarten experience, delinquency and youth and adult crime, and population density and transiency in each school's service area. A *Pupil Information and Attitude Inventory* was also devised by project teachers and administrators and administered to the children in the project schools from grades 4 through 12. This survey, after compilation of the data, is a part of each child's cumulative record.

Two instruments have been devised to examine the crucial factors of teacher information and teacher attitude. The *Teacher Information Questionnaire* was constructed by a group of sixteen classroom teachers in the project schools. This survey has been administered to all the teachers in the experimental and control schools. Frequency distribution and second-order runs with selected questionnaire items have been tabulated at the University of Michigan Computer Center.

Dr. Henry Meyer and Miss Donna MacLeod, from the University of Michigan, School of Social Work, designed an instrument in 1959, entitled *Values Questionnaire,* for measuring the attitudes of social workers. In 1960, Drs. Meyer and Litwak and project staff members modified this instrument to make it appropriate for administration to approximately 750 experimental and control school teachers in the Detroit Great Cities Project. This modified instrument titled *What Do You Think About These Social Questions?* measures nine dimensions (see Table 1).

Table I.

Value Dimension Number	Value Dimension Title
I	Individual worth versus system goals
II	Personal liberty versus societal control
III	Group responsibility versus individual responsibility
IV	Security-satisfaction versus struggle-suffering-denial
V	Relativism-secularism versus absolutism-sacredness
VI	Innovation-change versus traditionalism
VII	Changeable human nature versus inherent human-fatalism
VIII	Diversity-heterogeneity versus consensus-homogeneity-conformity
IX	Interdependence versus individual autonomy

The values questionnaire's seventy-two questions, plus the information survey's eighteen questions, have been processed through the Computer Center at the University of Michigan. Although we can acknowledge that the data from these instruments have most significant implications for the project's program and perhaps for education in Detroit, any reporting of these data as such would tend to contaminate seriously the results of the projected post-tests, particularly in our control schools.

Indeed, the midpoint of a five-year demonstration project is an awkward time for reporting in detail the significant results of evaluation and research. Base-line data have been gathered and are in the process of being analyzed and interpreted. Yet we have only subjective evidence that we have increased the competence of particular individuals and groups of children, youth and adults.

We have data to indicate that IQ scores have been substantially increased in certain situations; that achievement scores have been materially affected by specialized coaching and enrichment programs; that parent participation in school and after-school programming is far beyond our expectations; that public and private agency involvement and cooperation is increasing rapidly as these agencies come to know the objectives of the project.

We know all these things, yet we do not know, at this point in time, the lasting effect of changes in IQ and achievement, nor the degree of reinforcement of the school by parents and agencies, nor the positive change in the aspirations of parents and of children. We know we are providing significant service to the children and the families of the children. But only depth evaluation over a sufficient period of time can tell us those aspects of our program which are appropriate for movement to school areas beyond the demonstration project.

In addition, therefore, to the evaluation procedures mentioned above, it is important that we examine in detail those larger educational and sociological aspects of the project which will be determinants in movement of the project through the school system. To assist us in the examination of three of these aspects, Dr. Eugene Litwak, School of Social Work, University of Michigan, has prepared three working papers. These papers are:

1. "Notes on the Relationship Between Family, Educational Achievement and Good Citizenship," July 25, 1961.
2. "Notes on the Relationship Between Neighborhood, Educational Achievement, and Good Citizenship," July 31, 1961.
3. "Notes on the Relationship Between Administrative Behavior, Educational Achievement and Good Citizenship," August 22, 1961.

The concepts which have been delineated in these documents and reviewed and modified by project staff and Drs. Litwak and Meyer, will be tested in a research program involving the project elementary schools, two control schools and two elementary schools outside the project. With the financial support of the Detroit Area Study of the University of Michigan and funds from additional sources, interview schedules and questionnaires are being prepared and staff organized to test the hypothesis outlined in the working papers. As Dr. Litwak says.

The full and systematic exploration of these problems is a necessary prerequisite for setting up programs which will be meaningful to the Great Cities Improvement Project. The simultaneous consideration of all three memorandum involving family, neighborhood, and administrative behavior should eventually permit the establishment of better relations between school and community (2).

Conclusion

What are the "short-term" forecasts for the Great Cities Project in Detroit? It is believed that a considerably larger number of children attending project schools will leave them with positive self-images, higher goals, greater scholastic achievement, and improved citizenship; they are expected to be more adequately prepared for continuing school or going to work—independent rather than dependent citizens.

It should be stressed that the Detroit Great Cities Project is not unique in its premises or in its purposes. Individual teachers and schools in Detroit and across the nation are striving to meet the needs of the child with limited background. With little organized help, and no extra funds, their work has been done with dedication and enthusiasm. Such efforts are inspirational, but they are often a stopgap, and we cannot hope that they will resolve a dilemma which has grown to such proportions that it can be met only with concerted, total-community effort. Now, as the community becomes fully aware of wasted manpower, the hard core of unemployed, the high-school drop-out and his inability in most cases to compete for a place in today's overcrowded, skill-demanding job market, it will turn more and more to educators, first for explanations, and then for positive and workable solutions. And educators must be able to provide these solutions, by bridging the gap between what the schools now offer and what life with increasing technology and urbanization demands of an individual.

And that gap does exist. In spite of the fact that more youth are finishing high school and going on to college, increasing numbers of young men and women, including a good percentage of the most able and most intelligent youth, do not find what they need in school, do not learn, lose purpose and direction, and drop out. They are abetted by indecisive parents, tolerated by an apathetic community, often tacitly disestablished by the school.

Certainly we have a commitment as a society to these youth. We should live up to that commitment, preferably before the sad decision to drop out is made. We should consider ways to prevent this crisis. It is far more wasteful of human and fiscal resources to wait until rehabilitation is necessary; particularly when we know the ways we must go to reduce drastically the number of drop-outs, and to make schooling more effective as preparation for life.

Perhaps the most significant thing about the Detroit Great Cities Project, and similar projects in many great cities, is that it stands as a statement of need, as a formal attempt on the part of a superintendent and a board of education to establish a structure which has the funds, the personnel and the support to do a thorough job of proving that all children, no matter how difficult their situation may be, can be well-educated and positively motivated.

I will close with a short list of observations about youth in today's society, made by Professor Earl Kelley (1). He states that all adults, and educators in particular, need to keep always before them these points:

1. Our culture is in jeopardy unless we can adequately care for our young.
2. Our young people are all right when we get them. If all is not well with them, it is due to what has happened to them in an adult-managed world.
3. If youth have not been too badly damaged by the life that has been thrust upon them, they enjoy and desire a good society as much as we do.
4. In urban society, our young live under more difficult circumstances than they used to.
5. The amount of juvenile delinquency in any community is a measure of that community's lack of concern for its young.
6. There is really no valid, responsible place in our urban communities for youth. They are a displaced segment of our society.
7. A place must be made for them and it seems to me that the only feasible place is the school.

It is our hope that the Detroit Great Cities School Improvement Project, in consultation and coordination with other Great Cities projects, can make schools in depressed urban areas the really "feasible place" for youth to grow to independent competent citizenship.

REFERENCES

1. Kelley, Earl C., *In Defense of Youth,* Englewood Cliffs, N. J.: Prentice-Hall, 1962, p. 145.
2. Litwak, Fugene, "Notes on Relationships Between Administrative Behavior, Educational Achievement, and Good Citizenship," mimeographed working paper. University of Michigan, Ann Arbor, August 22, 1961, p. 13.
3. Mitchell, Charles, "The Culturally Deprived—A Matter of Concern," *Childh. Educ.,* May 1962, 38 (9):412-415, 419.
4. Rosenthal, Robert, and Fode, Kermit L., "The Effect of Experimenter Bias on the Performance of the Albino Rat," unpublished manuscript, University of North Dakota, University, n.d.
5. Taylor, Harold, "The Whole Child: A Fresh Look," *Saturday Review, Educational Supplement,* December 10, 1961, pp. 42-43.

Henry Saltzman | The Community School in the Urban Setting

That the public schools in America cannot shut themselves off from the communities they serve has been a long-accepted tenet of our educational philosophy. As a result of the thinking and experimentation of men like Francis W. Parker (7), John Dewey (6), Joseph K. Hart (5), and Henry Barnard (1), generations of school men have sought to increase the points of contact between their schools and their communities, to make the life within the school meaningful in terms of the life outside the school, and to consciously seek to use the school as an instrument for community improvement.

A "community school," therefore, has been variously defined (2) in terms of:

Its pursuit of the solution of community problems.

The extent to which its curriculum is centered on the study of the economic, social, governmental, and political activities of the community.

The special services it renders to both children and adults.

The extent to which the school building is used as a community center.

The responsibility assumed for adult education.

The scope of the vocational-training program.

As educators have developed various aspects of the community school, four main types have emerged (4).

Type 1: The school with a community-centered curriculum. In such a program, the school sees the community as a "resource for the enrichment of the program of the school . . . community resources . . . also help determine the kind of learning experiences children have" (4, p. 50). Community improvement activities do not necessarily grow out of the studies, but the emphasis is placed on understanding the community and making the curriculum meaningful.

Type 2: The school with a vocations-centered curriculum. The school here uses the opportunities provided by the community for work experiences. Counseling, adult training and retraining programs, and supervision of working students are usually included along with the preparation for employment. Most vocational schools more or less follow this pattern.

Type 3: The community center function. In this type of school, the emphasis is put upon developing the fullest use of the physical facilities of the school by various community groups. Most of the schools in urban areas to which the label "community" has been affixed, are of this type.

Type 4: The community-service program. Here the aim is to improve the conditions of life in the community. Children and adults study local problems. Efforts are made to coordinate the activities of many agencies with the school's program. Here the school deliberately sets out to do community-development work.

The essential unity of the school and its environment is the philosopical basis for these four concepts of the community school. Until this unity is established, the school cannot begin to feel the pulse of the community or build a program which will be relevant and realistic.

To develop such unity, many authors have stressed the obligation which school administrators assume for analyzing and understanding the communities they serve (3). Using survey techniques, school personnel learn the problems of the communities and their resources, and then design curriculum, special services, and community-center activities accordingly.

Most community-school proponents assume that educators have the capacity to understand the needs of their communities and that they have both the imagination and the willingness to meet these needs. These assumptions are generally proven correct in situations where the educator not only understands the community, but *identifies* with it. There is an important distinction to be made here. *Understanding is cerebral; identification is partly visceral.* Either can be present without the other. One without the other, however, precludes the creation of the community school. Where both are present in the educators, community schools flourish.

Wherever the social-class level of community and educator are similar, both understanding and identification can be developed. For the teachers and administrators who work in communities whose dominant values they either hold or respect, whose child-rearing practices they approve (and tend to follow themselves), whose margin of economic security enables the parents to take an active interest in their children's education and the welfare of the school, and/or where the education level or motivation of the parents is adequate for them to work with school authorities with some competence, the obstacles to developing community schools are few. Under these circumstances, the educator can go beyond understanding the community; he can identify with it.

Thus, there will be relatively little difficulty in establishing the community school in urban middle-class neighborhoods. Where we are having our greatest difficulty is in those neighborhoods of the city where the middle class teacher confronts the lower class child and parent and/or those who differ from him with regard to culture, ethnicity, or race.

In the classrooms of these schools we discover the antitheses of middle-class expectation:

Pupil transiency rather than stability.

High percentages of reading and arithmetic retardation rather than strong mastery of the fundamentals.

Weak rather than strong motivation.

Above average drop-out rates.

Serious discipline problems.

Uncorrected health defects which impair learning.

In the homes we often find the single-parent family, the unemployed father, low educational levels, and high adult- and infant-mortality rates.

These conditions, the fruits of poverty, are the by-products of our slum neighborhoods, often voiceless, disorganized, and alienated from the institutions which hope to help them.

In such a confrontation, understanding is difficult to achieve. To ask for something beyond this—identification—is to ask a great deal.

But until we at least can approximate the identification felt by the middle-class teacher in a middle-class community, or the country-born teacher in the rural community, the effort to build urban community schools will be half-hearted and largely unsuccessful.

The barriers to real communication across social-class lines are many and subtle. The very words we use, their enunciation, the rate at which we speak, the clothes we wear, etc., all can contribute to separation, suspicion and misunderstanding. In such a setting a well-meant gesture can be misinterpreted, good intentions may be regarded as condescension, criticism may be taken for prejudice. The ability of the school staff to communicate with the people of the slum will determine the extent to which a broad, varied, and effective school program can be developed. The social-class barrier between the school and the slum is a formidable one and must be taken into account in the structuring of community schools.

We are often told that we need to have the "best" teachers in these schools. This is an easy and basically meaningless panacea to offer. Certainly we can do much to increase the understanding of future teachers with regard to the slum and its problems. We can, as will be discussed later in this paper, insure better communication. But personalities differ

—and to this extent, the abilities of teachers to professionally identify with the communities will vary.

We all know teachers and principals in slum schools who have succeeded, by some magic of mind and personality, where so many others have failed. While we must try to educate others to emulate these great ones, I doubt that we can ever do this effectively with enough people, given the many intangibles involved, to meet the needs of the city.

The urban community school will always face the fact of teachers who fail to understand enough, fail to identify sympathetically, and tend to perform perfunctorily in the classroom. With this expectation, or perhaps, certainly, we must try to compensate by refining the school's ability to project the understanding, the concern, the warmth and the skill of the masterful teachers.

If the school, as an *institution* can be structured so that it is recognized as an authority that cares about the neighborhood and its children, and one which can translate this concern into action that is seen as significant by the *community,* we can hope for an urban community school. As such, it will depend less upon virtuoso performances on the part of its talented personnel, and more upon the shape of its collective action. Thus, the school's activities will be designed:

To give the talented personnel the widest scope.

To give the less talented opportunities for developing understanding and identification.

To provide the maximum opportunities for interaction between classroom teachers and parents.

In a sense, this school will create its own in-service program by the nature of its special programs.

Conspicuous collective school action depends heavily on a principal who is flexible, and who understands and works with community needs more than with bureaucratic prescriptions. Without him, all the formulae and conceptualizations of the community school are meaningless. From him, can come insight and know-how which really make the community school work. We are convinced that such principals can be developed systematically. This becomes the first step in the creation of the urban community school.

School Planning and the Community School Principal

The following discussion is based upon two assumptions: (1) The planning for community schools in slum areas must begin *before* the design and construction of the school building. (2) Present procedures of school planning makes for inadequate preparation of the administrative talent required by the urban slum school.

Pressures upon school construction divisions in our cities are so great that they are being forced increasingly to build schools on an assembly line basis. Factors contributing to such pressures are the large numbers of obsolete central city schools, the rising expectations of the urban population with regard to education, the increasing mobility of urbanites with the consequent redistribution of the school age population, and, the effects of urban renewal programs in shifting population and in changing land use patterns.

Short of time, money and personnel, the school systems are forced to grind out mass-produced schools. Too often, the fact that the school will serve a lower-class neighborhood may not be deeply considered by the planners. We have noted that the class barrier is difficult to pierce for those who work directly with the children; this communication barrier is even more serious for those insulated from the community. Designing schools with inadequate reference to the needs, strengths, and aspirations of the community is the very antithesis of the community-school concept.

Therefore, we must develop a planning procedure for community schools which will:

1. Supply the architect with insights into the nature of the community's problems, with the thinking of the community itself regarding its school, and with a total program around which he can wrap a building.

2. Put the future principal of this building into the position of "honest broker" between the community and the school planners.

3. Recognize the existence of other specialized agencies, public and private, which also work with the community and consider their function in the community school's program.

These objectives might be accomplished by bringing together four major urban agencies (8)—the Board of Education, the Urban Renewal Agency, the social agencies which expend public funds in the gray areas, and the health and welfare council. These groups are not coequal. Only three are in a position to commit funds and staffs on a long-range basis to the effective planning and operation of community-based programs. The health and welfare council is strategic, however, because it has the capacity for recommending to its member agencies participation and commitment to the program.

The basic commitment of each agency would be as follows:

The board of education would select key school staff members (principal, community coordinator, guidance coordinator) two years before the new community school is opened; agree to plan the physical structure of the school to follow as closely as possible the recommendations of the planning group; keep the school staff free to participate actively and, during the planning period, on a full-time basis with the other agencies and citizens' groups who will have a share in the community served by this school; make available from its files the data needed by the other agencies to set up coordinated programs.

The housing and redevelopment authority would make available its community survey data to other agencies; adjust timetables and program objectives to harmonize more closely with the plans of the other agencies; make its professional staff available to the planning group to consider physical plant requirements of the community school; through planning, insure against major dislocation of population which would render null the specific plans of the agencies; modify its construction plans to fit neighborhood needs as these are expressed by local citizens and agencies.

Public agencies would make staff available for regulation consultation and planning; introduce new action programs to meet specific problems; adopt more flexible staffing practices to permit tie-in with other programs.

The health and welfare federation would survey the gray area to discover which agencies are already making major commitments of time and staff; develop interagency programs which give high priority to the areas; and insure, if possible, long-term commitments from agencies to stay involved in the area.

What might result from such an effort?

1. A school would be built whose facilities would be available for use by social agencies, health agencies, and interested citizen groups on a seven-days-a-week, twelve-months-a-year basis.

2. The staffs of every agency involved would find new and significant roles to play in a number of new settings.

3. Much closer cooperation would result between schools and agencies.

4. Public agency support would be strongly felt by social workers from the voluntary agencies.

5. Fuller sharing of data would be facilitated.

6. There would be a neighborhood base of operations for many centralized agencies.

7. Closer contacts among citizens and agencies would ensue.

8. Preventive programs could more easily be launched.

9. Each institution could establish a closer tie with its neighborhood.

10. A climate of mutual interest among agencies would aid the trial of new programs.

11. Through closer contact with many institutions and agencies, professionals would broaden their understanding and develop more generalized skills than heretofore. Thus, a new breed of generalists might arise among social workers. This could correct the atomizing effects of the overspecialization now evident.

12. Opportunities would open for observation of and communication with children and adults in a wide variety of situations.

13. All workers would come to have a neighborhood "bias" rather than an agency bias.

At the center of this process will have been the key staff of the future school. They will have been liberally educated with regard to the community and their colleagues in other agencies. Working with committees of citizens and professionals, they would have considered all aspects of the school's program and be in a position to make specific recommendations to the architect.[1]

This group would open the new school and administer it for at least the first few years of its operation. It is difficult to believe that, having been involved in such a community-planning process, these administrators could not then develop an effective community-centered program. Certainly their understanding of the community would be deepened and a strong sense of identification could develop without the loss of precious years.

While we have described a process which basically involves the advance selection of administrators for new schools, we recognize the problem of making existent schools community oriented. Here again, the advance selection of a new principal might be useful, or the temporary release of the assigned principal. In either case, six months of community involvement, free of school responsibility but tied to the design of a community school program, might be useful.

The Intelligence Function of the Community School

Observation of community schools presently functioning in several urban slum or gray areas reveals two inadequacies which narrow the effectiveness of otherwise good programs. First, there is a failure to sys-

---

[1] Under a pilot program, Community Planning for Community Schools, being carried out in Detroit, subcommittees of lay people and professionals worked out recommendations for a new high school in the following categories: employment; home and family; environmental factors in physical health and safety; mental health; recreation, group work, social functions and physical education; individual values; school-and-community relations; civic and political activity; auxiliary services; and educational trends. For further information, contact Dr. Arthur Parkllan, Board of Education, 1354 Broadway, Detroit, Michigan.

tematically collect a variety of information about the school child and feed this information back to the classroom teacher and to other professional personnel. Second, there is no feedback procedure for enriching the daily curriculum of the school from the community activities carried on after the regular school day.

We have already emphasized the need for school liaison with other agencies. The specialization of these agencies is such that each may possess valuable insights into the family and the child as these relate to the agencies' interests. But specialization has also led to the scatteration of this information. Access to this information might provide the teacher with knowledge which could be translated into more effective classroom work. Without fuller knowledge, we can only pay lip service to our determination to educate the "whole child."

The teacher's major sources of information are her own observations and the school's guidance and administration staff. This provides too narrow a base for fully understanding the child and his home situation. The urban community school should experiment with a variety of procedures for the collection and evaluation of data which are relevant to the educator's purpose. It may be necessary, for example, to schedule the guidance department of the school for *regular* case conferences with non-school agency personnel and to assign responsibility for transmitting suitable information to the classroom teacher.

In several cities, slum schools are providing varied and useful after-school activities for children and adults. For example, in the Couzens School in Detroit, about seventy such activities are scheduled each week. Many of these programs are led by the parents themselves. Many of the activities are related to aspects of the regular school program—current events, homemaking, science, art, etc. Because the urban community school will continue to expand the range of after school activities, this program itself should serve as the basis for the expansion of the school's information about individual children.

The teachers and lay people who direct these programs are in an especially strategic position to observe children in relatively relaxed and informal settings. Their observation of the strengths, weaknesses, special talents, and interests of the children could usefully guide the classroom teacher in offering individually designed opportunities for expression of skills and interest within the regular curriculum, *if the teacher knew about them*. At the present time, this feedback also is largely unstructured and incidental. A community school must eliminate the communications barrier between its school program and its community-centered activities. The performance of this intelligence function should be considered a vital part of the community school's program warranting special staffing and scheduling.

A similar weakness exists with regard to curriculum development. We have noted that the community school needs to make its curriculum as meaningful as possible in relation to the neighborhood it serves. Where the principal is knowledgeable and sensitive to community needs, the after school program will reflect this. This after-school program will represent a part of the collective action of the school to meet community needs.

The substance of these programs should also serve to enrich the school's regular curriculum. A two-way reinforcement of learning would thus be possible. The classroom could contribute to the child's skill, understanding, and interest in various after school activities. These activities, in turn, can expand and enrich the curriculum and children's skills. To carry out a community centered program without regard for the school curriculum is to create activities for activities' sake rather than for the improvement of learning. The after school program should not only offer useful educational and recreational programs, but should be intimately connected to the regular curriculum.

A variety of ways might be explored to do this. One could involve the assignment of a good teacher with an interest in curriculum innovation who would spend a large part of her time observing the after-school programs and develop curriculum units based upon these programs. Such a person would be responsible for meeting with regular teachers to present this material and to explain the reasons for their use. She would help to more fully orient the classroom teacher to the nature and scope of the after school program.

Another method might involve the double platooning of teachers so that some report late enough in the day to carry on after-school programs. The teachers would alternate, thus providing the experience of actual responsibility. Such direct contact might enable teachers to add aspects of the community program to their regular classroom work.

Summary

The development of urban community schools in deprived neighborhoods will involve:

1. A multi-agency planning process.

2. The development of understanding and identification with the community through the advance placement of principals and key staff.

3. Programs of collective school action that project the school's awareness of and concern for the needs of the community.

4. A structured plan for gathering intelligence about children and families.

5. A feedback mechanism for curriculum enrichment and development.

REFERENCES

1. Brubacher, J. S., *Henry Barnard in Education,* New York: McGraw-Hill, 1931.
2. Cook, L. A., and Cook, E. F., *A Sociological Approach to Education,* New York: McGraw-Hill, 1950.
3. Goodykoontz, Bess, "Selected Studies Relating to Community Schools," *National Society for the Study of Education Yearbook,* Volume 52, Part II, Chicago: University of Chicago Press, 1953.
4. Hanna, Paul R., and Naslund, Robert A., "The Community School Defined," *National Society for the Study of Education Yearbook,* Vol. 52, Part II, Chicago: University of Chicago Press, 1953.
5. Hart, J. K., *Democracy in Education,* New York: Appleton-Century, 1918.
6. Mayhew, K. C., and Edwards, Anna C., *The Dewey School,* New York: Appleton-Century, 1936.
7. Parker, Francis W., *Talks on Pedagogues,* New York: E. L. Kellogg, 1894.
8. Saltzman, Henry, "The Great Cities Program," *in* Thomas Shirrard (Ed.), *Community Organization,* New York: Columbia University Press, 1961.

A. Harry Passow | Education in Depressed Areas

The work conference united for two weeks two groups with a professional interest in the complex problems of education in centers, especially in their depressed areas.[1] One group, the conferees, consisted of "school people" with immediate and direct responsibility for operating programs effectively from day to day and for providing leadership for long-range educational planning. The second group, the speakers, included behavioral and social scientists disposed to separate from the aggregate of school problems those aspects they could study systematically. These specialists were asked to report research dealing with a particular phase of education in depressed urban areas, to present theoretical assumptions, and to confront the practitioners with the implications for educational planning. The hope was that such a bringing together of theorists and practitioners for two weeks of intensive interaction would generate, first, understanding of each other's concerns and ways of working and, second, better formulation of problems and programs.

Academic achievement and personal attitudes towards self and community—these focused much of the discussion. The most central questions were of this order: What are the significant differences between those students who do and those who do not achieve academically, have high educational and vocational aspirations, and conform to broad societal norms? What causes these differences? What will overcome the academic and other deficiencies which plague children and youth from depressed areas? What is the school's particular role of prevention and rehabilitation? There is the temptation to explain these differences solely in socioeconomic terms—middle-class children achieve, in general, at a higher level than lower-class children; teachers tend to be middle-class oriented, as is the curriculum of the school. However, the conference discussions

---

[1] I am indebted to Mr. David Elliott for his assistance in the preparation of this chapter. Mr. Eliott's notes and summaries were especially helpful.

rejected as too narrow and sterile an analysis which deals only with socio-economic status, only with ethnic or racial minority status, or only with in-migration and urbanization as separate and dominant stands. Some general ideas emerged from the discussions, which seem basic to many other proposals or hypotheses.

Coordinated, Multi-Level Approaches Are Needed

Many images might clarify the various distinct, interrelated levels of involvement and social organization which offer explanations, plans, and programs for overcoming gaps in individual achievement and motivation. One possibility is to view the young learner as the bullseye of a series of concentric forces which influence his attainment. With the child at the hub, the concentric spheres might be these:

The child, with his genetic potential; his experiential background; his stage of intellectual, emotional, and personality development; his attitudes and values; his self-image and view of himself in relationship to others.

The family of the child, as well as his other immediate primary (peer) groups; ethnic and racial group characteristics; newcomer or old-resident; socio-economic and educational level; family stability, including the absence or presence of positive male models or matriarchy; extent of acculturation to urban setting.

The neighborhood in which the child and his family live; its religious, social, political, and economic characteristics; the nature of the housing available; the relationships with other neighborhoods, in the city; the sense of social health.

The school and *the classroom* which the child attends; student population, staff, program; the resources available in implementing the program; teacher characteristics and expectations; curriculum goals; the school climate.

Other agencies and institutions active in the neighborhood and the larger urban setting, such as community centers; welfare agencies, health and medical facilities, public and private; personnel, programs, organizational characteristics; working relationships among institutions and agencies; power and decision-making forces.

City and larger metropolitan area—social, economic, and political characteristics; relationships among various units and divisions within the area; relationships with surrounding areas; effectiveness in solving problems.

Larger regional, national, and international setting—social, political, economic characteristics; relation of its philosophy to local education goals and budgets.

Each of these major spheres is constructed of intricate details. For example, economic conditions depend on such factors as the labor market, discrimination in employment, availability of trained personnel, automation, industrial output, over-all business developments, international conditions. The various levels are, of course, interrelated, somewhat mutually limiting and equally significant for planners, because the plans cannot be fully implemented by operations at any single level. For instance, classroom modifications by a single teacher may be futile unless supported by the climate of the school, the neighborhood, and the family.

Since planning and involvement take place at different levels, coordinated efforts are required of many groups, agencies, and institutions. There are limits to the possible impact of a program at any level if that program ignores the multidimensions of the problems of urban life. Several papers emphasized the need for integrated planning aimed at altering the conditions in the school, the home, the community, and the urban area as a whole, involving health, educational, social, economic, political, and religious agencies and institutions in the process. This idea of "multiphase approach" does not mean that smaller, more restricted efforts are doomed to failure but, rather, that such plans must be weighed realistically in terms of their potential.

The Health and Welfare Council of the Baltimore Area sees the implications for action to capitalize on the total resources of the community as follows:

> . . . it will require a *comprehensive and coordinated* approach rather than a piecemeal attack;
> . . . it must envision *experimentation, integration, self-analysis, and innovation* as well as coordination and intensification of existing services;
> . . . while leadership must come from those agencies which offer direct services to people, successful prosecution will require *wide community support* and commitment;
> . . . if real impact upon serious community problems is to be made, *the effort must be carried beyond the area and time of a single demonstration* (2).

Differentiation Between Preventative and Remedial Programs

Throughout the conference, it was emphasized that in the search for factors that influence achievement, distinctions need to be made between practices which are primarily *preventative* and *developmental* and those which are essentially *compensatory* and *remedial*. For example, at the junior high school level, academic retardation may be so severe that programs must be mainly remedial in nature, to compensate for past school failures. With the younger child in nursery, in kindergarten, or even first grade, measures are more likely to be preventative in nature, designed to prepare the pupil for school achievement and the avoidance of remedial procedures. The philosophy behind a program—prevention or remedy —affects the points of emphasis, the methods to be used, the organizational arrangements and the levels of involvement.

The preventative aspects imply modifications and adaptations of programs and services to help the child hurdle his educational handicaps, cultural limitations, inarticulateness, short attention span, underdeveloped abstract-thinking abilities, lack of motivation for academic success, and similar deprivations that hobble a child's scholastic development. Unless steps are taken to compensate for these shortcomings, retardation and failure inevitably will raise a demand for remedial projects. Because success in reading and other language arts constitutes the key to academic progress, most programs stress methods, materials, special personnel, and other audio-visual and guidance services to improve as the verbal and other basic skills.

Remedial services have many different aspects. Most familiar is remedial reading instruction for pupils who lack facility in this field. Reading clinics may be established for the diagnosis and treatment of severe reading disabilities. Special service personnel of many different kinds may work either with children or with classroom teachers. For example, the New York City system assigns to schools in depressed urban areas teacher-specialists in remedial reading, science, mathematics, and core curriculum; guidance specialists, teacher trainers, Puerto Rican coordinators, behavior attendance counselors, and substitute auxiliary teachers (Spanish-speaking teachers who aid the regular classroom teachers with English instruction). Dade County, Florida, employs a team of a certificated American teacher and two bi-lingual Cuban-refugee teacher aides to work with approximately sixty Cuban-born youngsters whose English is too limited for the regular classroom. Similarly, New Haven has appointed "helping teachers" who are relieved of some of their regular teaching assignments to provide leadership for a teaching team to work with a specific group of students. The helping teacher works with other teachers in the development of materials and methods of instruction. These programs illustrate how supplementary personnel can aid in upgrading reading achievement by improved instruction and remedial assistance.

The Quincy, Illinois, program of enrichment in the primary grades is essentially preventative in intent. It seeks to determine whether more time with a single teacher, an extended kindergarten day, and work with parents will make a difference, especially in reading and in attitudes toward school. Will such a program reduce the number and severity of behavioral problems, preferably before they become delinquency? Many children see themselves as failures, thanks to early defeat in school. The lethargy, negative self-image, and loneliness patterns lead to further failure and eventually hostility, escapism, and aggression as the child grows older. At the kindergarten-primary level, the problems are perceived as lack of those success experiences which contribute to positive self-concepts. Early thwarting of deficiencies, it is hypothesized, may avoid the need for remedial services later.

Building Early Readiness for School Work

Several papers focused on the need for programs to develop certain intellectual, language, and learning traits in children to help them anticipate and handle school tasks. Professor Deutsch emphasized the factors in the pre-school milieu which sentence the lower-class, deprived child of impoverished family to almost certain initial failure. Thus, the negative concept of school is reinforced. Professor Goldberg suggested that the school may be the most accessible place to breach this circular negative-reinforcement process and to compensate for the ineptness toward learning.

Action guides emerged as follows: Early intervention programs, such as nursery and pre-kindergarten classes, day-care centers, and similar pre-school arrangements should aim to promote readiness for formal school instruction. School-centered compensatory activities, from nursery through primary grades, would provide experiences generally absent from the home and neighborhood of disadvantaged children. These would attempt to offset the experiential poverty that affects what Deutsch calls the "formal, contentual, and attitudinal systems" of the child. Educators would adapt school programs, materials, teaching methods, and organization to differences in children's learning styles and cultural expectations, rather than treating all differences as handicaps and deficiencies. Various curriculum modifications aim at broadening the child's experential base and increasing his ability to express himself verbally. Parents should be involved in an educational program beamed at a higher level of home management and child care, at increasing the parent's desire and skills for enriching the background of the child with a minimum of disruption of ongoing family life. Direct help will be channeled through pre-school curricula, possibly through increased use of educational television and other media for communicating with busy parents.

To sum up, promising ways of overcoming immaturity are embodied in enriched pre-school and kindergarten activities designed to develop auditory and visual discrimination, verbal expressive ability, sustained attention, observation skills, ability to follow directions, and a generally receptive learning style. Beyond this stage, the follow-up in primary years must feature study and experimentation with revised methods for teaching reading; increased use of different materials; emphasis on verbal and symbolic experiences; small group and individualized instruction; adaptation of methods to different learning styles. Such programs may require postponement of formal instruction in favor of developing learning-how-to-learn skills and motivation for successful achievement in reading and arithmetic. The need for pre-school education of both children and parents is quite clear; the structure of such programs is not quite so clear. Preventative programs rich in materials, day-care centers or publicly supported nursery schools, early school attendance, parent education programs, and similar efforts would demand either multi-agency coordination or a drastic expansion of present school functions. To be resolved would be the problems of funds and facilities, plus recruiting and training personnel whose roles would contrast with those of present teachers.

Speeding Acculturation to Urban Life

Professor Ravitz pointed out the cultural differences between recent in-migrants and established city residents and the consequent cultural conflicts. Just as the reasons for the various waves of immigration in the past varied, so the impetus for migration from rural areas to cities varies. Speaking of Southern Appalachian migrants, Porter pointed out that while they are white, native, Protestant Americans of several generations' standing, they are still different "in speech, in dress, in culture, in habits and mores, in education, in social status, in work experience, and in health" (4). The impact of the required adjustments may subject such a family to "cultural shock" as grim as any foreigner's.

Rural-urban migration breeds one set of problems; race and nationality create others. Ausubel maintained that ego development among segregated Negroes suffers from "differences in interpersonal relations, in opportunities for and methods of acquiring status, in prescribed age, sex, class, and occupational roles, in approved kinds of personality traits, and in the amount and type of achievement motivation that are socially sanctioned for individuals of a given age, sex, class and occupation." The psychological, emotional, attitudinal, aspirational unity of the child who grows up in the depressed area—what has been called the "slum complex"—enters the classroom. But, there are other behavioral aspects of children from depressed areas: the realities of life have matured him faster in certain respects; he may be more vigorous and spontaneous in expressing his emotions; his language may be more colorful, if less grammatical; and he may have learned the strengths which come from group support and cohesiveness.

How can the school contribute most effectively to the urbanization of the new arrival? How can it acculturate the lower-class child—teach him middle-class skills so that he can cope with the problems of living and earning a living in the middle-class-dominated city? Two answers come from Wilmington and New York. The Wilmington Public Schools project has highlighted human relations, in terms of diagnostic techniques and instruments to help children understand and develop skills as group members. The focus of classroom activities has been on helping children develop concepts about family, neighborhood, groups and community as a basis for improved behavior in social situations. The 5-year Puerto Rican Study in New York City created for teachers published guides and resource units which melded learnings about living in the city with the traditional basic skills required for success in school.

Changing the School and Neighborhood Climates

Professors Havighurst and Wilson both examined the effects of social class composition of the school neighborhood on the behavior of both the students and teachers. Both agreed that predominantly lower-class neighborhoods produce schools in which children achieve less well and have lower aspirations, both educationally and vocationally. Havighurst argued that students of the sociology and psychology of education concur that "the fact of attending a lower-class school does have something to do with the lower academic achievement of the pupils from that school." Wilson presented evidence of lower-class areas and described some of the impact of school climate as it affected the attitudes of students and their aspirations. Havighurst, concluding that neighborhoods with too low a "status ratio" (that is, too small a proportion of middle-class to lower-class children) tend to produce inferior results, suggested that planners do more to develop all-class communities and mixed-class schools. Some individuals accepted this documented evidence, but expressed caution about the propriety and the possible consequences of the school's attempting to alter these conditions.

The school may choose from several courses of action: making drastic internal improvements to enable itself to function as a lever for upgrading the standards of the area as a whole; or serving as the catalyst for "social urban renewal." Perhaps an excellent illustration of the former approach is the Banneker Group schools of St. Louis, under the leadership of Dr. Samuel Shepard, Jr., assistant superintendent. Dr. Shepard administers the twenty-three elementary schools in one of the city's most depressed areas with a population 95 per cent Negro. Except for four "borrowed" teachers who help prepare materials and charts and who participate in the guidance aspect, the Banneker program operates without extra personnel or financial resources. In a sense, Banneker is not a program but rather a continuing challenge to the entire community—children, parents, teachers, administrators, and others—to strive to do better because they are capable of doing better now.

By literally saturating the district with parent meetings, communications of all kinds, and radio programs, Dr. Shepard has influenced significantly the community's attitudes toward the importance of education and toward understanding the need for higher school achievement. In each school, assemblies, contests, field trips, and radio programs (including a mythical character named "Mr. Achiever") urge children to attend regularly and to work for higher accomplishments. Beginning with the signing of a "Parent's Pledge of Cooperation," parents are advised how to help their children schedule homework time, how to provide proper facilities and atmosphere for home study, how to "get tough" about finishing homework. "Hints for Helpful Parents" itemizes suggestions for parents. Children in the area are surrounded by the motto: "Success in School Is My Most Important Business," with achievement charts for extra reminders. Non-school agencies allot homework time in their programs. Teachers are instructed to "stop teaching by the IQ score," to abandon their attitudes of condescension toward the children, to keep standards high and to help the children attain high standards. Even the area merchants are enlisted; they discourage loitering and truancy during school hours and display educational materials.

Anything that will inculcate a respect for learning, enhance pride in academic achievement, boost morale of students and staff, and alert children and parents to new opportunities for Negroes is viewed as worth trying. Under the charismatic, dedicated leadership of Dr. Shepard, the schools have become the antidote for some of the defeatism of slum living. No administrative means are used to integrate the schools racially or alter the status ratio of middle-class to lower-class students. Instead, the program operates on the premise that educationally qualified individuals will find work and therefore, a socio-economic upgrading as well.

New Haven's Opening Opportunities Program involves five large-scale renewal projects which will include replacement of the city's fourteen oldest school buildings. The rebuilding involves relocation, homemaking, education, and housing programs aimed at promoting social goals. Community schools, operating 12 to 15 hours a day on a year-round basis, serving all races, creeds, and classes, will be the instruments for an integrated and total approach to neighborhood needs. The school's basic roles will multiply, becoming those of an educational institution for children and adults; a neighborhood center for leisure and recreational activities; headquarters for community services such as health clinics, family and employment counseling, legal aid and other social and welfare services; and a focus of neighborhood life for confronting and resolving problems.

New York City's Commission on Integration recommended that one cardinal consideration in the selection of a site for a new school building be its effect on preserving or promoting ethnic and racial integration. Other criteria follow, such as "distance, topological features, transportation to existing school plant and pupil population destiny" plus other fiscal and real property considerations. Population shifts and neighborhood changes—rapid and unpredictable—retard integration in elementary schools, particularly in the fringe areas. The "open enrollment" plan wherein youngsters from schools with heavy concentration of Negro and Puerto Rican children are transported to predominantly white, middle-class schools is still being assessed in terms of its effects on both sending and receiving schools. Professor Goldberg's paper indicated that, from the little evidence available, the gains one expects from unsegregated contacts is not automatic.

What is the critical status ratio or "toppling" point in the proportion advantaged of to disadvantaged children—in-migrant, racially different, lower-class—above which school and/or neighborhood climate changes? What are the crucial factors operating? Are efforts at changing the social composition of a school and neighborhood more promising than efforts aimed at changing only the educational program? While the regional high schools Professor Havighurst recommends are probably easier to set up than integrated elementary schools, is the secondary school too late to overcome the effects from a lower-class, segregated school in a depressed area? In his paper, Dr. Fischer argued against a school system organized primarily on racial criteria; he would provide for maximum free choice for all children, limited only by unnecessary overcrowding. Dr. Fischer was disturbed by "the growing pressure to locate schools, draw district lines, and organize curricula in order to achieve a pre-determined racial pattern of enrollment." The consequences of alternative approaches on children, families, staff and community require further study.

Curriculum Modifications Are Essential

The academic performance of children from depressed areas, so marked by scholastic retardation, demands curriculum reappraisal in depth. To begin, a thorough analysis of educational goals can determine their appropriateness for disadvantaged children and youth. Does "equal educational opportunity" change its meaning when linked to the concept of compensatory services and experiences? To what extent would these children's needs for acculturation to urban life affect the curriculum objectives? What unique aspects of urban life lend themselves to the curriculum as resources? Are goals dealing with personal and family life; with basic citizenship and social skills; with understandings of the cultural, political, social, and health frameworks more urgent for the disadvantaged child than for the middle-class child?

Americans generally resist the notions of different education for different classes, of education as the gateway to socio-economic mobility, of class barriers to educational opportunity. And yet, the idea of equal educational opportunity, the desire that all children "with their human similarities and their equally human differences, shall have educational services and opportunities suited to their personal needs and sufficient for the successful operation of a free democratic society"(1), remains a commitment for the public schools. Such an ideal of individualized instruction implies recognition and acceptance of variations in both ability and needs among the public school population.

If, despite the normal spread of educational ability, large numbers of children are not achieving, are not learning the basic skills required for academic success, are failing to develop their talents to the fullest, then educators must not lower the goals or write off blocks of children as non-achievers. McClelland, discussing the approaches used to identify gifted students, suggests that far too much emphasis has been put on talent potential as a fixed attribute. Instead, "talent potential may be fairly widespread, a characteristic which can be transformed into actually talented performances of various sorts by the right kinds of education"(3). Developing an understanding of "the right kinds of education" is basic to helping youngsters from depressed areas realize the objective of equal opportunity. The aspects of the educational program that are being modified, studied, or tested are many, affecting all levels and all elements of curriculum.

Pre-school and early childhood programs. Assuming that kindergartners' learning suffers from early impoverishment in verbal and cognitive experiences, pre-school programs for 3- and 4-year olds are being tested. Richer than the usual nursery school activity, the curriculum aims to develop cognitive and sensory motor skills, auditory and visual perception and discrimination, motor coordination, observation skills, and ability to understand and follow directions. The coordination of verbal experiences

and enrichment activities seeks to raise the motivation for school achievement and to enhance the learning-how-to-learn skills. In some instances,
an accompanying program for mothers promotes home management and
child care, as well as understanding of the educational enterprise.

Content modifications. Because the school program has such high verbal
content—indeed, the child's success depends on his mastery of fundamental communication and linguistic skills—the development of reading
competence and related language skills is of prime concern. A variety of
techniques for teaching pupils to read are employed, including experimentation with methods, materials, groupings, and special personnel. Reading
improvement teachers are used in some school systems to apply early
diagnosis and corrective services. For those youngsters for whom English is a second language, special materials and techniques are being developed.

New emphasis in the elementary school is also found in such projects
as Wilmington's project for schools in changing neighborhoods which
stresses deepening insights and skills in human relations as a supplement
to academic skills. Specific methods appropriate to the program's objectives include role playing, open-ended stories, use of film and other
aids for human understanding, utilizing community resources for curriculum trips.

Special modifications have been made for potential school leavers.
Among these, work-study programs, in which youth are placed and supervised in part-time jobs, are widely used. The employment experiences
are then dovetailed with work-oriented English, social studies, mathematics, and guidance experiences. The work-study approach is seen by
some school systems as "an alternative pathway to adulthood" beginning
with youth ages 13 and 14.

The perimeters of a program which would capitalize on the educational resources of the city, without curtailing opportunities or drive
for achievement are still unclear. There are healthy elements, for example, in social studies programs which focus on urban life, which use
the cultural resources of the city, and which contribute to enhancing self-
image through understanding the contributions of various ethnic and
racial groups to American life and culture. New York City offers family
living education, as so many youngsters lack security of a sound family
life and its precedents in facing their adult responsibilities. Other approaches to using the city as an educational resource include discovery of
the community's social service needs and volunteer service to others.

Probably in no area of curriculum is a question so often begged as are
these: What knowledge, skills, and attitudes should be acquired by young-

sters in depressed areas? How do these differ from the general objectives of public school programs? How can sequence, continuity, and articulation be structured for a highly mobile population? Programs in the category of so-called "basic" or "general" mathematics or "consumer" English are being increasingly questioned. However, for certain students, what alternatives are better? Not all students can or should be studying nuclear physics or fourth-year Latin, but the fact that he lives in a depressed area should not cause him to be guided automatically into vocational preparation for semi-skilled or unskilled work. As one participant put it, in developing curriculum for depressed area children, we tend to underestimate their intellectual potential and to overestimate their experiential background. Programs which open up intellectual opportunities, which are meaningful, and which are seen as contributing to both immediate and long range development must be developed for children in depressed areas.

Curriculum enrichment. Perhaps the most widely known enrichment program is the Higher Horizons Program of New York City, now being adapted in numerous other communities. The program encourages those identified as the most able students in schools in low socio-economic, culturally deprived neighborhoods, to develop their potential more fully and to climb to higher educational and vocational levels. Among its several aspects are remedial and enrichment services in reading, mathematics, and a foreign language; clinical services (psychological, psychiatric, and social work); a cultural enrichment program (concerts, plays, films, athletic events, field trips to colleges, hospitals, industrial plants); parent education meetings and interviews; a public information program for the community at large. Evaluation of Higher Horizons and its variations suggests positive results in such areas as reading achievement, school grades, pupil morale, improved staff morale and enhanced motivation. However, the studies raise prickly questions as well as providing answers. The need for isolating those aspects and factors which influence the program—aside from the charismatic qualities of the principal—has been noted. Whether improved instruction outweighs enhanced motivation or whether both are indispensable is unknown. Whether the enriched experiences are effective with a particular kind of child only is not known. Which facet of the program contributes which net gain is still not clear. As one conferee commented, to raise these questions is not to deprecate the Higher Horizons Program but rather to determine whether "a well-planned program of social and cultural experiences plus an improved educational program can significantly upgrade the educational achievement and aspirations of a substantial number of youngsters from deprived areas or just a small core." To date, the emphasis has tended to be on those youngsters who are identified as the most promising and able.

Improved instructional materials. A great deal has been said about the need for creating instructional materials for both pupils and teachers which strike a spark in the learner from a narrow, cultural background. The major objections to much of the existing material for reading instruction, for example, are its so-called middle-class bias and its over-all blandness. Instructional materials need to be interesting, exciting, and tempting for children from depressed areas. What kinds of materials, as one participant put it, will get these children mentally out of the squalor and poverty, the imprisonment of their home environment and brighten their self-images? Out of their urban setting, some teachers have produced materials which reflect easily-recognized experiences of the children in their charge. Now available is a set of materials which weaves every-day living into reading-improvement worksheets: how to make sound purchases, how to find one's way around the neighborhood, how to locate and use community services and resources, and how to apply for a job are some of the topic treated. Functional content which deals with personal care, vocational orientation, and similar concerns seems promising. The possibilities of programmed instructional material—such as its aptness for individualized instruction, its manipulative qualities, its self-pacing—are being explored both for direct teaching-learning as well as for remedial purposes. The uses of various kinds of audio-visual and manipulative materials are being expanded.

School organization and classroom modifications. Techniques of developing divergent thinking abilities of inarticulate youngsters indicate another trend in instructional emphasis. The emphasis is on encouragement of children to think outside the conventional verbal channels and to use intuitive thinking, curiosity, exploration, and guessing rather than memorized rote verbal responses.

Some schools are experimenting with team teaching arrangements of various kinds as well as block time arrangements. Ungraded primary units are being tested as to their effects on disadvantaged children. Pittsburgh's Team Teaching Project is designed to cope with the problems of "excessive mobility of population served, a high rate of teacher turnover, and the depressing cultural and socio-economic conditions in some of the areas from which their pupils come." By using different-sized teaching teams to work with classes and groups of various sizes, by drawing on personnel resources from the community, educational experiences are being extended and brought to life. Some instruction takes place in groups of 70 to 120 pupils; elsewhere, small groups of five to fifteen concentrate on subjects in which they require special help or have unusual ability. Varying in purpose and emphasis, four kinds of teaching teams have been organized for the primary, intermediate, special subject and junior high school areas. A mental health team enrolls a psychiatrist, two psychiatric social workers, two school social workers (home and school visitors), a clinical psychologist and a research consultant. This team has been organized for the early identification and referral for therapy of children with emotional and social handicaps which inhibit their learning. Finally, social agencies, educational and religious institutions, civic and welfare organizations, and governmental units help provide personnel, facilities and funds which complement and undergird the educational effort.

The ungraded primary unit and its offshoots gear their pace to individual ability, in an effort to insure continuous progress for a child or at least to reduce the trend of failure for the youngster who moves haltingly. The unit generally treats the first through third grades as a block with grade lines eliminated so that the youngster may spend as few as two or as many as four years in the primary grades, progressing as he is able to, without being retarded.

Diagnostic and remedial programs. Like the Pittsburgh Mental Health Team, programs are being initiated in other cities to diagnose learning difficulties as early as possible in order to help prevent handicaps or disabilities. New York City's Early Identification and Prevention Program, for instance, typifies efforts to identify, as early as possible, children with problems of emotional or social adjustment. Here again, a functioning team aims to clarify the scope and nature of the child's problems and to foster the kind of mental health, educational climate, counseling and treatment services that will reduce potential incidents. Prime attention is for children with reading problems; diagnostic procedures refer such youngsters to various clinics and agencies. Lack of adequate facilities in school and community, which aggravate the urgent need for more remedial services in all curriculum areas, is a need recognized by educators in most cities. Most pressing, perhaps, are the reading and special programs, such as additional classes for disturbed youngsters who can only remain in school if special assistance and instructional arrangements are made.

Reading clinics are available in many cities for youngsters who are too retarded to be helped either by the classroom teacher or by supplementary reading personnel. Staffs usually include selected teachers functioning as reading counselors, plus a clinical team consisting of psychologist, social worker, and psychiatrist. In New York City, to be referred to such clinics, children must be of normal intelligence although severely retarded in reading.

Additional staff. Extra personnel are being assigned to schools to help children, classroom teachers, school administrators, and parents; to increase remedial and diagnosis activities as well as referrals; and to work with home and community agencies. Some of the special personnel found in the schools of New York City, for instance, include these:

Reading improvement teacher—relieves the classroom teacher for reading instruction, assists new and probationary teachers with reading instruction methods and materials, assumes responsibility for classes in schools where teachers have had to forego full lunch periods.

Other teaching personnel—provides remedial reading help in schools with large groups of non-English-speaking pupils, teaches English as a second language to small groups of children in part- or full-time classes.

Non-English-speaking coordinator—helps other teachers improve the learning techniques and general adjustment of non-English-speaking pupils.

Substitute auxiliary teacher—links the school with the home, particularly of non-English-speaking pupils.

Junior guidance teacher—instructs children with normal intelligence who reveal patterns of serious social or emotional adjustment; works with psychologist and guidance specialist to determine whether the child can be helped or needs to be institutionalized.

Teacher of children with retarded mental development (CRMD)— works with small units of mentally retarded children in a self-contained classroom.

Teacher-trainer—works with newly appointed or probationary teachers on a helping-teacher basis.

Detroit has added coaching teachers to support the work of the regular teachers by their extensive diagnostic, remedial and developmental work in the language arts and arithmetic; full-time visiting teachers (school social workers) to diagnose and refer pupils and their parents for aid from appropriate agencies and specialists; school-community agents to provide liaison between the school and its community, parents, other adults and agencies. Other cities have increased available personnel for specific services for children in depressed areas, services which are usually of compensatory or remedial nature.

Extension of school day. Schools in depressed areas have long served as neighborhood recreation and leisure-time centers. Some school systems are going beyond the usual after-school recreation programs and are providing places for individual and group study, reading and science centers, cultural enrichment centers. The after-school program is viewed as more than a day-care or custodial activities and, instead, presents schools with enrichment centers for children and youth, as well as adults. The community-school concept—using the school plant for coordinated community services with programming from early morning to late evening, 7 days a week, 12 months a year—is extending into depressed areas more and more.

In New York City, the Mobilization for Youth Homework-Helper Project employs high school youth from low-income families as tutors for elementary school youngsters with academic problems. The tutor is paid on an hourly basis, which yields a small income for after-school work. Selected grade-school pupils attend after-school tutoring sessions on a one-to-one basis. The high school students are trained for the work and are supervised by adult teachers. The high school tutors are not expected to provide remedial help but they do contribute the extra reassurance, support, and immediate impetus for helping elementary schoolers with their studies, especially in the language arts area. The program has the dual virtues of recognizing and rewarding concretely high school students who are achieving and of helping culturally disadvantaged children with their school work.

After-school programs will continue to feature recreational and informal pursuits, civic meetings and performances of various kinds, but the expansion of these into culturally enriching activities will enable some youngsters to escape from the slum society into the centers for support, entertainment, instruction, and social intercourse.

Extension of school year. Several kinds of programs are lengthening the school year. One is a schedule change using a 12-month program with all of the implied modifications in staffing, programming, and facility use. Widespread is the practice of school's operating summer programs and camps. The summer school may be an extension of the normal academic program to enable youngsters either to make up for past deficiencies or to enjoy advanced work or other forms of enrichment. Normally, students at the elementary school level are invited to attend without credit, marking, or formal examination but rather to experience educational growth. The primary objective of summer-school programs in the depressed areas is more usually that of enrichment and remediation. The atmosphere can be less formal, particularly if advantage is taken of day-camp possibilities for school activities. Here, the program can be enriched within and outside of the building, drawing heavily on the camping approach. Some school systems are operating summer residence camps for youngsters from depressed areas as a means of getting them away from the city and from disadvantaged neighborhoods. A low-cost camping program and outdoor recreational experiences are combined with academic and educational opportunities in such arrangements.

Extended guidance and student personnel services. Increased guidance and counseling services are found mushrooming in many depressed area schools. Team approaches to working directly with youngsters on a counseling or therapy basis are involving guidance specialists, social workers, psychologists, and classroom teachers. Often, services are being extended to the family to help parents better understand the educational program and their own children's behavior and achievement. Guidance services have been scheduled for the evening hours and summer months to make them more readily available to depressed area families. Non-school people with competencies in particular vocational or professional areas are supplementing the more traditional guidance services. Student personnel services are one of the prime areas in which diagnotic and counseling services are being extended to reduce clinical needs of youngsters from depressed areas.

Work-study and continuation programs. Keeping youngsters in school so that they do not join the drop-out statistics is no longer viewed as an adequate goal by most school systems. Instead, secondary schools are attempting to develop retention programs which are meaningful, which are perceived as contributing to the youth's personal and vocational goals. An illustration of the concentrated efforts in New York City to retain high school students is found in the Youth Achievement Program. Boys with records of truancy, poor behavior, and academic failure are grouped together under the full-time guidance of an experienced, sympathetic teacher. Besides two regular-program classes, the boys attend a two-period class with their special teacher who uses curriculum materials designed for the group. In the afternoon, they work at part-time jobs for private employers with the special teacher responsible for job placement, job visitation, and contact with the home. Their curriculum materials emphasize job orientation and preparation for adult responsibilities.

Work-study programs, by giving equal importance to academic achievement and work skills, increasingly are viewed as the means for secondary schools to hold youngsters with meaningful, gainful experiences. Particularly important for alienated youth, this practice is catching on also for preventive programs. The Detroit Upgrading Program provides a short-term work experience for out-of-school unemployed youngsters, combined with in-school instruction. Other projects modify school programs to combine continuation of academic work with pre-employment instruction. Such programs equip youngsters with information about work tasks and training standards and aims at stimulating the academic achievement pre-requisite to job success. Courses include work-sampling, trips to plants and stores, and classroom visits by local employers. The field trips are designed to launch discussions about training demands, rewards, opportunities, and personal satisfactions. There is close scrutiny of the role of trade unions and various legal and quasi-legal organizations whose purpose it is to upgrade workers and eliminate discriminatory practices.

Work explorations, on-the-job training, subsidized work experiences are all being arranged along with programs to convince youth of the need for education. Efforts are being made to offer a climate conducive to more school for the drop-outs, at least on a part-time basis. The 16-to-21-year-old group is particularly critical; thus, the post-high school technical training and job retraining are both seen as promising practices. Basic education for individuals with technical skills but threadbare educational qualifications represent another facet of school retention or continuation efforts.

Parent education programs. The need for interpreting to parents the school program and its stress on educational achievement and motivation has resulted in the transfer of some parent education programs from school to home and neighborhood. School systems have found parents of children in depressed areas indifferent and apathetic, rather than hostile to education. Frequently, such parents are uncomfortable in the presence of a teacher or a person who represents authority. Many would be glad to have their children achieve, but—having had little formal schooling themselves—they know little about the whole process or how they can assist. Some school systems are attempting to reach parents by informal, apartment-house-based programs rather than the formal, structured, parent-association approach. These programs seek to help parents directly and practically with their day-to-day problems and to avoid dealing with general discussions about child care.

New methods of instruction. Relatively little research has sought to pinpoint methods that reach culturally disadvantaged youth. Many kinds of reading instruction methods are being tested for their contribution to developmental and corrective needs of children in depressed area schools. However, little is known about what methods will contribute to a more trusting relationship between pupil and teacher, will provide for variety and motility, will modify the need for immediate gratification, will contribute to overcoming the specific learning disabilities of depressed area children. The particular teaching procedures that influence classroom climate have not been clearly seen as yet. Experience has shown that some teachers succeed better than others with pupils in disadvantaged areas. It would be invaluable to know more about the constellation of forces which contribute to this differential success: how much is due to personality, including the ability to be supportive and accepting, imaginative and creative; is "middle-class oriented" teaching necessarily a negative factor or can it effect growth positively; how does the teacher reach the hard-to-reach youngster? Study may yield some leads to methods, tempo or pacing of instruction, attention span, involvement, and emphasis on different sensory modes as they effect pupil attainment and drive.

Coordinated efforts among youth-serving agencies. The duplication of effort, overlapping of services, lack of coordination, and failure to share information continue to plague various social and welfare agencies in many a community—particularly in depressed areas. Several projects are using the school as the catalyst for coordinating efforts amongst the educational, social, municipal, and service agencies.

In-service teacher and staff training. Almost every educational upgrading program involves some kind of in-service training of teachers to equip them to meet the challenge of working in depressed areas. These training sessions may aim at wakening the teacher's sympathy and understanding of the cultural heritage, economic and social problems and individual life styles of pupils in depressed areas. Beyond that, in-service programs attempt to help the teacher directly with methodology, subject matter, instructional resources, methods, classroom management and the availability of special services in depressed areas. The potential rewards and personal and professional satisfactions which come from working with disadvantaged children are stressed.

In conclusion. The multi-dimensions of the problems of education in depressed areas and the various efforts to give meaning to the ideal of equality of opportunity demand unclouded perspective, a prophet's eye for planning, and a predilection for the larger context. The above listing of various efforts to improve education and life in depressed areas represent a sampling only and is neither comprehensive nor qualitatively selective. They simply illustrate the many ways to attack the complex and crucial problem. Agreeing that more and better research and experimentation are needed, the social and behavioral scientists will certainly be increasing the production of studies and their complexity. Educationally, the gaps are awesome in our understanding of the factors whose total is cultural deprivation and its consequences. What are the effects of various social and psychological factors on the attitudes of different groups toward the schools and toward education? The importance of looking at the problem in terms of its educational, sociological, psychological, economic, political, health, welfare and housing dimensions is increasingly clear. Knowing that the decision makers or the influentials must become involved, we do not know how to attract their commitments nor how to organize the unaffiliated in the depressed area so as to increase the indigenous leadership.

During the conference several expressions were repeated over and over again:

"We need more data ..."
"We need to test ..."
"How will this affect other programs if ..."
"Where will the teachers come from to ..."
"With limited resources, would it be more profitable to ..."
"Where will the money come from for ..."

Over and over, participants stuck on the question of whether the school alone can make the necessary impact without society's opening up really equal opportunities in employment, in housing, in civic affairs. The importance of full and equal employment opportunities cannot be overemphasized and is directly tied to educational attainment. We need to know much more about the nature, the consequences, the effects of the total societal milieu on educational opportunity. We need to know how each of the subfactors interacts with others to create the conditions for equal opportunity. We need to capitalize on the positive elements of life styles in the depressed areas, of ethnic and racial minority groups, of the city as an educational center in order to move ahead purposefully and unitedly to overcome the disadvantages of millions of Americans.

The outlook is both discouraging and hopeful. It is discouraging in terms of its size, complexity, bitterness, and the human cost involved. The outlook is hopeful in the forces which are being mobilized to dissect and resolve this wasteful, destructive problem of displaced citizens in a rejecting or ignoring homeland. The ideal is clear, the directions well marked; now, the initial steps must be taken so that Americans all can move ahead toward the fullest realization of each individual's potential.

REFERENCES

1. Educational Policies Commission, *Education for ALL American Youth: A Further Look,* Washington, D.C.: National Education Association, 1952, p. 29.
2. Health and Welfare Council of the Baltimore Area, Inc., "A Letter to Ourselves: A Master Plan for Human Redevelopment," Baltimore: the Council, January 18, 1962, p. 5.
3. McClelland, David C., "Issues in the Identification of Talent," in David C. McClelland et al., *Talent and Society,* Princeton, N.J.: D. Van Nostrand, 1958, p. 25.
4. Porter, E. Russell. "When Cultures Meet." Cincinnati, Ohio: Mayor's Friendly Relations Committee of Cincinnati, May 1962, p. 1.

PART VI

Bibliography

Books

Ashmore, Harry S., *The Negro and the Schools,* Chapel Hill: University of North Carolina Press, 1954.

Back, Kurt W., *Slums, Projects, and People,* Durham, N.C.: Duke University Press, 1962.

Banfield, Edward C., and Meyerson, M., *Politics, Planning, and the Public Interest,* New York: The Free Press, 1955.

Barron, Milton L., *The Juvenile in Delinquent Society,* New York: Knopf, 1956.

Bendix, Reinhard, and Lipset, Seymour M. (Eds.), *Class, Status, and Social Power,* New York: The Free Press, 1953.

Berger, Bennett, *Working Class Suburb,* Berkeley: University of California Press, 1960.

Bloch, H. A., and Flynn, F. T., *Delinquency: The Juvenile Offender in America Today,* New York: Random House, 1956.

Bloch, Herbert A., and Niederhoffer, Arthur, *The Gang: A Study in Adolescent Behavior,* New York: Philosophical Library, 1958.

Brunner, Edmund DeS., and Hallenbeck, Wilbur, *American Society: Urban and Rural Patterns,* New York: Harper, 1955.

Burchill, George W. (Ed.), *Work-Study Programs for Alienated Youth, A Casebook,* Chicago: Science Research Associates, 1962.

Center, Richard, *The Psychology of Social Classes,* Princeton: Princeton University Press, 1949.

Clift, Virgil A., Anderson, Archibald, and Hullfish, G. Gordon (Eds.), *Negro Education in America: Its Adequacy, Problems, and Needs,* 16th Yearbook of the John Dewey Society. New York: Harper, 1962.

Cloward, Richard A., and Ohlin, Lloyd E., *Delinquency and Opportunity: A Theory of Delinquent Gangs,* New York: The Free Press, 1960.

Cohen, Albert K., *Delinquent Boys: The Culture of the Gang,* New York: The Free Press, 1955.

Conant, James B., *Slums and Suburbs,* New York: McGraw-Hill, 1961.

Davis, Allison, *Social Class Influences Upon Learning,* Cambridge, Mass.: Harvard University Press, 1948.

―――――, et al., *Intelligence and Cultural Differences: a Study of Cultural*

Learning and Problem-Solving, Chicago: University of Chicago Press, 1951.

Dunham, H. Warren (Ed.), *The City in Mid-Century: Prospects for Human Relations in the Urban Environment,* Detroit: Wayne State University Press, 1957.

Educational Policies Commission, *Education and the Disadvantaged American,* Washington, D.C.: National Education Association, 1962.

Floud, J., Halsey, A. H., and Martin, F. M., *Social Class and Educational Opportunity,* London: Heinemann, 1957.

Ford Foundation, The, *The Society of the Streets,* New York: The Ford Foundation, 1962.

Fortune Magazine, Editors of, *The Exploding Metropolis,* Garden City, N.Y.: Doubleday, 1958.

Ginzberg, Eli, et al., *The Negro Potential,* New York: Columbia University Press, 1956.

Ginzberg, Eli, Anderson, James K., and Herma, John L., *The Optimistic Tradition and American Youth,* New York: Columbia University Press, 1962.

Gittler, Joseph D. (Ed.), *Understanding Minority Groups,* New York: Wiley, 1956.

Goodman, Paul, *Growing Up Absurd,* New York: Random House, 1960.

Gottman, Jean, *Megalopolis: The Urbanized Northeastern Seaboard of the United States,* New York: The Twentieth Century Fund, 1961.

Greer, Scott, *The Emerging City,* New York: The Free Press, 1962.

Gulick, Luther H., *The Metropolitan Problem and American Ideas,* New York: Knopf, 1962.

Gutkind, E. A., *The Twilight of Cities,* New York: The Free Press, 1962.

Halsey, A. H., Floud, J., and Anderson, C. Arnold (Eds.), *Education, Economy, and Society: a Reader in the Sociology of Education,* New York: The Free Press, 1961.

Handlin, Oscar, *The Newcomers,* Cambridge, Mass.: Harvard University Press, 1959.

Harrington, Michael, *The Other America: Poverty in the United States,* New York: Macmillan, 1962.

Harris, Irving D., *Emotional Blocks to Learning: a Study of the Reasons for School Failure,* New York: The Free Press, 1961.

Havighurst, Robert J., et al., *Growing Up in River City,* New York: Wiley, 1962.

Havighurst, Robert J., and Neugarten, Bernice L., *Society and Education,* 2nd ed., Boston: Allyn and Bacon, 1962.

Hollingshead, August B., *Elmtown's Youth: The Impact of Social Classes on Adolescents,* Wiley, 1949.

————, and Redlich, Frederick C., *Social Class and Mental Illness,* New York: Wiley, 1958.

Hunt, J. McV., *Intelligence and Experience,* New York: Ronald, 1961.

Hunter, Floyd, *Community Power Structure: a Study of Decision Makers,* Chapel Hill: University of North Carolina Press, 1953.

Hyman, Herbert, *Political Socialization,* New York: The Free Press, 1959.

Jackson, Brian, and Marsden, Dennis, *Education and the Working Class,* London: Routledge and Kegan Paul, 1962.

Jacobs, Jane, *The Death and Life of Great American Cities,* New York: Random House, 1961.

Jaffe, Abram J., *People, Jobs, and Economic Development,* New York: The Free Press, 1959.

Kahl, Joseph A., *The American Class Structure,* New York: Rinehart, 1959.

Kravaceus, W. C., and Miller, W. B., *Delinquent Behavior: Culture and the Individual,* Washington, D.C.: National Education Association, 1959.

Lichter, Solomon, et al., *The Drop-Outs,* New York: The Free Press, 1962.

Lipset, Seymour M., and Bendix, Reinhard, *Social Mobility in Industrial Society,* Berkeley: University of California Press, 1959.

Lonsdale, Richard C. *The School's Role in Metropolitan Area Development.* Syracuse: Syracuse University Press, 1960.

Lynd, Robert S., *Middletown in Transition: A Study in Cultural Conflicts,* New York: Harcourt, Brace, 1937.

————, and Lynd, Helen M., *Middletown: a Study in American Culture,* New York: Harcourt, Brace, 1929.

Mayer, Martin, *The Schools,* New York: Harper, 1961.

Mays, John Barron, *Education and the Urban Child,* Liverpool, England: Liverpool University Press, 1962.

————, *Growing Up in the City: A Study in Juvenile Delinquency in an Urban Neighborhood,* Liverpool, England: Liverpool University Press, 1955.

McClelland, David B., et al., *Talent and Society,* Princeton, N.J.: Van Nostrand Company, 1958.

Mercer, Blaine E., and Carr, Edwin R., *Education and the Social Order,* New York: Rinehart, 1957.

Miller, David R., and Swanson, Guy E., *Inner Conflict and Defense,* New York: Holt, Rinehart, and Winston, 1960.

Mumford, Lewis, *The City in History,* New York: Harcourt, Brace and World, 1961.

Myers, Jerome K., and Roberts, Bertram H., *Family and Class Dynamics in Mental Illness,* New York: Wiley, 1959.

National Society for the Study of Education, *The Community School,* 52nd Yearbook, Part II, Chicago: University of Chicago Press, 1953.

Park, Robert E., *Human Communities: the City and Human Ecology,* New York: The Free Press, 1952.

Queen, Stuart A., and Carpenter, David B., *The American City,* New York: McGraw-Hill, 1953.

Riessman, Frank, *The Culturally Deprived Child,* New York: Harper, 1962.

Rodehaver, Myles W., Axtell, William B., and Gross, Richard E., *The Sociology of the School,* New York: T. Y. Crowell, 1957.

Sears, Robert R., Maccoby, Eleanor E., and Levin, Harry, *Patterns of Child Rearing,* Evanston, Ill.: Row, Peterson, 1957.

Sexton, Patricia C., *Education and Income: Inequalities of Opportunity in Our Public Schools,* New York: Viking, 1961.

Simpson, George E., and Yinger, J. Milton, *Racial and Cultural Minorities: and Analysis of Prejudice and Discrimination,* rev. ed., New York: Harper, 1958.

Vernon, Raymond, *Metropolis 1985: an Interpretation of the Findings of the*

New York Metropolitan Region Study, New York Metropolitan Region
Study, Vol. IX, Cambridge: Harvard University Press, 1960.
Warner, W. Lloyd, Havighurst, Robert J., and Loeb, Martin B., *Who Shall Be
Educated?*, New York: Harper, 1944.
Warner, W. Lloyd, Meeker, Marchia, and Eells, Kenneth, *Social Class in
America*, Chicago: Science Research Associates, 1949.
Whyte, William F., *Street Corner Society*, Chicago: University of Chicago
Press, 1943.
Williams, Robin N., and Ryan, Margaret, *Schools in Transition*, Chapel Hill:
University of North Carolina Press, 1954.

Selected School Reports and Bulletins

In addition to preparing a paper analyzing in depth the problems its system faced, each team was asked to send curriculum bulletins, instructional
guides, research reports and other materials which dealt with education in depressed areas. These materials, mostly mimeographed or duplicated, were
made available for study by the participants during the work conference.
From the large quantity of publications submitted, a selection has been made
for inclusion in this bibliography.

Atlanta and Fulton County, Georgia

Local Education Committee of Atlanta and Fulton County, *Educational Development Program: Increased Excellence and Efficiency for Schools in the
1960's*, Volume I: The Commission's Findings and Recommendations;
Volume II: Report to the Commission by Its Educational Council, Atlanta:
Metropolitan Development Council, January 1961; September 1960, 68
pp.; 51 pp.

Baltimore, Maryland

"Analysis of Jobs—Unskilled and Semi-Skilled, Junior High School Special
Curriculum Students," 1960.
"Coordinated Work-Study Programs in the Baltimore Public Schools," n.d.,
6 pp.
Furno, Orlando F., and Hendirckson, Harry C., "Pupil Mobility—Implica-
tions for Curriculum Development," May 1962, 21 pp.
Health and Welfare Council of the Baltimore Area, "A Letter to Ourselves:
A Master Plan for Human Redevelopment," Baltimore: the Council, Jan-
uary 18, 1962, 15 pp.
"The Vocational Program," 1961, 37 pp.

Chicago, Illinois

Cook County Department of Public Aid, "A Study to Determine the Literacy
Level of Able-Bodied Persons Receiving Public Assistance," Chicago: the
Department, August 1, 1962, 166 pp.
Cook County Department of Public Aid, "A Study to Determine the Possible
Impact of Automation on a Selected Group of General Assistance Recipi-
ents in Chicago," February 1961, 40 pp. plus Appendixes.
"Quality through New Directions: Annual Report of the General Superin-
tendent for 1960," 1960, 48 pp.

Cincinnati, Ohio

Handbook on Human Relations, October 1959, 39 pp.

"Human Relations and Learning Summary," Jackson School, 1960-1961. No page numbers.
"Language Development through Creativity," February 26, 1962, 5 pp.
Porter, E. Russell, "When Cultures Meet . . . Mountain and Urban," Mayor's Friendly Relations Committee of Cincinnati, May 1962, 9 pp.
"Talent Development Projects: the Guilford School," 1962, various pagings.

Cleveland, Ohio
"Great Cities Grey Areas Program: Hough Community Project," 1961, 31 pp.
"Profile of a School in a Disadvantaged Urban Area," 1961, 24 pp.
"Unemployed Out-of-School Youth Survey," 1962, 30 pp.

Dade County (Miami), Florida
"The Cuban Refugee in the Public Schools of Dade County, Florida," January 1962, 28 pp.
"Dropout Study, First Year Report 1960-1961," August 1961, 13 pp.

Dallas, Texas
"Dallas County Youth Study: An Abridged Report," June 5, 1962, 23 pp.

Denver, Colorado
Hurd, Gwendolyn M., and Rimmel, Erma L., Preparing Your Child for Reading, 1961, 129 pp.
"Reading Improvement Program: Asbury Summer Elementary School," 1960 14 pp.
"Three Special Projects in Reading: A Progress Report," November 21, 1962, 42 pp.

Detroit, Michigan
Boyd, Cleo Y. "Detroit's Southern Whites and the Store-Front Church," (Abridged) Detroit Council of Churches, n.d., 14 pp.
Mitchell, Charles, "The Culturally Deprived—A Matter of Concern," February 9, 1962, 18 pp.
"A Plan for Evaluating Major Activities in Great Cities School Improvement Programs," August 1961, 27 pp.
Rasschaert, William. "Evaluation by Design." Prepared for ASCD Conference March 12–16, 1961, 31 pp.

Los Angeles, California
"Divergent Youth: A Report Presented to the Los Angeles Senior High School Principals' Association," June 1962, 13 pp.
"The Manpower Challenge for Youth in the Nineteen Sixties," June 27, 1961, 37 pp.
Bender, Eugene I., "A Profile of Four Communities: Compton-Pacoima-Wilmington-Willowbrook," Research Department: Welfare Planning Council of Los Angeles County, March 1962, 30 pp.
"Remedial Reading Program in the Elementary Schools," 1962, 47 pp.
"A Guide to Work Experience Education and Employment Placement Program," 1960 revision, 35 pp.
Point of View: Educational Purposes, Policies and Practices, 1961 revision, 56 pp.

Milwaukee, Wisconsin
"Helpful Classroom Techniques. Supplement to Progress Report, Committee on Educationally Underprivileged," September 1960, 7 pp.

"Orientation Classes for In-Migrant-Transient Children, First Report, Two Parts, Part Two: Some Curriculum Provisions," October 1961; December 1961, 55 pp; 75 pp.

New Haven, Connecticut

"Opening Opportunities: New Haven's Comprehensive Program for Community Progress," April 1962, 50 pp. plus Appendixes.

New York, New York

Curriculum Resource Materials for Meeting School Retention and Pre-Employment Needs, 1962, 228 pp.

"Demonstration Guidance Project at George Washington High School: Report on Class of June 1961," 11 pp.

"Division of Child Welfare, 1960–1961," 1961; 28 pp.

"First Annual Progress Report: The Higher Horizons Program, 1959–1960," 73 pp.

Kahn, Alfred J., "New York City Schools and Children Who Need Help," Citizens Committee for Children of New York, June 1962, 78 pp.

"Portals to the Future." *Annual Report of the Superintendent of Schools 1959–1960,* March 20, 1961, 77 pp.

"The Story of the First Graduating Class of the Demonstration Guidance Project in George Washington High School," February 1961, 24 pp.

Toward Greater Opportunity. A Progress Report Dealing with Implementation of the Recommendations of the Commission on Integration, June 1960, 196 pp.

What We Teach: Annual Report of the Superintendent of Schools 1960–1961, 1962, 123 pp.

Philadelphia, Pennsylvania (Did not participate in the work conference but did send materials.)

"The Dunbar High Roads Project: Paul Laurence Dunbar School," September 1961, 70 pp.

"Eagle Program: John Wanamaker Junior High School," September 1961, 30 pp.

"Evaluation of the Harrison Heights Program: William Henry Harrison School," September 1961, 19 pp.

"Ford Projections: The Ford Foundation Project Schools," May 1961, 20 pp.

"Ludlow School Beacon: James R. Ludlow School," September 1961, 59 pp.

"The Peak Program: William McKinley School," n.d., 56 pp.

"Heights Program: William Henry Harrison School," September 1961, 30 pp.

"The School-Community Coordinating Team," December 1959, 13 pp.

"Star Program: Joseph C. Ferguson School," September 1961, 48 pp.

"Wider Horizons Program: H. J. Widener School," September 1961, 29 pp.

Pittsburgh, Pennsylvania

Pupils, Patterns and Possibilities: 1961 Annual Report of the Superintendent of Schools, 1961, 31 pp.

Quincy, Illinois

Liddle, Gordon P. "Modifying the School Experience of Culturally Handicapped Children in the Primary Grades," Quincy Youth Development Project, n.d., 10 pp.

Richmond, Virginia
"Summer Centers for the Extension of Cultural Opportunities and Enrichment of Experiences," Summer 1961, 15 pp.
"A Tentative Guide for the Certificate Program, Grades 8 and 9," 1961, 269 pp.

St. Louis, Missouri
"The School and Community Work-Related Education Program. Progress Report," August 1960–June 1961, 44 pp.

San Diego, California
"Information Pertaining to the Major Culturally Deprived Area of the San Diego," March 27, 1961, 12 pp.
"Study Committee for the Instructional Program of Socially Handicapped Youth: Logan Area Home–School Community," Feburary 6, 1962, 5 pp.
"Study Committee for the Instructional Program of Socially Handicapped Youth: Memorial—A Unique Junior High School," March 6, 1962, 5 pp.

San Antonio, Texas
"The Visiting Teacher in Education: A Handbook," tentative edition, May 1962, 15 pp.

Texas, State of
Preschool Instructional Program for Non-English Speaking Children, February, 1961, revision, 62 pp.

Syracuse, New York
"Analysis and Proposals for the Madison Area Educational Program," June 1961, 116 pp.

Washington, District of Columbia
The Amidon Plan for Education in the Sixties in the D.C. Public Schools, n.d., 35 pp.
"Curriculum Portfolio: Charts for the Amidon Plan," n.d., seven charts.
"An Evaluative Study of Basic Education and Related Services in the District of Columbia Public Schools," May 1961, 27 pp.

Wilmington, Delaware
An Adventure in Human Relations: A Three-Year Experiment Project on Schools in Changing Neighborhoods, 1963, 135 pp.
"Three Year Experimental Project on Schools in Changing Neighborhoods: Summary of Progress and Plans of Agencies and Organizations Participating in the Community Aspect of the Project, 1961-62, April 12, 1962, various paging.

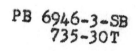